When it comes to God,
you can always draw...

CLOSER

A 365-DAY DEVOTIONAL

KAYTEE MITCHELL

Ark House Press
arkhousepress.com

© 2021 by Kaytee Mitchell
First published in 2021.

All rights reserved. The use of any part of this publication reproduced, transmitted in any form or by any means, electronic, mechanical, photocopying, recording or otherwise, or stored in a retrieval system, without the prior consent of the author is an infringement under the Copyright Act 1968.

Requests and enquiries concerning any information
or reproduction should be addressed to:
1655 Jett Road, Owensville, MO 65066, United States of America
or via email to Inextravagance@gmail.com.

All Scripture quotations, unless otherwise indicated, are taken from the Holy Bible, New International Version®, NIV®. Copyright ©1973, 1978, 1984, 2011 by Biblica, Inc.™ Used by permission of Zondervan. All rights reserved worldwide. www.zondervan.com The "NIV" and "New International Version" are trademarks registered in the United States Patent and Trademark Office by Biblica, Inc.™

Cataloguing in Publication Data

Mitchell, Kaytee, 1994- .
    Closer: A 365-Day Devotional
    ISBN 978-0-9752228-2-9 (paperback)
    ISBN 978-0-6453370-0-6 (epub)

Typeset by Sarah Ko & www.initiateagency.com
Cover Design by Rachelle Castro and Katie Elliott

In Memory Of:

DANNY GERARD MITCHELL

I love you "this much", my forever hero.
xx

AUTHOR'S NOTE

Here's the beautiful thing about this devotional—it started as a God-whisper and transformed into a reality over a five year process. Therefore, you will read a range of devotions, poems, and words written from the young 19-year-old dreamer, who just graduated high school, writing in wonder as she discovered the heart of God, to the highly passionate 24 – year-old young adult, who had been molded to craft every devotion prophetically, as a glorious work of art. My heart is that as you read, you will get to see firsthand the beauty of simplicity and complexity, which I decided to leave unrefined. My heart is that you could fully experience my journey of becoming an author who simply said yes to God and danced into a dream far beyond what she could have imagined. **My prayer is that He will speak to you something wild in coming closer to His heart, and that you will wildly say <u>yes</u>, regardless of your age or qualifications.** *Follow His whispers; embrace the adventure, and trust His heart. No matter how long they take to come true, they always will, so long as you believe in the God of the impossible.*

xx

TABLE OF CONTENTS

JANUARY

1. Closer 13
2. A Deeper Calming 14
3. My One and Only 15
4. Beautifully Broken 16
5. In His Eyes 17
6. Never Say Never 18
7. A Delight 19
8. I AM 20
9. 45 21
10. Extravagant 23
11. Create To Love 24
12. Leaving Lebanon 25
13. An Adventure 26
14. More Than Many Sparrows 27
15. Be Content 28
16. The Battle Plan 29
17. Beauty in the Ashes 31
18. In Writing 32
19. First Choice 34
20. Promises like Peonies 35
21. Shaped 36
22. By His Spirit 37
23. Peace in His Plan 38
24. Be You to the Full 39
25. Sticks and Stones 40
26. Take a Breath 41
27. The Voyage 42
28. The Strength in Joy 43
29. An Artwork in Progress 44
30. Keep On Running 46
31. Transformed 47

FEBRUARY

32. Ardent 49
33. Letting Go Is How A Bird Learns To Fly 50
34. Chosen 51
35. Living in Value 52
36. Pleasant Places 54
37. The Details 55
38. A Power In Praise 56
39. A Radicle 57
40. A Full Life 58
41. Vivid 59
42. Beauty in the Placement 61
43. In the Face of Fear 62
44. Beloved 63
45. Rewritten 64
46. For Such A Time As This 65
47. Divine Days 66
48. Not There, but Here 67
49. Persistence in Prayer 68
50. Praising in the Pieces 69
51. Raging Against the Wrong Wars 70
52. The Embrace of Love 71
53. The Designer 72
54. Humility at its Best 74
55. A Choice to Choose 75
56. Into Existence 76
57. Timeless 77
58. Living Under Expectations 78
59. Pouring Into Rest 79

MARCH

60. Gold Glittered Paths 80
61. Abiding Faithfully 81
62. A Glorious Glimpse 82
63. The Little Foxes 83
64. Even If 84
65. Being Still in the Silence 86
66. The Librarian of Secrets 87
67. To Live a Plan 89
68. Small Beginnings and Everlasting Kingdoms 90
69. Hide and Seek 91
70. Time's Side 92
71. To Gain Something Greater 94
72. Out of the Cave 95
73. Everything We Are 96
74. In the Gap 97
75. In Seasons 99
76. Favor and Grace 100
77. Pisteuo 101
78. Seeing Lasts a Lifetime 102
79. Anchored Promises 103
80. Fearless in the Fields 104
81. The Greatest Father's Vows 105
82. Sealed Secrets 106
83. The Only Exception 107
84. All the Days of My Life 108
85. The Most Powerful Trust 109
86. Patient Built Palaces 110
87. The Prince of Peace 112
88. Contained 113
89. Thirst No More 114
90. Beyond the Borders 115

APRIL

91. To Trust in a Living Dream 116
92. The Depths 118
93. Catalyst 119

#	Title	Page
94.	To Walk With God	120
95.	Undone	121
96.	1000 Times	122
97.	Designed	124
98.	Take A Risk	125
99.	You Belong Here	126
100.	Pray. Discover. Go.	128
101.	Remain	129
102.	Be Strong and Courageous	130
103.	In Wonder	131
104.	A Greater Trust	132
105.	Hold Your Breath	133
106.	A Light For My Path	134
107.	No Limits	135
108.	Beauty or Chaos	136
109.	Eclipse	137
110.	The Bigger Picture	138
111.	Selah	140
112.	The First Dance	141
113.	To Be	143
114.	From Giants to Glory	144
115.	Out of Time	145
116.	No Greater Love	146
117.	Entwined	147
118.	An Explosion of Light	148
119.	Expect God	149
120.	Brokenness Made Beautiful	150

MAY

#	Title	Page
121.	Kiss the Waves	151
122.	Existing	152
123.	Everyone has a Testimony	153
124.	Arrows of Flames	154
125.	As Delicate as a Rose	155
126.	Behind the Mask	156
127.	Better Together	157
128.	A Daily Letter	158
129.	Open Hands	Open Hearts	159
130.	Through the Ordinary	160
131.	Rise and Shine	161
132.	Pondering the Pieces	162
133.	From Curses to Blessings	163
134.	Beauty in the Balance	164
135.	A Promise Worth Persevering For	165
136.	Battlegrounds of Victories	166
137.	More than "Just an"	167
138.	Moments	168
139.	The Greatest Promise	169
140.	Untouched	170
141.	Bold	171
142.	Go. Set. Ready.	172
143.	The Power of PS	173
144.	A Little Bit of Magic	174
145.	Beyond	175
146.	To Overcome	176
147.	Waves of Grace	177
148.	I am Nothing but Value	178
149.	_____ is LIFE	179
150.	In Seasons of Waiting	180
151.	Endless	181

JUNE

#	Title	Page
152.	Let Go and Let God	182
153.	Embrace the Journey	183
154.	God-Colored	184
155.	Imprints	185
156.	Stop Snoozing	186
157.	A Higher Calling	187
158.	Pulse	189
159.	The Church	191
160.	None Compare	192
161.	All I Need	193
162.	Patience in the Rain	194
163.	One Good Thing	195
164.	Once Upon A Beautiful Time	196
165.	Fresh	197
166.	Searched	199
167.	Stay the Path	200
168.	Glimpses Of Glory	201
169.	Your Attitude is Everything	202
170.	Inside Out	203
171.	Ablaze	204
172.	More Trust, Less Understanding	205
173.	More Than a Cover	206
174.	Unveiled	207
175.	Live In Such Truth	208
176.	Immeasurably More	209
177.	To Chase A Dream	210
178.	Right In-Between the Eyes	212
179.	Be Silent	213
180.	The Call of Neverland	214
181.	The Shown in the Unknown	215

JULY

#	Title	Page
182.	Within Us	216
183.	Hello Discouragement	217
184.	Close Your Eyes	219
185.	Tapestries of Seasons	220
186.	Present Over Perfect	221
187.	His Grace	222
188.	Clothed for the Days to Come	223
189.	Unchangeable	224
190.	Waiting for the Mansion	225
191.	Without Ceasing	226
192.	With Everything	227
193.	Rescue Your Warrior	228
194.	Raise Your Flag	230
195.	True	231
196.	The Mist	232
197.	All or Nothing	233
198.	Go Abroad—Dream Bigger	234

199. Seeking Peace in Troubled Times......235
200. Fall as Heroes; Stand as Warriors 236
201. Attracted to the Distractions.............238
202. More Of You 239
203. Beyond You 240
204. BOTH 242
205. Calm 243
206. Waiting for the Whisper.....................244
207. Morning's Delight................................245
208. Victory in the Valleys 246
209. Deep Waters...247
210. The Unknown 248
211. Just Keep Swimming 249
212. Consider the Contrast........................250

AUGUST

213. Robes of Righteousness.......................252
214. The Rose and The Warrior.................254
215. A Churched Unchurched City............255
216. With Honor 257
217. Expect the Unexpected 258
218. Bold and Unashamed..........................260
219. Fields of Gardens 261
220. Being His 263
221. Glorious...264
222. Like Magic 265
223. Wild Love 266
224. Greater Beginnings.............................267
225. Fiercely Beautiful................................268
226. Painted Facades 269
227. Take Sail; Take Courage 271
228. The Prize..272
229. Thorns of Grace 273
230. Led by Love..274
231. Prayer Warriors...................................275
232. Came To My Rescue 276
233. Treasures in Jars of Clay 278
234. The Finishing Touch 279
235. To the Moon and Back........................280
236. Think Kingdom....................................281
237. More 282
238. Own Your Flame..................................283
239. The Karate Kid....................................284
240. Our Fortress 285
241. Firm and Secure 286
242. Don't Desert the Desert 287
243. The Rare 288

SEPTEMBER

244. His Chosen Ones 289
245. Go In Peace..290
246. Still do..292
247. Love Letters...293
248. A Promised Land.................................294
249. In the Boat...295

250. Weightless..296
251. Breaking Free......................................297
252. Crowned...298
253. Generosity's Kindness........................300
254. Love's Awakening 302
255. Here..304
256. Wake up, Sleeping Beauty 305
257. Before One of Them Came To Be.......306
258. "You Choose".......................................307
259. Armed and Ready................................308
260. Fear or Dare 310
261. Foxes and Lions...................................311
262. Take Captive the Captivating 312
263. The Frontline......................................313
264. What's In Your Hands?.......................314
265. Take a Seat 315
266. Note to Self: 317
267. Free...318
268. Catch Fire..319
269. The Present 320
270. My Everything.....................................321
271. Beautiful Details 322
272. Stay Wonder-Filled.............................323
273. Don't Look Back 324

OCTOBER

274. Lead Your Heart.................................325
275. Restart 326
276. With White Lines of a Lion's
     Marking 327
277. Stand Firm; Stand Tall 328
278. Embracing Expectation......................329
279. Sigh Away 330
280. P. S. – I Love You 331
281. Grounded in Gratitude 332
282. Here or There 334
283. Value in the Kingdom 335
284. Unfathomable......................................337
285. He's In The Waiting............................338
286. A Hidden Treasure 339
287. Wildcard...340
288. Beyond Your Wildest Dreams............341
289. One...342
290. Burning Bushes...................................343
291. Come to Life...344
292. Whispers..345
293. You Are More 347
294. Before the Glass Slipper 348
295. Shaped in Him.....................................350
296. Stronger Alone.....................................351
297. Where Is Your Delight?......................353
298. "I Do"...354
299. [Extra]ordinarily His 355
300. Identity vs. Sovereignty.....................356
301. Stillfully...357
302. Awakened Vessels................................358

303. Designed Differently 359
304. [I]limited 360

NOVEMBER

305. Adventuring Understanding 361
306. Child of God..362
307. The Greatest Calling..........................363
308. In the Midst 364
309. Fixated..366
310. Legacy...367
311. Seek God...369
312. Into the Sea 370
313. Ignite...371
314. Just Wait...372
315. With Honor and Beauty 373
316. Perspective..374
317. The Deception of Glamour 375
318. Don't Let Go..377
319. Enough..378
320. Always and Forever 379
321. Remember the Sparrows....................380
322. Somehow...381
323. Beauty in the Simplicity 382
324. From the Outside In...........................383
325. Shaped in Advance.............................384
326. Waiting on a Word in Bloom 385
327. Veni. Vedi. Vici...................................387
328. A Prayer of Freedom 388
329. Renewed..389
330. Royal 390
331. Sparks of Fire.....................................391
332. Speaking Words Into Existence.........392
333. In and Out 393
334. You Won't 394

DECEMBER

335. Eternal Foundations 396
336. Begin Strong. Finish Stronger...........397
337. Trusting > Understanding 398
338. Without Words....................................399
339. Lock Your Eyes 400
340. Perfect Love 401
341. Ten Degrees 402
342. Delicate Desires..................................403
343. An Open Journey................................404
344. Always...405
345. Shaped in Precision............................406
346. His Victory 407
347. I Love You 408
348. "Mirror, Mirror"...................................409
349. Defend the Destined...........................411
350. What If, Not Ever? 412
351. Be More...414
352. You Are What You Eat.......................415
353. Being Loving/Being Right..................416
354. Fit for the Kingdom............................417
355. More Than A Feeling..........................418
356. Idk 419
357. Hallelujah 420
358. Embraced in Grace.............................421
359. Beautifinement....................................422
360. In Fear and Wonder 423
361. Refined 424
362. The Aroma of Heaven.........................425
363. In You 427
364. Putting His Garden To Bed 428
365. Adventure On 429

CLOSER

1

CLOSER

We are at this moment as close to God as we really choose to be.[i]
- J. Oswald Sanders

@rachellegrace

It is an unquestionable truth that we are created for relationship with others, but to realize we are created for relationship with the Creator of the universe is an unfathomable awakening. James 4:8 reads, "Come close to God, and God will come close to you."[ii] The truth is, you can be as close to God as you want to be, but sometimes it takes more than one step. We can so easily *desire* to be as close to God as possible, yet we are more likely to *see* what we want, rather than to *seek* what we want. In 2 Peter 1:3 we read, "His divine power has given us everything we need for a godly life through our knowledge of him who called us by his own glory and goodness."[iii] He has given us *everything* to be as close to Him as possible. In verses 5-7, we read a list of qualities that tell us exactly how to get closer; it is a list that gives us many steps, but the question is, how close do you want to be? In verse 8, we read on to hear Paul say, "For if you possess these qualities in **increasing** measure, they will keep you from being ineffective and unproductive." (emphasis added) In other words, the more steps you take, the closer you get. The closer you get, the closer you'll want to be. And the closer you are in increasing measure, the more these qualities will begin to form within you in increasing measure, and the more you will become increasingly effective for the kingdom of God. As Francis Chan said, "You could be the godliest person in this room. That's up to you."[iv] You can **always** get closer.

*And closer yet, and closer the golden bonds shall be
Enlinking all who love our Lord in pure serenity;
And wider yet, and wider shall the circling glory grow
As more and more are taught of God,
That mighty love to know.*[v]
- Frances Havergal

2

A DEEPER CALMING

At times, it feels as though we are swimming at the surface of a vast ocean of mystery. Looking down into its ocean deep, this longing stirs within us to go deeper into its sweet unknown. We wonder where we could go that we have never gone, and what lies beyond the deep, that we have never seen. Still the endless possibilities of what could go wrong can create fear within our hearts. A fear that not only consumes our thoughts but paralyzes us from going deeper → from seeing and experiencing *more*.

I once had the opportunity to go scuba diving in the Keys of Florida. One of the key elements I learned in scuba diving was to *relax*. Right as you are trying to go beneath the surface, your gear and body-weight want to float back up to the top. In order to go under, you have to breathe normally and relax, to sink, *before* you can experience the extravagance beneath. So if you can't relax, you will tense up and take shallow breaths, which will keep you at the surface—paralyzed, because of your own fear. When we are afraid, our breath becomes shorter, we become a little frantic, and even though God has given us the gear we need to experience *more* of Him, we just can't seem to go deeper. *Yet when we learn to steady our hearts, our deeper breaths allow us to go to the greater depths of His love.* I like how Psalm 36:5-6 describes God's extravagance, "God's love is meteoric, his loyalty astronomic, His purpose titanic, his verdicts oceanic. Yet in his largeness nothing gets lost..."[vi] (emphasis added) In other words, His love is always surrounding us, always there for us. Yet when you are out of your depths, it is easy to frantically try to go deeper in your own strength. In return, however, it's only exhausting you more, taking more breath, and causing you to rise to the surface, which is opposite of the direction you'd like to be going. But here's the good news—just because you feel empty, it doesn't mean the ocean has run dry.

It's easy to become so focused on trying to live out our calling that we exhaust ourselves out of God's wonder. It can turn from a desire to see more of God to reaching for a "justified" reward. And yet, I believe with all of my heart that God is calling some of us to a *deeper calming*. One where we live effortlessly in His love that drives out fear, in His loyalty that drives out doubt, in His purpose that drives out uncertainty. To a place that is still and calm, *to see* all His wonders around you, even if you can't *feel His peace* within you. His love is no greater in the deep than it is on the surface. It will always be the same. *Yet He calls us to this calming because it's what we were made for.* He sees our deepest longings and says, "Be calm. Be still. Do not be afraid." So that we can go deeper and know Him more, to experience the extravagant life He offers. You already have the gear, you just have to take heart. Proverbs 25:3 says, "Like the horizons for breadth and the ocean for depth, the understanding of a good leader is broad and deep."[vii] I believe the Pulpit Commentary describes it best, "As you can never rise to the illimitable height of the heavens, as you can never penetrate to the immeasurable depth of the earth, so you can never fathom the heart of a King, can never find out what he really thinks and intends."[viii] That's where the deeper calming calls. We may never fully know what He may be orchestrating at the surface, or in the middle, for us to go deeper, but it always is to go deeper to His heart. He is a good God. He is a wondrous God. And this mystery around you is a beautiful opportunity to breathe in and out. The unknown will fade, and Jesus' wonder will become clearer and clearer, and at last, when you open your eyes, you will realize you are deeper than you have ever gone before.

ISAIAH 7:4
Keep calm and don't be afraid, do not lose heart.[ix]

3

MY ONE AND ONLY

"The One." I grew up with this mindset of believing that someday, somewhere, *the one* would come and sweep me off my feet. That it would be love at first sight. That it would be my very own real-life fairytale. I dreamt of who my prince in shining armor would be. I grew up looking for love and acceptance in all places, but every guy wasn't *it*. He wasn't the one I had spent so many nights dreaming about. On the night of June 2, 2009, I, Kaytee Mitchell, **fell in love**. I met someone by the name of—Jesus. <u>Everything</u> has changed since.

It was filled with many "just so happened" moments, and a lot more divine orchestration than I could understand then, but it was the love I had dreamt of and so much more. Never have I ever fallen so fast. Matthew 19:17 reads, "**There is only One who is good.**"ˣ This was the beginning of seeing His goodness allure me in an entirely new way for the days to come. To my surprise, this day wasn't by accident, it was planned and purposed by a Prince who had patiently waited for me to *come* to Him and *accept* Him into my heart. Long before that moment, He had been protecting me in the wilderness, providing for me in the deserts, and taking care of the details of my life quite intricately and delicately, every step of the way. I just didn't know it then. We can so easily put all *this* pressure of a perfect partner on a person who isn't Jesus. Yet, there is only One who is good.

My belief is that who we marry will never satisfy our hearts in the way Jesus can. Because the truth is, **who we marry isn't supposed to take the place of Jesus... they're supposed to lead us closer to Him.** To be Jesus for someone is a lot of pressure, and disappointment should be expected. It is the same way when we place these perfect expectations on a human whom we love deeply. On the other hand, we can fall in love with someone who will lead us *to Jesus,* and that makes all the difference. With Jesus at the center, grace will always catch and keep what is true and good together.

Some of us have been waiting for "the one" for so long, when the only One who is good has been waiting for us. We have been placing expectations that couldn't be lived up to, and setting standards on our lives that we could never reach alone. It is good to dream big and to go after what is in your heart, but there is only One who is BIG enough to make those wishes explode before your very eyes. Jesus is as real as your dreams, and His pursuit of your heart will always be greater than the expectations you place on Him. Yet we can so quickly run from Him when we are disappointed, which in fact, is the opposite of what we should be doing. Somewhere in between the dreaming and the disappointments, fear can place false accusations in our hearts that our hopes aren't worthy, and neither are we. This so quickly makes us run from a God who loves us entirely more than we could imagine. He doesn't take His hand from our own when we're disappointed in Him. He reaches out His hand and squeezes ours gently, letting us know that He is still there and that greater is coming. He embraces us, and loves us uniquely as we are, where we are.

Do I believe that everyone has someone out there that they will fall madly in love with? YES! I will believe in true love till the day I die. But what I also know is that when our hearts are empty and desperate for love, it is Jesus alone who will satisfy. For there is only One who is good, and only One who can fulfill our wildest dreams. One day, when we all find our person, we will love them for who they are, not for who they are not. They may not be perfect, but they actually don't need to be, because we already have the One who is. One day, you will see the faithfulness of Jesus' love over every tiny, minute detail of your dreams, and you will fall in love all over again with *your One and only,* for He is, and always will be, the definition of **good.**

4

BEAUTIFULLY BROKEN

Beautifully broken the grape that pours out a fresh anointing of His grace.
Return to Me, oh Israel, and sing.
Return to Me, and I will return to you.
Your time for singing has come.

Return to Me, O Israel, and believe in your purpose.
Outside of the palace is where you belong.
Where the vineyards are ripe to pick.
Here in the quiet your heart sings—your heart remembers—your heart dreams. "A dream is a wish the heart makes."[xi] A promise is a wish the Lord keeps.
Here the wine is sweet. Yet you see only grapes. It's transformed now. You're transformed now. See what's become. Taste the new thing I have given you. Refreshing it will be to the soul that seeks the Lord. Fresh from the vine. Fresh in its time. See My hands, covered in its remains, that your love may remain wild for Me. Crushed it may have been, but greater it has become. Pour out of your heart—taste and see what's been made new inside as you open up again. My heart bursts open inside your heart—trust its whispers in the quiet. Pressed you were so precious you could become. Shaped in the still to rise above the noise.
You know who you are. How beauty-filled you'll stay because of redemption's kiss.

Inspired by:

Those who have been ransomed by the LORD will return. They will enter Jerusalem singing, crowned with everlasting joy. Sorrow and mourning will disappear, and they will be filled with joy and gladness.[xii]
ISAIAH 51:11

This is the way God put it: "They found grace out in the desert, these people who survived the killing. Israel, out looking for a place to rest, met God out looking for them!" God told them, "I've never quit loving you and never will. Expect love, love, and more love! And so now I'll start over with you and build you up again, dear virgin Israel. You'll resume your singing, grabbing tambourines and joining the dance. You'll go back to your old work of planting vineyards on the Samaritan hillsides, And sit back and enjoy the fruit—oh, how you'll enjoy those harvests! The time's coming when watchmen will call out from the hilltops of Ephraim: 'On your feet! Let's go to Zion, go to meet our God!'" God will create a new thing in this land: A transformed woman will embrace the transforming God![xiii]
JEREMIAH 31:2-6, 22

5

IN HIS EYES

Reading: Psalm 139

You look in the mirror and see so unclear

With a mind full of lies
it's hard to see yourself right
When you hear all around
what's in and what's out
Your heart starts to pound
wondering: *do I fit in now?*
You frantically seek approval in their eyes
but they can't see past your crafted disguise
That covers every blemish and scar
written on your fragile heart

But you see, your appearance is a fake
if your heart isn't awake
Beating for the One
Who sent His only Son

So you could see the truth
that doesn't lie in what you do
No make-up can cover your hidden shame;
no perfect smile can hide your silent pain

No words can change your fractured
heart; no actions define who you are
Only God can show you proof
of what He created out of you
How you're made in complete perfection,
your face doesn't need correction
Your strength doesn't always
need to strive on, just let go,
and let God be the ONE Who holds your
impossible world in place
and floods your reality with His grace
Who desires for you to see
you're created exactly as He wanted you to be
And who you truly are
lies within the mysterious
depths of His open heart
The scars you thought you had inside
were healed the day God made you alive

That you could finally see again the
unquestionable beauty that lives within

The very heart you long to share
God molded and shaped with
precision and care

To reflect His very heart
in the person that you are
For who you are was made unique
so that you wouldn't feel the desperate need

To be someone you're not and change,
to finally stand out and not be the same
You are beautiful and so are they
but you're both made in different ways

You each have talents to express your heart
to reflect God's gifts in who you are

So realize the beauty you have within
that God made before your life began

So that not one person would be the same
but made unique in Jesus' name
Don't let your insecurities blind your heart
from seeing yourself for who you truly are
Be secure in the God above
Who created you fearfully in His love
Look to His heart and you'll see your
own, far more precious than diamonds,
far more worthy than gold
The answer to your heart lives deep inside
just give God a chance to open your eyes

You'll be awestruck—with no words to describe
the undeniable beauty He's seen all this time
For in those moments when fear
and beauty decide to collide
Look to the Groom, who only sees you
for who you *really* are
reflected
in His eyes

6

NEVER SAY NEVER

> "It's a terrible thing to see and have no vision."[xiv]

These words by Helen Keller impact the silence of any person's ordinary dream to make it come to life. What once seemed so far away now seems so near, and what once seemed like a dream now walks into reality. Or at least it should. It should seem impossible, but possible; impractical, but practical; unreasonable, but reasonable. Some critics may be reading this saying → she is completely contradicting herself. But let me shine truth on this statement. The first unbelievable word is in our own strength and ability. The second faith-filled word is in God's strength and ability—and that is what makes this exciting! Proverbs 29:18 tells us, "Where there is no vision, the people perish, but he that keepeth the law, happy is he."[xv] Or as Mark Batterson puts it, "Show me your vision, and I'll show you your future."[xvi] When it comes to seeing, we look at all that we can do; when it comes to vision, we look at all God can do. And that is what makes it so exciting—it's beyond us.

I know so many people who could go many places and do many things, but their vision is so small, and so is their view of God. They sit back waiting and watching to see if something—anything—will happen, but they don't even have a vision of what they want to happen. They will say, "I will never have enough money" or "I will never have enough time." They wish with a "will it ever happen" mindset, but stay stuck with a "never have enough" vision, and it contains them from all that God can do. My advice: never say never. Because when you have a vision of where you want to go, you will always have enough money to save up for your dreams to come true, and you will always have enough time to set aside to chase them. Your vision may not always stay the same, but it will always allow you to see further along the way than if you were to stay right where you're already at. But the critical thing to know about having a vision is that you can't do it alone. John 15:5 tells us, "I am the vine; you are the branches. If a man remains in me and I in him, he will bear much fruit, apart from me you can do nothing."[xvii] We can't do it alone. We can't make the impossible possible, the impractical practical, nor the unreachable reachable. In other words, you can't live a God-sized dream without God. Otherwise, it is just an oversized dream beyond you. But with God, anything can happen. And that is why having a vision is so important. It allows you to see that your life has meaning and purpose, that there is always something worth fighting for, and that along the way, you won't just see God's heart, but you will discover your own. Anyone can stay where they are at and have wishful thinking; but it is those who dare to dream that will go many places and do many things, because they believe in a God who can, and who will, do the unfathomable.

7

A DELIGHT

> *Keep my Sabbath days of rest, and show reverence toward my sanctuary. I am the Lord.*[xviii]
> Leviticus 19:30

Rest. The concept of it sounds lovely, yet it's a wrestle to live out. To think that the God of the universe rested Himself, that He may give us an example to do the same, is beyond amazing. Yet it can be easier for us to follow Him in obedience, in sacrifice, and in giving than it is for us to follow Him in rest. Kerri Weems says, "Sabbath is God's metronome, marking out a weekly rhythm of rest and renewal."[xix] Rest is not merely suggested, it's actually commanded. Not because God wants to force us to trust Him, but because He knows it's good for us to remember Him. As Isaiah 58:13 says, "Call the Sabbath a delight."[xx] It is a day of trusting God can do more in one day than you could with seven. It is a day to be, to soak in truth away from distraction, and to live the life God intended for you to love. It is a day to remember, to refocus your heart on His, and to reprioritize your schedule for what actually matters. *Sabbath sets the pace of your week and tunes it to the rhythm of His grace.* Some weeks may be more high-paced, yet not all of life is meant to be a sprint. Much of it is a walk, an adventure, a wandering. So the Sabbath is good! Yet, seldom is it welcomed. May you take the time to look at your year and mark out your Sabbaths. I can bet your finances would increase, your joy would skyrocket, and your relationships would be so much more complete. As Ezekiel 20:12 says: "And I gave them my Sabbath days of rest as a sign between them and me. It was to remind them that I am the Lord, who had set them apart to be holy."[xxi] Take a risk on God, and see what happens—you'll never know if you never try. Set your Sabbaths, and you'll set apart an unforgettable journey with God.

8
I AM

@sarahbgraves

When He says, "I AM," He says, "I know."
When He says, "I AM," He says, "I see."
When He says, "I AM," He says, "I can."
When He says, "I AM," He speaks a promise of love and truth.
Though no eye can see, He sees. Though no ear can hear, He hears. The unimaginable is His design for those who love Him. There are no words to describe, no image we can create, no dream we can wonder, that will be more beautiful and life-giving than what He has already planned and placed before you. And when He says, "I AM," His words tug on your heart promising that there is a purpose for every mountain you have climbed and for every valley you have passed through. He whispers knowing there is a place you will reach at the end, where you'll see His every design on the path you walked of His plan outworked, and those two words that urged you on every step of the way you'll hear spoken again: "I AM." Like a whisper of love, you'll know: He knows, He sees, He can, He is... and it doesn't makes sense and does makes sense all at the same time. But the one thing you are sure of undoubtedly is:
He is forever I AM, and you are forever His.

Revelation 1:8
"I am the Alpha and the Omega--the beginning and the end," says the Lord God. "I am the one who is, who always was, and who is still to come--the Almighty One."[xxii]

9
45

I cannot be like Jesus and live inside my four walls. Inside my four walls, I cannot live like Jesus lived. This thought replays in my mind like a broken record on repeat. It all started with a walk. I was enjoying the sun like any ordinary day, when a bright red door caught my eye. The numbers 4 and 5 sat by each other on its frame.

Thus, I lingered, my imagination flew wild, my heart anchored in the depths of this moment. Four... like the 4 walls of a home. Five... like the 5 fingers of an outstretched hand. I grabbed my journal and started to scribble my thoughts ferociously as quickly as they came:

I wonder how many times we live on one side or the other. Between the four walls of safe and the five outstretched fingers of giving. Do we ever truly discover its combination? Or do we separate their value time and time again. Never forty-five, but four or five, one without the other. Do we add

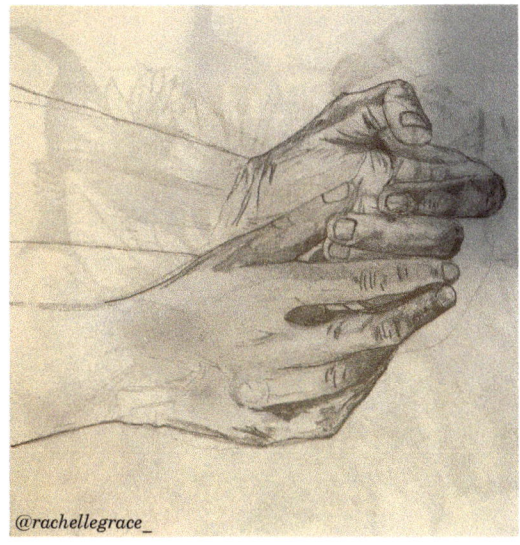
@rachellegrace_

it, subtract it, multiply it, or divide it to change or do we let the two rest together? Do we ever think that life is not a sum of all or nothing, but

instead it is this in between balance of beauty and grace that equals life. 45: the two become one but stay one. They stay whole. Us and Christ. The holes of Him for the whole of us. The more complete He is through us the more completion He brings around us by being who He already sees within us. It's a partnership. Two wholes. Just like a dance. All of me poured out before all of Him. 4+5. One resting. One giving. One receiving. One loving. The total sum and value of rest is found in relationship. We can never just rest, we can never just give. We can never be just one. We can't be a bottomless jar that doesn't receive the water trying to fill it because it's trying to be given in the same moment. We can't also be containers of liquid, keeping to ourselves what can quench the thirst of our beloveds with our poured out hearts. We feel loved in receiving. We feel loved in giving. Not 9. Not 1. Not 20. Not 25. Not 1 ¼... But 45. 45 is the sum of two whole hearts knowing their parts and breaking apart to beautifully create love outside of them and inside through them. Christ exists as we let love exist. Learning to be like Christ is learning the lavished grace of love poured out and poured in. Like washing the feet of ash with grace. Like being washed from your pain by pouring out for your loved ones. And in return, returning to you. Returning to God. Returning to love. Love returning you over and over in His hands. Living outside of our four walls is where we find the surprises we desire. It's there care comes. It's there heaven comes to earth.

And just like that, I can never see 45 the same. Somewhere in the whisper of the air, I sense there's so much more to life when we overflow from rest to the rest of the world. It's not addition, subtraction, multiplication, or division... it's two wholes resting, belonging, remaining, reminding us that this is home. *Home is found in the pouring out and pouring in; it's becoming emptier to become fuller as there's new space for love to refill your soul once again*. Sometimes it takes a bright red ordinary door to remind one how to find home again, and sometimes it repeats like a broken record, waking you up from your four for their five, so that you can break time, to take a walk outside, and maybe find a way to reach out in its time, to come back more whole inside than before. Sometimes God is just kind like that.

> *I can't wait to hear what he'll say. God's about to pronounce his people well, The holy people he loves so much, so they'll never again live like fools. See how close his salvation is to those who fear him? Our country is home base for Glory! Love and Truth meet in the street, Right Living and Whole Living embrace and kiss! Truth sprouts green from the ground, Right Living pours down from the skies! Oh yes! God gives Goodness and Beauty; our land responds with Bounty and Blessing. Right Living strides out before him, and clears a path for his passage.*[xxiii]
> Psalm 85:8-13

10

EXTRAVAGANT

One definition describes it as "spending much more than is necessary or wise."[xxiv] Another closely relates saying, "Exceeding the bounds of reason, as actions, demands, opinions, or passions." And yet, both scream the message of "completely out of the question" when it comes to the word "extravagant." And even though we seldom hear the word, we dream of its boundless measures all the time. We constantly think about what is beyond the borders and focus on what we want to be instead of acknowledging what is. We have extravagant dreams that exceed the bound of reason. And no matter how many reasons we can find to not step towards the borderline, we will always keep dreaming, thinking, and wishing for the extravagant. One of my favorite lines is from the movie, *Letters to Juliet*. Sophie, the main character, says, "What and if are two words as non-threatening as words can be. But put them together side-by-side and they have the power to haunt you for the rest of your life... What if?"[xxv] I wonder how many of us have allowed those two harmless words to have such a hold of our hearts, our dreams, and our passions. I wonder how much farther we could go if we switched the two words around to, "If what?"

In the story of Joshua, we read in Chapter 3 about the process of the Israelites crossing the Jordan. I don't want us to look at the extravagant miracle, but at the extravagant steps. In verse 5, Joshua tells the people, "Consecrate yourselves, for tomorrow the Lord will do amazing things among you."[xxvi] Isn't that what we all want to hear? That God is going to do amazing things among us? But we see by verse 8 that Joshua tells the priests who are carrying the Ark of the Covenant, "When you reach the edge of the Jordan's waters, go and stand in the river." And it wasn't like the water was warm and welcoming. No, it was at flood stage, but they were faith-full and so was God, He parted the waters and the priests walked across on **dry** ground, in the **middle** of the Jordan River. Talk about the unthinkable. Not only did He create a path, but He made the ground dry. *It started with an extravagant step to see an extravagant dream come to life.* We must ask ourselves like the priests must have before they stepped into the floodwaters of the Jordan: "If what?" rather than "What if?" *If what* focuses our faith on God whereas *what if* shows our faith in ourselves. One holds the power of courage while the other overpowers you with fear. The question isn't about the extravagant miracles God will perform, but rather, about the extravagant steps you are willing to take. Because an extravagant dream comes with extravagant measures. And like the quote in the movie goes onto say, "You need only the courage to follow your heart."[xxvii]

Many times we want to see before we believe; but more often, God asks us to believe in Him before we can see what He can do. So whatever you are dreaming, thinking, and pondering that is beyond reason, step out in faith that God will simply be God. Although we can't ever give God enough, we can always give Him our all. If you are with the Lord, then you know the Lord will be with you.

11

CREATE TO LOVE

Joy is our greatest strength and most powerful weapon. Laughter is only a fruit from it. Love its reason for existence. Kindness its branch of expansion. God created the earth as a work of art, yet I believe He created man out of love. He created in love to love. To *love* man. To *share* with someone the greatness He holds within. He has so much stored within that He gives each person uniquely a gift of Himself to put His glory on display. *Does the gift go to waste if the man goes to waste? Or does the man go to waste if the gift goes to waste?* If we do not create, then, do we not cultivate our ground? If we feel like we are wasting away, then maybe we put to death the very thing that makes us come to life. To create—a dream, a design, a decision—based on *love*, still taps into that part of life for which we exist. To feel cut off from our ability to create then feels like our hands are tied up behind our backs, while holding the key to turn off the ticking time bomb that's about to go off worldwide. The thing is, we know there's an answer within our creation. When held back, it is only a matter of time before it will impact somebody. Our yes can impact somebody's eternity. Yet, our no can impact somebody's eternity the same. The weight of this is only binding to the bound, but freeing to the freed. Still, He is making all things new. He is creating to love. He is transforming everything. Jeremiah 31:22 says: "God will *create* a *new* thing in this land: a transformed woman will embrace the transforming God."[xxviii] (emphasis added) Our yes matters. Our creations matters. We matter. I write these words alongside this verse: *I do not carry the weight of the world in my heart; I carry Jesus in my heart, and He carries the weight of the world.* It's not our burden to bear, but it is our blessing to multiply. Something within us dies when we hold back our gifts, so we mustn't hold back. Create in love to love… to share with someone outside of us the greatness God has placed within us. Thus joy will be our greatest strength and most powerful weapon. Thus we will laugh without fear of the future. Thus love will be its reason for existence, and kindness its branch of expansion, as we create with the Creator the new thing in this land.

12

LEAVING LEBANON

*Come with me from Lebanon, my bride.
Leave Lebanon behind, and come.
Leave your high mountain hideaway.
Abandon your wilderness seclusion,
Where you keep company with lions
and panthers guard your safety.*[xxix]
Song of Songs 4:8

Mountains are beautiful, yet dangerous. Though we like to sit at the top and gaze at all that is around us, we miss so much of experiencing what could be ours. It's breathtaking from a distance, but there's so much more at the bottom waiting for countless moments to take our breath away. Theses mountains are high, welcoming, and comfortable, and we all have them. They are our greatest insecurity, the highest of our fears, the height of our pride. And it keeps us running to the top where we can hide and see everything, instead of embracing life-changing moments at the bottom. When I read this verse, this is what I hear, "Come with me to an unimaginable hope; leave your insecurities behind. Abandon the comfort you once called home, where safety was the god of your life." It goes on in verse nine to say, "You've captured my heart, dear friend." And we see that the call to come down the mountain is because something greater waits at the bottom. It may not be as safe or comfortable, but it will make all the difference. Instead of *seeing* what could *be*, overcome whatever is holding you back, to *be* what He *sees* in you.

13

AN ADVENTURE

I tend to see life as this self-discovery journey with this overwhelming desire to see the world, to travel to every country, to see every sight in existence, to experience every thrill possible, to make a difference everywhere I go, and to hold the love of my life's hand through it all. It's an awesome plan, but a plan that is missing awe-filled wonders. A verse that has been pounding on the doors of my heart for weeks is Luke 12:34, "For where your heart is there your treasure will be also."[xxx] The Passion Translation is even more convicting as it says: "Where you deposit your treasure, that is where your thoughts will turn to—and your heart will long to be there also."[xxxi] To be honest, this verse frustrated me. I kept thinking, "I'm only human." But I've learned that this phrase can tend to be a self-righteous excuse. The reason being, I wanted my life to be everything I desired it to be, when this verse showed me that all these desires had nothing to do with God. I dream of adventures and discovering new things every day, and my goal in life is to make a difference wherever I go in everything I do, but I will miss life's goal or point if my heart is only for the desires I seek. A journey doesn't begin with a left or right turn, it begins with an open door, and that's what I missed. A turn may direct you, but an open door leads you with a purpose. I was seeking direction but was overseeing the point. Every lesson and every door has a point that always and forever points to Jesus, and that's what life is all about—God. Let's take the "I" out of life and discovery, and replace it with God who gives us life to discover Him. The journey we desire isn't around us, actually it's within Him. Instead of desiring to see the world, let's desire to see His heart. Instead of wanting to discover who we are, let's discover who HE is. Instead of wondering who's hand we are going to hold in life, let us be held in His hands to see life's wonders. Life is not about the depths of the water we're in, but the depth of the Word we seek.

It's not about where we go, but Who we're going for. It's not about us making a difference, but about the difference God is making. Merriam-Webster's definition of adventure is "an exciting or remarkable experience."[xxxii] (emphasis added) "Adventure" comes from the Middle English word "aventure," which refers to *a chance or risk*. Instead of taking an adventure around the world to be a remarkable experience, let's take an *aventure*, or chance, within God's Word to experience Him. It is when we see His heart that we will begin to appreciate the greatest beauties of life, and our journeys will be awe-filled. So let's turn pages instead of directions. Let's experience mountains and valleys instead of traveling them. Let's discover with our hearts and not our eyes. Let's "aventure"—let's take a risk, and let's delve into the beautiful mystery of all He is.

*Things never discovered or heard of before, things beyond our ability to imagine—
these are the many things God has in store for all his lovers.*[xxxiii]
1 Corinthians 2:9

14

MORE THAN MANY SPARROWS

One by one they landed on the line of the telephone pole, and their number continually increased. As one flew along the line with fluttering wings, feet shuffled to the right and to the left to make room for one more. Then, almost as if it were timed, they take off and fly into the sunset, not leaving one behind. Not one is ever forgotten, I softly hear, as Matthew 10:31 comes to my heart: "You are worth more than many sparrows."[xxxiv] That moment still amazes me, because as I thought about how God took care of each of those fifty sparrows all sitting on the line, five more would come, and then another four, and then another seven. They just kept coming, and God took care of every single one. The thing about birds that I admire is that we have similar dreams: to go higher, to test the boundaries, and to go everywhere possible! Birds are constantly going different places and leaving everything behind, flying in faith that their supply will be provided at the next place they land. And God is always faithful; they always end up with what they need. The thing is, He provides for every single one, as five more come, or four, or seven. And He does the same for His children, for us. Some of us are called to go to different places, or to do different things, and that involves a risk of leaving everything behind, but in losing everything, we will gain everything. He is simply saying, "You are worth more than many sparrows," and so we have nothing to fear; because when we fly off into that sunset, He will always have a place for us to land on the other side.

15
BE CONTENT

Today, be intentionally content with all that comes your way. As Philippians 4:12 says, "I have learned the secret of being content in any and every situation,"[xxxv] I think that's a secret we all need to discover. The deeper our trust goes in God, the deeper our roots will go in contentment. And so, **do not undervalue your today**, but seek beauty in it, and be content no matter how things go. When it comes down to it, every day is as ordinary as the next; the difference is in how you see it. Being content isn't about settling for ordinary or striving to be extraordinary, it's about being His and knowing you have everything even when nothing goes right or everything does. In any and every situation, you forever have Him.

16

THE BATTLE PLAN

I can hear it and see it all happening in my head: "Gideon! Get up! I need you to thresh the wheat this morning," his mom shouts from the kitchen. Gideon sits up and rubs his eyes as everything comes into focus around him. His first thought, "Why am I up right now?" His second thought, "Here's to another ordinary day." Hesitantly, he stands up and stretches his arms out before he gets dressed to head out to the winepress again. Little did he know that today wouldn't be like the rest, his day would be quite extraordinary. (emphasis and details added)

In Judges 6, we read how the Midianites had experienced oppression from the Israelites for seven years. Because of this, the Israelites had been preparing shelters for themselves in the mountain clefts, caves, and strongholds. Yet further on, we see that the Midianites, Amalekites, and other eastern people invaded the country, destroying everything that the Israelites had grown and owned. They were left with nothing.

Verse six says, "Midian so impoverished the Israelites that they cried out to the Lord for help."[xxxvi] I can only imagine the Father's heart thinking, "Finally." At this point, the Lord sends an angel to speak to Gideon in the winepress, and this is where we press resume on the story of Gideon. While Gideon is threshing the wheat, the angel of the Lord comes and speaks, "The Lord is with you, mighty warrior."[xxxvii] Seven words that are so simple, yet so powerful. Seven words that Gideon desperately needs to hear. Even though these words are reassuring, Gideon's response seems pretty expected as he says, "If the Lord is with us, why has all this happened to us? Where are all his wonders that our fathers told us about when they said, 'Did not the Lord bring us up out of Egypt?' But now the Lord has abandoned us and put us into the hand of Midian." If I had been experiencing hiding and poverty for seven years, I would probably react the same way. But I love the response God Himself speaks, "Go in the strength you have and save Israel out of Midian's hand. Am I not sending you?" Their conversation continues as Gideon asks, "But Lord, how can I save Israel? My clan is the weakest in Manasseh, and I am the least in my family." And even though the Lord Himself spoke to Gideon again, "I will be with you,"[xxxviii] Gideon still questions, he still doubts, he still fears. Still the Lord continually reassures him. Even more so as Gideon asks God to prove Himself to him by making a fleece wet with dew while leaving the ground dry, and that is exactly what He does. But because that was slightly practical, Gideon asks God to prove Himself a second time by having the fleece stay dry instead while having the ground wet with dew, and so it happens. And just like God spoke earlier, Gideon goes on to destroy the Midianites, as God promised.

It's a happy ending, the ones that we love to read and hear or even watch on television. But there are so many vital points to this story that we can't just glance over. One is that Gideon was just as human as us. He doubted, he questioned, he feared, and God knew this before He chose Gideon to defeat the Midianites, because God saw something in Gideon that he couldn't yet see in himself. Two is that Gideon asked God to prove Himself to him. He literally was asking God to comfort his doubts and quiet his fears by keeping the fleece dry and making the ground wet with dew. And God still doesn't look at Gideon any differently when he asks for the opposite the second time. Three, Gideon had the weakest clan and God used only half of them to bring about victory for the Israelites. In other words, Gideon was the least prepared and able, and God used him to fulfill His purpose.

We all have different purposes that God has spoken over our hearts, not just once, but multiple times (because when God does speak, He will always repeat it). But just because we hear it time and time again, doesn't mean that our doubts and fears won't resurface. Like the angel spoke to Gideon, God speaks to us, "The Lord is with you, **mighty** warrior." Still we can turn around, looking over our shoulder, wondering if He is really speaking to someone behind us. Because all that we see is a façade of who we think we are rather than a reality of who God says we are. Meaning: we feel like we can keep it altogether on the outside, but on the inside we believe we are anything but a warrior. But God sees you, and He only speaks truth, and He makes you start to wonder that maybe it's not a façade, but a reflection of who God created you to be. The thing is you don't have to have it all together, you don't have to be the best prepared, because *you can't be prepared for what He is about to do anyway*, all you can do is go in the strength you have, and He will do the rest. When it comes to your purpose, it will be beyond you. It will seem impossible, impractical, and you'll probably question God through the process of Him proving Himself to you. But it doesn't make you any less worthy in His sight. What you can know is that He is for you and with you; that He desires to give you the best and loves to see His victory come to pass through His chosen. The Israelites, for so long, tried to stay hidden and safe, but God calls us out of our comfort zones to go onto a battleground before us. *One that is dangerous to the eye, but more dangerous to leave untouched for comfort's promise.* So when He does call you, know that the enemy isn't just going to leave you alone with God during the time before the battle/before your purpose. But that isn't a discouraging statement, it's a strengthening mindset. To know that the enemy is going to try to deceive you and talk you out of God's greater purpose for your life allows you to create a battle plan for when he does attack. The attacks might be the subtle thoughts of "I'm not enough" or even the opposite of "I'm better than this," or they may be bigger attacks convincing you that you don't belong or that this isn't your purpose at all. You know yourself best and you know the vulnerabilities and insecurities that the enemy will try to use against you, but that's what a battle plan is for.

1. *Be aware when the enemy speaks lies, and remind yourself of God's promises when he does.* Say whatever God spoke to you out loud, write them down, believe them, and know them as your truth.
2. *Believe in who God says you are.* When you start to feel discouraged, remember who God sees you as, which is a mighty warrior, one that He chose to fulfill His purpose long before you were created. You were literally made for this.
3. *Don't be afraid to ask.* When you feel like you can't see God around you, don't be ashamed to ask Him to prove Himself to you. He gladly will. His heart desires to show you Himself more than you desire Him to.
4. *Go in the strength you have.* When the enemy uses comparison of people, dreams, or gifts to distract you from your purpose, know that God has given you the exact weapons you need to fight your battle and fulfill your purpose. He isn't selling you short. Keep going in the strength you have with the gifts you've been given, and He'll do the rest.
5. *Repeat and be brave.* His Word will come to pass. Happy endings don't just happen in movies and books.

As the Lord spoke to me one day, so He speaks to you: "Here's what the enemy knows—that he can use your greatest desire to distract you for a time being. But what I know is that no matter how hard he presses, you won't break. And the more he does, the **stronger** you become." And through it all, know that God is for you and with you. *You can't prepare for what He's doing, for it is great, but you can trust in what He is doing for He is faithful.* As Elisabeth Elliot says, "The heart set to do the Father's Will need never fear defeat."[xxxix] His victory ***will*** come to pass! The Lord is with you, *mighty warrior*.

17

BEAUTY IN THE ASHES

The Spirit of the Sovereign Lord is on me, because the Lord has anointed me to preach good news to the poor. He has sent me to bind up the brokenhearted, to proclaim freedom for the captives and release from darkness for the prisoners, <u>to bestow on them a crown of beauty instead of ashes</u>, the oil of gladness instead of mourning, and a garment of praise instead of a spirit of despair.[xl]
Isaiah 61:1, 3 (emphasis added)

Fire: *a rapid, persistent chemical change that releases heat and light and is accompanied by flame.*[xli] There is a moment, a sudden set of time, that we, as Christians, have each walked through flames. Who we were died and fell into ashes; who we became flamed for all to see. Fire to fire we burned, from one to the other we ignited. From a refining fire around us to a brilliance within us, a liveliness of imagination before us. Out of luminosity of love to a vivacity of passion, we rose and we were bestowed a crown of beauty. It wasn't a fire that burned those who came near, but a fire that drew near the lost at its greatest intensity of light. It was evident. It was enchanting.

To those around that were fireproof, they couldn't feel the fire burning within us, but the flame around us was unquestionably seen. What they did see, they couldn't deny but believe, to then see and lay down their fireproof walls to be filled with the flame of passion and feel the fire of love. In a moment, everything can change. We can go from fireproof to living on fire, from ashes to beauty, from dead to alive.

18

IN WRITING

> *In view of all of this, <u>we are making a binding agreement, putting it in writing,</u> and our leaders, our Levites and our priests are affixing their seals to it.*[xlii]
> Nehemiah 9:38 (emphasis added)

Before we go back and find out why they say these words, I want you to think about the importance of having something in writing. I can think of a few things off of the top of my head: a marriage certificate, an ownership of a house, a diploma, or even a copyright statement. All of these are written agreements to have proof that they are real and binding. Now let's get back to the story. Just earlier, we see how God sustained the Israelites for forty years. It says in Nehemiah 9:21, "They lacked nothing, their clothes did not wear out nor did their feet become swollen…" for forty years! He gave them kingdoms and prosperity, he protected them and provided everything that they needed, and they were even as "numerous as the stars in the sky," and yet we see they rebelled against the God who provided all of this. We see that they had everything, but they forgot about God. Yet, when their enemies began to oppress them, they remembered Him. Verse 27 reads, "From heaven you heard them, and in your great compassion you gave them deliverers, who rescued them from the hand of

their enemies." However, we read on and see that, "As soon as they were at rest, they again did what was evil in your sight." Yet when they cried out to God again, He heard from heaven and in His compassion, He delivered them "time after time." The Israelites kept turning from God because they kept forgetting about Him. When they had everything they needed, they forgot He was everything, and so once again they'd fall.

There is a beautiful significance in writing, because not only is it proof, it's a reminder. And that's what the people came to realize. They didn't want to keep living in their present conditions, but they didn't want to forget His unconditional love either. So they wrote a binding agreement, so they could not forget, and to show how important it was to them. When it comes to you and God, what do you need to stop forgetting? Is it the dream that He placed on your heart and you kept pushing off? Is it writing Him into your planner so that you will make time for Him? Or maybe it is needing to write out your goals for the week/month/year to remind you that this is what you are aiming to do or become in a set period of time. It can even range from your prayer list to your sermon notes. There is just a beautiful significance in writing because no matter how many times you forget, the written agreement will always remind you of the reason and purpose instead of just the finish. *The beauty of promises made in our weakness is that they are faithfully kept by His strength*. So whatever God is speaking to your heart, write it down→ every single detail.

For you'll see the beauty in writing as every detail in your book becomes written into your reality by His love.

19

FIRST CHOICE

My child,

All that runs through your head are plans for your life. I am the maker of life and yet you focus your eyes on what's ahead rather than Who's beside you. Wait in patience for I speak in multiple ways. I am listening, but My Sovereignty speaks louder than My words. The silence isn't an unanswered prayer, but a faith-filled reply. My silence will draw you closer to My Word, which will draw you closer to strength. Stop looking back at what could have been and pray forward for what will be. I am faithful. I am true. I am love. I am God. I want to be your first choice and not your second plan. Trust in Me and I will show you where to walk. When life carries on, and you depend on Me, I carry you.

> "Regarding the covenant I made with you when your *ancestors* came out of Egypt, My Spirit remains with you, living among you. Do not be afraid. Yet once more I will shake not only the earth, but also the heavens, the sea, and the land. I will rattle all the nations, and all that is valuable in *the eyes of* the world will be *willingly* brought to My house. I will see to it that it is filled *to the brim* with My glory. *You see, all* the silver and *all* the gold *in this world already* belong to Me. *You will stand by and watch as* the magnificence of this new house will eclipse the magnificence of My first house. And in this *new* house, I will give *you* peace. On that day, I will choose you, my servant Zerubbabel (Shealtiel's son); this I declare. I will make you *My choice* as a signet ring *represents the wishes of its owner* because I have chosen you."[xliii]
> Haggai 2:5-9, 23 (emphasis added)

20

PROMISES LIKE PEONIES

I love that when Marco Polo saw peonies for the first time ever, he described them as "roses as big as cabbages."[xliv] It was so unfamiliar to him that he grabbed two familiar things, completely contrasting in substance, and repainted a picture with words of what he saw. Likewise, when God placed the phrase "Promises like Peonies" on my heart, it was such a wild combination that I knew it was from Him. The more depth I looked into the unique qualities of a peony, the more I saw why the two could so easily relate to the realm of faith.

When we dig deeper, we close our eyes to what we know to seek—that which we have not yet discovered. With closed eyes, we see glimpses of promises God has made, things that have never been made known before. On the contrary, with open eyes, we may see somewhat of an ordinary reality that can be overlooked as natural soil. Yet when God is in something, nothing is really ordinary; every detail is extraordinarily interwoven with supernatural designs. We must learn to dig deeper with a wild imagination to hear His whispers in their form. Faith may see far, but it still only sees a two-dimensional view of God's plan. It may see something rising up, it just doesn't fully know how great of a God-thing it truly is. At first glimpse it may look like a cabbage-sized rose, yet in coming closer with an open heart to the unimaginable, a completely different species may be found.

I live far out in the country, which creates a perfect backdrop of stars over my house. One night in particular, while driving home with a friend, a shooting star flew across the sky. She was so in wonder that she nearly cried. In that moment, I whispered a small prayer to always have that childlike wonder. As we sat on the roof this night, I looked up at the stars for the hundredth time, yet for the first time in a long time, I really saw them. I didn't see in a two-dimensional view, but in a three-dimensional wonder. I was stunned, wondering if the makeup of constellations were even the closest of distances to each other, or if they too were galaxies apart. My prayer is that we may live in an infinite wonder, forever dreaming of our days like this. That is what it's like to see cabbage-sized roses.

As Isaiah 43:19 says: "Behold, I am doing a new thing! Now it springs forth; do you not perceive and know it and will you not give heed to it?"[xlv] In taking our ordinary into His wild, allowing our focus to shift to His, we will discover things we never noticed before. In shifting my focus, I found: peonies symbolize honor, wealth, marriage, and beauty. Therefore, the whispers He had been speaking to my heart previously now had an image to layer their glimpsed promises with. Once I dug deeper, I saw a glimpse of what God was seeing from His three-dimensional view, and I was again, lost in wonder for the longest time.

When you're walking the paths designed by God's hand, they surely will be aligned with unfamiliar designs for they are new! New meaning: not existing before, a wild thought, never having been seen. *When it's God, He loves to create in wide-open spaces, where we know no thing, that He may do a new thing in three-dimensional designs.* If it can't be made up, it is unquestionably God at work! As Hebrews 10:23 says: "Let us hold unswervingly to the hope we profess, for he who promised is faithful."[xlvi] You may have two familiar thoughts like promises and peonies to describe your unfamiliar glimpse. Hold onto them with every bit of fierce courage within you. You will see what's never been done before. Grasp tightly what you have seen, not letting the unknown steal its wonder, and move forward into its territory as brave and fierce as you are. If you know nothing about what's next, you may just be in for a wonderful surprise. You can never truly know what it may behold, but you can wait for it with a childlike wonder and a dreaming heart. I wonder what multilayered promises, as unique and wondrous as peonies, God has been thinking up for you—what deeper depth and dauntless dimension waits beyond the star-like glimpses you've seen.

21
SHAPED

Inspired by Proverbs 27:17

Iron sharpens iron
Your heart shapes my heart
All watch it grow to greater heights

My heart is open Your love revealed
Now I see with eternal eyes

As iron sharpens iron,
so one person sharpens another.[xlvii]

A hope ahead The past behind
A new story has become

I am new
My chains unshackled Victory is won

A fire for love
A passion for rain Everything is clear

My broken ruins Your floods of grace
Love has conquered fear

@ kathleenmadethis

22

BY HIS SPIRIT

If there were a man in the Bible who I feel like had it altogether, it would have been Samson. From a young age he was set apart for greatness. He had strength, God's favor, a woman he loved, and he was victorious in all that was placed before him. Or as some would describe, a perfect life. But somewhere in the midst of God's preparation of Samson, for his battle against the Philistines, Samson started to believe it was by his own strength instead of the Lord's Spirit. So much so that by Judges 16:20 we read, "But he did not know that the Lord had left him."[xlviii] It's one of the most heartbreaking verses in the Bible, and it's one of the most humbling. Looking back at Samson's victories, we realize that before each one it says, "The Spirit of the Lord came upon him in power." But instead of giving praise to the Lord, he took the praise himself. And that was Samson's greatest imperfection—he failed to acknowledge that every form of perfection he had in his life came from the Lord. And in turn, he lost everything without realizing it. Everything referring to the greatest promise of all—God Himself. Reading the story reminds me of a moment God whispered to my heart something that left me taken aback for a few minutes: "When you have everything, will I still be your Everything?" It was one of those stand still moments where I imagined having everything I ever prayed for, my idea of a perfect life, but without God in it. And all of a sudden, I realized how empty it felt. Then I thought about my "now," with all the little details I loved about it, seeing God over everything, and I realized I loved the life I already had. I saw everything I had in Him instead of everything I wanted for me. And it was there that Psalm 23 really stuck out to my heart, "The Lord is my shepherd, I shall not be in want. He makes me lie down in green pastures, he leads me beside quiet waters, he restores my soul. He guides me in paths of righteousness for his name's sake… Surely goodness and love will follow me all the days of my life, and I will dwell in the house of the Lord forever."[xlix] Sometimes I wonder how different things would have turned out if Samson realized his everything was in God—if then he would have not been in want of Delilah, leading him astray. If he would have lived his very own "perfect life" with the perfect God over it all. If we were in Samson's shoes, would we have realized everything we had was from the Lord's love for us? To know <u>He is everything</u> we want even without having everything we asked. Our perfect life is having Him as our everything, and when we realize this, how much more differently will we live our lives knowing His Spirit is our one desire. Because I believe it is there that our faith is strengthened, our courage discovered, our love intensified, our passion adventured. When we realize that it's by His Spirit that **all** happens, we will see all of our gifts and blessings come from Him. And when they do come, it will be in His will and in His timing. And that is where freedom is found—in knowing that by His Spirit our everything is found in Him.

> *"Not by might nor by power, but by my Spirit," says the Lord Almighty.*[l]
> Zechariah 4:6

23

PEACE IN HIS PLAN

> *"For I know the plans I have for you," declares the Lord, "plans to prosper you and not to harm you, plans to give you a hope and a future."*[li]
> Jeremiah 29:11

When we say, "I can't do this," God replies, "I can." When we feel lost, God knows exactly where we are. In our insufficiency, God is made known. This brings me to a point of understanding. It's something we all desire, to know everything as soon as we can. We like to say, "We can handle it." But I believe that if we knew the answers we sought too soon, we would run in fear instead of courage. We tend to sit and wonder of how God will use us, overlooking the fact that we are already being used. God will prepare us with baby steps to achieve His great plan before us. Yet notice how I said plan, not dream. A dream is thought up in the mind and usually wanders there. A plan has been well thought out and is already in the working with a finish in mind. His plans are greater than our dreams, and they are already at work in us. There are moments that we will be walking blindly by faith, but we won't be wandering aimlessly. Just remember, it is greater to have peace with no understanding than understanding with no peace. Because when we have understanding, it usually is to our plan. But when we have peace, it is often for His plan. Someone once told me, "God is wanting to reveal His will to you more than you want Him to." And He so does, but we just need to trust Him enough to let Him work for our good, for He always works for the good of those who love Him. It is because of His great love for us that, even when love is blind, we can find peace in His plan.

> *You will never find an answer apart from God; you will only find a solution.*

24

BE YOU TO THE FULL

Dr. Seuss said, "Be who you are and say what you feel, because those who mind don't matter and those who matter don't mind."[lii] There is such a freedom that is found in being yourself. But did you know that this quote applies to your ministry too? I'm not sure about you, but I know that I have had *many* moments of feeling insignificant, inferior, inadequate, and any other "in" word that made me feel **so** small in the call of the Great Commission. I didn't feel good enough, I didn't feel qualified, and I surely did not feel like I was making a difference wherever I was. I was just simply "me." There's one night in particular that my "me" side decided to run. I had moved from a town of 2,500 to a church size of around 12,000, and as our youth service started to end, I, the leader, felt so small. I walked out of those church doors after six months of attending, about to quit. I went up on a hill nearby and started to call my church leader to talk things over with; I am thankful now that she didn't pick up. One lesson I learned then is that when we do come to a place with a fork in the road, we shouldn't call for wise words from just anyone, but from the One who knows all. I was ready to leave that fork behind, but God spoke so clearly and told me to go back inside. To be real, I did contemplate with God for a few minutes before I listened. I walked right back into those doors and tried to be myself—to pour out, to let others pour in, and something changed. Actually, a lot from that day on changed. Girls started to open up to me, God started speaking through me, and people around me kept reminding me of what they saw in me. It was a complete turn around. This moment reminds me a lot of the story of Jonah. He was called to preach to the city of Nineveh, which happened to be a fork he did not want to take, and so instead God gave him a huge fish. Or really, I guess it was the other way around, the huge fish got a Jonah. Talk about feeling small. But we see that Jonah cried out to God in this moment. And again God spoke in Jonah 3:2, "Get up and go to the great city of Nineveh, and deliver the message I have given you."[liii]

I believe God is speaking this same message to many of us today, and yet, I wonder how many of us have let our feelings of insignificance dictate our comfort. Or how many of us have willingly fled from the call because of having failed so many times before. God is simply saying, "Get up! You are whom I have chosen. You are the one that I have called. You **can** do this, not by might, not by power, but by my Spirit, for I am with you." *You are the greatest qualification that you have.* There is no one else like you that speaks, creates, or even thinks the same way. And that is what "being you" to the FULL is all about. You can be anybody, but not anybody can be you. When it comes down to what matters most, you will discover it is found at the fork in the road. In the moment of standing with fear and courage on your left and right, just remember, *you were made for this*. You, the one like no other, were made, handcrafted and shaped, for this, this moment, this place, this season. Then **go** and deliver what you were made for. Be you to the full.

25

STICKS AND STONES

Sticks and stones may break my bones, but words can never hurt me.[liv]

Words. They are unquestionably powerful and yet we use them without question. They can be an expression of our identity, emotions, or moods, but they can also shape and create a moment, a situation, and ultimately a person. In Genesis 1:26 it reads, "Then God <u>said</u>, 'Let us make man in our image, in our likeness...'" to go on to say in verse 27, "So God <u>created</u> man in his image."[lv] (emphasis added) God created what He spoke, and I believe our words do the same. As Rudyard Kipling put it, "I am by nature a dealer in words, and words are the most powerful drug known to humanity."[lvi] Simply put, <u>words are powerful.</u> Growing up with Marvel movies, my vivid imagination can only piece together that words are a lot like a superpower we all have. They create, reshape, break, or destroy, and you control them all. You see, just like a superpower! But we treat words as if they were nothing when they are always creating something. So my question is: what words are you allowing to create you? Because, honestly, everything we read, hear, and think about is in some shape and form of a word. It can be things through social media, movies, books, conversations, and events. They all hold power that create and shape you a little more every time. And the thing is, change is constant, but it's slightly invisible, because you don't realize its impact until you look back. If you look back a week from now, you may not see much. But if you look back a year, you'll see various seasons of change that formed and shaped you in someway to who you are right now. But what we must look at is not whether or not we changed, but <u>how</u> we changed, either for better or for worse. Like Proverbs 18:21 says, "Words kill, words give life; they're either poison or fruit—you choose."[lvii] Are the words you're letting in creating life within you? Or are they taking away from the life God intended for you? Because words are powerful—they can create and reshape or break and destroy. So be aware of the words that are impacting your moments, because they can also impact your lifetime.

26

TAKE A BREATH

There's an indescribable peace that calms us in the depths of taking a breath.

Breath. It's what keeps our hearts beating, keeps us going, and keeps us alive. And like many things, we forget about the importance of breathing. We typically don't notice it until we are short of breath and are desperate to breathe to function normally again. It's important. We see in Genesis 2:7 that God <u>breathed</u> life into man, and he became a living being. His eyes opened, his heart beat, his strength grew, he was alive. But many of us can feel like we are dead, failing, hopeless. We can devalue ourselves and the willingness God has to breathe life into us. We can allow life-changing dreams to die, allow ourselves to keep living with emotional struggles, give up when we fall, run from open doors in fear, and forget that we've been made ALIVE in Christ. We disbelieve that our dreams matter; our hearts matter; He hears us; He cares for us; He adores us, and He wants to help us. We forget His love is willing to breathe life into our dreams, willing to breathe hope into our hearts, willing to breathe good into our situations. As Ezekiel 37:9-10 says, *Then He said to me, "Prophesy to the breath; prophesy, son of man, and say to it, 'This is what the Sovereign Lord says: come from the four winds, O breath, and breathe into these slain, that they may live.'" So I prophesied as he commanded me, and breath entered them; they came to life and stood up on their feet—a vast army."*[lviii] The thing is that these were merely dry bones, and the breath of God brought them to life. He made flesh come upon them, created skin to cover them, and they came alive—simply by His breath. Even if we see our dreams, values, and wishes as dry bones, He can still change everything about its composition. He *breathes* and miracles flow. How much more will He do when He *speaks* for His beloved ones? When you feel like your heart's desires aren't worth it anymore, God still believes they are, because you're forever worth it to Him. So instead of allowing yourself to be dry, ask God to breathe into your dreams, values, and wishes! You see, when your heart is dry, it's like you are short of breath—your vision is impaired, your heart is racing, and you feel weak. But when God breathes into your lungs, you see clearly. His peace steadies your heart and thoughts, and He makes you strong again. As Ezekiel 37:14 says, "I'll breathe my life into you and you'll live."[lix] So take a deep breath, breathe in His love and breathe out His peace; and know deeply, you are fully loved, and again, fully alive!

27

THE VOYAGE

To look behind you can lead to compromise; to look beside you can lead to comparison;
Yet, to look forward beyond you can cultivate much more power, self-discipline,
and love, Leading you from glory to glory on grace-filled paths of freedom.

A voyage is an uncommon journey that a rare handful of us are willingly able to experience in life. It's "a course of travel or passage"[lx] that is typically by water or through air or space. Merriam Webster defines it as: "a long journey to a distant or unknown place."[lxi] On a voyage, you have no idea where you are going, and very few factors remain known. A few of them being: one, you're not going to be on land for a long time; two, seafood or pretzels will be your favorite meal for the next few months to come; and lastly, you are going to be your very own best friend until you see civilization again. Now obviously number two and three are a little sarcastic and can vary depending on the voyage. But number one, that is as straightforward as you can get. Land—the solid, reassuring, safe place you have lived on for so many years, you will miss it like crazy on the rocky and turbulent days ahead. Still, not everything about a voyage is dreadful and scary. You will see things no one has seen before, discover places you've never known, and grow in an entirely new way as the captain of your voyage prepares you for your next destination.

One prime candidate in the Bible, who was well-known for his voyages, would be Abraham. He went from place to place on the word "go," not knowing where he was headed, not knowing how the Lord would provide. Just like we each have our own definitions for the voyages we are on. Moses wandered for forty plus years for a land he heard of and hoped existed. Noah was on a voyage, literally by sea, for way too many months before land came into sight. And for you, it may be leaving the life you have grown comfortable with to go live an unheard of dream, to go to a place you are not sure the Lord will provide for, or to simply draw closer to your Captain in trust, in which you're not certain of what your end destination may be. What you do know is that you are now on the boat and there is no turning back—you are *all* in.

Do you know what God spoke to Abraham after he obeyed? His heart's greatest desire—a son. God told him, "Look up at the heavens and *count the stars*—if indeed you can count them… so shall your offspring be."[lxii] (Genesis 15:5, emphasis added) Abraham finally landed on his distant unknown land so many years later, and God gave him a promise he wasn't expecting, but was dreaming up on his voyage. Little did Abraham know that the Captain of his heart was listening to him on all those long, starry nights. Now the stars he had seen so many times before were about to be looked at through a completely new perspective. They now represented his offspring, and where there was once much mystery, there was now much promise. Likewise, God is telling you "look up," to have a new perspective for the voyage of trust you are on, and He is reassuring you with "count the stars" because He can. It's His way of saying, **You don't have to have this figured out. It doesn't have to make sense. You don't need to know where you are going because I do, and I am able to do ALL things.** As He says in Isaiah 43:19: "SEE, I am doing a new thing,"[lxiii] (emphasis added) God is going before the voyage you are now on, making a way to fulfill the promises you chatted about on the voyage to make them come to life right before your very eyes! And on your voyage, this is my saying for you to remember: "Don't look behind at what was once good because greater is ahead. Don't look at someone else's voyage in envy because God knows the route He needs to take you on to get you to your destination. And finally, look forward in a way that sees all that God is doing right before your very eyes here and now." For as Marcel Proust says: "The real voyage of discovery consists not in seeking new landscapes, but in having new eyes."[lxiv]

28

THE STRENGTH IN JOY

In the deepest of sorrows, joy is there. In the greatest of unknowns, joy is there. In the most hidden of valleys, joy is there. Joy is everywhere. I believe it is one of the most powerful things next to prayer. It is in the moments we feel lost, in the times where we face fear, and in the pause of something lost. *Joy is our reminder that life goes on*—that there is still beauty out there; that everything is going to be okay. Nehemiah 8:10 says, "Do not grieve, for the joy of the Lord is your strength."[lxv] There is a weight in sorrow, but a strength in joy. And joy is everywhere—so it is always with you, which means—you are going to get through this. You are stronger than you know.

29

AN ARTWORK IN PROGRESS

> Kintsugi: the art of repairing metal with gold or silver lacquer and understanding that the piece is *more beautiful for having been broken.*[lxvi]

In Japanese philosophy, there exists this idea of "wabi-sabi." It is the act of embracing the flawed or the imperfect. Kintsugi is used to mend together broken pottery. In this method, the cracks are highlighted, rather than hidden, and filled instead of ruined. The art is about seeing less as more and embracing imperfection for its worth. However, imperfection to most is defined as a fault, blemish, or undesirable feature, being faulty or incomplete.[lxvii] It's harder for the world to grasp imperfection as beauty because we live in a world that "fixes" things that are not perfect. *Yet, maybe imperfection is actually incompletion waiting to be completed again.* It is not a matter of whole or ruined, but rather a work of art that is continually reshaped to highlight the beauty even more through time. Perhaps, our lives are what we label as imperfect in which we have been in strife trying *to fix* all this time, when it is merely space in our hearts for God *to fill* time and time again. Maybe all along, your life has been art in the making to become more beautiful having been broken, and instead of hiding the cracks, you can allow the gold to highlight your designed strength.

I wonder what it is that you have labeled as ruined, imperfect, and unchangeable, which is wholeheartedly in need of filling? Or what have you settled with because you've given up on hope for its completion? No matter the case, God treasures their value. He cares for your cares. As He delights in the details of your life, He also hurts for the breaking of your heart. And though you may not see it or completely understand it yet, there is beauty to be completed within an artwork in progress.

A work in progress is an unfinished project that is still being added to or developed.[lxviii] Just like our hearts are simply an artwork in progress, being continually developed, designed, and reshaped by the filling of gold. A few weeks ago, I heard an invitation: "Let me see your heart. Do you want it to be fixed?" And my response was, "I want it to be filled." I wanted the same Holy Spirit to fill me with what was spoken of in Exodus 31:3-5: *I have filled him with the Spirit of God in wisdom, in understanding, in knowledge, and in all kinds of craftsmanship, to make artistic designs for work in gold, in silver, and in bronze, and in the cutting of stones for settings, and in the carving of wood, that he may work in all kinds of craftsmanship.*[lxix] I wanted my broken heart to be filled—with glory and gold and overflowing with joy because of it. There is a power in the broken, for that's where God creates **gold.**

A fact about gold: Scientists estimate 80% of the world's gold still remains *undiscovered.*[lxx] I can only imagine the amount of gold undiscovered in our lives. Let me encourage you that when you are in that standstill moment of discouragement and disappointment, know a miracle is about to take place because His power has become the atmosphere around you.

In this parable of the breaking of bread, we read:

One of his disciples, Andrew, Simon Peter's brother, said to him, "There is a boy here who has five barley loaves and two fish, but {what are they for so many?}" Jesus said, "Have the people <u>sit down</u>." Now there was much grass in the place. So the men sat down, about five thousand in number. Jesus then took the loaves, and when he had given thanks, he distributed them to *those who were seated. So also the fish, as much as they wanted. And when they had eaten their fill, he told his disciples, "Gather up the leftover fragments, that nothing may be lost." So they gathered them up and filled twelve baskets with fragments from the five barley loaves left by those who had eaten.*[lxxi] *(John 6:8-13, emphasis added)*

In the process of breaking, you easily can wonder what you have in your hands for so many? When you're overwhelmed with all that God's placed in your heart *(the 5,000 dreams and needs)*, and you just don't know what good the pieces are in your hands, Jesus has you sit—for a miracle is about to take place. Sitting still, you become MORE aware of your emptiness. Yet, it brings you to this desperation for God that results in breaking. But take courage, for in the breaking miracles happen, and you *see God Himself* remain faithful to your heart. Not only that, He picks up the leftover fragments because He wastes no thing, even when you are full, He still treasures the fragments, because they still matter. As Isaiah 58:11-12 reads:

I will always show you where to go. I'll give you a full life in the emptiest of places—firm muscles, strong bones. You'll be like a well-watered garden, a gurgling spring that never runs dry. You'll use the old rubble of past lives to build anew, rebuild the foundations from out of your past. You'll be known as those who can fix anything restore old ruins, rebuild and renovate, make the community livable again.[lxxii]

I promise you this, you are not empty to be left empty. God is so ready to pour out His Spirit on your longings and your needs. He's ready to fill in the spaces with gold, to highlight the weak with strength, to build anew with love and generosity, an artwork worth waiting for. My friend, the Holy Spirit will bring completion to the incomplete and will fill those who empty their hearts before Him. Know you are only becoming more beautiful having been broken that you may see His beauty in this broken world. Know He cares for every fragment and detail of your life, that nothing is unseen and He stops to listen to you. Know you are an artwork in progress in which He is filling empty spaces with gold. May you believe that He is faithful—for if you'll sit just a little bit longer, you'll see His hand perform miracles overflowing with His glory and goodness all around you. Don't give up in the process, for when you discover the gold, you will discover His great love that has always been for you.

> *All beautiful things carry distinctions of imperfection. Your wounds and imperfections are your beauty. Like Kintsugi, the Japanese art of mending broken pottery with gold, we are all perfectly imperfect. Breakage and mending are honest parts of a past which should not be hidden. Your wounds and healing are a part of your history; a part of who you are. Every beautiful thing is damaged. You are that beauty; we all are.*[lxxiii]
> Bryant McGill

30

KEEP ON RUNNING

In running a race, <u>the race</u>, set out before you. You will have people come and go—some who are at the same speed, some who take a different course, and some who hold a different level of endurance. But we are <u>all</u> called to run it. There was once a cross-country meet I was competing in, and as I was jogging next to my friend in this race, ¾ of the way through, she needed to take a break. Yet being completely fine and energetic, I told her I was going to go on, only to find out that within the last stretch, the person in front of me was the last one I needed to pass to win a bronze medal. Let's just say, I easily got that medal with all the stored up energy I had. My friend was upset, but my coach was *so proud*. How much more, I wonder, is God cheering us on to go after what is in our hearts, yet we are being held back by the company of comfort, fear, or pride. Maybe even a better word would be familiarity—to cling to what makes sense, what you see and know, instead of "pressing on" to what God has before you, as Paul puts it. He states, "But I press on to possess that perfection for which Christ Jesus first possessed me. No, dear brothers and sisters, I have not achieved it, but I focus on this one thing: Forgetting the past and looking forward to what lies ahead, I press on to reach the end of the race and receive the heavenly prize for which God, through Christ Jesus, is calling us."[lxxiv] (Philippians 3:12-14) Some of us are still running someone else's race, being dragged behind from the potential within. Others of us are waiting for someone to run with us, missing the greatness that's right before us *now*. And some of us are heaving on the side, thinking we can't go on. Let me encourage you— PRESS ON! Don't give up. God didn't call you to a race you couldn't finish. It's okay to move on from familiarity to experience the unimaginable. It's where God wants to take you. Press on to possess the perfection for which Jesus first possessed you. Keep on running!

31

TRANSFORMED

Do not conform to the pattern of this world, but be transformed by the renewing of your mind. Then you will be able to test and approve what God's will is— his good, pleasing, and perfect will.[lxxv]
Romans 12:2

This verse has been impressed on my heart for years, honestly. But trying to figure out exactly what it meant always would stump me. I knew that to be transformed was to change in character or appearance technically. But I still had that weighted question within me, "Am I truly being transformed?" It wasn't until I decided to look up the term for "renew" that the meaning dawned on me. The definition according to Google was: *"to resume* after an interruption." In a more biblical sense: "to resume what God was speaking over one's destiny before the enemy interrupted with distractions."

In the story of Hosea, God speaks, "Therefore I am now going to allure her; I will lead her into the wilderness and speak tenderly to her. There I will give her back her vineyards, and will make the Valley of Achor a door of hope."[lxxvi] (emphasis added) He speaks about *renewing* her. How? With His love. Where? In her brokenness. Why? Because she was "interrupted" and distracted, and "went after her lovers, but God she forgot." (2:13) The same way God wanted to allure Israel back to Him is the same way He wants to *resume* His love and promises in our lives. It is in that brokenness, where we walk in the Valley of Achor, that God fights for our hearts. But the thing is, it is there that the enemy is especially fighting for our attention too. We can recognize that we are in a different season, but we usually overlook the fact that we are also in a battle. In all the pieces around us, God will come in and speak truth over us, reminding us of His promises before us, and ultimately lavishing His love on us. But it is also in those pieces that the enemy will try to creep in and speak what we expect to hear, "You're not strong enough. You just have to accept who you are. This is something you can't overcome." And the crazy part is, we often listen to them as our own thoughts, and we recite them over and over feeling defeated. But this is where God whispers, "Wake up." And our eyes all of a sudden can see *all* that the enemy has been doing to overpower us, instead of recognizing God's power within us. It's where God speaks, "What are you thinking?" To realize those aren't our thoughts or His words. It's where we are called to put on the full body of armor in Ephesians 6:10-18 to be strong, not in ourselves, but "in the Lord and in His mighty power."[lxxvii] Because the thing is, *you are so much* **more**. And the enemy knows that, and he will try to contain you by interrupting the plans God has for you.

The enemy will do anything to try to distract you from seeing God's power at work in you. But it's when you fight back in God's strength, in His name, and in His power, that you are renewed—because your focus is back on *Him*. What God can do through you is greater than anything you can do alone. But that is the most amazing thing! Because that means that you are more, and you can overcome anything! You aren't who you were any longer. You are *new* and *better* and *stronger*. Who you once were is gone, and who you believe to be now is who you will be. But make sure whoever that person is, is the same person God *sees* and *believes*. It's not this broken, helpless person who is ordinary. No. It's this outstanding, wonderful, child of God who has been transformed. Like 2

Corinthians 3:18 says, "And we all, who with unveiled faces contemplate the Lord's glory, are being **transformed** into His image with ever-increasing glory, which comes from the Lord, who is the Spirit."[lxxviii] (emphasis added) When we set our eyes on the Lord's glory, on all the greatness He is doing in us and around us, we press resume on our lives. We focus on what He sees. We believe in what He says. You are powerful in Him. You will overcome with Him. And you are transformed by Him. And that is *renewing* from the inside-out. Then you will see that His will is good, His will is pleasing, and His will is perfect.

32

ARDENT

Be expectant; be filled with hope. Be fearless, My love, for there is more before you. There is more of Myself I will reveal to you, for you seek Me wholeheartedly and devotedly. I am found in the details—seek with wonder-filled eyes and you will always find Me. Come to Me with all you find, and I will bring life to your discoveries. What you plant, I will garden. What you choose, I will pursue. What you seek, I will find. For My love is ardent for you. Let worry be far from you, it has no room in your heart, then you will be at home in Me. My Word is My Word. I know trusting is crazy, but it is also gentle. My love is fierce, but it's also refined. It is pure, and it is gold. That is why what you touch will turn to gold, for My love has marked it. Your love is enough for Me, but you will see Me more in all that you do. It's not a requirement, but a reminder of who I am. All that I am is yours, and all that you have is Mine. Keep it, treasure it, and steward it, and you will see an overflow of abundance. You will see every whisper come to life.

"For the Lord is always good and ready to receive you. He's so loving that it will amaze you—so kind that it will astound you! And he is famous for his faithfulness toward all. Everyone knows our God can be trusted, for he keeps his promises to every generation."[lxxix]
Psalm 100:5

33

LETTING GO IS HOW A BIRD LEARNS TO FLY

"The sun rises, the clouds shape, and the melodies start to ring in the air. Safe—that is how I feel. Comfortable—that is what I am. Everything I need is right here. My family, my necessities to live, my home, and yet I always wonder—what if there is more? As I look out into the forest and at the land, I see others soaring, flying, higher and lower—they're free. It's something I've always wanted to try, but I'm scared. Afraid to leave everything I've ever known to do something I've never done. But today is different, because I don't want to merely live anymore; I want to be alive. My feet tremble in fear as I walk to the ledge. My thoughts race with all that can go wrong, but I feel it in my heart—that soft faint whisper saying, "Go." It's the whisper I hear when I wonder, yet now it's stronger than ever, and so I let go and fall. I hear the whistles of lullabies in my ears, I feel the wind wrap around me, and I open my wings—I am free."

The thrilling experience a bird must have in learning to fly is indescribable, but it starts with letting go. Growing up, I think we all had dreams and ideas built up within our hearts of what we were going to do in our future. We'd talk about it with the ones we loved, and it'd fill our hearts with so much excitement. Then, we do. We grow up, and there's this moment when we look over the view of our safety, our eyes grow open to again wonder, and all of a sudden, the thought comes into our hearts, "What if?" During that moment everything changes. So many needs are seen and discovered, and ever so softly we hear that faint whisper, "Go." We feel unstoppable and we take a step, but it is within that first step that our reality shakes. We realize we are leaving everything we know. We are leaving comfort, safety, and relationships behind, and it is scary. But it takes change within us for change to happen around us; and *sometimes it is within the waves of change that we find our true direction*. Every difference made has required risk. Every revolution began with a step. Every dream began with letting go of fear to fly. You see, you cannot perfect change; it is not something you can truly prepare for. However, change can perfect you, for in its embrace, you will learn how to soar. It is not those who hear the Lord that will change the world, but those who listen to the Lord. It is those who risk falling that find their wings.

*But those who trust in the Lord will find **new** strength. They will soar high on wings like eagles, they will run and not grow weary, they will walk and not faint.*[lxxx]
Isaiah 40:31 (emphasis added)

34

CHOSEN

> *All that is gold does not glitter, not all those who wander are lost;*
> *the old that is strong does not wither, deep roots are not reached by the frost.*[lxxxi]
> - J. R. R. Tolkien

I'm going to tell you a story. One of a beautiful orphan girl who is wandering the streets. She runs into a man. He looks ordinary, but there's something kind that lights up within his eyes when he sees her. They find a nearby bench where the man listens to the girl talk about all she has seen and experienced that day, and it brings such joy to his heart. When she finally runs out of words to say, he reveals his true self to her. He is a king who has much and loves much. He asks if she would like to be his new daughter. Overcome with excitement, she says, "Yes!" And so he allows her to live in his kingdom, teaches her to be intelligent, crowns her with treasures, and calls her his child. But as time passes, she begins to wander from the castle, becoming distracted by the beauty the world offers. She becomes so infatuated with all that is around her that she forgets about everything her father has done. She becomes so focused on filling her heart with what is in front of her, that she can't seem to fill the part of her heart that is missing. Months pass and she sits down on the corner of the street wondering where it is that she lost her joy. Out of the corner of her eye, she sees the bench where her father found her—not her beauty, her riches, nor her status. He just loved her for her. And so she courageously sends him a letter, not knowing if he'd welcome her back. He replies instantly with an instruction to meet him at the bench at noon. On the dot, he arrives and asks her to walk with him. He leads her into a beautiful forest where she begins to talk about all she remembered from when they first met. He sees the light come and go from her eyes as she talks about her search for meaning. As she looks around the forest that has nothing to offer, she looks back at her father and says, "But here. Here I feel complete. Because you are here, and now I realize, that has been my heart's desire all along. You are my soul's delight." As she kneels by her father, he takes her hand, with compassion in his eyes, tears softly rolling down his cheeks, and he replies, "I have always chosen you. It was just you that had to choose me."

This is a story of Israel found in Hosea. Israel was chosen by God to be His people, and yet they kept wandering off trying to find meaning elsewhere. Like the daughter, Israel wandered from God and ultimately forgot about His love. We find God's response in Hosea 2: "Therefore I am now going to allure her; I will lead her into the wilderness and speak tenderly to her."[lxxxii] This beautiful picture is painted as He brings His chosen back to a place with no distractions, to remind them of His great love. Hosea goes on to read in 2:15, "There I will giver her back her vineyards and will make the valley of Achor a door of hope. There she will sing as in the days of her youth, as in the day she came up out of Egypt."[lxxxiii] Once again, we see that Israel has found the joy of the Lord and replaced their delight in Him.

Now, we can reread the beginning poem a little differently than before. For as one returns, one cannot deny: *Not everything that is pleasing to the eye is as pleasing to the soul, and wandering doesn't always mean you're lost, but choosing where you're found. The most defining moments in life cannot be forgotten, for love's truth goes far deeper than treasure's roots, which shan't ever be touched by nature's sound.* The end of the poem goes onto read, "From the ashes a fire will be woken, a light from the shadows shall spring; renewed shall be blade that was broken, the crownless again shall be king." [lxxxiv] The orphan's story was remembered, and hope arose everywhere because she was with the king again. She remembered his kindness, and she chose him. Israel remembered God's love and choose Him. Now it's our turn, to remember His heart and choose Him as He chooses us, again and again.

35

LIVING IN VALUE

Something I have realized is that there is so much more room for God's plan when you finally stop holding onto your own. As humans, we sometimes think we have everything all figured out, when we actually have no clue. God has so much more in store for us than we can even fathom, but we must learn to let go of what is behind to move forward into the beauty that is ahead. A bit of small advice: Live life day-by-day, and you'll be following God's plan. It's as simple as that! And yet, our little minds of understanding try to make it so much more complex. *Maybe a revelation really just starts with a realization that where you are is where you're supposed to be.* It's not a give-and-take, share-and-compare, type deal. It's a trust that God has your world in His hands. Of course, walking with God isn't going to be a breeze. Although we have sight and senses, we have to learn to love God beyond our senses, to truly trust with our minds and souls. Let our every thought wrap around Him as His arms wrap around us. Let us seek His will and face in every opportunity and every circumstance. Let us fall in love with God every day. As we draw closer to His heart, He reveals more and more of Himself to us. Oswald Chambers beautifully puts it this way:

The nature of spiritual life is that we are certain in our uncertainty, consequently we do not make our nests anywhere. Common sense says, "Well, supposing I were in that condition..." We cannot suppose ourselves in any condition we have never been in. Certainty is the mark of common sense life; gracious uncertainty is the mark of the spiritual life. To be certain of God means that we are uncertain in our ways, we do not know what a day may bring forth. This is generally said with a sign of sadness, it should

rather be an expression of breathless expectation. We are uncertain of the next step, but we are certain of God… Leave the whole thing to Him, it is gloriously how He will come in, but He will come. Remain loyal to Him.[lxxxv]

My words of wisdom for you to never forget are: Everything that you are going through is worth it for the One who finds worth in you. Living in value is simply living knowing you're valued. As Psalm 139:16 says, "You saw me before I was born. Every day of my life was recorded in your book. Every moment was laid out before a single day had passed."[lxxxvi] You can trust nothing takes Him by surprise. He most likely has a surprise waiting around the corner just for you. Thus, you just have to trust Him, and wait and see, to find out!

36

PLEASANT PLACES

> "To *be* or not to *be*. That is the question," says William Shakespeare.[lxxxvii]
> Which also reminds me of my absolute favorite quote by Jim Elliot:
> "Wherever you are, *be* all there."[lxxxviii]

To "be" can be described as to live or to exist.[lxxxix] It can also be defined as to take place. As it says in Acts 17:28, "For in Him we live and move and have our being."[xc] But in the placement of being, it's easy for our minds to wander to other places—that's where the question lies and arises. Because around our being we find those boundaries. They are usually known but not commonly welcomed. But boundaries were never meant to deprive our lives but to protect our hearts. Take Adam and Eve, for example. They had boundary lines in pleasant places all the way up until the tree of knowledge. But why did they eat the fruit? Because they thought they were being deprived, not protected. They wanted to know and understand, instead of trust and be where they were placed. Now let's relate this to us—because we often let our minds wander to the fruit of the tree of knowledge, instead of standing on the Rock of truth. Isn't it interesting how the tree of knowledge was outside the boundary lines? They didn't *need* to know everything, it was simply their human nature to *want* to literally take matters into their own hands. (Sound familiar?) Some of us have a great dream and call on our life. One that is unquestionably extraordinary. But it just doesn't look the way we thought it would. Where we are right now doesn't make sense at all in light of where we feel the strong desire to be. Financially, it doesn't make sense, and strategically it doesn't quite line up. Quite honestly, the tree of knowledge looks so sweet and tempting as the enemy whispers, "God is depriving you. *You* need to do something now or it will never happen." For some of us that's being married, or pastoring a church, being on the mission field, starting a nonprofit, opening a business, writing or finishing a book. Whatever it is, it's in your heart, but it doesn't seem to be just yet in your boundary lines. You may keep wondering, "Why is this in my heart if it's not in my hands?" But as Psalm 16:6 says, "The boundary lines have fallen for me in pleasant places; surely I have a delightful inheritance."[xci] They are there to protect us and shape us into who we are meant to be in Him—for it is in Him that we live and move and have our being. Instead of *placing* yourself where you want to *be*, **be** where you **are** placed. For outside of His boundary lines, you only bring confusion and hardship on yourself. But when you trust Him with where you are placed, and be fully there, you'll see His favor come to life all around you. He will go before you, and as you grow, the boundary lines will expand; and as you continually trust Him with what's placed before you, you'll see your dreams come into being—to come into place.

37
THE DETAILS

If there's one thing I have learned about the heart… it's that we'll never know it or understand it completely and fully. But there is One who will never fail it or lead it astray. There is One who sees the good and the bad, the pure and the ugly, and He loves and wants it all. What He creates out of those mixed emotions, those unknown desires, those unseen longings, is the most beautiful and wondrous art. What we simply place as material into His hands, He remakes into something glorious by His hands. *There's no treasure that could be bought, no sight that could be sought, and no journey that could be discovered, that could compare to the beauty God has before us.* There's no one who will ever want to give us greater than the One who shapes the definition of greatness. Oh, how He sees and knows the deepest details of our hearts and shapes them into the steps of our lives.

> *The Lord directs the steps of the godly.*
> *He delights in every detail of their lives.*
> *Though they stumble, they will never fall,*
> *for the Lord holds them by the hand.*[xcii]
> Psalm 37:23-24

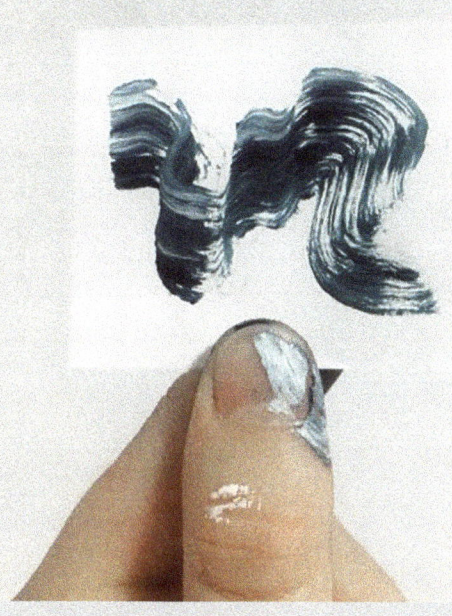

@ kathleenmadethis

38

A POWER IN PRAISE

Read Joshua 6

"There is a power in praise." This is the thought that has been running through my head for days, days filled with a few mountains, a lot of valleys, and many "in-between" moments. But the thing is, those moments were not typically my greatest memories, but the ones I wanted to get through quickly. They were the moments I was being human and stressed and honestly taken off guard. They were the moments that did not go according to my plan, and God was softly nudging me to praise instead of complain. We have all had those moments. But the thing that shocked me the most then was the actual power in praise—because it wasn't my situation that needed to change, but my perspective. In recalling the story of Jericho, I noticed the same nudge also being revealed to Joshua. God told Joshua to march around the walls of Jericho one time for six days to give him this great city. And on the seventh day He wanted them to march around it seven times and, on the seventh, to shout while the trumpets blared. And truthfully, this sounds kind of crazy. I'm sure if I was Joshua I would have been like, "Why don't you just do it now?" But I believe God was teaching them the power of trust and praise. Joshua strictly told them to not "give a war cry" or to even say a word until they were to shout. And so they didn't for six days. And when that trumpet sounded on the seventh march around the wall, it came falling down. "There is a power in praise." The Hebrew word for shout literally means "to make a joyful noise, to split the ears (with sound)."[xciii] Not only were they silent for six days, but then, they also praised God *before* the walls came down *because* of how much they trusted His word. And that's my challenge to you: to praise God for the small things and the great things in advance that are done for you or can be done unto others. Like in verse 10 of Joshua 6, do not give a war cry or complain about your circumstances, instead praise through them! When we complain, we build up spiritual, emotional, and physical walls that keep us trapped from seeing the beauty we can make out of the in-between moments. But when we begin to praise God even for the unexpected, our perspective changes to expect God to make the situation beautiful. It may not be the beauty we were expecting, but it won't be the repulsive idea we were making it out to be either. Instead, it will hold more details of delicacy that we wouldn't have seen otherwise. It's usually in the moments that God says something crazy that our walls of Jericho go up. But like Joshua and his men, we should trust and not complain, and praise through until the walls fall down and His blessings follow. There is a power in praise, so give a great shout when the unexpected happens, because you can expect God to shake things up as you do!

> *God is magnificent; he can never be praised enough.*
> *There are no boundaries to his greatness.*[xciv]
> Psalm 145:3

39

A RADICLE

"The first part of a seedling to emerge from the seed."[xcv]

It starts as a thought, a seed, and in our prayers, the roots grow deep.
Then all of a sudden, a breakthrough is seen. It's more than a vision, it's finally a dream.
To be wanderlust is to travel far, but we oversee the wonder in our hearts.
From fire to sparks or sparks to fire, a reaction is made by our own desire.
From where we are to where we want to be, a fine line stands in between.
There are ups and downs and places we can't see, when it comes to the path of discovery.
We wonder to live more than live in wonder, hide from our dreams as if life had a cover.
Because with every mountain, there is a cost, for what is behind may be lost.
It's a risk, a fear, an uncomfortable place, to not know the end with no replay.
But there's so much more than the eye can see; it goes above and beyond our wildest dreams.
With fear and wonder we were made, and our greatest loves are shaped the same.
Where there is no risk, there is no faith, so take a step where the road's unpaved.
All of the difference lies in a day, of the reasons and risks we do or don't take.
In looking back our faith will grow, but it's looking forward we must begin to go.
Within a radicle, everything can change. But the choice is ours, to live by fear or faith.
For those who choose fear, dream to one day see, for those
who chase faith, see their most radical dream.
And so it goes from glory to glory, from grace to grace, from radicle to radical, for the brave.

"But the seed planted in the good earth represents those who hear the Word,
embrace it, and produce a harvest beyond their wildest dreams."[xcvi]
Mark 4:20

40

A FULL LIFE

> *I will always show you where to go. I'll give you a full life in the emptiest of places.*[xcvii]
> Isaiah 58:11

What seeds has God placed in your heart? What talents has He placed in your hands? What people has He placed in your path? These are the three questions that separate an empty life and a full life. I believe that God has created us all perfectly, but also specifically, in a way to live life to the fullest in a completely different way than the person on our left or right, in front of us or behind us. Our full could be their empty, their full could be our empty, because we were made to live life differently. One of my favorite things to do is to listen to people's stories. I love to first see their personality, all their little kinks and quirks, the bits and bolts that make up who they are. Then I like to hear their passions, their dreams, and their greatest loves. Then finally, how God has brought them to where they are, for every story is so orchestrated and intertwined with those seeds, talents, and people that they couldn't have done on their own. You see God's grace and favor is over their lives; it always leaves me in awe, not only of the person, but of how awesome our God is. It amazes me to see what He already saw in us from the beginning, and that He has been hemming behind and before us in a timely fashion. Through it all, we are simply living the life we love, and in doing so glorifying the God we love.

When I think about these three questions, I think about multiple parables in the Bible. One of them being the parable of the mustard seed in Matthew 13:32 which says, "Though it is the smallest of all seeds, yet when it grows, it is the largest of garden plants and becomes a tree…"[xcviii] The second is the parable of the talents, where each man was going on a journey, and each was given a certain amount of talents to use. And then I think about the countless people God placed in others' journeys to help them along the way. There was Ruth with Naomi, Elisha with Elijah, Deborah with Barak, Jonathan with David, and so on. Tying these all together, I feel like the little seeds, or the little dreams, God places in our hearts are not just simply something we are supposed to stick in our pockets; they are designed within us to be planted and to grow into an unimaginable reality. But we usually get stumped at the question, "How do I grow this seed?" or "How do I pursue this dream?" This is where the talents come in. God simply says, "Use what is in your hands."

He has given each of us specific and unique gifts to match perfectly with the desires of our hearts. But the thing is, it's a journey, and that's where people come in. God places specific people in our path to help us when we are weak or blind, and to encourage us on in the journey we are walking. Not only that, but in the process of being impacted, you will yourself be impacting others beyond what you could know. **The separation between an empty life and a full life is either going after what God has placed in your heart or simply letting your dreams be dreams.** There's something fulfilling and purpose-filled when we live our lives intentionally for a God that is far greater than we could ever imagine. There's something desirable about that journey that takes us through the deepest of deeps and highest of highs to be with the One who knows you best. There's something exhilarating to planting a dream and using your talents with people around you who believe in you. It's unexplainable, but it's worth everything. He will always show you where to go, and He will always give you a full life in the emptiest of places.

Never forget: *Who you are in Him is greater than anyone you could ever be alone.*

41

VIVID

> "Loving me empowers you to obey my word. And my Father will love you so deeply that we will come to you and make you our dwelling place. But those who don't love me will not obey my words. The Father did not send me to speak my own revelation, but the words of my Father. I am telling you this while I am still with you. But when the Father sends the Spirit of Holiness, the One like me who sets you free, he will teach you all things in my name. And he will inspire you to remember every word that I've told you."[xcix]
> John 14:23-26

Trust the whispers of your heart as you grow older, for it only becomes more entwined with My own as you age. Forgive and forget, say sorry and love. Do not wear a mask to any at all. Have a sense of adventure with everything you do. Say no to what's outside My grace, and it will empower your yes for what I've anointed you for. This will go far beyond what you could imagine. Taking risks takes time, so don't be disappointed with its present circumstance, instead be joyful, for what you know awaits. Listen constantly. The wind isn't a weight; it's a push, a covering, a sensitivity. Distraction camouflages much of My goodness, not taking it away, but hiding it. When it comes, close your eyes, then open them. The morning will always be ours, your time to rise—no matter the hour, and night, My time to tuck away—no matter the day. Fortune isn't always found in the fields, but in the heart. Keep the two separate. It will be a vine if kept close. Let not the world deceive you of what I have spoken. Love open, enlarged, not for just one, but many, yet keep your family closer. Trust in the desires that awaken within your heart. They're singing to the sound of your Father's heart. They're quite clear, quite unquestionable. So still—let your heart sing! Leave no room for waiting, for time is of the essence. Act and see. Seek and find. Knock and doors will magically open. I go before you, as if the God in heaven opened them Himself. Always believe in the toughest times, and I will see you through. The world awaits your story! It will shock and awaken the world with wonder having withstood the hands of time. My faithful servant, because you have believed, they will see Me. There is freedom in forgetting the words I am to keep, yet there's also much vision in remembering their direction. Stay its course, and stay true until it turns. You will see everything I've promised. You will see my Word as clear as day. As vivid as the beginning, it will be in the end.

But, first, remember, remember, remember the signs. Say them to yourself when you wake in the morning and when you lie down at night, and when you wake in the middle of the night. And whatever strange things may happen to you, let nothing turn your mind from following the signs. And secondly, I give you a warning. Here on the mountain I have spoken to you clearly: I will not often do so down in Narnia. Here on the mountain, the air is clear and your mind is clear; as you drop down into Narnia, the air will thicken. Take great care that it does not confuse your mind. And the signs which you have learned here will not look at all as you expect them to look, when you meet them there. That is why it is so important to know them by heart and pay no attention to appearances. Remember the signs and believe the signs. Nothing else matters.[c]
· C. S. Lewis

42

BEAUTY IN THE PLACEMENT

*My daughter Emma—nearly six years old—came to me all aglow this morning. She lay at my feet on my bed all stretched out as if she hadn't a care in the world. "Mommy," she said, "I had a wonderful dream last night." What was it about?" I asked. "I was a Queen," she answered. And as she did her cheeks blushed pink. "Really!" I replied. "What happened in your dream?" "I was wearing a long, beautiful dress," she said with her hands gesturing downwards, flowing. "Was there anything on your head?" I wondered aloud. "Yes, a crown." "Hmmm, why was that such a wonderful dream?" "I just love feeling that way!" "What way?" And with a sigh she spoke one word… **Beauty.**"*[ci]
<u>Captivating</u>

This story has more of an emphasis on a girl's sense of beauty. But I also think a guy's sense of nobility can relate. Just a little bit more heroic, filled with honor, plus a crown of gold instead of diamonds. But I didn't choose this story to look at the image of royalty, but the heart of royalty. The heart of a princess and the heart of a prince that are oh so beauty-full. We read countless verses about the heart in God's Word— full of stories and moments of courage, deception, joy and even pain. We also countlessly see why the heart needs protection, because it is the greatest treasure a person has to offer. It's where our beauty is strengthened or weakened; it's where our dreams thrive or diminish; it's where our worth is known or forgotten. All in the heart of a woman and a man. But there's one story that I want to focus on—that story is in John 12. It begins with Jesus at Lazarus' house where a dinner was served in his honor. Then comes the line of pure beauty, "Then Mary took about a pint of pure nard, an expensive perfume; she poured it on Jesus' feet and wiped his feet with her hair. And the house was filled with the fragrance of perfume."[cii]

There are two main points I want to make about this act of love. One, Mary poured out her highest value at the feet of Jesus. Two, Mary laid her highest form of beauty at His feet and humbled her honor to honor Him. They say the perfume she used was worth a year's wages, and yet she so freely placed it before Him in a way that couldn't be undone. Then she used her hair, a girl's prized beauty, to dry His feet with, showing she would honor His heart with her highest form of honor. It only makes me reflect on my own personal relationship with Jesus to wonder, "Have I completely laid what my highest value is at His feet? Trusting that no matter what, what brings the most glory to Him is what I desire." For some girls, that may be your greatest dream, for some men that may be your greatest security. And after that, will we choose to honor God over honoring our hearts by laying our highest beauty at His feet? Trusting that He can do more than we can—filling an entire room with the fragrance of His worth instead of our own. Some of us may have to check our hearts and see, "What is it that I value the most?" "What do I feel defines my worth?" I think it's safe to say that these questions are uncomfortable. They are for me. I'm still in the process of answering them. Because that little princess and prince who wants to feel "beautiful" must first realize their worth by trusting God. On my trust journey, God spoke so clearly, "It's not about the place; it's about the placement." Mary could have sold the perfume and given the money to the poor as Judas stated, and God could have blessed that money easily. But there is so much more worth in how Mary placed the perfume before His feet—it was the placement of her beauty before Him that showed her undeniable love. Like Isaiah 52:7 says, "How beautiful on the mountains are the feet of those who bring good news…"[ciii] The beauty isn't in the place, but the placement. Placing our beauty before His feet is when we become most beautiful. Some of us are in a place of stillness, but place your beauty before Him. Some of us are in a place much like a valley, but place your beauty before Him. Some of us are in a place on a mountain, but place your beauty before Him. And you will find you'll always feel in your heart the highest form of "**beauty.**"

43

IN THE FACE OF FEAR

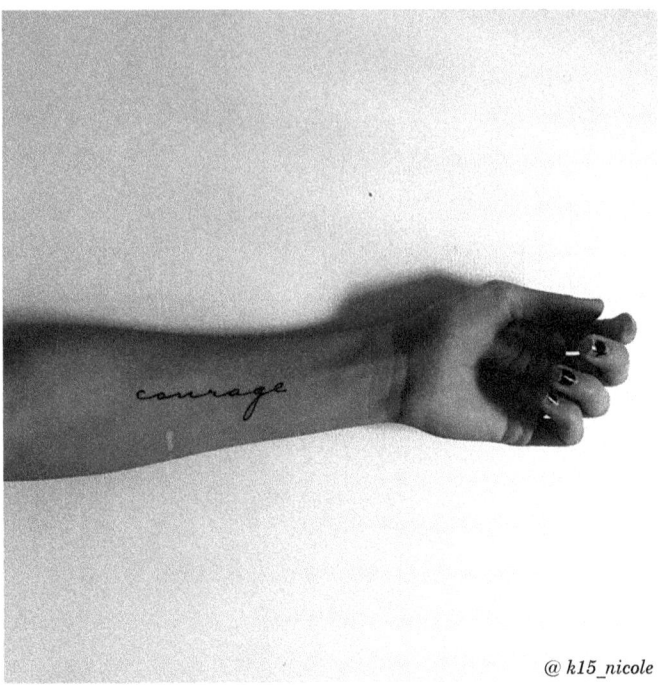

@ k15_nicole

When we become afraid, we tend to run; but instead of running, I believe we should face fear. As the book *Divergent* puts it, "Fear doesn't shut you down, it wakes you up."[civ] When we are faced with fear, we should be wide-awake knowing that we are about to be faced with greatness. My friend once mentioned that fear is sometimes defined fear as "False Evidence Appearing Real," and that is exactly what it is. It's false, fake, and anything but real, but it intends to hold us back from something so real, true, and great, so that instead of keeping our eyes open to greatness, we will shut our eyes in fear. And that is where courage comes in. God is continually reminding us throughout the Bible, "Do not be afraid," not only because we have nothing to be afraid of, but because fear remains powerless until we agree to let it have power over us. Fear is not an emotion that your heart holds; it's a spirit that wants to hold your heart. In those moments, our faith must arise to remember that fear is not more powerful than us because God's power lives within us.[cv] Many people say that faith and fear are far apart, and though they are different in intentions, they are also complementary. When fear tries to hold us back, faith encourages us to move forward, for it is in the face of fear that our faith is truly tested. In the moments where fear tries to paralyze us, our faith will adrenalize us, and we will always overcome in His strength. Thus, in the face of fear, be filled with courage, for great things are to come.

> *You give me your shield of victory, and your right hand sustains me; you stoop down to make me great.*[cvi]
> Psalm 18:35

44

BELOVED

Beloved. Just saying it sounds alluring. But it's more than a word; it is a title, a gracious name, spoken by the most beautiful and loving God. It's what He calls His chosen. Some have come to know *beloved* as a word used in romance between two lovers, yet the depth within this word is much stronger. In the Old Testament, twenty-six out of forty-two times it's used as the word "ahebh," to "breathe" or "to long for."[cvii] In the New Testament, it's commonly used to describe the beauty and unity in His love in which Jesus addresses His disciples with twelve times. It's the very title God calls His own son by in Matthew 3:17, 12:18, and 17:5. Furthermore, this is the same name God calls **us** by. He has the same longing to be with us.

He sees us the way He sees His son, as His children, as His chosen. Try to wrap your mind around that. It may take a few days, weeks, months, or maybe years—but it is so vitally important to see ourselves the way God sees us individually. Because the way He sees us, uniquely, is the beginning of us seeing our true selves. However, there's usually this barrier, this holdback that comes up when we try. It usually comes from this little voice that says, "This can't be true for you. You're not worthy of being enough." Sadly, that voice has contained *me* for many years. But I'm so thankful for a God who pursues me relentlessly, calling me by name, Who is always fighting for my worth—because He knows it is *great*. He does this for each and everyone of us. But there is someone else who knows of your great worth too—and that is the enemy. In Ezekiel 28:12-14 we read, "You were the model of perfection, full of wisdom and perfect in beauty… Your settings and mountings were made of gold; on the day you were created they were prepared. You were anointed as a guardian cherub, for so I ordained you. You were on the holy mount of God; you walked among the fiery stones."[cviii] Then, by verse 17 we read, "Your heart became proud on account of your beauty, and you corrupted your wisdom because of your splendor." As Stasi Eldredge says it in her book *Captivating*, "Satan fell because of his beauty. Now his heart for revenge is to assault beauty… But most especially, he hates Eve. Because she is captivating, uniquely glorious, and he cannot be."[cix] This is the enemy we not only hear, but more often we will listen to. "You aren't enough" versus "You are chosen." Which one is easier to believe? And which one does God say is true?

God is constantly reminding us, relentlessly pursuing us, and graciously calling out to us, "Beloved," because He wants and longs to be with us. I will never forget when He first whispered, "If you would know My love for you, you would change the world." If we all knew His love for us, we wouldn't question how *all* He can do through us is *limitless*. There is a verse in Song of Songs 4:12 that says, "You are a garden locked up, my sister, my bride; you are a spring enclosed, a sealed fountain,"[cx] followed by stanzas of all that is in her garden. He is saying this to his beloved. God is saying the same to us. "There is so much more for you. I *know* the plans I have for you. I know what you are capable of doing with Me and for Me. I have the BEST in store for you. Just trust Me. You are enough." It's unfathomable. All the closed doors He protects us with to lead us to the right doors He pursues us with, where He allures us to the unimaginable and the best before us. But before we can believe what He has prepared for us, we have to believe what He has prepared within us. Rick Warren says it this way, "God changes caterpillars into butterflies, sand into pearls, and coal into diamonds, using time and pressure. He's working on you too."[cxi] God took something that looked unchangeable and ordinary and made it beautiful and captivating. The same way we were changed when we became His. As 2 Corinthians 5:17 says, "This means that anyone who belongs to Christ has become a *new* person. The old life is gone; a new life has begun!"[cxii] We were once lost, but now we're found. We were once broken, but now we're whole. We were once unworthy, but now we're beloved. And with that truth, we can believe and know, we can change the world with Him.

45

REWRITTEN

Dear God,

Let me see myself as You see me, that I may be free from the power of comparison, inadequacy, and shame; that I may begin to grasp how perfect I am in Your eyes, made uniquely with care and precision. From my human traits to my God-given gifts, let me begin to praise You for how I am fearfully and wonderfully made. There is no question that You made me perfectly with a purpose, that I am beautiful, that I'm loved, and that my value is found in You. I praise You because my story is rewritten every day with a fresh new start, and I'm thankful it never gets boring. I thank You for not answering every one of my heart's desires so that I may one day discover the best of Your heart's desires. And most of all, I am eternally grateful for Your selfless love that has held me together, always. In my highest moments, You are there. In my lowest moments, You are there. And in the in-between, You are there. When I'm stuck You run to me. When I'm broken, You mend me. When I'm scared, You comfort me. When I'm weak, You carry me. And while I mess up often, You still died for me, to be with me. That is the love I fell in love with—the love that changed my life. Which brings me to my last thought: let me love like You love me. Let me be a shoulder to cry on, a hand to hold, a good worker for Your name, and a humble servant to Your will. That in everything I do, everywhere I go, people may see Your love through me. That they may know You and be able to see, that You have been with them always too. Let me see myself through Your eyes, let me trust Your heart, and let me love as You love. I know that will change everything. Amen.

> *I feel put back together, and I'm watching my step. God rewrote the text of my life when I opened the book of my heart to his eyes.*[cxiii]
> 2 Samuel 22:24-25

46

FOR SUCH A TIME AS THIS

"For such a time as this,"[cxiv] He speaks through Mordecai to Esther. "For such a time as this," He speaks to our hearts. "For such a time as this," we were prepared to be brave, obedient, and faithful. "For such a time as this," we were called to make a difference. It is in this time that we usually start to feel comfortable, secure, and content → but it is in this time that everything can change. Esther was prepared since birth to every detail of her character that set her apart as a woman that one day won the heart of the king.

But the thing is, she didn't know she was being prepared while God's presence was going before her. God had greater for her. Soon, she became queen and was blessed beyond what she could imagine. But God didn't stop there—no, He raised her up to stand for her people, His people—and in that moment she had to decide if she was truly going to give Him **all**. And a lot of us come to that place—where the future is unknown, His promises sound bigger than comprehension, and then, there's the heart. The very thing that can take us forward or lead us astray. And "for such a time as this" our hearts can speak pretty loud. It can persuade us to do anything and everything apart from His promise with just a simple phrase, "Follow your heart." But the thing about our hearts is that they hold onto what's behind when they can't see what's ahead.

When His heart calls us to leave whatever is behind us, it's so we can step into whatever He knows is waiting ahead of us. And in this moment He speaks, "You said you'd give Me all." That moment defines whether your statement was just words or truth. It is there that we must trust and believe that He has gone before us.

It's where He whispers, "You can go your way, but My presence has gone before you *this* way." Like Esther, we may have to go against our hearts and trust in His and follow in complete faith. And it is there that our love is beyond words—for whoever loves Him will obey His commands. It is there that God will do the impossible and show us He made it possible for us in the steps He prepared us for—"for such a time as this."

So I said to the Lord God,
"You are my Maker, my Mediator, and my Master.
Any good thing you find in me has come from you.
Lord, I have chosen you alone as my inheritance.
You are my prize, my pleasure, and my portion.
I leave my destiny and its timing in your hands."[cxv]
Psalm 16:2,5

47

DIVINE DAYS

Give Him a seed, and He will make a forest.
Give Him a brick, and He will make a palace.
Give Him a spark, and He will make a wildfire.
For He will take what you bring, and breathe life into its form.
*He will meet you halfway, and go **far** beyond your dreams.*

Sometimes we see a seed, a brick, or a spark as something so small, and we dismiss its value as insignificant so quickly. Like the man with one talent, we bury it deep in disbelief rather than sharing it with a hint of hope. Easily we can treat our days the same. We live in a world that loves the "go, go, go," more than the "be, be, be," and it creates much space for depression, anxiety, strife, and loneliness to move in. When we expect our tomorrow to go by routine, we bury it in the dirt. Like manna that fell from heaven for the Israelites [daily], our days are given to us—fresh and anew. We don't have to carry old agendas and worries into the next day. We have an open heaven with a limitless supply of surprises. Yet we so easily place God in a box when we label what's been given as insignificant, when in all actuality, we could so easily give it to Him to see what He could create and do in *one day*. If He spoke the word "light" and it still exists to this day, I want to live in wonder every morning of whatever else He could do. Lamentations 3:21-23 says: "But this I call to mind, and therefore I have hope: the steadfast love of the Lord never ceases; his mercies never come to an end; they are new every morning; great is your faithfulness."[cxvi] My challenge to you is this: wake up expecting the unexpected, then look heavenward and live on fire. As you give God every ordinary day, you never know what He could create or do. Lastly, don't put a period where God has placed a comma. *Being inspired is what I live for, but God doesn't add up our days into a reasonable equation that reads extraordinary; He multiplies them by interweaving seeds with bricks with fires, by going beneath the surface and above the clouds, by working deeply and gently within us and through us, and by creating an ebb and flow in between the spaces and blessings to spell out divine.* That's why every day is new. You never know what to expect—but it will be fresh, and depending on your perspective of the small or big day, it could be limitless with a bit of multiplied commas. Because God is creative and His mercies never come to an end. He loves the something small more than the pile of disbelief. As Ephesians 2:21-22 says: "Now he's using you, fitting you in brick by brick, stone by stone, with Christ Jesus as the cornerstone that holds all the parts together. We see it taking shape *day after day*—a holy temple built by God, all of us built into it, a temple in which God is quite at home."[cxvii] (emphasis added) God isn't boring when you give Him the chance to light up your life. It may not make much sense, and it may look ordinary at first, yet if you trust your every day to the Lord, you'll see a comma goes far beyond a period, and it travels to many more heights and depths, never ceasing to be amazed by His wonders.

*@rachellegrace_*

48

NOT THERE, BUT HERE

When we are asked what we want to do in the future, we tend to have a big vision that we want to live out, but the part of getting there is where we get stumped. We like to pray for open doors, but we always want them to lead to something **big** and **powerful** instead of *promising* and *guiding*. We tend to seek greatness around us rather than within us, because we'd rather do great than be great. *But greatness cannot come from you if it is not prepared within you.* Yes, going around the world and being used by God is awesome, but sometimes God has a greater plan for where you already are. He is saying, "Not there, but here." It's not that He doesn't have great things for you, it's that He wants to do greater things within you. Ezekiel 16:7 says, "I made you grow like a plant in the field. You grew up and developed and became the most beautiful of jewels."[cxviii] And that's exactly it. We are developed to become the most beautiful of jewels when we dwell in Him. It's not about the place where we are, but the placement of our hearts, which should be to be in His will. Sometimes we just need to bloom where we are planted, to be used where we are, and to be refined in beauty by His greatness. Philippians 1:6 says, "Being confident of this, that he who began a good work in you will carry it on to completion until the day of Christ Jesus."[cxix] Be confident in knowing that you are exactly where you are supposed to be.

Do what you can, with what you have, where you are.[cxx]
Theodore Roosevelt

49

PERSISTENCE IN PRAYER

And so I tell you, keep on asking, and you will receive what you ask for. Keep on seeking and you will find. Keep on knocking, and the door will be opened unto you.[cxxi]

Luke 11:9 Prayer is an extraordinary thing. The fact that we are communicating with the Creator of the universe, the God of the impossible, the Orchestrator of life itself, is often a belittled, yet mind-blowing concept. As Psalm 8:4 describes it, "What is man that You are mindful of him, or the son of man that You care for him?"[cxxii] I don't think it is something we will ever really be able to grasp—that He sees every one of us in the crowd of 5,000 knowing our every want, desire, need, doubt, hope, and fear. He bends low to answer our spoken prayers as much as our silent prayers. He is incredibly loving, and that makes prayer even more sacred. Yet, we can easily treat prayer either as an "Abra Cadabra," hoping it will happen as soon as we ask, or as a last resort doing everything in our power before we seek His power. Very rarely do we see prayer as a state of being and resting in

the Lord, having our hearts become more like His. They are not so much of a "give me," like when you ask your parents for $10 to go see a movie. It is a blessing, yes. But so much more than that, it's an answer from God's deepest love of His heart to the deepest desires of our own. It is what Jesus says in John 14:13, "You can ask for anything in My name, and I will do it, so that the Son can bring glory to the Father."[cxxiii] It's also a hope and faith in persistence. The verse before in Luke 11:7-8 reads, "And suppose he calls out from his bedroom, 'Don't bother me. The door is locked for the night, and my family and I are all in bed. I can't help you.' But I tell you this—although he won't do it for friendship's sake, if you keep knocking long enough, he will get up and give you whatever you need because of your <u>shameless persistence</u>."[cxxiv] (emphasis added) I'm not saying God won't answer your one-time prayer, because He can. But just like faith can speak and move mountains, faith can also persist and climb the mountain. There is a man by the name of George Muller, who would write the starting date of his prayer, and pray until it happened. He would keep track of the days, and for one man's salvation up to twenty-seven years. It was an answer from deep to deep, from God's heart to man's. Muller saw prayer as more than a desire, but a hope and faith that wasn't worth giving up on. It's the same way Moses sought favor for his people against God's wrath in Exodus 32:9-10, where God responded, "Now leave me alone."[cxxv] Yet his persistence moved God's heart. Jim Watkin says, "A river cuts through a rock not because of its power but its persistence."[cxxvi] Persistence is more than seeking God's favor; it is a process of faith. How and when He answers may be different from what we expected, but it will be in a way that is perfect. Persistently pray with an <u>undeterred heart</u> for whatever God places in you like a flame, and never give up. Keep asking, seeking, and knocking, for prayer's persistence is what cuts through the impossible.

Undeterred: "persevering with something despite setbacks."[cxxvii]

50

PRAISING IN THE PIECES

There are times where our trust will be tested and our faith will be stretched. It's in these moments where all the pieces of our life seem scattered and do not seem to connect. But in Genesis 15:17 we read, "When the sun had set and darkness had fallen, a smoking firepot with a blazing torch appeared and passed between the pieces."[cxxviii] And this is our promise—that God walks with us through the pieces. Jeremiah 29:13 says, "You will seek me and find me when you seek me with all your heart."[cxxix] Don't try to put the pieces together, but fix your eyes on God, and they will fall together in the perfect timing. Trust in His character, praise through the pieces of doubts, worries, and trials, and seek Him always, for His heart is forever for you.

51

RAGING AGAINST THE WRONG WARS

For our struggle is not against flesh and blood, but against the rulers, against the authorities, against the powers of this dark world and against the spiritual forces of evil in the heavenly realms.[cxxx]
Ephesians 6:12

We would be blind and deaf to not acknowledge the war and chaos in the world around us. But sometimes we are raging against the wrong wars. We have this armor known as self-pride in our life that can be fighting this battle of, "I want to do what I want" and "I can handle it alone." We don't want help and mostly we want to be seen as strong. We don't want to be seen as weak, and so we put up this guard and hide our faults. But when things don't go our way, we fight against the very refuge that is meant to protect us. We will scream, yell, and break in frustration of our will overlooking His perfect will for us. We fight to be strong. We fight to be loved. We fight to feel worthy. But we start a war of chaos within ourselves when we are surrounded in an atmosphere of peace. Why? Because our self-pride says, "I can do this." When God's spirit says: *Let Me do this. Take off your armor of war, and step into My armor of love. Put on the belt of truth; pull it tight. Place the breastplate of righteousness over your heart.*

Hold onto the shield of faith, and let it protect you. Put on the helmet of salvation and hear Me, follow My commands. Fearlessly hold the sword of the Spirit, and stay close. For this battle is not yours, but Mine. Instead of creating a war of confusion, trust in His promise. As we pray: "We do not know what to do, but our eyes are upon You…" Our Almighty God sends His word: "Do not be afraid or discouraged because of this vast army. For this battle is not yours but God's. You will not have to fight this battle. Take up your positions; stand firm and see the deliverance the Lord will give you… Do not be afraid; do not be discouraged. Go out to face them tomorrow, and the Lord be with you."[cxxxi] (2 Chronicles 20) We have nothing to fear, because God is on our side. Therefore, we can lay down our fight, because the battle is the Lord's. He can do this. We can trust His might.

Just stay close, and see the deliverance the Lord will give you. He's speaking to your heart:

Do not be afraid. Do not be discouraged. This war is already won.
It is finished. It is finished.
It is finished.

"So much of winning the battle is understanding who we're fighting."
- Anonymous

52

THE EMBRACE OF LOVE

I had walked the trails of faith, sure as a mountain, filled with awe and wonder, but still a landscape in the sky. I had learned the melodies of hope, heard more than seen, felt more than known, like a star on a lonesome night. And then, I was embraced by love, overwhelmed with care, flooded with sunlight and warmth, an inescapable fall into the unknown becoming free.

Of all, we may yearn for the landscaped skies, and we may seek the melodies of light, yet it is love I would choose. Not to be the greatest talent; not to be the greatest person, but to love and be loved. To be the hands and feet of Jesus, yes, but to also be embraced by the hands of Jesus through the outstretched arms of His beloved ones. This, I have discovered, is what keeps hearts pure, fires burning, eyes wonder-filled, and life enchanting. This is God Himself, our belonging in Whom we've always known, always knowing us.

Forever loving us, and forever surprising us.
It is in the embrace of love Himself that we quickly discover:
He wasn't simply a missing piece, but all the pieces were simply Him.

Love never stops loving. It extends beyond the gift of prophecy, which eventually fades away. It is more enduring than tongues, which will one day fall silent. Love remains long after words of knowledge are forgotten. Our present knowledge and our prophecies are but partial, but when love's perfection arrives, the partial will fade away. When I was a child, I spoke about childish matters, for I saw things like a child and reasoned like a child. But the day came when I matured, and I set aside my childish ways. For now we see but a faint reflection of riddles and mysteries as though reflected in a mirror, but one day we will see face-to-face. My understanding is incomplete now, but one day I will understand everything, just as everything about me has been fully understood. Until then, there are three things that remain: faith, hope, and love—yet love surpasses them all. So above all else, let love be the beautiful prize for which you run.[xxxii]
1 Corinthians 13:8-13

53

THE DESIGNER

I love the concept of design: *a plan or drawing produced to show the look and function or workings of a building, garment, or other object before it is made.*^{cxxxiii} I love that designs embraced for their intended shape are the most beautiful art. I love how we are a royal priesthood with destined crowns and designed garments to carry out the call of God on our lives. There's a story in 2 Chronicles 20 that emboldens my heart for destiny's sake. The set up is found in verses 2-3: "Some time later the Moabites and Ammonites, accompanied by Meunites, joined forces to make war on Jehoshaphat. Jehoshaphat received this intelligence report: 'A huge force is on its way from beyond the Dead Sea to fight you. There's no time to waste'…Shaken, Jehoshaphat prayed. He went to God for help and ordered a nationwide fast."^{cxxxiv} Some of my heart's greatest prayers are found in the verses that follow. "They were up early in the morning, ready to march into the wilderness of Tekoa. As they were leaving, Jehoshaphat stood up and said, 'Listen Judah and Jerusalem! Listen to what I have to say! <u>Believe firmly in God, your God, and your lives will be firm</u>! Believe in your prophets and you'll come out on top!' After talking it over with the people, Jehoshaphat appointed a choir for God; dressed in **holy robes**, they were to march ahead of the troops, singing, 'Give thanks to God, His love never quits.' **As soon as** they started shouting and praising, God set ambushes against the men… and they all ended up dead."^{cxxxv} (20-22, emphasis added)

A warning is sent of the battle that is coming, and Jehoshaphat doesn't sit in silence and fear, instead, he calls a nationwide fast. The result is that wind words are heard, warriors are armed, and a choir is appointed. Funny enough, I did say a choir, and oddly enough, they were the very vessels God used to bring victory. They didn't have to do a thing, but sing. I wonder, how many more wars would be won if we realized our worship does the same? As His chosen, we each have garments to march victoriously in. They are interwoven with His purpose and colored with His sovereignty. Funny enough, they are what make us who we are, and oddly enough, they are our most powerful weapons to win the war. To embrace who we are as enough overflows with praise to the Lord from the depths of our hearts for Him to sit enthroned upon.

The garments are interwoven, but some strings have to go beneath the surface for the designed work to come together purposefully. In the moments where you can't see anything, take courage and meditate on Psalm 139:15: "My frame was not hidden from You, when I was being formed in secret, and intricately and skillfully formed *as if embroidered with many colors* in the depths of the earth." (emphasis added)^{cxxxvi} What is hidden from your sight is not hidden from His. As Ephesians 1:11-12 says: "It's in Christ that we find out who we are and what we are living for. Long before we first heard of Christ and got our hopes up, he had his eye on us, had designs on us for glorious living."^{cxxxvii} Embracing who you are allows you to step into the Designer's sketched-up heart and find His love interwoven through the garment's design with purpose, freedom, and life. These garments were created to be the most flexible armor, one you never have to remove. Although wars are daunting, believe fully in your God and stand firm.

The truth is, a battle may be on its way to take you out, and I pray that I can be the messenger running ahead to warn you: "There's no time to waste." My hope is that instead of retreating in fear and silence, you may take precautions by praying and praising, by stepping into the garments your Designer knows fit you best. I am believing this for healing against cancer, miraculous provision, and restored relationships. Not only just that, but for hearts to be set free from anxiety, depression, and addictions. I am praising God now for the wars that were coming to take your royal crown, yet are now ambushed and diminished in the name of Jesus! When you hear the sirens of the battles coming, may you hold onto this truth: **we are always armed when we are ourselves.** Being your most authentic self is the secret weapon that the enemy can't *ever* take away. Thus, you can march boldly from victory to victory, with His praise always on your lips.

54

HUMILITY AT ITS BEST

"I am nothing."

This is a phrase that I commonly began to hear among Christians. They would finish it with the phrase, "But He is everything," in a way of justification. So I myself began to say and believe the same words, "I am nothing," justifying it with, "He is everything." But I came to a moment of realization that those who lived for God would look at others who lived without God, and would tell them they were something so valuable, to then speak the exact opposite over themselves. When in fact, those who know God have everything, but they defeat themselves with believing this phrase of "humility." But I do not believe that phrase holds any truth, because we all *are* something. Humility is not tearing yourself down to lift God up; it's giving God all the glory and credit for what we achieve through Him by His grace. A quote by C. S. Lewis says, "Humility is not thinking less of yourself, but thinking of yourself less."[cxxxviii] It is not degrading the person you are, it is just always uplifting who God is. I truly believe we need to stop beating ourselves down with words and start laying ourselves down at His Word. *We need to see sons and daughters when we look at the lost, and we need to see the same when we look at the saved.* We need to see that we are something unique and not worthless, that we were bought with the highest price and hold great value. That we are as perfected in His image, as we are purposed for His glory. 1 Peter 2:9 reads, "But you are a chosen people, a royal priesthood, a holy nation, God's special possession, that you may declare the praises of him who called you out of darkness into his wonderful light."[cxxxix] We don't need to shy away from being powerful when His power lives in us. We don't need to stay in the shadows and hide. For He's called you by name out of darkness to live set apart in His light to bring and bear the glory of His name. Maybe then we should change the phrase to, "I am something, but He is so much more," so that we could begin to see the way God sees us and would believe *all* that *He can* do through *us*. I believe that is humility at its best.

55

A CHOICE TO CHOOSE

There are times in life when God doesn't give us a definite yes or no in the search for direction, and so, we come to stand still paths, because no matter what we choose in the end, He is still for us. He says, "Do not let your hearts be troubled, and do not be afraid,"[cxl] in John 14:27, which means, don't suffocate yourself in fear of what to do. God is within you; you will not fall, and *even if* you do, He will *always* catch you.

In the day-to-day decisions, always remember: **our choice doesn't define our calling**, it just leads us in preparation to it. Think about it this way, if we thought about every step we took, we'd miss out on the beauty of life, because we'd only see footprints and feet. It is in our walk with God that we are guided in beauty, because we are able to look up and see life for its value. *God won't always give us a definite yes, but He'll always provide a clear no whenever needed.* So take a step of faith, do not be troubled, and do not be afraid.

@ashtynekole

56

INTO EXISTENCE

A friend used to tell me that we can "speak things into existence." But usually the **words** we speak aren't really the **things** we want to exist. It just comes so much more naturally to us to be critics rather than thankful and optimistic of the things that we see. Whether it is how we view our image or our situation, it's easy for us to pick out everything we are not versus everything God is. My childhood pastor put it this way, "The way you live your life is the way you view God." So if we live in disbelief or an inadequate lifestyle, what is this saying about our view of God? I can tell you one thing, it's not what His Word appoints as truth. Now there are two stories I want to look at, the first beginning with 1 Samuel 17—the story of David and Goliath. We read about Goliath in verse 4 → he is over nine feet tall, a champion of Gath, and he just came out of a Philistine camp! To make it even crazier, his armor was five thousand shekels—125 pounds! Not only that, but also, his challenge was to send someone to fight <u>him</u> for whose people would become rulers or servants to the other. Do you sense the pressure? Then all of a sudden, a boy named David, who had no training with men, but only with bears and lions, came up and offered to be <u>the one</u> to fight the nine feet tall Goliath. Now, we see that earlier in 1 Samuel 16:7 God had said to Samuel not to look at his appearance or height, referring to David's. Yet even in 17:42, that is the first thing Goliath sees→ a boy. Even Saul replied with, "You are only a boy, and he has been a fighting man since his youth".[cxli] But you know what won the battle? Not David's strength or "degree of throw." It was his view of God and belief in what He could do through him. David didn't even take a sword as back-up just in case the stones didn't work, he believed in the power of God and spoke it into existence, "For the battle is the Lord's, and he will give all of you into our hands."[cxlii]

The second story is in 1 Chronicles 29:1 where we read, "My son Solomon, the one whom God has chosen, is young and inexperienced. The task is **great**, because this palatial structure is not for man but for the Lord God."[cxliii] (emphasis added) Once again, we see that God has chosen the <u>one</u> who is young and inexperienced, and we see in 28:5, it was out of many sons that he was chosen to do the *great*. Even more so, Solomon is David's son. We see this pattern here that God doesn't call the qualified, but qualifies the called, and that is something we must learn to believe, heart and soul. *Our greatest setbacks will not come from defeat, but by believing in the appearance of what we are not, instead of believing in the identity of who God <u>says</u> we are.* Like David and Solomon, we should speak into existence Who God is and how He can use us, for we are chosen. Henry J. Eyring said, "Don't worry about how inexperienced you are or think you are. But think about what, with the Lord's help, you can become."[cxliv] And that is what we should speak into existence.

Open your mouth with a mighty decree;
I will fulfill it now, you'll see!
The words that you speak, so shall it be![cxlv]
Psalm 81:10

57

TIMELESS

There is... a right time to hold on and another to let go.[cxlvi]
Ecclesiastes 3:6

Have you ever felt change like a gust of wind? Like a moment where everything shifts? From planting to reaping, embracing to parting, holding on to letting go. For a season, it was right to be in that place at that time, but sometimes we come to a new place where that faint whisper blows, "Everything is about to change." We hear it as a preparation to not hold onto familiarity and instead grasp onto God when the time comes. It's a moment where we must remember—He is for us. Change requires us to let go of what once was to grasp onto the once upon a time we are called to live **now**. When it comes, there is no moment to waste, and much to be embraced. When it's time to go, you will know, for your greatest desires will become magnified within the overview of His heart. His timing speaks up in the most intimate way to lead you by the most unexpected way. He doesn't fast-forward these moments for less than His best; He lingers for His beloved. For at all times, His goodness is timeless.

I'm not sure if you've heard of Amanda Cook's song, "You Don't Miss a Thing," but I love her lyrics: *What a wondrous thing I can stand to sing, cause when I fall to my knees, You're the one who pulls me up again. What a mystery that You notice me, and in a crowd of ten thousand, You don't miss a thing.*[cxlvii] I'm not sure if you get a little teary-eyed while reading it, but it sure does move my heart every time I do. When we feel like we are completely unseen, God doesn't miss a single thing. When we feel like the world is going on and we ourselves don't know how to go on, God doesn't miss a single thing. When we feel it's impossible to believe in anything good or beautiful or freeing, God doesn't miss a *single* thing. And He will stop the world to make sure you never forget it. In Mark 6:34-44, we read about Jesus who had compassion on this crowd of people and [stopped] to spend time with them. Not only does He see their hearts, but also their needs, and He doesn't just let them go untouched. Instead, He sees the dryness of their hope, the brokenness of their dreams, the unbelief of providence, and He says, "What *do* you have?" Perspective shift. In the midst of our pain, Jesus goes deeper and shows us there's a little bit more that we don't see just yet. If you don't know this story, stop and take time to read this incredible passage, and when you're done, be prepared for God to speak a timeless message to your heart: *There is power in the broken*. Jesus sees the need, He sees the heart, and He also sees the power. He doesn't say, "Oh, I understand your life isn't perfect, I'll be here when you get it altogether." No. He acts, He pursues, and He draws us *closer* to His heart. In the midst of people letting go, in the midst of lives parting, in the midst of undesirable change, Jesus sees power in the broken. The miracle isn't just placed inside the disciples' hands, it's met with the crowds willingness to *stay*, to *come closer*, to *trust*. There are miracles everywhere! Because Jesus, He doesn't miss a **single** thing. The disciples had to *let go* in order to see God's power displayed. The crowd had to *hold on* to receive the immeasurably more of God. In one place and one time, there was a single thing each person needed to act upon, and because they each did, He didn't miss any one of them. There was no one left unseen, untouched, unchanged. *The thing is, Jesus doesn't only see what we [do] have within our hands, He sees what we were made to do within our hearts.* When we're obedient, and when we step out in courage, we will be a part of His miracle's unfolding. What a wondrous thing when we can stand to sing, for even when we fall to our knees, He's the one who pulls us up again. What a mystery that He notices **each of us** in a crowd of ten thousand, and still, He doesn't miss a *single* thing. So when we come to the place where we feel that faint whisper say, "Everything is about to change," we'll be fearless for we know...His goodness is timeless.

58

LIVING UNDER EXPECTATIONS

William Shakespeare said, "Expectation is the root of all heartache."[cxlviii] As humans we can expect so much and see so little. In fact, *expectations steal the opportunities for us to be real*. We sometimes allow our perception to become our reality, and the expectations of others to be our guide. Yet, we can become so afraid to make mistakes living under this pressure of perfection. Expectations have a way of capping growth; instead of being the person we now see, we feel obligated to stay true to the same person of the past, and this tension can tear us apart. It can feel like a constant search for something real under high pressure, unrealistic expectations. So that when our reality changes, our perception is thrown off because it's not what we expected.

Yet, we can so easily put these limitations on those around us too. On people who want to change or situations that are trying to. We can become blinded to who someone is trying to be when we place expectations on them of who we knew them to be, and that's why we see so little—because expectations show us who they were, but not who they now are. But I think change is beautiful because it leaves room for God's beauty to renovate our lives. *If we all stayed the same forever, there wouldn't be any chance for discovery*. And that is why expectations steal the opportunities for us to be real, because even if we discover something new, we feel as if it's almost wrong to change and be made new. Yet Ezekiel 36:26 says, "I will give you a new heart and put a new spirit in you; I will remove from you your heart of stone and give you a heart of flesh."[cxlix] A heart of stone is sculpted and never changing unless by wear; a heart of flesh is constantly beating, changing in shape, and being made new. **Expectations are sculpted, but freedom is shaped.** It is in God that we learn to live in freedom—He shapes us daily and takes us on a journey daily that has no end. Everything is changing around us, and it will only begin to change within us, when we break free from the hold of expectations. *We have to stop living under them, and we have to stop giving them out.* Maurice Setter puts it this way, "Too many people miss the silver lining because they're expecting gold."[cl] In other words, we will keep missing all of the beauty that is around us, and even within us, if we only expect the most beautiful things to be behind us.

Live with God; come daily into His green pastures. Let Him take the coat of pressure off of you and replace it with a glorious crown. For there, in His transformed grace, you'll be the most glorious you, in its atmosphere of freedom.

59

POURING INTO REST

Matthew 11:28 says, "Come to Me, all you who are weary and burdened, and I will give you rest."[cli] Pouring out for God is one of the most life-changing moments we can experience, but if we do not allow God to pour into us, we will be burdened down in weakness rather than rested in strength. It is good to go for God, but we can't forget to come to Him. We must remember that we are our greatest ministry, and if we are not allowing our hearts to get poured into, we will run out of _____ to pour out. Grace. Kindness. Forgiveness. Love. We cannot give what we do not have ourselves. Today, pour out the rest of your strength at His feet, so He can pour into your heart sweet rest and strength.

@aimeewhitm

I am the Vine, you are the branches. When you're joined with me and I with you, the relation intimate and organic, the harvest is sure to be abundant. Separated, you can't produce a thing. Anyone who separates from me is deadwood, gathered up and thrown on the bonfire. But if you make yourselves at home with me and my words are at home in you, you can be sure that whatever you ask will be listened to and acted upon. This is how my Father shows who he is—when you produce grapes, when you mature as my disciples.[clii]
John 15:5-8

60

GOLD GLITTERED PATHS

> *Awake, awake, Zion, clothe yourself with strength! Put on your garments of splendor, Jerusalem, the holy city. The uncircumcised and defiled will not enter you again. Shake off your dust; rise up, sit enthroned, Jerusalem. Free yourself from the chains on your neck, Daughter Zion, now a captive.*[cliii]
> Isaiah 52:1-2

Did you know that Zion means wilderness? You wouldn't find this on a Google search engine. Yet whilst in Israel, a Messianic Jew explained to me that Zion, above any other meaning, meant <u>wilderness</u>, and secondly, <u>fortification</u>. Thus as the scripture says, "Awake, awake, Zion," I want you to imagine these two very things: the wilderness as God's garden where you've been resting and your fortification by the anointing of His presence. Whilst you were resting in this season, He'd been preparing the garden with resources for the journey ahead. He packed your luggage, wrapped your food and water, and even included your favorite books and games. For what I have come to realize is that *the opposite of resting is not moving, but arising.*

Whether we do everything or nothing in a day, time doesn't stop. But for most of these days, we don't live up to their full potential. We often sail into its motions and come back to harbor at sunset with the idea of rest for the next day that is to come. So when we read this passage, know it's not saying, "You've been doing nothing, now get up and go." It's more like, "Listen. Hear the wind words awakening your heart to arise. There is more for you today than your mapped out plans. I've bought you some new outfits for the journey ahead, put them on; it's going to be wild. Trust Me. We are going far into the unknown where life is FULL of unseen gardens and magical horizons awaiting. A life for the free to walk the gold glittered paths designed uniquely for them."

The enemy would love nothing more than for you to think you have it all figured out and leave God out of it. But to bring God into your everyday "ordinary life—your sleeping, eating, going-to-work, and walking-around life,"[cliv] that is arising and placing the armor of God on to face this extraordinary life faithforward. Friend, dare I say, you have been living your life more captive than you think if you've had a handle on everything with little to no risk. Instead, arise and embrace the ordinary with enchantment. God prepared you more in the resting than you know, and He is alongside you for every other need along the path. What lies before you already dwells within you, and it is truly unique and perfect for the gold glittered paths that await. As you decide to rise up and embrace this God life, I fully believe you will find more gold within you than around you, and obviously, if your path is of glittering gold, you are in for a beautiful journey. I'm not ignorant to the fact that the enemy will try to allure you off the extraordinary path to the side paths that look like short cuts at the time. So when I say this, don't take it lightly: *come into the throne room before you walk out onto gold glittered paths*. Don't just get up and go. Clothe yourself with strength and put on your garments of splendor; be on guard with all things true and lovely; be alert to what is the opposite of what God spoke to you in the throne room, and sit enthroned with the authority of God within you to shut up the devil and his pleas. You never know what magical seeds may land in your hands when you're being faithful with what's in your heart. <u>For the path isn't just paved to walk on, it's designed to plant seeds along the way for others to follow.</u> As you arise to this new life, let it be done with laughing and singing as you trust in Him![clv] (1 Peter 1:8) The enemy hates nothing more than smiling soldiers. Smile, laugh, and live! Beneath the dust is so much sparkling gold. And always remember… this is just the beginning.

61

ABIDING FAITHFULLY

Every step you take is a big step outside of your walls. It is not only there your destiny lies, but also there the enemy waits. Don't play it safe and don't hold back, for I am your armor, and My peace is your protector. Yes, anxiety rises, but rise higher when it comes, and run further when it leaves. For you know if it came, something greater is coming. Keep growing. Keep expanding. Your roots are deeply embedded in Me, and as you draw from the source, you flourish.
My power abides in you as you abide in Me.

"Your anointing has made me strong and mighty. You've empowered my life for triumph by pouring fresh oil over me. You've said that those lying in wait to pounce on me would be defeated, and now it's happened right in front of my eyes and I've heard their cries of surrender! Yes! Look how you've made all your lovers to flourish like palm trees, each one growing in victory, standing with strength! You've transplanted them into your heavenly courtyard, where they are thriving before you. For in your presence they will still overflow and be anointed. Even in their old age they will stay fresh, bearing luscious fruit and abiding faithfully. Listen to them! With pleasure they still proclaim: 'You're so good! You're my beautiful strength! You've never made a mistake with me.'"[clvi]
Psalm 92:10-15

62

A GLORIOUS GLIMPSE

Have you ever dreamed with God? I'm talking about really dreamed. Like the thoughts that make your heart race with peace and joy in the same moment? The thoughts that you believe only could be possible in heaven? The thoughts that are so creative that they had to be designed by God? They're like Holy Spirit drops. Where, for a moment, it feels as if heaven is all around you. Have you ever expanded the imagination of your mind to, for a moment, believe anything could happen? What if I told you it could? That kings and kingdoms are real? That all that is in your heart is for a purpose? Have you ever created the space to let a glorious glimpse take place? For a glorious glimpse is seen through the eyes of faith and walked with the steps of courage. And let me be so bold to say that it may not be just a glimpse of heaven, but a glimpse of your future reality. Isaiah 54:2-3 says: "Clear lots of ground for your tents! Make your tents large. Spread out! Think big! Use plenty of rope, drive the tent pegs deep. You're going to need lots of elbow room for your growing family. You're going to take over whole nations; you're going to resettle abandoned cities."[clvii] When God speaks this to Israel, He is talking about their future glory—He's giving them a glorious glimpse of what is to come. When all that is around them is ruined and incomplete, God gives them a glimpse of what He can see that they can't, and they only have to believe it in their hearts to start moving towards it with hope.

If there was someone who believed BIG, it would be Walt Disney. He kept dreaming beyond cartoons and movies, he dreamed up the kingdoms of Disneyland and Disney World, and today they stand as every child's go-to dream. What if you chasing after your kingdom dream sparked others to think up dreams for the kingdom? My favorite thing I've read about Disney took place on Disney World's grand opening. It was October 1, 1971, five years after Walt Disney died, and someone turned to his wife saying: "Isn't it a shame that Walt didn't live to see this?" And her response was, "He did see it, that's why it's here."[clviii]

I wonder what glorious glimpse you need to see in order to chase its reality. What wild wonders wait in your days ahead? I pray that as you read this, your heart begins to stir, for the MORE before you is not a question. No matter your age or status, we all have glorious glimpses of kingdoms waiting in heaven for our hearts to see. It may be of your future family, your future home, your future ministry, and it may be closer than you know. Acts 2:17, 25-28 says: "'In the Last Days,' God says, 'I will pour out my Spirit on every kind of people: Your sons will prophesy, also your daughters; Your young men will see visions, your old men dream dreams.' David said it all: I saw God before me for all time. Nothing can shake me; he's right by my side. I'm glad from the inside out, ecstatic; I've pitched my tent in the land of hope. I know you'll never dump me in Hades; I'll never even smell the stench of death. You've got my feet on the life-path, with your face shining sun-joy all around."[clix] Clear your tents, and make time and space for God to give those Holy Spirit drops to you. Let your tents be the size of kingdoms. Think HUGE! You have plenty of rope, plenty of gifts and talents that are God-given—use them! Let the convictions in your heart dig deep to be unshakable, and it will stand on the land of hope. See the glorious glimpse and walk the life-path before you. God is all around you at all times. So when you dream, dream big. When you think, think wild. When you love, love deep. For more is ahead, and you can trust Him with the kings and kingdoms in your heart. Expand! Expand! Expand! Nothing is too much for God. Nothing is too crazy to create. See it, even if no one else does—for one day, they will, and they will marvel at the glory of the Lord.

63

THE LITTLE FOXES

There's a little game called, "Never have I ever." It can be a quite hilarious game, but it's also a great game to examine ourselves with. Typically you say, "Never have I ever," followed with something you have never done, and then people around you put a finger up as a point if they have done what the person said. Eventually when they reach ten points, or all fingers are up, they are out! But what if we did this with our thoughts? Never have I ever... felt enough. Never have I ever... felt beautiful. Never have I ever... felt valued. These are the little seeds that when planted in our heart, they grow roots that shouldn't be grown. Song of Songs 2:15 says, "Catch for us the foxes, the little foxes, that ruin the vineyards, our vineyards that are in bloom."[clx] These foxes are the thoughts that we think every day and sneak into our heart; these little foxes are the thoughts we don't even realize we believe about ourselves. *But the smallest thoughts are just as destructive as the obvious ones.* You see, we are constantly growing, but if we allow these thoughts to seed within our heart, we will never be able to bloom into the person God created us to be all along. So we should examine our hearts and switch the thoughts to, "Always have I always been enough," or, "Always have I always been beautiful," and, "Always have I always been valued..." Because you are—each of us are. But you have to stop allowing the foxes, even the little ones, from destroying the beauty God is creating within you. So first, <u>think about what you think</u>. Be cautious of the little foxes that can sneak into your heart. Second, guard your heart with His Word, for every thought, action, and belief comes from it. Let His Word build a picket white fence around your heart that is in bloom, so the foxes won't try to break in as often. Third, let God be the Gardener. Let Him uproot the lies or weeds that have grown in your heart, and let Him plant truth or beauty in replacement. And lastly, see yourself through God's eyes, and not through anyone else's, that you may remember how precious you are to Him; that you may see how perfectly, and how beautifully you are in bloom.

64

EVEN IF

Have you ever waited on something for so long that by the time it showed up, you almost lost heart for its coming because it took longer than you anticipated? It's like when you discover the new iPhone 8 is out, and you can't wait to have it, but by the time you finally receive it, the iPhone 20 is out, and you already moved on in your heart from the 8. Or when you schedule a catch up, but by the 11th time of them being "unable" to show up, you lost every bit of desire to even be their friend (jokes… but kind of). Or how about a passion? You step into the field of your calling at the bottom of the pyramid, and what you thought would take a week to climb up, actually takes years. So much so that you almost forget why you came to the pyramid in the first place. You were expectant, but how many times do you knock before you realize no one is home? How long do you wait for the answer to become a yes? How much strength do you need to keep taking heart in a desolate desert? When you're waiting, it does feel like forever, and forever isn't easy to embrace.

I love the story of Shadrach, Meshach, and Abednego. I love that when all odds were against them, they *still trusted* God to come through. If you don't know the story, these three men served a king named Nebuchadnezzar. As king, Nebuchadnezzar ordered every person to bow down and worship the image of gold he had set up. Now these three knew that they were only to worship the one true God, and so… they wouldn't worship his. This outraged the king because they stood against his command and stood for their God. So he gave them a second chance, threatening them to bow down or to be thrown into the fire. Instead they threw back words of fire: "O Nebuchadnezzar, <u>we do not need to defend ourselves</u> before you. If we are thrown into the blazing furnace, the God whom we serve is able to save us. *He will* rescue us from your power, Your Majesty. But *even if* he doesn't, we want to make it clear to you, Your Majesty, that we will never serve your gods or worship the gold statue you have set up."[clxi] (Daniel 3:16-18, emphasis added) Thus, into the furnace

@sarahbgraves

they went, and out of the fire they came unblemished. What I love most about this story isn't the **big impossible** miracle, but the stance of their hearts that said, "Even if," when defending the name of God. *For what lied within them was a greater fire than the odds against them.*

In the waiting, we can easily lose heart when it doesn't look like much is happening. But I dare say, a lot more is happening beneath the surface. God reveals Himself as *faithful, powerful,* and *loving* in thin places. **As we find the contentment to linger with God, we gain a glorious inner strength to stand for God.** Even if you were promised an iPhone 8 that never comes, even if this person tells you no for the 1,000th time, even if you stay at the bottom of the pyramid—you *know* God, and you know He is with you and for you, no matter what the enemy says. We are not meant to lose who we are in the waiting, but rather, to gain perspective of who we are. We are not meant to bow down when the world says the opposite of what God speaks, but to stand taller. Most people won't understand the God-thing that's taking place within you, *yet it's here in the forever space that the thin place of heaven dwells,* and God meets you. So when fear tells you to cave in, may a greater flame arise within you that stands for the God who is with you to walk out unblemished!

65

BEING STILL IN THE SILENCE

We tend to see silence as a burden or a closed door, and it tends to build up a fear in our hearts that somewhere, we took the wrong turn, and now we're left stranded and alone. But Psalm 46:10 says, "Be still and know that I am God."[clxii] It is in the complete silence that we become the most dependent on God. It is in the complete stillness that He is made known. Being still is a way of letting go, and in doing so, our hearts can be strengthened in God. In trust, we discover **silence isn't a burden, but a beauty**. For sometimes it just takes silence for the beauty shining around us to be found. An interesting fact that I learned is that when one of our senses is gone, our other senses intensify! So when our hearing is gone, our sight becomes stronger, causing us to be more aware of everything surrounding us; which in turn, enables us to discover beauty in a new way—especially His beauty, for He is being made known. God is speaking to our hearts, "Be still and move in My steps. Stop trying to figure everything out and let go." You can trust Him in the silence; you can be still for He knows what He's doing. You can go where He leads—for He will show you. They say seeing is believing, but sometimes it starts with believing to see; then again, it may all just begin with stillness. Be still to believe; be silent to see, all His goodness around you, all His beauty surrounding you, and all His love for you, intensified, in all its brilliance.

66

THE LIBRARIAN OF SECRETS

I am not a condoner of magic, but I do love a good Harry Potter movie. One of my favorite scenes is from the first movie. Harry goes into a particular wand shop, just recently having discovered his true identity, not knowing his magical capabilities, and is greeted by the owner of the shop with a: "Good afternoon, I thought I'd be seeing you soon, Harry Potter. You have your mother's eyes."[clxiii] One, I love how he knows him by name. Two, I love how he recognizes him by his eyes, like his mother's. But the scene continues for Harry to find his wand—the old man says: "Every Ollivander wand has core of a powerful magical substance, Mr. Potter. We use unicorn hairs, phoenix tail feathers, and the heartstrings of dragons. No two Ollivander wands are the same, just as no two unicorns, dragons, or phoenixes are quite the same. And of course, you will never get such good results with another wizard's wand."[clxiv] 1. The wands were created beforehand. 2. They were as uniquely given as uniquely crafted. As Harry tried wand after wand, he found his one. The plot twist is that the wand he was destined for was created with a tail feather from a phoenix, and the only other feather that phoenix gave belonged to the one who gave Harry his scar. Mr. Ollivander goes on to say: "Yes, curious indeed how these things happen. The wand chooses the wizard, remember... I think we must expect great things from you, Mr. Potter." Walking away from the shop, Harry must have realized two certain things: 1. He was chosen 2. His life was never going to be the same from that moment on. He had walked into a whole new world—and in this one, everything was already prepared for him. His parents left him their inheritance, he had a school set up, he had someone to watch over him, and well... he was famous for his scar. Prior to this, he was sleeping under a stairwell, being called worthless, and slaving for his so-called family. So to say that this was unexpected to him would be an understatement.

Likewise, Israel is God's chosen, yet before we come to Isaiah 48, Israel has not been living the most God-fearing lifestyle. Yet, we come to this chapter where a God-shift occurs. In verses 3-5 God speaks: "For a long time now, I've let you in on the way I work: I told you what I was going to do beforehand, then I did it and it was done, and that's that. I know you're a bunch of hardheads, obstinate and flint-faced, so I got a running start and began telling you what was going on before it even happened. That is why you can't say, 'My god-idol did this.'"[clxv] This is where the two relate. Before Harry walked into this "new world," there was a secret door he walked through that looked like an ordinary brick wall. Yet, by having someone with him that knew the combination to get to the other side, he entered into the greatest discovery of a completely new landscape. Likewise, God has gone before us and has everything prepared—an inheritance, a messenger, pioneers that have led the way, and a home ready. Because we had no idea, we can't take any credit for it. *We simply have to trust the voice that knows the secret to the secret door*. But this isn't just about the secret door, it's about how much more is within you that you've never noticed before. If you can learn the art of knowing His voice, God is willing to let you in on secrets He knows about you. Amos 3:7-8 reads: "The fact is, God, the Master, does nothing without first telling his prophets the whole story. The lion has roared—who isn't frightened? God has spoken—what prophet can keep quiet?"[clxvi] When God is preparing a new thing, He isn't silent. He is the librarian of secrets, and He knows exactly who to use, when to use them, and where to place them to lead them to where they need to go. I love that Mr. Ollivander knew each wand he created and gave out, without forgetting one. Likewise, God remembers which word He has designed and shaped and who He used to speak it through to get to you. And until the secret sinks into your heart, words will keep coming, like each wand kept trying, until the light bulb moment occurs. The "this is what I'm created for" knowledge comes to life.

Before you even came to know God, He knew you by name, and He could see in your eyes His child. You coming into His shop was only the beginning of the journey. While walking the journey, you're sure to discover much more about yourself that you didn't know before, and the more that was crafted uniquely in you that He's always known. The One whose power marked you is the same who placed great power within you. As we read in Isaiah 48:6-7: "You have all this evidence confirmed by your own eyes and ears. Shouldn't you be talking about it? And that was just the beginning. I have a lot more to tell you, things you never knew existed. This isn't a variation on the same old thing. This is new, brand-new, something you'd never guess or dream up."[clxvii] I'm writing all this because I believe God is going to let you in on the new thing that He has prepared beforehand for you and has chosen you to do GREAT things through to bring Him glory. I believe God will whisper to you in this moment to hear His voice and know it. He will bring old words back that have been forgotten to lead you forward into what is promised. Pages and pages of words have led up to this moment, and may you remember them with the One who is the librarian of your heart. He is the keeper of all dreams and wishes, hopes and needs. Keep following Him when it makes no sense and store up all those words within. For He does not speak to merely speak, but to be heard. The further you go, the more He'll let you in on. Then, when you least expect it, one last secret will be kept from you where a secret door awaits. He will open the door for you, you need only to walk through it to soon discover, you're the greatest secret that's been kept all along.

67

TO LIVE A PLAN

> "We plan the way we want to live but only God makes us able to live it."[clxviii]
> Proverbs 16:9

Journal entry: March 8, 2014

*To plan to live is one thing, to live a plan is another. When we begin to plan without prayer, we begin to trust in a life that **sounds** promising. Yet, when we begin to pray with a plan, we lay it before God to **discover** His promises. Mark Batterson puts it this way, "Keep planning like it depends on you, but make sure you pray like it depends on God."[clxix] So trust in God with all your heart for **He will** make your paths straight. For wisdom will not forsake you, and God will not either.*

Journal entry: October 25, 2018

Promises are like rainbows, like incomplete circles stretched out to the earth. Colorful in His glory, unstructured to our plan. Touching heaven, touching earth. A mark of peace, a reminder of hope, a signature of love across the skies of grey. When storms cloud our hearts, there He paints rainbows to not depart the path of promise. There we ground ourselves until the rainbow stretches to the ground beneath our feet. In His timing, not in mine, I say. I stand and sing in the rain, for I know Love is on His way, His sign to come and color the empty again with light. What if it is in our stretch that we bear most His Light? Like the rainbow stretched out across the sky, we display Him as we become like His outstretched arms? As He died stretched out on the cross to bring forth an eternal glory, our dying to flesh displays a clear reflection of His power of love at its fullest—all seven of its vivid colors grounding to earth His heart.

His Word: January 3, 2019

If I could write you a devotion, it would go a little like this: Fear not the waves of fear, forget not the power of My word. Come: as much of a ground than an invitation. Go: as much of an assurance than peace. Peace is a piece of My heart in the depths, but on the run, go is as much of a promise to seeing what's ahead. It's been a voyage for many to believe in what's been promised; it's been a triathlon for you. For all to come true, all had to first taste death. Not as a test, but as a sacrifice. Not because I needed it, but because it freed its hold from on you to on Me. Still coming true, but by My hand and not yours. "I have a plan." You've heard me say it countless of times, like the millions of stars staring down at you from the sky. Now trust My voice again. It is trust that sees the unseen, but where there is no trust, all remains unseen; thus the heart's trust is rare, for only caring can cultivate the heart to stay open in the tension of its two worlds. Faith alone is its fire, love its only strength, and grace its sufficiency. And so, My love, I end with saying this: believe in love again. Let love lead your heart into wilder pastures. Let true love wildly surprise you. Let all My love come true; and most simply, let love be love.

68

SMALL BEGINNINGS AND EVERLASTING KINGDOMS

Zechariah 4:10, "Do not despise these small beginnings, for the Lord rejoices to see the work begin…"clxx One of my favorite parts of the day is getting ready. That time is typically set apart for an hour. Yet there are days where I get ready only to find out I still have 45 minutes until I need to go. Do you know what I do with most of those 45 minutes? Keep getting ready. Often, we spend our entire lives feeling like we need to keep preparing. If we are handed more time, we will use it to keep fixing what we see as imperfect. Preparation has its strengths, but if it is overly done, it becomes a motion that is not driven to where God is calling us to go. It may just be that He has given you time between the getting ready and the motions to be driven enough to break from life's comfort and engage in the extraordinary dream He's placed within you. It's easy to keep thinking that today is just another day, to set your treasures aside until your vision comes to pass. It's easy to despise small beginnings when we don't realize that we're missing them because we're preparing for them. What if a gardener kept putting on their gloves, buying soil, purchasing tools, and studying how to plant correctly, but never actually put the seed in the ground? They'd end up with a very small garden. I've come to learn that those who wait for everlasting beginnings will find a rather small kingdom, while those who act on small beginnings will reap an everlasting kingdom. I believe wholeheartedly: [Those who change the world will not see small beginnings as small, but as beginnings.] They are the ones who will find treasure beneath the dirt; they are the ones who will dig up wells instead of waiting for rain. There is a grace to having a set apart time to get ready, but there is favor to setting apart time for small beginnings. Some of us have been expecting an extravagant garden without even planting a seed. Even "Jack the Giant Slayer" planted the few seeds he'd been given and discovered growth beyond what he could've dreamed. My friend, sow into what you believe in. *You don't have to know everything for impossible things to grow*. Some of you need to surrender your vision to the Lord, to pour out every detail at His throne of grace, like the woman who poured all of her perfume upon the feet of Jesus, and just start *fresh*. Sometimes small beginnings start as new beginnings. Some of you need to *see* what's been placed in your hands, and to ask God what to do with it. It may be as simple as planting where you're at and giving your all to that one seed in a field ready for ten thousand. Sometimes the seemingly insignificant beginnings are the very miracle to your kingdom's

@ kathleenmadethis

foundation. Then some of you don't have a seed, no details, no direction, so you just need to go. Go high and low, far and wide. Sometimes beginnings are just to begin. Begin setting out, searching, praying. For where your treasure is, there your seeds will be also. Begin with those seeds and watch their wild multiplication. Small beginnings are about trusting the Lord with what you have and where you're at for His kingdom's sake; whether it's pouring everything out at His feet, planting the one thing that's in your hands, or having nothing and going after the treasure in which you seek, it begins and ends with Him in mind. The smallest beginnings become everlasting kingdoms for those who believe in magic.

69

HIDE AND SEEK

*For you died and your life is now **hidden** with Christ in God.*[clxxi]
Colossians 3:3 (emphasis added)

To be hidden in God is such a beautiful thing. When we died to who we were, we became alive to whom we're *becoming* in Christ. His love branded our hearts in His design, and an evolving love started to take place in a process of shaping and being remade in His image. Yet, being hidden in His image is one of the hardest things we face because it is not always easy, and that is where "hide and seek" comes in. It's about becoming hidden in God in seeking His heart. When we seek our heart, His image becomes hidden within us; but, when we seek His heart, our lives become hidden in Him. And that's a daily process—becoming: it's an intentional being. Being is a way of saying, "This is who I am," while becoming is a way of saying, "This is Whose I am." Who we were before always has a way of trying not to be forgotten, and that's why being hidden in Christ is a daily process. It's about seeking His heart and becoming more like who He is, instead of seeking our heart and being reminded of who we were. It's a constant process of laying our image down, so that His image can be seen, and ours can be hidden in Him. You see, being hidden in God is a beautiful thing, because it's also an evolving love. The closer you draw to His heart, the quicker He can shape your heart in His love—in His love that molds and perfects and shapes in precision; in His love that made you fearfully and wonderfully, and in His love that treasures your worth above all else. In a way, being hidden is just being close, close enough to hide within His heart as a form of trust for Him to guide your own heart to where it is destined to go.

We lose ourselves in the things we love... we find ourselves there too.[clxxii]
- Kristen Martz

70

TIME'S SIDE

*This is what the Lord says:
"Stop at the crossroads and look around.
Ask for the old, godly way, and walk in it.
Travel its path, and you will find rest for your souls."*[clxxiii]
Jeremiah 6:16

I wonder how slow time would fly
If we'd just take a moment to look in its eyes
To give each day its value and every moment its chance
Than to be of no worth with no second glance
For as fast as we would like it to be
The greatest moments wouldn't ever be seen
There'd be no valleys, with no victories as well
We would never know our strength with no stories to tell
But if we decided to stand on time's side
I think we'd take the journey instead of the ride
Some days would be long and others would be green
But we'd see light in the dark, and hope in the unseen
There is grace in the battle, and courage in the fight
But bravery is found when we walk without sight
To wish upon a shooting star is hoping for change
Yet all begins within the heart to live beyond its range
There is more to the puzzle than the finish line
And more to a poem than a crafted rhyme
For the artist knew its purpose beforehand
That someday the pieces would speak to man
These bits of peace time has placed in our hearts
Will come together to shine in the dark
And it is there that we will be
More than conquerors, more than we'd dreamed.

Life is a dream when today is our wish.

71

TO GAIN SOMETHING GREATER

> *You're blessed when you feel you've lost what is most dear to you. Only then can you be embraced by the One most dear to you.*[clxxiv]
> Matthew 5:4

I remember the times in my life that I was so confused with God, when I had some huge doors slammed in my face. There were times of tears, times of shouting, and many nights of feeling lost in confusion. But as time slowly passed, and my seeking of God gradually grew, understanding came, and this phrase slowly imprinted on my heart: *To lose something great is to gain something greater*. He sometimes takes away what is dear to us, so we can be held closer by the One most dear to us, and in this response, we are shaped to fight for Who we love over what we love. Job 37:5 says, "He does great things beyond our understanding,"[clxxv] and that is something we have to have faith in. God calls us to remain faithful to Him over our understanding, and sometimes He even calls us to let go of the great, but we can know that He always has in store for us something greater. I have come to discover that a closed door doesn't mean a dead-end, but it's just an open door to another journey. Walt Disney says it this way, "We keep moving forward, opening new doors and doing new things, because we're curious and curiosity keeps leading us down new paths."[clxxvi] So let us replace fear of change with curiosity, let go of understanding to experience greatness, and be embraced by the One most dear to us through it all.

72

OUT OF THE CAVE

There's a common story that many of us know in the Bible where Elijah talks to God on a mountain. But a lot of us don't pay attention to why he even went to the mountain in the first place. In 1 Kings 19:3 we read, "Elijah was afraid and ran for his life."[clxxvii] Then we read onto verse 4, to see that Elijah is done and is ready for his life to be taken. Shortly after, he falls asleep, and God provides food and water for Elijah to start a forty-day journey ahead of him. But here comes the minor detail that stuck out to me, in verse 9 it says, "There he went into a cave and spent the night." After traveling for forty days and nights, Elijah finally finds his place of rest. I sometimes wonder, what if Elijah would have stayed in the cave, in the protection of their comforting walls. What if when God spoke, "Go out and stand on the mountain…" (where anybody could find him), he responded with the mindset he displayed in verse 4, "I have had enough, Lord. Take my life, I am no better than my ancestors." Do you see what he would have missed? Not only meeting with God, but meeting with somebody who would not only travel with him loyally from there on out, but somebody who would receive a double portion of God's blessing on his life to continue to carry out God's purpose for years and years after. *What if in the cave, Elijah would've caved in and listened to his comfort instead of his calling?* Or here's a better question for the situation you're in, when you're faced with the same two options, will you choose to cave in or to come out of the cave? The verb of cave is: "to cause to fall or collapse—usually used <u>within</u>."[clxxviii] Somehow and someday we will each get to a cave in our lives that, like Elijah, we were driven to out of fear. And once we sit there, it can be so comforting and nice to be out of the motions. It's silent; it's calm, and mainly, you're safe. I know of many people who have run to the cave out of fear, insecurity, or even exhaustion—ready to give up on God or the church or their calling. And in their comfort their mindset is, "I have had enough, Lord." Sadly, I have seen people collapse from <u>within</u> by listening to the comfort of their *own* voice. But then I have seen others who listened to *His voice* in remembrance of His character, and they experienced even more blessings in their lives, and continued on with their purpose by listening to *His calling*. So this is my hope for us: that when we find ourselves within a cave of comfort, we will listen to His calling over our fears, insecurities, and exhaustion. That we will not focus on the fear in front of us, but will remember the character of God before us. That when we come to the place of giving up or caving in, we will instead rise up and step out to experience God in a completely new way. That like Jesus replied to Satan in the wilderness, "It is written," we will proclaim the same over our lives, "If God is for me, who can be against me?"[clxxix] "For He knows the plans He has for me… plans to prosper me and not to harm me, plans to give me a hope and a future."[clxxx] And, "Don't be afraid, dear heart for God is with me. Don't be discouraged, for He is God. He will strengthen my heart and help me. He will hold me up with His victorious right hand."[clxxxi] Don't let the cave contain you from all that God has before you. Instead, remember His Word, come out of the cave, and listen to His voice, because the best is yet to come.

73

EVERYTHING WE ARE

Trust your heart—for it is deceitful above all things
< Trust God— for He searches the heart and examines the mind

I have come to learn that the first phrase is what many of us listen to, yet it is not necessarily the wisest thing to do. The second phrase is the smartest thing to do, and yet our actions and thoughts seldom cling to its truth. We like to switch up the ending of the statements to say: Trust your heart—for you know your own heart and mind. Even though we know this not to be true, our actions reflect otherwise. I'm not simply talking about having a crush on someone, or wondering which opportunity to choose, what I'm focusing on is how we see ourselves—our image. Jeremiah 17:9 reads, "The heart is deceitful above all things and beyond cure, who can understand it?"[clxxxii] The truth is that our heart can be very deceitful, even about our own image. It's like this picture I saw long ago of a girl, about 100 lbs, looking in the mirror. But what she saw reflecting back was a girl who weighed 180 lbs. We see ourselves so much differently than others do, and we try to change ourselves to be something or someone we are not because of it; when honestly, people see you as beautiful and strong, but we can become our greatest critics. You may want to be fiercer or more caring; you may want straight hair or curly hair, or you may want to be more serious or more playful. Basically, it's easier to see everything we are not instead of everything we are, because we listen to our heart's deceitfulness quite readily over God's truth. But, I want you to visualize this picture with me: You're out in an open field, and it's just you and God; He is placing an extravagant garland on your head, presenting you with a glorious crown full of treasures, deeming you, <u>insert your name,</u> as

@ kathleenmadethis

His beloved. It's a breathtaking thought, right? And *these* are the thoughts God has of you. Proverbs 4:9 says, "She will set a garland of grace on your head and present you with a crown of splendor."[clxxxiii] When He sees you, He sees perfection, He sees grace, He sees beauty, He sees value, love, purpose, and He sees His child. And the overwhelming joy that comes into His heart when He sees you is indescribable. That is the heart you should listen to—the One who searches your heart and is in love with it; the One who examines your mind and smiles with delight. So let us seek understanding from His heart over our own. There's a quote that says, "We lose ourselves in books, we find ourselves there too."[clxxxiv] I think it's safe to switch out the word "book" with "God's Word." Because it's where we lose everything we are not, and find everything that we are. It's in Him that we belong, and it's in Him that we are found. So when it comes to listening, trust in His heart over your own.

> *What a piece of work is man! How noble in reason, how infinite in faculty!*
> *In form and moving how express and admirable.* [clxxxv]
> -William Shakespeare

74

IN THE GAP

> *I looked for someone who might rebuild the wall of righteousness that guards the land. I searched for someone to stand in the gap in the wall so I wouldn't have to destroy the land, but I found no one.*[clxxxvi]
> Ezekiel 22: 30

I don't know if you've ever wanted to change the world, but I'm pretty sure most of us would agree it'd be an incredible thing. Difference is undeniably alluring, and is almost like a spotlight nowadays. But truly, have you ever deliberately sat down and tried to think out how a difference could be made possible? If you haven't, it's likely the world will seem a lot bigger and you will feel a lot smaller in that instant. These instants are both logical and impractical, for change only happens greatly outside of us when we first embrace change daily within us, like a ripple effect. Yet, I wonder if that's how the people in Ezekiel 22 felt for their unrighteous city. With so much corruption, it seemed useless to them to try and stand up against it. Therefore, God searched high and low for anyone to stand in the gap for this nation, but no one dared to be the difference they longed for in their hearts. *Deliverance was possible, change just had to start within.*

I struggled for years with the burden of wanting salvation for my friends and family, so much so that I felt like it was my fault that they were still unsaved. Because I felt like a failure, I was too discouraged to stand in the gap. Maybe some of you have this same burden on your heart, and it's likewise been weighing you down. Can I share with you something that forever changed my life? *That feeling isn't from God. You aren't Jesus.* This pressure and guilt, which has been holding you captive in defeat isn't from Jesus. It sounds ridiculous typing it out, but the truth is—it can feel very real until you know this truth. Here are some things I've learned about standing in the gap that I hope will help you realize, it's not as daunting as it seems.

First, "Give all your worries and cares to God, for he cares about you."[clxxxvii] (1 Peter 5:7) You are not Jesus. Though the enemy may try to convince you otherwise. You were not made to carry the salvation of others on your shoulders. That's what He died on the cross for. When you care for others, trust that God cares for them too. Pray for them and hand them to Jesus. Prayer will go a lot further than our words, actions, and efforts ever will. Stand in the gap, but know that His yoke is easy and light. Second, as written in Hebrews 4:16: "So let us come boldly to the throne of our gracious God. There we will receive his mercy, and we will find grace to help us when we need it most."[clxxxviii] Prayer is the most powerful weapon we will ever access in fighting for our loved ones, friends, and nations. It's incredible that we are able to approach the throne boldly on behalf of those who desperately need it. It's not coincidental that in Esther 4:16 she says, "Go and gather together all the Jews of Susa and fast for me...And then, though it is against the law, I will go in to see the king. If I must die, I must die."[clxxxix] Both verses found in chapter 4, verse 16, talk about approaching the throne of a king. We can also talk to our Father-King and approach Him for our loved ones. We can stand on their behalf; we can stand in the gap, we can make a difference.

Jonathan Edwards prayed, "Lord, stamp eternity on my eyeballs."[cxc] Likewise, this prayer keeps our eyes open to the people He places around us, and the need they have in their heart for a Saviour. By deciding you're going to be different, the world's eyes will be drawn to you standing in the gap. Who knows, maybe they'll even come to you to discover the God you're standing for. *By being the change you wish to see, you start a revolution that stands in the gap for a nation that has never known anything different from the world.* Don't be afraid to just be you, and don't be afraid to pray. It's so much simpler than you think, and a whole lot lighter than the enemy is trying to make it out to be. God's freedom is for you as much as it is for them. Therefore, approach His throne boldly, for He cares for your cares. Let's stand in the gap.

75

IN SEASONS

There is a time for everything and a season for every activity under the heavens.[cxci]
Ecclesiastes 3:1

There are only four seasons in a year, but there are multiple seasons in our lives. Sometimes it's hard to realize when we are going through a season of discovery, but every season has a lesson to be learned. A saying I have learned to be quite true is, "Comparison is the thief of joy." When we begin to compare our seasons to others, we miss the beauty of the lesson we are in. Each of our lives are stories filled with experiences and written by lessons; but we must begin to realize that we are in God's perfect timing and perfect season. We tend to measure ourselves up against others and wish for their lives, but we haven't seen what they have gone through to be where they are. It's easy to see what we want, but are we willing to go through what it takes to get to what we want? Some seasons have chapters, so instead of wishing our season away, let's learn to love the lesson we're in. It's only a stepping-stone to discover what *wild* plans God has ahead of us. As Philemon 1:15 says: "Perhaps you could think of it this way: he was separated from you for a short time so that you could have him back forever."[cxcii] Perhaps this promise made to you has been separated from you for a short time, yet when it does comes back, you can and will undoubtedly keep it forever. Some seasonal waits are for forever promises; and if the promise is worth waiting for, the process is worth enduring for. Let love exist even when it seems forever away, because God is on His way, and He will break through like a hero, suddenly—redeeming and rescuing as the story comes to an end, as the season comes to its finish, and promises come unimaginably true.

76

FAVOR AND GRACE

Let's begin today with the story of Noah. The man who God chose to build an ark that was 450 feet long. But I don't want to look at what God asked Noah to do, instead I want to look at what Noah asked, or in other words, prayed. We read in Genesis 6:9 that, "Noah was a righteous man, blameless among the people of his time, and he walked with God."[cxciii] It doesn't just stick out to me that Noah was righteous and blameless, but Noah *walked with God*. What kind of questions did he ask? What is it that Noah wondered and talked to God about? What did he desire to learn and know? What kind of dreams did he pray for? Because this is the only man who stayed true to God when all of the world became all about themselves instead of all about God. Noah found favor in the eyes of the Lord. What type of conversations did they have that Noah "knew that he knew" that God was greater than anything this world could give. And one word sticks out to me—grace.

One definition of grace is favor. When I reread 2 Corinthians 12:9 knowing this, my heart saw grace in an entirely new light: "My (favor) is sufficient for you, for my power is made perfect in weakness."[cxciv] The same favor that Noah had in the eyes of God is the same favor that is sufficient for us every day. Which signifies, we can be just as close as Noah was; we can do greater things than those who found favor in God's eyes in the Old Testament; we can walk with God in our every moment. We can wonder with God, ask Him questions, and pray for our dreams, and believe with all of our heart that He will work for the good of those who love Him. He will let His favor shine upon those who obey Him, and seek His heart continually. We can be just as righteous or blameless as Noah because we have His grace, which means we have His favor. But it is vital to remember that favor is not about us, but about God. It is a grace that is sufficient for us, but it is also a call of obedience. *We may ask for the favor of God to do great things in our lives, but we must also be willing to do great things for Him in return with our lives*. Today, set apart a time to go on a walk with God, ask Him some questions, pray some bizarre things, and then see how He answers. For the best part about being favored is being in relationship with God Himself. You never know what secrets He is yet to speak; you never know what wonders you are yet to find.

77

PISTEUO

<u>Man of Steel</u>:
Martha (Mom): "Sweetie, how can I help you if you won't let me in?" Clark (age 9): "The world's too big, Mom." Martha: "Then make it <u>small</u>. Just, um, focus on my voice. Pretend it's an island out in the ocean. Can you see it?" Clark: "I see it." Martha: "Then swim towards it, honey."[cxcv]

I wonder how many times we **all** have felt like Clark. So small in a world so big. Seeing all that we aren't and can't handle. Seeing all that is before us, yet, simultaneously keeping in focus what is behind us. God is lovingly knocking on the door of our heart saying, "Let Me in. Listen to My voice and follow it. Life is simpler than you think. Just take one step at a time." As soon as God speaks a promise over us—our minds can speed up by 189% to expect it will magically grow overnight, that somehow in your sleep, you were made into this superhero, ready to live your dream! I'm sorry to say that is not exactly how it works. Moses heard from the Lord to deliver God's people, but he didn't walk straight from that meeting with God into the promise. Abraham wasn't told, "You are going to have a son," to immediately find his wife pregnant. Noah wasn't warned about the coming flood to find an ark prepared and polished waiting for him. No. In all of these promises of hope, there was a process too. That's just usually the part we don't want to hear. "Oh hey, Moses! Also. Forgot to tell you. There's going to be ten plagues before that." "Oh and Abraham, you will actually be 100 when your son is born." "One last thing, Noah. That ark I mentioned is going to take you about 120 years to build. But you've got it!" If God told us the process beforehand, we would probably give up all hope on the promise. But because He does give us a promise, we can hold onto the hope that, "The word of the Lord holds true, and we can trust everything He does."[cxcvi] When the Lord gives us His Word, it won't return to Him void. He tells us so we can prepare to be directed. Mary was engaged when the angel spoke to her about being *the mother of Jesus*. (Talk about speeding up your mind 189%.) I'm sure these thoughts had to run through her head: "My fiancé will leave me. My family disown me. My culture shun me." But deep down, she trusted God. In Luke 1:45 it says, "Blessed is she who has **believed** that the Lord would fulfill his promises to her!"[cxcvii] (emphasis added) The word *believe* in Greek is pronounced *pisteuo*.[cxcviii] The same word can be translated as "faith" and "trust." All three are necessary when persevering in the process. In Moses' perseverance, he was made into a great leader for his people. In Abraham's perseverance, he matured into a great father of many nations. In Noah's perseverance, he grew as the role model for the new human race. In Mary's perseverance, she was shaped in the secret, for *the secret* she would carry for years to come. Every one had a specific word from the Lord to cling to in belief. Likewise, God has a specific promise to entrust you with for His glory. See it as your island out in the ocean. Keep swimming towards it. Keep persevering and believing you will see its completion. When you reach the shore, you will know, every moment of strength, weakness, courage, and doubt, was worth it to see His word hold true. Just listen to His voice, make the world smaller, and *pisteuo* in His purpose for you.

78

SEEING LASTS A LIFETIME

During March of 2013, I travelled to Africa for my first missions trip. People kept warning me of how the poverty would be absolutely shocking, but the most shocking part to me was how peaceful I was within all the poverty. At first, I was a little stunned, thinking, "God how is this not tearing me to pieces? Why don't I feel?" And then I heard His voice ever so clearly reply, "I am not allowing you to feel so that you can see." *Feelings last only a moment, but seeing lasts a lifetime.* I think we base our life off of feelings *so* often. Feeling things out and letting it break us open, but then re-mending, turning back around, and never doing anything about it. Feeling super happy, but forgetting that feeling within a day. You see, you can look back on life and remember the "image" of being super happy, broken, or lost, but you can't "feel" that "feeling" again. It's fuzzy... like a blur. Jeremiah 17:9 states, "The heart is deceptive above all things and beyond cure. Who can understand it?"[cxcix] Our heart may feel many things, but it doesn't see everything, and that is why it is impossible for us to understand it. Only God who sees everything can understand it. But, this just shows why we should stop being so driven by desires without sight. Allow God to show your heart things it has never seen before, and then when you see much, you will feel much with a new understanding. On this trip, God allowed me to see these simple things. He let me see the *beauty* within each person—how they are all unique, beautiful, children of God. He let me see their *hunger* after the God who is greater than life. He let me see *who* He is, instead of just what He does. It was life-changing. Why? Because I can still "see" it all vividly. We

feel so much, but see so little, and I think it's time that we allow our hearts to see and our eyes to feel. That's a little mind-stretching thought because our eyes can't feel literally, but they can reflect feelings when you look into someone's eyes. Within your eyes, others can see kindness, value, compassion, and that expresses a feeling of *love* that far outlasts the hands of time.

79

ANCHORED PROMISES

> *When God made his promise to Abraham, since there was no one greater for him to swear by, he swore by himself, saying, "I will surely bless you and give you many descendants." And so after waiting patiently, Abraham received what was promised.*[cc]
> Hebrews 6:13-15

Hope. It is an anchor for our soul, a peace for our unknown, and a strength for our every moment. It is what lets us look forward to our tomorrow and live bravely in our today. It is what President Snow describes as hope in *The Hunger Games*: "A little hope is effective. A lot of hope is dangerous."[cci] Dangerous in the ability to cause change. And that is the hope Abraham had in Hebrews 6:13-15. God made a promise to Abraham that was so great that He swore by Himself, and so Abraham waited patiently with hope for the promise that we read of in Hebrews 11:12, "And so from this one man, and he as good as dead, came descendants as numerous as the stars in the sky and as countless as the sand on the seashore."[ccii] He had a hope that was an anchor for his soul and unshakable for his promise.

And there are three things that stand out to me about his anchored promise: one, that it is unmoving; two, that it is unseen, and three, that it is unquestionable. In Hebrews 6:19 we read, "We have this hope as an anchor for the soul, firm and secure."[cciii] His promise was unmoving, no matter what situations arose or what circumstances were around him, because the hope that was within him was not moving and neither was his promise. Then, in Hebrews 10:35 we read, "So do no throw away your confidence; it will be richly awarded."[cciv] Though an anchor is beneath the surface and cannot be seen, Abraham's confidence was that God still could see what he couldn't. He had a confidence in God that allowed him to believe in God's promise as his own, and that is what made it unquestionable. Like Hebrew 11:1 says, "Now faith is being sure of what we *hope* for and *certain* of what we do not see."[ccv] (emphasis added) He was sure of what he hoped for and certain of his promise—because he had an anchor in his soul of God's Word.

I believe that God has an anchored promise for each and every one of our lives: one that is beyond ourselves, beyond our comfort, and beyond our sight. But it is our hope! And the thing is—***it's a hope that is dangerous because it can change everything***. And the enemy knows that, so he will try to do whatever he can to keep you from it. But our hope will always be greater than our adversity. Anchors come in all shapes and sizes for different reasons and purposes, but they are all unmoving, unseen, and unquestionable. Each anchor has flukes to secure it in place. Likewise, our prayers are like flukes that help keep our anchor firm and secure, so that when we can't see what is under the waves of life, we don't give up. Instead we hold onto our confidence that reminds us of our promise. Until then, we can wait patiently for the day our unseen will breakthrough the surface of our lives, just as He promised.

80

FEARLESS IN THE FIELDS

Growing up, we are told we can be anything we want to be. As children, we'd dream up the most creatively constructed futures and have the simplest attitude that it would be so. This same child-like faith is found in Luke 1:37 which reads, "For with God nothing will be impossible."[ccvi] Another version says, "For no word from God will ever fail."[ccvii] What if when God spoke over our lives, our belief in His creatively constructed future for us was the same? Sometimes, as we grow up, it becomes harder to believe, to have faith, and to trust in what God is doing. But really, it's not crazy at all.

In 2 Samuel 23, we read a story of a mighty warrior named Shammah. We find him here standing in the middle of a field of lentils, a place full of value, treasure, and worth. But the sneaky thing about life is that the enemy doesn't like to leave goodness untouched. The Philistines band together to take the field as their own, and all the Israelites flee...except for Shammah. Shammah takes his stand, in the middle of the field, and he defends his ground. And then, the Lord brings about a great victory.

Here's the thing, the enemy is sneaky, but he is not silent. 1 Peter 5:8 says, "The enemy prowls around like a roaring lion."[ccviii] Yet, Proverbs 28:1 says, "But the godly as are BOLD as lions."[ccix] (emphasis added) The enemy roars *like* a lion, but he's *not* a lion. He's not greater than you, because God is within you, and is also with you. These two truths are what give us the boldness to stand in the middle of a field under attack.

My three questions for you are: one, <u>what is your battle?</u> Is your battle really against flesh and blood? Or is it actually against the enemy trying to steal the value of your portion? Two, <u>what are you defending?</u> Psalms 45:3-5 says, "Put on your sword, O mighty warrior! You are so glorious, so majestic! In your majesty, ride out to victory, defending truth, humility and justice."[ccx] What truth has God spoken to your heart that has been planted within your spirit, and is still growing in your field of promises? I know the middle makes you feel stuck, vulnerable, and defenseless, but get this next part of the verse, "Go forth to perform awe-inspiring deeds! Your arrows are sharp, piercing your enemies' hearts. The nations fall beneath your feet." Do you truly believe that what He has spoken over you is worth defending? Three: <u>what are you holding onto?</u> What are you trying to fight the battle with? Are you picking up your sword?

Did you know the very Bible that is on your shelf is your *greatest* weapon against the enemy, and within it is TRUTH and POWER. ***I think honestly we give too much power to doubt and take hold of the power of the Word too seldom.*** The Word is sharper than any double-edged sword. It pierces the enemy's heart, and I'm thinking it's time to start defending your heart. The enemy knows your motions well, but what he can't foresee is how you'll react. He will attack yes, but he comes into the middle of the field hoping you'll flee instead of defend. Yet, you can STAND fearless in the fields. Here's why, because you are chosen.

Cain was marked by God so that no one could kill him, and you are marked by God so nothing can defeat you. (Genesis 4:15)[ccxi] I don't know if your courage is rising yet, so let me put it this way. If the enemy can't kill God's chosen, why do we need to run from him? He can attack us all he wants, but he will never be able to defeat us. *Though your kingdom may be under attack, your heart cannot be penetrated.* There is great victory that is before those who defend what God has spoken, and are crazy enough to believe it. **You** can be *fearless*, because you, as a *mighty* child of God, are <u>marked</u>. Withstand, withstand, withstand, and watch as God moves. Victory shall come; He will come through!

81

THE GREATEST FATHER'S VOWS

I vow to love you tenderly, to never let you go.
I vow to cherish every secret you share with Me, and to hold your deepest wishes close to My heart.
I vow to go after what's in your heart to pursue your heart to the fullest.
I vow to always stay by your side, even through the darkest of times, for My
love to be a fire to keep you warm. I vow to protect you, even in the harshest of
climates, for you to always remain who you are, to always be Mine.
My vows are to keep you, to save you, and to hold you, that you'll never
feel alone in such a big world. Though the stars at times are hidden, they
always exist. So My Love always exists, even in the unseen.
My vow is My Word to love you every day, that I may be the greatest Father in the world to you.

@k15_nicole

"It is very common for people to swear an oath by something greater than themselves, for the oath will confirm their statements and end all dispute. So in the same way, God wanted to end all doubt and confirm it even more forcefully to those who would inherit his promises. **His purpose was unchangeable, so God added his vow to the promise.** So it is impossible for God to lie for we know that his promise and his vow will never change! And **now we have run into his heart to hide ourselves in his faithfulness**. This is where we find his strength and comfort, for he empowers us to seize what has already been established ahead of time—an unshakeable hope!"[ccxii] (emphasis added)
Hebrews 6:16-18

82

SEALED SECRETS

Her heart was wild, but I didn't want to catch it, I wanted to run with it to set mine free.[ccxiii]
- Atticus

"Do you want to hear a secret?" I imagine my young self shaking my head up and down excitedly, eyes lighting up with sparks, heart quickening at the thought. Not only was I being trusted with top secret information, but I now had a new friend who confided in me. That secret was treasure to my heart for it created a unique bond between us—one only we would now share. The secret probably was about a boy she liked that we would giggle about and give boy reports on when we caught him "looking" at her—you know, the signs? And at this time, the boy probably had no interest whatsoever in her at the age of seven, and most likely still believed in cooties. But it was our secret, and it created such a fire inside of me.

As you may know, the older we become, the bigger the secrets become. There's the big ultimate engagement day secret to the smaller hidden secrets of your heart's desires. They expand over ranges of life's territory and yet there's always a small spark within each one—for every secret has a tag of love attached (or should, at least). Then there's us and God—as a Father, He knows everything, and as a best friend, He lets us in on some of His hidden mysteries. Every time He whispers, we light up—something sparks in our hearts—for He trusts us as we are and is a friend who knows where we are going. He reveals sealed secrets to us—ones that others don't know are hidden deep inside our destiny; ones that burn brighter in our hearts than any other sense of doubt or discouragement—and we must keep them aflame. In Genesis 18:17, God so casually says in front of Abraham: "Shall I keep back from Abraham what I am about to do?"[ccxiv] Followed by whispers of unforgotten dreams that had remained hidden deep in Abraham's heart. It ends with: "So that God can complete in Abraham what he promised him." I believe God lets us in on Godsecrets, not only because He trusts us, but because they are breath to the fire in our hearts. *What secrets we do hold, we can run wild with.* His whispers, His promises, His revelations, are tagged with love and sealed with purpose, releasing us to live wild in the truth of what He's spoken with complete freedom. Catching them wouldn't make much sense, but running with them is igniting!

As R. H. Sin writes: "She was a fire enough to light the way and burn anything attempting to stop her."[ccxv] Our God-secrets should burn so brightly that they do the same. Yet with every secret, there is a seal. The heavier the promise, the thicker the seal is pressed. A secret is truth revealed ahead of time; therefore, every secret has its perfect timing. Like an engagement, if someone spoke up about it ahead of time to the soon-to-be-fiancé, they would've ruined the entire surprise! Yet with the secret, the right preparations could be put in place for the big reveal. Are you following? Like Song of Songs 8:6 reads: "Place me like a seal over your heart, like a seal on your arm; for love is as strong as death, its jealousy as unyielding as the grave. It burns like blazing fire, like a mighty flame."[ccxvi] Seals were precious to their owners and were as personal as their names. Therefore what God has spoken over you is sealed with His forever faithful identity! When He whispered into your ear the BIG secret, you heard from the BIG God whose I AM stamp was sealed over your heart. The secret wasn't only a fire to your heart but a light to your path so that you could see the direction in which He was taking you. All so that God could complete in you what is promised. Though it may be sealed, don't forget to guard it, for the enemy is sneaky with his crafty doubts. But as you treasure His word in your heart, no discouragements or lies or distractions can come close to stopping you—for your fire will burn ever brighter as truth reveals all.

83

THE ONLY EXCEPTION

I used to see courage as having no fear or being fearless. As I read, "Be strong and courageous," throughout the Old Testament, I felt even smaller and smaller when I realized that I was the furthest thing from fearless. But as I read the story of Esther, I began to see God's hand designing her life to be used, once again, in courage. I have had Esther 4:16 underlined in my Bible for a while now, because her statement is so strong, "And if I perish, I perish."[ccxvii] But I never realized that it was actually a fear-filled response. In the verses right before her statement, she hears Mordecai's urgent and pleading statement, and at first she replies with words of fear, because of the impossibilities of the situation. We sense her fear because there was only *one* exception for her to uninvitedly enter into the king's courts and her life to be spared. I'm sure that Esther's heart was racing as fast as her mind was searching for the right thing to do. Yet, we see her courage when she obeys in fear, even though her "what if" far outweighed the "maybe if." And so she goes before the king in reverent obedience with hope for the one exception. I believe that is what courage is. It is not about being fearless of stepping out, rather having a fear of God posture in stepping out. God is going to call many of us to things that have only one exception of hope, but courage will fight for that one exception, fearless or fear-filled.

> *Courage is not the lack of fear. It is acting in spite of it.*[ccxviii]
> - Mark Twain

84

ALL THE DAYS OF MY LIFE

I want you to imagine greatness. What do you see? Maybe it's fame—holding that golden trophy in your hand. Maybe it's an adventure—reaching the top of Mt. Everest. Maybe it's being at your favorite place in the world: France, Italy, or Russia. Or maybe it is experiencing a moment of using your gift in front of thousands of people. Now all of these things are absolutely great, but they would all have a lack of beauty if they were apart from God. These are things I would imagine when I heard the word "great." But, when these doors of greatness were right in front of me, God shut every one of them saying, "I have something greater for you." And so my imagination flew wild with awesome ideas of what God was going to do. But I discovered that greatness isn't found in what you do or where you are, it's in Him. He is the greatness that I have always desired. And where did I realize this? Sitting on the roof of my house. I wasn't halfway across the world, I was in an ordinary place, but I was in His will and with Him. I remember thinking, "I'd rather be in His will than halfway across the world out of His will." I was already in greatness for He was with me all along. Holding a golden trophy obtains greatness if He is with me. Reaching the top of Mt. Everest obtains greatness if He is with me. Being in a stunning place obtains greatness if He is with me. Using my gift in front of a stadium full of people obtains greatness if He is with me. **Greatness is found in big moments, but it's also found in small whispers.** Greatness is found wherever He is, so truly, He is the very desire we seek—God, who is greatness Himself. As Psalm 27:4 reads, "One thing I ask of the Lord, this is what I seek: that I may dwell in the house of the Lord all the days of my life, to gaze upon the beauty of the Lord and to seek Him in His temple."[ccxix] When He is the desire that we seek—we discover greatness all the days of our lives.

@ kathleenmadethis

85

THE MOST POWERFUL TRUST

150 psalms, countless stories of worship and praise, and one God who deserves all the glory. Isn't it amazing? The beautiful thing about genuine worship is that it's not at all about ourselves, but is completely and fully centered and focused on Him. Worship should be the cry of our hearts from the beginning of the day, as we wake up, to our every answer for our every circumstance. Because worship is **all** about Him, and it is the most powerful trust in the world. I have learned that there are many different reasons to praise, but when you bring them altogether—worship adds up to be a complete surrender, and there is no better place to be. One of the coolest stories of worship happens in Acts where Silas and Paul were praising and singing hymns to God in prison. We read in Acts 16:26, "Suddenly there was such a violent earthquake that the foundations of the prison were shaken. At once all the prison doors flew open, and *everyone's* chains became loose."[ccxx] (emphasis added) I love the way Darlene Zschech puts it, "Praise is declaration, a victory cry, proclaiming faith to stand firm in the place God has given you. Praise is a proclamation that the enemy's intent to plunder you will not rock you. Praise declares that you will not be moved by the enemy's attempt to snatch you away."[ccxxi] That is exactly what Paul and Silas did. They praised God in chains, not allowing adversity to steal their hope and faith in God. Not only did it break off their chains, but also everyone's around them. Praise is a game-changer, a heart-turner, and a faith-statement. And so my challenge to you is to praise before you pray. Before you pray to God to get you out of the situation you are in, before you ask Him for your wants, before you plead for change—praise Him. Because I have realized that praising God does three major things. One: it aligns our hearts with His heart. Two: praise is surrender, and surrender is praise. Three: it is the highest declaration of trust. When you praise Him first, your heart starts to surrender to His will praising Him for all He is doing and will do. It allows you to see beyond yourself and to focus on Him. And it places your entire situation before Him in trust. Praise is taking yourself out of the equation so that God can come into it. It's all about Him and who He is, and trusting in what He is doing. So praise before the breakthrough, for He will break through upon your praise.

86

PATIENT BUILT PALACES

> *Imagine yourself as a living house. God comes in to rebuild that house. At first, perhaps, you can understand what He is doing. He is getting the drains right and stopping the leaks in the roof and so on; you knew that those jobs needed doing and so you are not surprised. But presently He starts knocking the house about in a way that hurts abominably and does not seem to make any sense. What on earth is He up to? The explanation is that He is building quite a different house from the one you thought of—throwing out a new wing here, putting on an extra floor there, running up towers, making courtyards. You thought you were being made into a decent little cottage: but He is building a palace.* [ccxxii]
> - C. S. Lewis

The first time I read this, I wanted to curl up on my bed and weep because it resonated so deeply. I kept hearing the Lord say, "You can trust in what I'm doing." But it looked so much different from what I was expecting. What felt like a natural disaster was just Jesus honoring my prayers of, "Jesus, I trust You. Your will be done." But in order for His will to be done through us, He has to grow the capacity within us by making some alterations first. Dreaming bigger requires a will that allows God to shift some things around. It's like the parable of the wise and foolish builders. The wise man listened to the words of God and built his house on a rock. "The rain came down, the streams rose, and the winds blew and beat against the house; yet it did not fall, because it had its foundation on the rock."[ccxxiii] (Matthew 7:25) Yet, the foolish man ignored God, took the matter into his own hands—and thus his vision crumbled. One trusted and discovered a palace on a Rock, the other created a cottage that crashed over the course of time.

While a palace is being built, *trust* and *patience* are vital. Trust leaves the house in the Creator's hands and goes downtown to work on other projects. Patience drives by, sees the palace is not yet complete, and rents another house in the meantime. In Psalm 45:13-15, we read: "*All glorious* is the princess within her chamber; her gown is interwoven with gold. In embroidered garments she is led to the

king; her virgin companions follow her and are brought to you. They are led in with *joy* and *gladness*; they enter the **palace of the king.**"[ccxxiv] (emphasis added) I don't know if you also imagined Rapunzel looking out her high tower, but I empathize with her longing to leave the chamber and enter THE PALACE! Yet, patience prepared her in ways she couldn't foresee. While she was very aware of her dreams, her garments to wear were being interwoven with gold. While patience kept her company, it also engraved her with wonder. While resting in the chamber, she made lasting friendships who'd one day follow her to the king! Patience *builds* palaces— present tense and future-focused, by a King who's *always* wild for His beloved. Patience isn't stuck in a cell with nothing to do. *Patience prayerfully ponders the promise while destined thrones are being established by His love.* As 1 Chronicles 29:1 says, "The task is great, because this palatial structure is not for man but for the Lord God."[ccxxv] Your patience isn't for nothing; it's trusting Him with everything, holding nothing back, letting Him into the deepest desires of your heart to create unshakable promises that your kingdom will be built upon. Then, one day you will finally live in your patient built palace and know that it was all *well* worth the wait.

87

THE PRINCE OF PEACE

He whispered, "Peace is your portion." Little did I know what that truly meant. Little did I comprehend the vast array of that which it truly speaks of. To me, peace was the thought of how I felt at the break of dawn, near the stillness of the sea, or during the serenity of a morning's welcome. Yet, this peace He spoke of was more than a feeling, it was a promise. In Micah 5:4-5 it says, "He will stand and shepherd his flock in the strength of the Lord, in the majesty of the name of the Lord his God. And they will live securely, for then his greatness will reach to the ends of the earth. And he will be our peace..."[ccxxvi] This peace is defined as: *freedom from war as well as connoting prosperity*.[ccxxvii] It's this peace that promises everything is going to be okay, and yet, is still beyond what we have ever known. As Isaiah 11:6-9 describes the peace and safety of the Messianic age, it talks about the wolf living with the lamb, and a child leading a calf and lion together. To me, it is as magical of a place as C. S. Lewis's Narnia. It's a peace that shouts "your warfare is over" and whispers "the best is yet to come." It's a peace that rises in our spirits that we may smile without fear, walk without hesitation, and speak without doubt. It's an invisible order but a held onto substance. This peace is our portion. It is our triumph and our sword; it is the Prince of Peace Himself, and He is ours.

> *Wrong will be right, when Aslan comes in sight,*
> *At the sound of his roar, sorrows will be no more,*
> *When he bares his teeth, winter meets its death,*
> *And when he shakes his mane, we shall have spring again.*[ccxxviii]
> The Lion, the Witch, and the Wardrobe

88

CONTAINED

When sparks and flames arise
And the forest all surrounds
Don't be consumed by the fire
That seems so safe and sound
For emotions can spread ablaze
With chaos to impart
Where ashes are its love
And ruins are its heart
Though harmless to the eye
It's dangerous to the touch
Don't try to test its boundaries
It will never see enough
But a spark can be contained
With all its wild and still be free
If peace can be found
Before whispering screams
In a field that is so plain
With trees welcoming you in
Don't listen to its taunting
Stand against the wind
For fire cannot be refrained
If it starts to spread too far
For ashes are its love
And ruins are its heart

*Whoever is slow to anger is better than the mighty,
and he who rules his spirit than he who takes a city.*[ccxxix]
Proverbs 16:32

89

THIRST NO MORE

Have you ever been so hungry that all you can think about is what type of food you want to eat, where you want to go, when you get to go, and how fast you can get there? And all of this is running through your head while you are in the middle of something: a conversation, class, work, or even an activity. No matter how hard you try to stay focused, your mind keeps wandering to that one word, that one picture—food. I don't even think I'm exaggerating when I tell you that this happens to me probably once a day. I can be anywhere with something major happening, but all I can think about is satisfying my appetite. If I miss my lunch break, my whole day is thrown off. Somehow, I turn from myself into a robot that shuts off and can't activate without food. But you know what's interesting? It is said that we can survive three weeks without food and only three days without water. And it reminds me of the saying, "You're not yourself when you're hungry." But honestly, you're not yourself when you're thirsty either. Sometimes, when we "think" we are hungry is when we actually just need water. In John 4, a woman from Samaria comes to draw water from the well (probably to satisfy her appetite), and Jesus comes over, seeing her thirsty self and says, "Give me a drink." I don't think He was trying to trick her at all. Instead, He was making her more aware of her appetite and craving for satisfaction. He goes onto say in John 4:13-14, "Everyone who drinks of this water will be thirsty again, but whoever drinks of the water that I will give him will never be thirsty again."[ccxxx] Doesn't that just make you forget about everything you were doing? Here is something that will make you thirst no more. Like "count me in!"

Jesus is speaking the same thing to many of us.

We are running and running and running, feeling so hungry and dissatisfied, running to get food from our friends, our plans, our loves, a substance, that temporarily relieves our appetite. But then once again it hits us and we keep running. During this time, we grow tired of running, tired of trying, and bitterness starts to grow in our hearts. *We start to run away to all these things around us instead of running to the One who is calling out to us.* But when you feel that emptiness, it's natural to try to fill it in. But it may just be with the wrong satisfaction. As Robert Madu said: "The enemy can't stop you from being blessed, but he can distract you from feeling blessed with the spirit of discontentment. If I were the enemy, I would try to convince you that you would be satisfied when you had 'this' desire."[ccxxxi] When it comes to Jesus, He gives us His love, His peace, a drink of His water of everlasting life, and it quenches every hurt, confusion, doubt, weakness, and appetite within you. Because really, we weren't hungry, we were just thirsty for Jesus, but we were searching in all the wrong places. This doesn't mean that once you spend time with Jesus that you won't need Him anymore; it just means that when you do become thirsty again, He is the One who can fill your heart, the only One who can restore you, and the constant One who will always remind you of Whose you are. He is the fountain that will never run dry, will always satisfy, and will forever be enough. Jesus— there's no other name, no other source of life, like Him.

90

BEYOND THE BORDERS

When it comes down to it, our hearts long for purpose; they seek to make a difference, and they long to be known. But it is easy for us to see the borders that are around us over the capabilities within us to exceed them. The question turns from "Can I" to "Will I?" This is where many of us stay. We feel lost in the questions instead of found in His grace. His grace that has been sufficient for Moses, Noah, Job, and Abraham. All who went beyond their borders either physically, spiritually, or emotionally. God used Moses who had a stuttering problem to lead a nation to a hoped for promised land. He used Noah to build an ark leaving behind everything he knew. Job was faithful to God beyond the borders of his comfort, and Abraham left everything behind not knowing anything ahead. They all went beyond their borders and, in return, lived a life with purpose that we all read about today. But if you could imagine yourself in their shoes, I think you would realize that they weren't any different from you. **They all saw the borders; they just each had enough faith in God to go beyond them.** Isaiah 26:15 says, "O Lord, you have made our nation great; yes, you have made us great. You have extended our borders, and we give you the glory!"[ccxxxii] We all have borders in our lives that can range from: doubt, fear, worry, comfort, anger, or even pride, and we all know them. They are what hold us back from living life to the fullest. But it is when we overcome those borders that we discover a boundless hope, an unlimited strength, and an everlasting promise. We see what we have always been capable of, because in some way, whether big or small, we have always had a purpose ahead of us. But, it takes crossing every border to experience that glory that we all long for. It not only requires big leaps, but small steps, to inch our way closer to going beyond the borders. But it is when we cross that border that we will know every leap was worth it and every step counted. In the wait, we discover the weight of the call that is worth crossing oceans, mountains, and valleys of borders for. It is there we will experience His glory; it is there our purpose is found.

91

TO TRUST IN A LIVING DREAM

Often we trust in a living reality, but how do we trust in a living dream? In something that is so close, real, and vulnerable to our hearts. Not only is it invisible, but it's neither sensible nor practical in many ways. When you close your eyes and think of it, it's everything you could imagine. But when you open your eyes, will you allow your heart to be open too? Even if it means taking risks that may end up letting you fall? Even if it means losing everything you have to see the one thing you've always wished for to come to life? These are the questions we face, but often do not dare to ask, or even dare to answer. Yet, one thing I have learned is that your dream didn't begin with you, but God. There are desires in your heart for a reason, and it is your choice to either chase them or let them go. Or really to just let them go to sleep. We can tuck them away in the little beds of our hearts, but we don't truly ever forget them. But as long as you're awake, your dreams will live within you too. And not seeing them or holding them can be discouraging, lonely, and even empty at times. But that is why this journey of trust is vital. Because it depends solely on God for it to come to life.

Proverbs 3:5-6 says:

Trust God from the bottom of your heart; don't try to figure out everything on your own. Listen for God's voice in everything you do, everywhere you go; he's the one who will keep you on track. [ccxxxiii]

I don't know what impossible dream God has for you, but I do know that, as spoken by Elisabeth Elliot, "The heart set to do the Father's will need never fear defeat."[ccxxxiv] Some of you are having dreams birth within your heart right now, my encouragement to you is to write every detail down. Some of you have had a dream in your heart for a while, and the enemy has slowly been rocking it to sleep, and I say unto you to persevere into your promise. What God spoke wasn't a figment of your imagination. The process takes a little bit longer than planned sometimes. Others of you are about to have the opportunity for your dream to come true, but brokenness is blinding you from the blessings God has before you. I urge you to "chase your dream." For you may not feel like it, but you know silently, the dream is still wide-awake in your heart.

But for whosoever is reading this

book—never give up. Usually it's when you don't feel like trying that you're closest to seeing breakthrough. I'm sure the man with leprosy didn't want to dip a seventh time. Because what if he did and wasn't healed? Or what if Joshua went around the wall a seventh time and nothing changed? It's a vulnerable moment after you chase your dream for the sixth time knowing what God has spoken over the seventh. Yet, this is when God proves Himself and His word to be true. As written in Proverbs 3:12, "A father's delight is behind all of this." Every moment counts; *nothing is wasted*. Trust God with where you're at. It may not make sense. It may seem impossible. It may be quite vulnerable because you shake at the thought of it coming true and not coming true in the same moment. But that dream is living within you for a reason. Trust God with it. He has a plan. He is good.

92

THE DEPTHS

I'm learning that we should not fear the depths. Sometimes going deep involves being vulnerable, and typically, if it's a hidden thing, it's hard to face. But fear, doubt, worry, brokenness, they shouldn't be our depths. *His love should be.* If so much of the deep is painted in black, we need to allow His melodies to sing over its depths—to bring light to the beauty and color it contains. His love is not only high, but also deep, and to discover its fullness, is to let His light penetrate both. Again, *we mustn't fear the depths.* For He spoke it into being; therefore, His power and presence already reside there and reign over its darkness. If we hear the tunes He sings above land, and sing them within the depths, we will see His orchestration take place within its magical underwater land. **We needn't stay deep, but we also shouldn't fear it.** For without the heights, we can never truly live, yet without the depths, we can never truly love. Freedom is found in the balance of both, like rhythms of grace, and in its song, we dance.

I'm not sure what you've been hoping for, praying for, or believing for, and I'm not sure how slow it has been in its coming, but sing His melodies of light over what may seem dark that His love may fill the depths of your heart and dismantle fear. For I do know that His plans for you are greater than you can imagine, and that His love never fails. Know this too, believe it, let it sink deep, and it *will* light up what is unknown. It may not still be clear, but you'll see God, His presence, His colors, and that will be enough.

In Ezekiel 3:1-3 it reads: *He told me, "Son of man, eat what you see. Eat this book. Then go and speak to the family of Israel." As I opened my mouth, he gave me the scroll to eat, saying, "Son of man, eat this book that I am giving you. Make a full meal of it!" So I ate it. It tasted so good—just like honey.*[ccxxxv]*(emphasis added)* I believe the promises, the glimpses to come, the prophetic words God gives us, we should eat. We should let them sink deep in a way that their light keeps darkness out. We should taste the sweetness of its promise to know its outcome will be good. The melody above land is the same melody underwater, you only need to sing it out. His love in the heights is as great as His love in the depths, you need only to fill their spaces with the same wonder. His words are vision, as are yours. So eat what you see, and speak its light into existence. Then when you go, His song will be playing in every dimension of your heart, from the heights to the depths, and carrying into the every day its tune; its beauty will flood you with love and not fear, for it will remind you of His vision to become yours.

> *Is there anyplace I can go to avoid your Spirit? To be out of your sight? If I climb to the sky, you're there! If I go underground, you're there! If I flew on morning's wings to the far western horizon, You'd find me in a minute—you're already there waiting! Then I said to myself,* **"Oh, he even sees me in the dark! At night I'm immersed in the light!"** *It's a fact: darkness isn't dark to you; night and day, darkness and light, they're all the same to you.*[ccxxxvi]
> Psalm 139:7-12 (emphasis added)

93

CATALYST

Catalyst: "a person or event that quickly causes change or action; something that causes activity between two or more persons or forces without itself being affected. A person whose talk, enthusiasm, or energy causes others to be more friendly, enthusiastic, or energetic."[ccxxxvii]

Did you know that your prayers don't only shape you, but that they can shape others' destinies around you? That your prayers are a catalyst to a revolution? That in seeking His heart, you were able to hear theirs? And in listening, your heart was directed and led by His will through His words. And then that perfect time came when all of your prayers added up and you saw their power catalyst someone into God's perfect plan for them→ and it was absolutely beautiful. Because your prayers catalyst change.

Jeremiah 33:3 says, "Ask me and I will tell you remarkable secrets you do not know about things to come."[ccxxxviii] You see, when you draw near to God, you draw even closer to His heart and His will, not only for you, but even for others, simply because you are listening and He is always speaking. There will be times that He will speak through us, but not to us. There are seasons that will be as silent as space. And though we may not see a thing, we can know He sees everything, with hidden dreams included. 1 John 5:14 reads, "This is the confidence we have in approaching God: that if we ask anything according to His will, he hears us."[ccxxxix] Every prayer that we pray is heard, not one of them is missing, not one is forgotten. And each of them are making a difference, but it is in God's timing when they will become a catalyst to change the world. *Change starts with the small;* all of the small people, small visions, and small prayers eventually add up into one big dream. And that is the remarkable secret He knew all along. In other words, "Show me your prayers, and I'll show you your future." Be a catalyst.

The beauty of not knowing the future is knowing God Himself.

94

TO WALK WITH GOD

Noah walked with God and found favor in the eyes of the Lord. In Genesis 6:22, we read, "Noah did everything just as God commanded him."[ccxl] I believe his story helps us to have faith over knowledge. But first, let's step back and take a look at what is going on. The world is filled with wickedness, God is talking about flooding the earth, and thus He tells Noah to build this impossible project of a massive ark. Noah of course responds with great faith, and embarks on a wildly new journey he wasn't expecting. However, because Noah walked with God constantly, he knew God's character and did not doubt what was spoken.

In knowing the details of something, we are able to understand it and even see it differently. For example, if someone gave you a "scarlet emerald," you might say, "Thanks! It is beautiful." But if you *knew* that this "scarlet emerald" was known as one of the most rare gemstones, valued around ten grand per carat, all of a sudden it would become far more precious and sacred. You would start to hold value in it a bit differently and hold it a little more carefully. That's the same with Noah and God. Noah was simply walking with God, getting to *know* the details of His character, and in return, coming to behold the magnificence of Who God truly is. The more he gazed upon God's beauty, the more his confidence grew in God's ability, which brings us back to his response of unwavering obedience, in which he *knew* he had no reason to question God. It says that, "Noah was a right man, blameless among the people of his time…" As he walked daily with God, he was embraced by God, and therefore shaped in His love and kindness.

The glimmering hope within this story is that God still intends this same relationship with *us*. Psalm 37:23 says, "The Lord directs the steps of the godly. He delights in every detail of their lives."[ccxli] In other words, God takes great delight in those who walk with Him. It is where we cannot see that we long to go; it is what hasn't been done that we desire to do. We want to make footprints in unknown places and untouched dreams. But the greatest thing about discovery is that it's found in walking with God, being embraced in His love, and being shaped in His kindness. Our journey with God will not be everything we expect it to be; it will be so much more. The greatest places we will come to travel will not go according to our plan, but will go exactly as He planned; and as we discover the details of His life, He constantly directs the details of ours. As you walk with Him, you'll soon *know* He is worthy of being trusted; undoubtedly, you'll step out in faith because of it, and soon the stories will go: <u>Insert your name</u>, was a right (man/woman) of God, blameless among the people of (his/her) time.

95

UNDONE

When I look into Your eyes; I am undone. There is no shame; there is such great love. Your words penetrate my greatest of fears; Your kindness drives away all madness. Still You choose me, You know me, You see me, and You love me beyond what I'll ever know. I'll declare what You've destined; I'll speak what You say. {Bold and unashamed, I am Yours.} Without rival, I will be still in the midst of raging wars. I'll choose You then and there as I do here and now. There's no greater honor. I want everything to do with You. You are my Rock Eternal, my fortress in whom I hide. My deepest of desires is for Your fame; my greatest of longings is but to linger in Your presence. No time with You will ever be long enough, for I live to gaze upon the beauty of Your temple, to get but a glimpse of the grace in Your eyes once again.

> "For just one day of intimacy with you is like a thousand days of joy rolled into one! I'd rather stand at the threshold in front of the Gate Beautiful, ready to go in and worship my God, than to live my life without you in the most beautiful palace of the wicked."[ccxlii]
> Psalm 84:10

96

1000 TIMES

Abdul Kalam said, "You have to dream before your dreams can come true."[ccxliii] I think dreams are one of the many ways we can worship God; they keep us in a continual wonder of His greatness and in a constant seeking of His will. And it is because of so many dreams that our world has been changed. Yet, as I have asked people what their dreams are, I have come to realize that many of us have stopped dreaming; we have stopped believing in the impossible. Mark Batterson puts it this way, "The day we stop dreaming is the day we start dying."[ccxliv] The miracles and wonders that are found in dreaming are world-changing because they affect more than just one life. But I think many have a fear of dreaming because it follows with a fear of failing. We tend to see failure as a closed door, *but I have learned that a closed door does not mean failure, as an open door does not mean victory.* Because whether a door is opened or closed, God's will is being done and that should be our ultimate desire. All to say, the fear of failure should never keep you from going after what God has placed in your heart. Many people who have achieved their dreams today have experienced failure, but they didn't see the closed door as a closed opportunity but an open opportunity for another chance. Bill Gates' first business failed; Jim Carrey used to be homeless; Stephen King's first novel was rejected 30 times; Thomas Edison failed 1,000 times before he created the light bulb, and Simon Cowell's record company failed. And you know what Thomas Edison, the one who failed the most, said? "I have not failed. I've just found 10,000 ways that won't work."[ccxlv] Failure is as much of a necessary part of dreaming as success. So don't be afraid. The beauty of the impossible is that we can discover all the wrong ways to find the one right way that can change everything. 2 Samuel 7:3 says, "Go and do **all** that is in your heart for the Lord is with you."[ccxlvi] (emphasis added) I believe David started to dream here, and God simply spoke through Nathan to tell David "go." And this is one of the key elements of dreaming—a person who will achieve their dream will have the end in mind before the beginning. David had a vision of what he wanted the dream to become, he just needed to know that the Lord was with him in the journey of allowing it to come to life. And that is what matters the most. No matter how many people do or don't believe in your dream, if God believes in it, that should be your every reason to go for it. Proverbs 29:18 says, "Where there is no vision, the people perish."[ccxlvii] So dream, dream again, and keep dreaming. Expect failure, but also expect success, as you "go and do all that is in your heart, for the Lord is with you," for you never know what wild thing may just come to life.

97

DESIGNED

> *You go before me and follow me. You place your hand of blessing on my head. Such knowledge is too wonderful for me, too great for me to understand! You made all the delicate, inner parts of my body and knit me together in my mother's womb. Thank you for making me so wonderfully complex! Your workmanship is marvelous—how well I know it. You watched me as I was being formed in utter seclusion, as I was woven together in the dark of the womb. You saw me before I was born. Every day of my life was recorded in your book. Every moment was laid out before a single day had passed.*[ccxlviii]
> Psalm 139

Day to day, we wake, rise, and go. We see, seek, and accomplish. Then, we repeat. Yet if we stay still long enough, we may just catch sight of all the designs shaped in the time we spend waking, rising, and going, to find forms in the seeing, seeking, and accomplishing. To uncover patterns of art, beauty, and life in the repetition. When we look around us, it's easy to overlook the extraordinary as normal. Yet every object has been designed by an artist that you have come across this week. The cover of a book, the painting on a wall, the shape of the building you are in, all thought up by someone who dreamed, who sat still long enough to wonder, then brought the vision to life.

It's a beautiful thing for our eyes to see the vision the artist purposed their design for. It's yet another thing, for you to meet the maker and know their heart behind the vision. Every day and moment isn't by coincidence. Not every day has been perfect, but it witnesses the art of perfection, molding imperfections into a flawless finish. We have a Father who is quite crafty, and He is here, working in us and through us constantly. We are not some broken statue that's been left for ruin. We are beautifully designed pieces of art in the Potter's hands that are constantly seeing His love shape and design our lives for **good**.

We see God's art in the life of Esther, a strong, heroic, and brave queen. But first, she was known as an orphan taken in by her uncle. When all she saw was valueless, God saw royal. She had no idea what He had thought up; she had no sight or vision of what the Maker was doing. Yet, she was obedient and she was faithful, with no idea of the purpose of her days. As she learned under Mordecai's words, she was being designed. As each day went by, her maturity was being formed. As she pressed on, she was being pressed in beauty. All along, the Potter was preparing her for a royal position far beyond her dreams. All along, there was a purpose behind the designs that we now see.

So what's your story? That's not for me to hear but for you to know. Because it's that knowing that draws you to ask the Maker some questions, and in that questioning, you'll find beauty where you once saw flaws; you'll find purpose where you once saw monotony. You'll find designs where you once saw nothing. May you find the strength to let go of the brokenness of your past, and embrace the beauty of knowing the Maker of the universe hasn't forgotten about you through it all. In fact, He was molding and shaping your days, declaring and fighting for your value, and always, *always* right there with you. And if you'll stay still long enough, you'll see God's signature on your own life, for an artist always leaves His signature on His finest works of art.

98
TAKE A RISK

Inspired by Ecclesiastes 11:9

She looks at the forest as if it were a fire, full of flames and passion waiting to ignite. She sees the fear, yet she also sees mystery. She sees darkness, yet she focuses on the light. She sees the breath in the leaves, the dance in the limbs, and the roots of security, but the world of adversity in which it fights. Yet, she stands still. Her eyes locked, her heart racing, her mind battling. She sees everything, yet nothing in the same glance. Uncertainty is by knowledge, but opportunity is by faith. With fear she trembles, but with courage she sees: "Take a risk in the moment of stillness where choice is your friend. Take logic and take your desires hand-in-hand. And go forward, without looking behind, focusing on His presence ahead as your guide." As she steps into their very words, the forest's splendor springs to life.

99

YOU BELONG HERE

These three words first stole my heart's attention March of 2013: *you belong here*. I was in Kenya at the time, and yet the words repeated in my heart in London, America, Russia, and eventually, Australia. The words, at first, I believed to be a placement, yet as I adventured on, became a tale as old as time.

My professor once told me: "An *adventure* is there and back again, where in the end, you'll come back home. The call of God is a *quest*, one where you never return, and if you do return, you're totally different." The concept of leaving home to go on an adventure is alluring. Yet, the most freeing part about it is that you know the end sight. You know you'll be coming back home eventually, if not in hours or days, then typically in weeks or months. Yet, quests, they are a different tale to be told. They not only involve courage, but the same sense of adventure, combined with curiosity and love. On a quest, one must leave what once was behind to truly embrace what is ahead. On a quest, home no longer looks like home, yet, it will look like what you make it out to be. On a quest, there is no convenience and comfort, but the unimaginable, unpredictable, and unobtainable. For when it comes to our quest with God, chasing after His wind words, following His peace, and pursuing His righteousness, it can look a lot like what these three words promise: "you belong here." *You* as in there is no one like you, as in, you're set apart for this. *Belong* as in you're valued, you're not overlooked or forgotten. *Here* as in, this is exactly where you're supposed to be, you're on course with His Will. Sometimes it would be easier to hear the three words and see them as an adventure, a placement, or a set-in-stone concept. Yet truly, they are the beginning to each of our quests, the star to our unimaginable journey, and the dove to a voyage across uncharted territories.

The Parallel Study Bible Commentary on Genesis 12:1 says this: "Abram must leave the settled world of the post-Babel nations and *begin a pilgrimage* with God to a **better world** of God's making."[ccxlix] Our unsettled thinking sails oceans, unsettled dreaming breaks barriers, and unsettled believing transforms nations. It is this stirring, this rocking in our spirits, this momentum of hope, that gives us courage to face head on the mystery ahead. One that's far away from everything we've ever known; one where the God we've always known becomes more real than ever. As C. S. Lewis said, "Only a real risk tests the reality of belief."[ccl] Our quests are but the beginning of our beliefs lived out. They're an adventure begun where we know only the start, trusting He knows the end. Holding onto the truth: "The Lord your God is God; he is the faithful God, keeping his covenant of love to a thousand generations of those who love him and keep his commands."[ccli] (Deut. 7:9)

Quests at times are lonely, challenging, and risky, but when God is in it, they are favored, anointed, and powerful. Though they are not always easy, they are worth it in every way possible. And so we press on, and we travel forward knowing a prize is at the finish, that a reward is awaiting us in full measures of grace. As Deuteronomy 28:10-13 states: *All the peoples on Earth will see you living under the Name of God and hold you in respectful awe. God will lavish you with good things: children from your womb, offspring from your animals, and crops from your land, the land that God promised your ancestors that he would give you. God will throw open the doors of his sky vaults and pour rain on your land on schedule and bless the work you take in hand. You will lend to many nations but you yourself won't have to take out a loan. God will make you the head, not the tail; you'll always be the top dog, never the bottom dog, as you obediently listen to and diligently keep the commands of God, your God...* (Deuteronomy

28:10–13, MSG) and so it will be for you. You will live in the land of the living. You will taste and see the goodness of the Lord. You will become who He has promised. You will know Him as forever faithful. For you belong here. You belong with Him. He is all around you; there are no limits to what He can do. Go on a quest. Go in peace. Take a risk. Take His hand. You will discover the better world of His making. You will live a life of no regrets. Just "go" and He will be with you.

100

PRAY. DISCOVER. GO

_____ moves the hand of God.
But the _____ of the upright pleases him.
If you believe, you will receive whatever you ask for in _____.
But in everything, by _____ and petition, present your requests to God.[cclii]

The answer to each of these fill-in-the-blanks is *prayer*. Prayer can be defined as, "An earnest request or wish,"[ccliii] but it is also known as, "A form of communication, a way of talking with God." Dr. Ralph Martin puts it this way: "Prayer is, at root, simply paying attention to God."[ccliv] Paying attention to God, I think that's what we overlook the most. We see prayer as being about us, when it is always about Him. It's about drawing closer to His heart, and ultimately His will. It's about asking and watching His hand move in His timing. It's about pleasing Him with our heart and not just our actions. It's about presenting our smallest to deepest wishes to God, and trusting in His answer. It's about Him. But we have begun to undervalue prayer for its worth, and have started to overvalue the pleasing things like sleep, food, and ultimately our schedule. Leonard Ravenhill says, "This generation needs to learn to eat less, sleep less, and pray more."[cclv] You will begin to see who you are living for when you look at who you're trying to please. Our prayers will either be circling us or circling God—based on where our focus is fixed, and my deepest prayer is that they will always be circling Him.

I have seen many people who try to take on God-sized dreams, but sometimes they focus too much on the dream that they actually leave God out of it. They do everything that they can, then as they look back on all they have planned and put together, they quickly remember, "Oh! I should pray."

Prayer has become undervalued.

Prayer should be first, last, and in-between. It should be, at root, us paying attention to God at all times. That's where Matthew 7:7 has spoken so clearly to me, "Ask and it will be given unto you, seek and you shall find, knock and the door will be opened."[cclvi] It doesn't say, seek, knock, then ask. Or go, discover, then pray. The first is to ask, to pray to God! Communicate with Him, and let everything you do begin with Him. Then seek and discover all the greatness He has around you and for you. Then knock, or go, and change the world. Romans 12:1-2 says it this way, "So here's what I want you to do, God helping you: Take your everyday, ordinary life—your sleeping, eating, going-to-work, and walking-around life—and place it before God as an offering. Embracing what God does for you is the best thing you can do for him. Don't become so well-adjusted to your culture that you fit into it without even thinking. Instead, fix your attention on God. You'll be changed from the inside out."[cclvii] And even before that we read the reason for our prayers in Romans 11:36, "Everything comes from him; everything happens through him; everything ends up in him. Always glory! Always praise! Yes. Yes. Yes."

Don't undervalue your prayer, for it is powerful. Pay attention to God, for He is wonderful. Then go out and live your life to the full! Fully beyond measure, deeply rooted in His extravagant love.

101
REMAIN

rachellegrace_

Remain in My Love for you,
You need only to look; you need only to remember.
To see the light—it hovers over the dark;
it's there in the mystery.
To see the designs—they are a silver lining,
wrapped in grace in everything.
In My world, you start small, yet as you remain, you'll grow larger:
In confidence, in certainty, in trust.
Think big for My words are not empty promises, they are full of power,
Ready to breakthrough at My command.
To live on supernatural food is sweet, yet isn't always filling. You've learned this.
It is My eternal fruit that I give around you and through you that speaks of My love for you on earth—it is satisfying for it can be touched.
It's given through My people, My surprises, My church.
You'll always find Me there and see My silver lining if you look with wonder. When it's dark, remember the light, hold onto those moments of love.
Watch for the rise of the dawn and run with it. Run wild! Run free!
I'll be there in all the details. Rise with it and you'll remain in Me.
Though looking back is beautiful, even enchanting, more is ahead.
There is always more ahead of you—where your biggest thoughts are untamed.
Where My love, My power, My supply is unending—awaiting your arrival.
In My world, there is no question of My love for you.
In your world, when you remain in Me, you'll know the same.
It is always My love for you that will drive you forward:
In curiosity, in excitement, in passion of what's next. By answering your heart, you will know My love.
Always listen and you will always remain.

> *I love each of you with the same love that the Father loves me. You must continually let my love nourish your hearts. If you keep my commands, you will live in my love, just as I have kept my Father's commands, for I continually live nourished and empowered by his love. My purpose for telling you these things is so that the joy that I experience will fill your hearts with overflowing gladness! So this is my command: Love each other deeply, as much as I have loved you. For the greatest love of all is a love that sacrifices all. And this great love is demonstrated when a person sacrifices his life for his friends.*[cclviii]
> John 15:9-13

102

BE STRONG AND COURAGEOUS

We hear this simple phrase throughout the Bible, but I think some of us perceive it in the wrong way. Being strong is about not giving up, and being courageous is about overcoming your fear of the unknown. Yet, when we read this, we usually think of strong as being mentally strong and courageous as having no fear. Actually, this verse has nothing to do with you and everything to do with God! It's not about the strength you were seeking inside, but it's about trusting in His strength through anything. Putting our guard up isn't what God is commanding of us; He is wanting us to put our guard down. Exodus 14:13 says: "Don't be afraid. Just stand still and watch the Lord rescue you today. The Egyptians you see today will never be seen again."[cclix] Just <u>stand still</u> and <u>watch</u> the Lord rescue you. Verse 14 goes on to say, "The Lord Himself will fight for you; just stay calm." It was never about what we could do with our strength, but what we could do with His. Being strong isn't everything, and being courageous isn't everything. He is our everything, and He is fighting for us.

103

IN WONDER

Shout the news of his victory from sea to sea, Take the news of his glory to the lost, News of his wonders to one and all![cclx]
Psalm 96:2-3

There is a sense of wonder that lies within every human heart knowing there's something more out there; yet, I believe it is those who know God that have already found this wonder. We see it in the stars, in the fire, in the storms, and in the diversity of creation. And it is our call, our last command, to go and share this wonder with the world. As each person adventures to discover what their heart is for, they overlook Who is for their heart; they have heard, but have not really listened. Yet, it's when they'll be still and listen that they will find the answers they've been searching for—the Truth. It is in His truth that we begin to understand for it is in His story we find our own. It is then that we see He is our wonder, and He is our everything. And that is when the world comes to life, when we become alive in Him. We see Him everywhere and in everything: the stars, the fire, the storms, and in the diversity of creation—for *He* is there. Everything is the same, yet it is all different. Because now, we see. Now, we hear. Now, we understand—and words can't grasp or describe it; yet it is on our lives to show it—to show His story of wonder. Job 37 reads:

God's voice thunders in marvelous ways; he does great things beyond our understanding. He says to the snow, 'Fall on the earth,' and to the rain shower, 'Be a mighty downpour,' so that all men he has made may know his work, he stops every man from his labor. He brings the clouds to punish men, or to water his earth and show his love. 'Listen to this... stop and consider God's wonders.'[cclxi]

Never lose your wonder of His wonders,
but broadcast them to one and all,
that they might know His marvelous works of love,
that they might see their sense of wonder is His name.

104

A GREATER TRUST

From the moment I stepped into church, I learned about a two-letter word that has been emphasized throughout the many years I have attended: "Go." I heard about the commandment to **go** and make disciples of all nations; I heard about the needs in our community that I should **go** and volunteer at, and I heard about the huge youth event I should attend… to get even more on fire for God. And all these things are good; they were also life-changing. But something I didn't hear much about was the four-letter word, "Stay." And so when I came to this season where Jesus spoke "Stay with me," I was surprised. All I saw were the promises before me that I felt called to. And yet here He was asking me to stay with Him knowing that there were many promises I could "go" and do. But what I have realized in this season of staying is that my trust became completely in Jesus. I couldn't go before myself to build up my own promise, I had to trust that He was and that He had a plan. And not only was I learning a lot more about Him, but I was also seeing the deeper desires of my own heart, some good and some that really needed Jesus to redirect. You see, right before He asked me to stay, He spoke these big promises over my life; promises I wanted to run to, promises I wanted now. My first instinct was, "Go!" But after each prophetic promise, He spoke, "Stay." And that brought me so much confusion. It was like I was standing in position at the start of the race, the gun went off, and then Jesus spoke: "Stay with me," while I watched all the runners go on ahead of me. What I didn't get then was that His promises are not a sprint with a finish line, where there is only one first place. His promises are a journey, a marathon filled with moments of going, moments of resting, and also moments of pausing and simply taking in all that's around you. They are filled with valleys, mountains, oceans, and deserts, but all that matters is that your place is with Him. And when that gun goes off, there's no reason to look at the runner on your right experiencing His promise, or the runner on your left being led to her promise, because there is no first or second place to win. <u>Your place to be is found with Him.</u>

One of the most powerful verses in the Bible is spoken by Ruth: "Where you go I will go, and where you stay I will stay. Your people will be my people, and your God my God."[cclxii] (Ruth 1:16) Ruth didn't only promise to go, but she also promised to stay. It wasn't about what was before her, but Who was with her. The same is seen in the story of Mary and Martha. Mary decided to stay at Jesus' feet while Martha was looking at all that was before her. Martha saw the sprint of where to go, while Mary saw the journey of Who to be with. Thirdly, there's the story of Elijah and Elisha where Elisha promises, "As surely as the Lord lives and as you live, I will not leave you."[cclxiii] (2 Kings 2:2) He promises to stay, and because of it, he inherited a double portion.

Ruth stayed. Mary stayed. Elisha stayed. These are three stories, three completely different races, each one with different paths. They chose to stay with who they were with, over where they could have gone. And likewise, we will also have great promises we could go and run to, but ultimately, it is not about the place before us. Instead, it is about being with the One who is for us. Just like David promises Abiathar in 1 Samuel 22:23, "Stay with me… You will be safe with me."[cclxiv] God speaks the same to us. When you come to a season where you are called to stay, know that it is a promise of safety and protection, and that it is a place where your complete trust will be found in Him. Sometimes *staying is a greater trust than going*, because you can't do anything, and that's a way of trusting Him with everything.

105

HOLD YOUR BREATH

@sarahbgraves

Thinking about standing on top of a tenfoot cliff about to jump into a body of water excites my heart like no other. But thinking about preparing to jump off a 100-foot cliff, makes my heart race anxiously in every way and form. But it's in that moment of running towards the ledge that only one phrase comes to mind—*hold your breath*. I feel like for many of us, this is the call from God on our lives. At first, we have a faith that is greater than the hill we are about to climb, and when we get to the top, we have no fear for God to hold us up on top of the mountain proclaiming, "This child is mine!" Although many of us would like to put a period there, that's usually just the introduction to the journey God is about to take us on. Because right after the ten-foot hill comes a 100-foot cliff, and then a 1000-foot mountain, and so on. And it tends to be that the greater the mountain looks, the smaller our faith feels. But if there is one thing I have discovered about a journey, it's that the beauty is not found within the mountain, but within its Creator. No matter how beautiful the mountain may seem once you're comfortable at the top, there's always another mountain that God has created and shaped with open doors, perfect timings, divine appointments, lessons, and blessings. It's in that moment of descending the smaller mountain to take on an even greater faith before you, that you'll hear "hold your breath," because you know God has something unimaginable before you. Sometimes it is the most ordinary risk-takers that impact the world in the most extraordinary way.

But now, O Jacob, listen to the Lord who created you. O Israel, the one who formed you says, "Do not be afraid, for I have ransomed you. I have called you by name; you are mine. When you go through deep waters, I will be with you. When you go through rivers of difficulty, you will not drown. When you walk through the fire of oppression, you will not be burned up; the flames will not consume you. For I am the Lord, your God, the Holy One of Israel, your Savior. I gave Egypt as a ransom for your freedom; I gave Ethiopia and Seba in your place. Others were given in exchange for you. I traded their lives for yours because you are precious to me. You are honored, and I love you.[cclxv]

Isaiah 43:1-4

106

A LIGHT FOR MY PATH

One of the most common things that we seek, but don't always see, and want, but cannot always find, is <u>direction</u>. It can be the simplest answer until we try to change direction and make the question complex. It brings up the most commonly asked advice: Who? What? When? Where? And Why? Plus the huge time stopper of, how? As we try to walk towards a **new** journey God may be calling us on, we start to call out the **old** questions to bring clarity to the situation and peace to our hearts. And honestly, we become a little scared. We reach into our back pocket, pull out our compass, and hold it in the palm of our hand, trying to figure out where to go now; but the arrow is spinning as fast as our heart is beating, and we feel completely lost simply because we cannot see what lies ahead. The unknown is a mountain that many of us will face many times in life—and that is where we find faith. Faith isn't always telling the mountain to move, but moving towards the mountain despite what you cannot see on the other side. What I have learned in these moments, is that His word will light our way. As Psalm 119:105 puts it, "Your word is a lamp to my feet and a light for my path."[cclxvi] Sometimes we don't need an answer, we just need to follow the trail. We may not know the direction, but His word will direct us the way to go. It takes only a little bit of faith, *a lot* of trust, and an open heart to adventure into the promises of which He speaks. You don't need a compass to know He will be with you wherever you go. Just trust Him, for He is always good.

107

NO LIMITS

"My love for you has no limits. I loved you **first**."

When He laid eyes on us, He was struck in complete awe. There was nothing more beautiful that He had created. Fearfully, carefully, and wonderfully, we breathed our first breath; He was in love—greater than any measure we will ever be able to understand, a love with no limits. It's an extraordinary love. *The way He looks at us would make the greatest of wonders seem small.* The way He sees us is breathtaking. He is enthralled by our beauty. There is no greater worth in His sight. And yet, the magnificence of pursuit He had toward us within that first glimpse does not grow weary at His every glance towards us—for this beauty He created within us is as unfading as His love for us. How He longs to give us everything of great beauty and value; how in love with us He is. Yet His love is patient and kind. Knowing what's best for us, He allures us. He never lets us go. He never gives up. Instead, He leads us in a perfect love, in a perfect dance. Keeping our hearts' desires close, but our hearts ever closer. Treasuring every moment, while orchestrating moments of treasure. He spins us out and pulls us in, never missing a beat. Though He lets us dance freely before Him on our own, His hand is always open and held out patiently to dance together again. Whether we dance near, far, or together, He never leaves our side. He is as close or as far as we need Him to be. For He simply is *infatuated* with us and *wild* for us beyond compare.

> *Now listen, daughter, don't miss a word: forget your country, put your home behind you.*
> *Be here—the king is wild for you.*[cclxvii]
> Psalm 45:10-11

108

BEAUTY OR CHAOS

Emotions are real, but not always true.
They can make you come alive, but can also come to ruin.
Yet if there's one thing I have learned from their pride,
It's that they truly don't have the authority to decide.
For as we can choose a place to be,
We also can decide how our hearts will see.
Covered by our feelings, or guided by His heart.
He can redirect our gaze to tame a fire's spark.
Though chaos may arise, beauty will stand.
For where there is control, there is also chance.
A risk with fear, a choice with faith.
There's always a shadow to each step we take.
But with His love and by His grace,
Mountains shall move and treasures remain.

If I had to decide on my favorite person in the Bible right now, it would definitely be David. David starts off as a shepherd, and eventually turns into a leader over the people of Israel. Although he wins countless battles and gains numerous territories, he stays humble and loves the Lord with all of his heart. Not only that, but he also has moments where he could literally kill Saul, who was trying to kill David, and instead, David chooses grace, letting him live. Not only does he have mercy on Saul, but also on Saul's own son Absalom who also was chasing after David to kill him. David is constantly showing mercy, and though he does have moments where he messes up, he still perseveres and seeks after God. What I want us to consider is the differences between David, Saul, and Absalom. Saul was jealous, Absalom was being selfish, and David was still merciful. They all had different emotions driving them. Saul wanted to be greater; Absalom wanted the kingdom; and David was seeking after the Lord's will. And because of their emotions, they all either made rational or irrational decisions. That is why I find so much wisdom in Proverbs 25:28,"Like an open city with no defenses is the man with no check on his feelings."[cclxviii] When we base our decisions off of what our hearts are feeling, we already are setting ourselves up for chaos. It is those who can take a step back and let God's spirit lead them that are able to see beyond their own emotions. Every time Saul followed his jealousy, he chose chaos. Every time Absalom followed his flesh, he chose pride. Every time David followed God's heart, he chose mercy. In our own lives we will be faced with decisions that can either bring beauty or chaos, but it is when we are able to see through His heart that we will be able to take a stand against fire. Like the poem says, emotions are real, but not always true. We then must learn to seek His truth to have sight of beauty's beckoning and not instead become blinded by the deceit of chaos's call. *But with His love and by His grace, mountains shall move and treasures remain.*

109

ECLIPSE

"What's in your hands" and "What's in your heart?" are two questions that I've been asking myself quite a bit lately, yet the question is, do both align? Does the deposit in my hands match the treasure in my heart and vice versa? I believe that when the two come into alignment THAT is when a catalyst for change is sparked, but it is if and only then. Sometimes we have things in our hearts, that if not yet placed in our hands, we exhaust trying to fan into flame without the breath of life. Timing is everything—for it guards the atmosphere of your heart to flourish with time and not fall in time. Then sometimes we have things in our hands, that without being valued in our hearts, can miss the very opportunity that looked like nothing but actually would change everything. Faithfulness learns to go after what is placed in front of it, even if it's not yet in its heart, for anything in the heart over a length of time becomes a piece of home. And then, there's the collision, the alignment, the lunar eclipse of the two—and like my mom described it once: "When the sun and moon aligned, it was like the presence of God was all over it. Anyone could sense that. Even a nonbeliever would have had to know there was a God who existed." 2 Timothy 1:14 says, "Guard the good deposit that was entrusted to you—guard it with the help of the Holy Spirit who lives in us."[cclxix] I love that the earth and moon each have their own orbits, yet both, with consistency, come into full circle at this one moment in time—this is the rarity of the Lunar Eclipse. It is breathtakingly beautiful in every God-way possible. In the same way, you also may not understand what God is doing, but

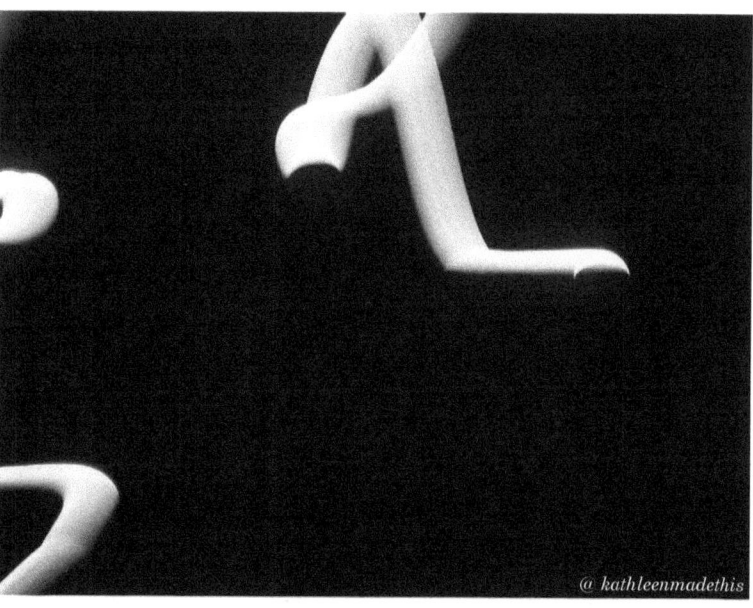

@ kathleenmadethis

with time, what's in your hands and heart will align, and you will know, the presence of God was over it all. We need only to remember that His ways are higher than our own, and that with time and faithfulness, the good deposit will reap a reward in full. The more diverse and farfetched the orbit of your heart's treasures and hands' deposits are, the more breathtaking it will be when the two do align, displaying God's glory for all to see. So guard, with every bit of your strength, what's placed before you and in you. Both are of great worth in God's eyes, and at the right place and right time, your Lunar Eclipse will occur!

110

THE BIGGER PICTURE

Love is patient, love is kind. It does not envy, it does not boast, it is not proud. It does not dishonor others, it is not selfseeking, it is not easily angered, it keeps no record of wrongs. Love does not delight in evil but rejoices with the truth. It always protects, always trusts, always hopes, always perseveres. Love never fails.[cclxx]
1 Corinthians 13:4-8

A while ago, a dear friend experienced a season that didn't completely make sense. As this friend of mine and I spoke over coffee, God gave me a vision, an insight, to the deeper purpose of her season. *Behind every season, there is a process.* Before rain falls, water from the ground evaporates, humidity is built up in the air until it's too heavy to hold, then back to the ground it goes. For every season, the earth turns and rotates in a timely fashion, circling around our solar system, until we happily transition again. Before one can be an expert in the field of their passion, comes 10,000 hours of practice. That's 416 days, or 832 half days, of nonstop effort, if either were practical. Yet when you love something so much, it's worth the time, patience, and perseverance. Now let me share the vision I had with you!

Imagine your hands are covered by grey and moldable clay. Here you are in a room, a decent size of sorts, completely white, as a blank slate to design. The room is smaller than you'd prefer, but since it's all you have, you figure it'll work for now. As you begin to shape the clay, an artist comes and shows you how to create different molds. Another teacher shows up and gives you tools to create intricate designs. Then a designer comes with canvases, and a painter comes with paints, and the entire room starts to flood with beauty. Before you know it, you step back and see the whole room designed in extravagance, from top to bottom, side to side, with *art*. It's breathtaking. As you ponder what could be done next, a businessman walks into the room. Having overheard the magnificent skill of your work, he offers you a job to design a room fourfold the one you finished. Suddenly you walk into the place God promised long ago.

Likewise, my friend was in a season where God was placing people around her to teach her skills she would need before the BIG picture could come together. The thing about being in a process is to **know** *God knows the desires of your heart*, but He doesn't rush us into something we cannot handle. Instead, the process is a glimpse of His protective and caring love for us. As the tools are handed to us to use, He gives us hope. As we learn new skills, He gives us perseverance. And the crazy thing is, it is for the BIG picture He has placed in our hearts. Because behind every season, there is a process. And that process is an assurance of the planted promise that is to come to pass. When you timely walk into the BIGGER picture, you will see His patience, His kindness, and His delight towards you, like prophetic paintings hanging on the walls, and you'll *know*, truly, His love **never** fails. In the words of J. I. Packer:

If life were an art lesson, we could describe it as a process of finding how to turn this mud into that porcelain, this discord into that sonata, this ugly stone block into that statue, this tangle of threads into that tapestry. In fact, however, the stakes are higher than in any art lesson. It is in the school of sainthood that we find ourselves enrolled and the artifact that is being made is ourselves.[cclxxi]

111

SELAH

I wonder what we declare as ruins that the Lord declares as palaces. I wonder what we declare as dirt that the Lord declares as gold. I wonder what we declare as ordinary that the Lord declares as destined. I wonder and I wait, and then I see as He sees, and everything is much more beautiful than I remembered. Have you ever taken notice of the word "Selah" in the Bible? It's actually repetitiously used throughout the Psalms. It means "to pause." I like to think of it as "to wonder." Because, honestly, we see and hear and take in so much every day that often we don't stop to take in the beauty of its value, and because of that we can easily feel lost in a place that was destined to be home. Somehow in the break of a moment, the pause of a breath, the stillness of a second, we can gather ourselves together to actually enjoy the wonders around us. We could do this every hour of every day and still be taken aback by the amount of blessings we have given to us in one day, yet *we lose the wonder of it when we lose our stillness to see it*. Those who let life fly by rarely find the gold beneath the dirt because they don't care enough take the time to, instead they grow complacent with living on dirt because they don't think life is worth the time to uncover. Complacency loses the beauty of hope. I believe hope wonders often. Hope becomes curious and cannot do nothing. It wanders through the days with open eyes and a still heart of what lies ahead. Faith carries that hope and love binds it all together. **The person with the littlest bit of hope will seize the littlest bit of gold and see its endless possibilities.**

When I read Isaiah 51:3, it is hope that I hear interwoven throughout its words: "The Lord will surely comfort Zion and will look with compassion on all her ruins; he will make her deserts like Eden, her wastelands like the garden of the Lord. Joy and gladness will be found in her, thanksgiving and the sound of singing."[cclxxii] Recently I walked through the ruins of Jerusalem, only to find out that it was ruins of a palace. You can only imagine the spark that lit up inside of me when this small bit of gold landed in my heart. The walls didn't seem so dusty and old and broken anymore. No. My imagination was wild with the royals that had walked past the maze of walls in their elegant clothes. Somehow everything went from ordinary to destined in the "selah" of a second. I was walking on the steps of a palace, where gold was plenty, and royalty was passing by. The walls were not confining but inviting. I wasn't lost, but found. In the "selah" of a moment, my heart became as open as my eyes, and that's the vision of wonder. Likewise, there is so much within every one of us that we can so easily see as ordinary that is divinely placed. I think when we pause, we listen to the Holy Spirit, who is walking in the ruins with us, and we find gold in what He has to say. It is what makes the deserts look like Eden and the wastelands like gardens of the Lord. It is where we flourish because it is where we are found. I believe there is gold waiting to be uncovered in who you are. I believe there are palaces of beauty waiting to be seen right where you're at. I believe there are destined moments waiting right around the corner for those who can only see it with wonder-lit eyes. There are words the Lord is wanting to declare over your every moment if you'll take the time to pause, wonder, and wait, just long enough to hear the one whisper that will turn everything in sight to gold, and what a palace of joy and gladness that will be.

112

THE FIRST DANCE

Weddings, oh how I adore them. Not because of the typical "true love" that is before our eyes, but because of the *faithful love* that guided them together beyond sight. I do have to say one of my favorite parts, unquestionably, is the first dance. It's not just how they look at each other, it's how they move together, how they fall in sync in one another's motions, how relaxed they become in their lover's strength. Then there's us and God; we've been in a dance all along. The moment you gave your life to Christ is the moment you took His hand for your very own first dance. At first, it was a little awkward trying to figure out the footing, but as He leaned in and whispered, "Follow My lead," you quickly begun to fall in motion with His steps. Where He moved, you moved. Your thoughts in sync with His thoughts, an effortless twirl into His love, to and fro, the timing perfect. Your head against His chest; His heart beating for your own. It was the beginning of your first dance that honestly, has never ended. In Isaiah 30:21 it says, "Whether you turn to the right or to the left, you will hear a voice behind you saying, 'This is the way walk in it.'"[cclxxiii] *But no matter how beautiful the dance is…evil won't give you the honor of being left alone.* The shocking betrayal isn't always obvious. It may just be as simple and tempting as an apple. One that would leave seven dwarves taken aback by the reality. When Snow White bit into the apple, she thought it was good, that it was okay. Yet, it had the same damaging effect as Maleficent's sleeping curse. Sometimes life happens in forms of green and red apples that seem harmless but can alter destinies. We know the fruit of the Spirit to be good, but even Satan tempted Eve with fruit that looked okay.

I think destinies are destroyed when we start to focus on the production of the fruit over the source of the fruit. It's easy to look at someone else's life bearing fruit. But just because a tree is still standing, doesn't mean its fruit remains unto uched. If a tree is rotten, so will its fruit be. But that's not what we see with our eyes when the fruit lands in our hands. It's not what Eve, or Snow White, saw either. Yet, even the tree didn't know it was being destroyed itself because it was focused on the production and not the source. Here is my advice friend, look to Jesus and trust Him. When you look to the source, you will see that it should match the fruit of the spirit—the Word of God. "But the fruit of the Spirit is love, joy, peace, forbearance, kindness, goodness, faithfulness, gentleness, and self-control. Against such things there is no law."[cclxxiv] (Galatians 5:22-23) As we lean into God and follow His lead, fruit will naturally produce in our lives beyond our understanding; but life will continue to unfold too, and we'll have many tempting apples still placed before us. As long as we are leaning into the source, we'll hear His voice guiding and protecting us. As long as we are dancing with the source, He'll take care of the fruit. Never forget the comfort you have in dancing in His arms when you see someone else's dance looking a little more tempting than your own. They may be just as uncomfortable as ever trying to find their way back to the source you already have. Motion attracts attention, so stay strong and follow His lead as He guides your way. He has a beautiful destiny before you that is only a dance away.

113

TO BE

Every dream is first believed into reality.

You are who you believe to be
This is true, can you not see?
Every morning when you rise
There is a choice that lies inside
To have courage and be victorious, to be loyal and be true
Or to have fear and be defeated, and not be you
For strength is not found in a place you seek,
It's not found in treasures or riches, nor princes or kings
Your strength is found in your heart
Where bravery abounds and magic sparks
There is no position or title to suffice
The pure heart who chooses his life
For what we believe is what we'll see
As nothing can hinder a true believer's dream

> *Embrace this God-life. Really embrace it, and nothing will be too much for you. This mountain, for instance: Just say, 'Go jump in the lake'—no shuffling or shilly-shallying—and it's as good as done. That's why I urge you to pray for absolutely everything, ranging from small to large. Include everything as you embrace this God-life, and you'll get God's everything.*[cclxxv]
> Mark 11:22-24

114

FROM GIANTS TO GLORY

I love the power of belief. Belief is armed with faith and tall in courage. Belief looks within, looks around, looks up, and it sees so much further than its sight. Yet once we believe, we then must begin. We can believe for the greater days ahead, and see its promise inside, yet it is the steps we take that will create it into a reality. Belief has its giants to face, for after knowing comes the going, and those are the battles that we must declare belong to the Lord.

In the book of Haggai, the prophet Haggai starts to speak to the complacent people of Judah to resume the rebuilding of the temple in order to give glory to God. God speaks through Haggai in 2:4-9: "'So get to work, Zerubbabel!' · God is speaking. 'Get to work, Joshua son of Jehozadak · high priest!' 'Get to work, all you people!' · God is speaking. 'Put into action the word I covenanted with you when you left Egypt. I'm living and breathing among you right now. Don't be timid. Don't hold back.' This is what God· of·the·Angel·Armies said: 'Before you know it, I will shake up sky and earth, ocean and fields. And I'll shake down all the godless nations. They'll bring bushels of wealth and I will fill this Temple with splendor.' God· of·the· Angel·Armies says so. 'I own the silver, I own the gold.' Decree of God·of·the·Angel·Armies. 'This Temple is going to end up far better than it started out, a glorious beginning but an even more glorious finish: a place in which I will hand out wholeness and holiness.' Decree of God·of·the·Angel·Armies."[cclxxvi]

Sometimes the greatest giants we will face will not be the gigantic evident ones around us—the figures the world can see, but the greatest giants will be closest to our hearts. They are giant not because of their size, but because of their closeness; it is their proximity to our deepest desires that make them so hard to defeat—for they know our vulnerabilities, because they're typically "us." We face the warrior who must be strong when it's okay to be weak, or feels weak but needs to be strong. We face the dreamer who knows their plans and is unwilling to back down, yet must bow down in submission to God's ways. We face the hero who is destined to change the world, who is equipped with every gift, who is anointed with purpose and grace, yet must choose to rise, to have courage, to be what they know is inside of them. Our greatest giants do not need a sword, but our bravery to be defeated as we face them. Telling yourself, "You can do this." Telling yourself, "It's going to be okay." Telling yourself, "Trust Him."

When we speak to our giants, they transform from our foes to our friends; we don't see someone against us, but we see the God for us in them. We see the warrior within us who rose, we discover there is much courage within us, and we walk forward into the greater glory with Him and for Him. When you speak, speak tenderly and confidently, as if God was speaking through you to you. Then, when your warrior is awakened, speak truth over the giants evident to the eye. Declare the battle is the Lord's, knowing the God·of·the·Angel·Armies is right behind you, spurring you on. As you begin each day, you may have to face these giants time and time again, but just remember, every glorious beginning has an even more glorious finish. Start with some gusto in your step and see how freely you will be dancing victoriously in the end. From grace to grace you will rise, from glory to glory you will go. You can do this, don't hold back, simply begin. What you're believing for will end up far better than what you're imagining.

115

OUT OF TIME

There's a movie I love called *In Time*. In this movie, each person is genetically engineered to stop aging at twenty-five, and that is when their "clock" is activated. This clock then becomes their currency to live off of. The rich can be immortal, but the poor have to work, steal, and borrow "time" to stay alive. There's a store in this movie that has {out of} time above the door. When the storeowner has no time, all the words stay lit. But if somehow the man can lend time, {out of} will dim away, and {time} will still remain. People then come running from everywhere desperate for more. Sometimes I wonder how differently we would all live if we also knew the value of time. Lao Tzu puts it this way, "Time is a created thing. To say, 'I don't have time,' is like saying, 'I don't want to.'"[cclxxvii] Personally, I feel like there are many of us who go through life waiting for that sign to switch to *time*, time and time again. But how many more of us will take time for granted and spend it without a second thought? In Matthew 11:28 we read, "Come to me, all you who are weary and burdened, and I will give you rest."[cclxxviii] But not many of us will do even that. Instead of resting, we take our flashing time and spend it carelessly. Then afterwards, we tell God, "I have no time," when He is the owner of time, freely giving it to us abundantly, to share even a fragment of it with Him. We can quickly become the ones who spend it on anything else, never truly appreciating its value; and like Lao Tzu said, basically saying, "I don't want to," to God's invitation to come and rest. One thing I have learned is that we will make time for what we love the most. Some of us are richer with time, and some of us are poorer, but we all already have our minds set on what we want to spend it on or who to spend it with. Time is a treasure, and where we spend it reflects our greatest priorities. So my challenge to you is to spend it with Jesus and resting in His promises and love for you.

For in every season of chaos, there is a beauty in rest.

> *Where you deposit your treasure, that is where your thoughts will turn to—and your heart will long to be there also.*[cclxxix]
> Luke 12:34

116

NO GREATER LOVE

He comes to us. No matter how far we run, no matter how far we stray, He never leaves. There's no greater love. He sees the darkest parts of our hearts, and the worst parts of our lives, and still loves us unconditionally. There's nothing that can separate us from His love, for still its depth runs deeper than our lowest valleys, still its height soars higher than the mountains for which we reach. He is always more; He is always enough. John 15:13 says, "There is no greater love than to lay down one's life for one's friend."[cclxxx] How much more powerful is it to lay everything down for a daughter or son? "But God showed his great love for us by sending Christ to die for us while we were still sinners."[cclxxxi] (Romans 5:8) There's no place too low you could hide, no point so high to which you could climb, to which you could lose His love. He will always choose you, and always have open arms for you to choose Him. There's no greater love.

117

ENTWINED

> *Escort me along the way, take me by the hand and teach me. For you are the God of my increasing salvation; I have wrapped my heart into yours.*[cclxxxii]
> Psalm 25:5

Dr. Brian Simmons writes, "The Hebrew word most commonly translated as wait is *qavah*, which also means to tie together by twisting, or entwine, or wrap tightly. This is a beautiful concept of waiting upon God, not as something passive, but entwining our hearts with him and his purposes."[cclxxxiii] I love the concept of thinking that in our waiting, we are not becoming undone, but instead are becoming entwined as one with the Lord. In a way, I reimagine the word "wait" as "sit still." To be entwined, being still must take place; otherwise, it's like trying to put a diaper on a baby running around the house, which is quite hilarious when you imagine the Lord chasing you down to wrap you in His garments. Yet, as we are still in our spirit, listening to the Lord, and following His lead, we learn His rhythms of grace and discover it to be quite freeing. To sit is not to do nothing with your days, it is to have complete rest in Him, to be able to *selah* when you sense His presence is near, to remember who the true vine is and to wrap your heart in His strength, promise, and truth. It is binding your heart to His and being escorted by His hand into a greater ball than you could've dreamed.

When we hear the word "wait," it's easy to shut off, become disappointed, or feel more impatient than before, for it's not always welcoming. Yet if we could hear "be entwined," we then have this visual of the vine moving, producing, and drawing closer to our heart. Not only is His love and purpose interweaving with our moments as we rest, but our heart, mind, body, and soul begin to become entwined with His ways. I believe a supernatural strengthening happens when we trust Him, for we somehow know what we did not know before; entwined, He lets us in on secrets that don't make sense but we can sense in our hearts. As Frederick Buechner says: "It's just where we least expect him that he comes most fully."[cclxxxiv]

What if when we heard the big "W-word," we became expectant instead of shutting off? Because we knew something was taking place worth waiting for. What if our hope awakened at the word for we knew a surprise was coming forth? *It wasn't Him holding something back; it was Him keeping you in place to receive what was promised.* What if we had it backwards all along? That being entwined created such an excitement in our hearts that all worry, fear, disappointment, and discouragement would flee. Whatever it is that is not yet in your hands, learn to entwine those dear desires around His heart. The more you long for it, the closer you press into His truth and purpose. The further it feels, the deeper you press into His love. The greater it seems, the more persistent you become in constantly wrapping it in His grace. In the end you will be saying: "Here's what I've learned through it all: Don't give up; don't be impatient; be entwined as one with the Lord. Be brave and courageous, and never lose hope. Yes, keep on waiting—for he will never disappoint you!"[cclxxxv] (Psalm 27:14) For even with the promise in hand, you will know it is His hand that is the greatest to hold onto. It is in the ending moments where we know He is enough that we are surprised most fully with the unknown blooms of delight that He had been planning all along. It is then and there we cannot be entwined enough with the Lord. Closer, deeper, and more fully, we will want to be near to Him alone, Him and His fullness.

118

AN EXPLOSION OF LIGHT

Reading: Psalm 107

O Child of God, why are your sails down? Lift them up! Don't you see the land in sight? Why aren't you dancing? Why aren't you parading with JOY! (laughs) The enemy is making a fool of himself. You can't attack a ship at port! You're grounded in truth. Safe with the crew aboard and on land! Get those pretty booties marching! It's a parade of beauty! Don't you see why? The King of kings is here, and He's asking for you! By name! What in the world? You don't need to know everything to know God loves you. Your heart is disturbed because He's silent. But He's only silent with surprise. Even if it seems impossible to be Him, believe it. He adores you, His child. Take cheer; take heart. Oh how the enemy knows and wants to hide what you're capable of. You're an explosion of light that can't be missed once sparked. His divine kiss is your spark. Again, you have no idea what's awakening. But these designed lands are for you to step into. Step on. Step forward. Move into your destiny.

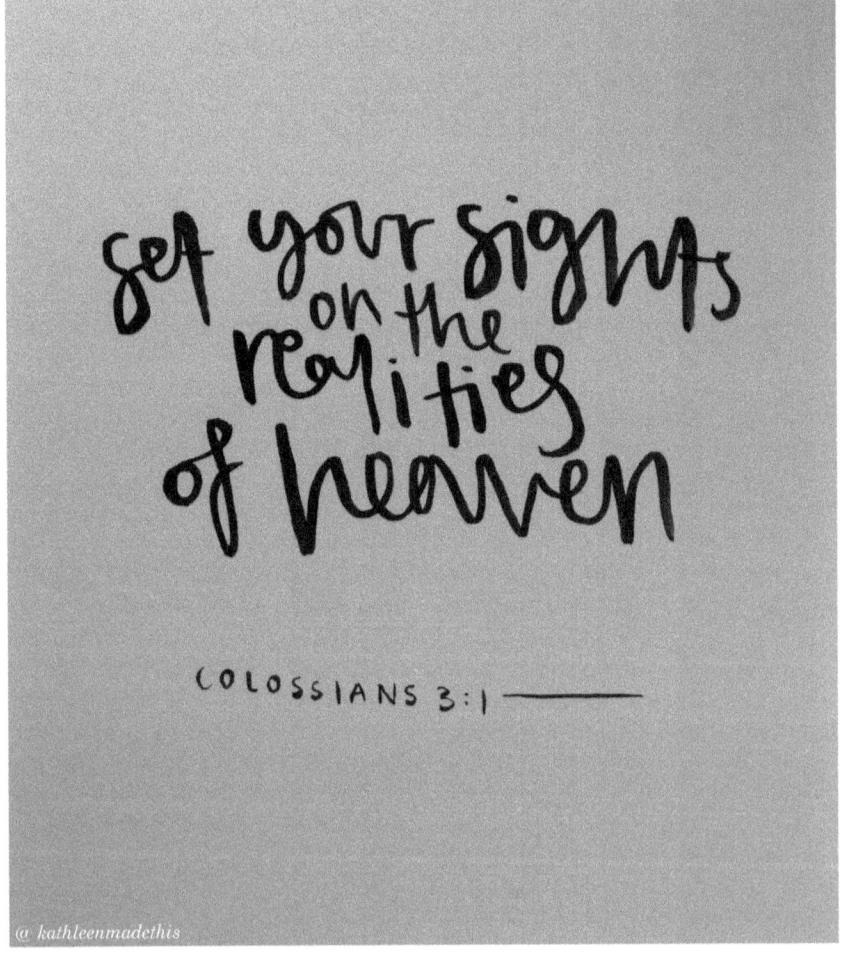

119

EXPECT GOD

> *She quietly expected great things to happen to her, and no doubt that's one of the reasons why they did.*[cclxxxvi]
> - Zelda Fitzgerald

I don't know if you've ever had great expectations—the kind that sound off the wall, the size of impossible and unbelievable, the color of unseen and unreal. They typically begin in the heart, whisper-like thoughts become a verbal expression we didn't expect to vocalize, which form cute little seeds, and then deposit in our wild garden of dreams. They say a dream with a deadline is a plan, but with some out of reach stars, a deadline cannot be attached. It's a God-expectation, and that shouldn't be placed in a 4x4 box. The risk attached to dreaming is disappointment. But to never try to live is a death in and of itself. Fear is simply a weed that is in competition with cultivated dreams. So the issue isn't a limited trial and error, but a limited thinking…a boxed in timeframe, a well-crafted to-do list, a law instead of a land. It's one that chains us to a settled place with a certain way of thinking rather than allowing us to roam freely from place to place. There are thousands of terrains around us and millions more to discover, but unless we can train our mind to be fearless, much life that was available to us will be missed.

I once was told a metaphor of a person who had died and gone to heaven. The man, walking with Jesus through a hallway, noticed his name on the door. He asked Jesus what was inside, and Jesus kindly replied, "You don't want to know." After the man insisted, he opened the door to see many taped up boxes inside. Jesus answered his wonders: "These were all the gifts and dreams that were available for you that you never asked for." It's one word that takes a second to speak, but requires much courage from our heart to let out: "Ask." Sometimes it's because we are afraid for God to not come through. Sometimes we block God from blessing us because we feel unworthy. Other times the gift comes and we walk away in pride of: "That's not what I was asking for." Each of these equals to a limited thought. But what if with each God-expectation, we expected God? The Alpha and the Omega, the first and the last, the beginning and the end, the I AM, who was and is and is to come. Proverbs 23:7 says, "For as he thinks in his heart, so is he."[cclxxxvii] Our thoughts lead to prayers or lead away from them. They lead to change or lead away from impact. They release or restrain. To think our thinking can create a wedge between us and the God of the universe is perplexing, but true, not on His end, but ours. He didn't set it up, we did, and until we allow those walls to come down, we will miss out on so many rooms in His house.

Psalm 84:5-7 reads: "And how blessed all those in whom you live, whose lives become roads you travel; they wind through lonesome valleys, come upon brooks, discover cool springs and pools brimming with rain! God-traveled, these roads curve up the mountain, and at the last turn—Zion! God in full view!"[cclxxxviii] The roads may be curvy, unpredictable, and have a few unexpected bends, but there's a full view awaiting that is breathtakingly designed. As you think, so you are in climbing the mountain—so think big, audacious, enlarging thoughts. Don't take the fun out of faith, but be adventurous with the God of the universe who can do exceedingly and abundantly more than all you can ask or think up. And then *ask*. Expect God with His patience and Sovereignty as much as His faithfulness and love. As Frank Dimazio describes a game-changer, so may you be: "A leader who thinks differently, explores continuously, breaks old molds, inspires faith, and impacts the future."[cclxxxix] Think outrageously huge thoughts, ask for what awaits, and pack your bags, for you're about to discover a wild adventure.

*(Your name) quietly expected for great things to happen to_____,
and no doubt that's one of the reasons why they did.*

120

BROKENNESS MADE BEAUTIFUL

> *I went down to the potter's house, and I saw him working at the wheel....*
> *Like clay in the hand of the potter, so are you in my hand.*[ccxc]
> Jeremiah 18:3,6

To be broken or shattered—it's easy to cringe at the very thought. It creates a world of change, and change tends to be what most of us fear. When change is gradual, it's not so noticeable. But when it comes without notice, that is when *we change*. We usually relate being broken with being worthless. However, it is in our brokenness that His worth is working within us. Somehow, it is in the moments that we are broken that we are *shaped, put together*, and *changed* into someone who is stronger, wiser, and even more beautiful. They often are the moments our flesh wants to run from, but truly, they are the miracles where our spirit most thrives. In Charlotte Gambill's book, *Turnaround God*, she beautifully puts it this way:

An interesting thing about clay is if it is left off the wheel without anyone shaping it, the clay will revert to its previous form. The same is often true for our lives. Like that lump of clay, we have to stay on the Potter's wheel if we want to become all God has designed our lives to be.... Without the Master's hands continually moving in our lives, molding our course, we settle for a shape that is far less than what God has in mind.[ccxci]

It is in our brokenness that we are made beautiful. He is simply remolding us and perfecting our design. He's shaping us for what is ahead and making our image more like His. We aren't being left in pieces; we are being put together by His peace. We are being made new.

121

KISS THE WAVES

A kiss. A sign of love. A touch with the lips. It is my absolute favorite part of any movie. Until then, the suspense in me can only wonder, when will it happen? But sometimes "the kiss" isn't the most romantic thing. Like when the princess kisses the frog or the kiss is a cure to poison. It's still powerful, but a bit less on the romantic side than two people who both confidently and nervously, awkwardly and perfectly, have their first kiss. A kiss can be beautifully defying with its gentleness. I love how Charles Spurgeon says: "I have learned to kiss the waves that throw me up against the Rock of Ages."[ccxcii] The waves that mock who you are, the waves that tell you to remain silent, the waves that laugh at your failed efforts; imagine beautifully defying them with the gentleness of a kiss, imagine the enemy going into an uproar over you ability to laugh fearlessly at his greatest attempts of war, imagine being thrown into the Rock of victory and knowing no defeat. It makes me smile, because *when we kiss evil with good, everything changes*. It creates ripple effects of beauty where the enemy tried to bring tsunamis of despair. The scripture that immediately came to my mind when I read this quote is found in Ezekiel 47:3-5: He walked to the East with a measuring tape and measured off fifteen hundred feet, leading me through water that was ankle-deep. He measured off another fifteen hundred feet, leading me through water that was knee-deep. He measured off another fifteen hundred feet, leading me through water waist-deep. He measured off another fifteen hundred feet. By now it was a river over my head, water to swim in, water no one could possibly walk through.[ccxciii]

@bulgerjoseph

I don't know what it is, but when I lock eyes with Jesus, and he is leading me through, on, or into the waters, I am fearless in His embrace. It's funny how we pray for more, but when He leads us there, we can so easily feel in over our heads. It's impossible for anyone, except... well, the One who has graced you to walk through it and into it with Him. When we do this, we kiss the waves. To live is the greatest mockery to the enemy, for we do not shut up in fear, yet rise in fearlessness. We laugh, we sing, we dance, whether we are sinking or swimming, and it is shocking to the world in every way. But I believe it is our kiss to the world's waves that proclaims God louder than our words could every write or say. It is a confidence that knows the Rock will always be greater than the waves, and it is as loud as it is bold. When the waves are rising around you, be fearless in His embrace. As the Bethel song goes: "Whether I sink, whether I swim, it makes no difference when I'm beautifully in over my head."[ccxciv] No matter how great the waves, God will always be greater. So kiss the waves that lead you to the eternal Rock. They're actually doing you a favor. (wink)

> *You will keep in perfect peace all who trust in you, all whose thoughts are fixed on you! Trust in the Lord always, for the Lord God is the eternal Rock.*[ccxcv]
> Isaiah 26:3-4

122

EXISTING

There are two definitions of "existing."[ccxcvi] One is to survive. The other is to have objective reality or to be found. I think we all have gone through seasons where we might have simply felt like surviving. We moved, but didn't feel; we would breathe, but not feel alive; we would have everything, yet have nothing. And we described it as existing—breathing and going forward, but never really living. I have come to realize that there is one difference between the two definitions—love. Love is what brings the world to life. Love is what moves us. Love is what makes us come alive. *Love gives us meaning in His meaning.* When we wander away from the love of God, the mindset of existing changes. Laws go from protective boundaries to restrictions. Doing good goes from being beautiful to being a burden. The church goes from a home to a house. Everything changes. We see in several places of the Bible to, "Love the Lord your God with all your heart and with all your soul and with all your mind and with all your strength."[ccxcvii]

It is in loving God that our existence is seen as being found and He is our reality. It begins when we love God with all of our passions, with all of our desires, with all of our knowledge, and with everything we do. As Acts 17:28 says, "For in him we live and move and exist... For we also are his children."[ccxcviii] We exist because we are His, not simply as a breath of survival, but a breath of life. And as we move closer to Him step-by-step, we become more alive in Him breath-by-breath. Everything we are radiates like glimmering hope as we draw home to all that He is; and as He holds us again, we belong again, and live again, like we belong.

Forever His and forever found.

We love because He first loved us.[ccxcix]
1 John 4:19

123

EVERYONE HAS A TESTIMONY

His story is our testimony; our story is His testimony. Now, let me explain. As I was thinking about testimonies this morning, and the power of them. In my mind, I was flipping through the many I have heard and the many I have experienced. But, I also started to think about how many Christians who were raised up in the church feel like they don't have a testimony, and others feel like they need to purposely mess up in order to even have one. This brought me to the conclusion that many of us have forgotten what testimonies are truly about, not about us, but about God. It's not about who we used to be or what we have done. Even though those are parts of our story, our testimony is constantly about Who *God* is, and what *He* has already done for us. So, if you have had the worst past or even if you had a past that was surrounded by the church, our testimony is the same, our stories are just different. Because our testimony will always show how great our God is, and our stories will always reflect what His greatness has done for us, which brings us back to the point that His story is our testimony, and our story is His testimony. Because from our story, His greatness is made known, and because of His story, we are made new. His story being His death on the cross for our sins... our stories being the testament of His faithfulness to us. These are the tales we pass down for generations, testifying not how good or bad *we* were before Christ, but how good and loving *Christ* has always been, and forever will be to us, to them, and to our legacies to come.

> *God's splendor is a tale that is told;*
> *his testament is written in the stars.*
> *Space itself speaks his story every day*
> *through the marvels of the heavens.*
> *His truth is on tour in the starry vault of the sky,*
> *showing his skill in creation's craftsmanship.*
> *Each day gushes out its message to the next,*
> *night with night whispering its knowledge to all.*
> *Without a sound, without a word, without a voice being heard,*
> *Yet all the world can see its story.*
> *Everywhere its gospel is clearly read so all may know.*[ccc]
> Psalm 19:1-4

124

ARROWS OF FLAMES

The thing about arrows is that once they are released, you can't take them back. You can only hope that their impact was not harmful or dangerous, and that their landing was safe. Our words, too, are like arrows of flame. They can either impact for good or for worse, be a light of inspiration or be a burn of fire. Psalm 64:3 describes it as, "Aim(ing) their bitter words like arrows."[ccci] Jeremiah 9:8 puts it, "Their tongue is a deadly arrow; it speaks with deceit. With his mouth each speaks cordially to his neighbor, but in his heart he sets a trap for him."[cccii] In both of these instances, words are described as arrows. Because not only can you not take them back, but their cutting edge also can truly impact someone's life. The word arrow literally means in Hebrew: *to divide, to cut into two parts; that which wounds, destroys, and, finally, an arrow with its cutting head.*[ccciii] But I believe that our words don't always have to wound or divide, because the bend of the bow begins in our hearts. If we shoot aimlessly or without thought, it is likely to cause harm. But if it is well thought-out, it could light a path instead of enflame it. I want you to picture this with me. Every thought starts as a flame; when we decide to speak, our words become the arrow that the flame attaches to. Our hearts then decide the direction the arrow will take. And as we release the bow, it can lead someone in encouragement, or wound someone in discouragement. But the choice of direction is ours. I believe that many of us have been impacted by arrows of flame in both situations—some that helped us find direction, and others that wounded our hearts. And though we can't always control the impact their words have on us, we can decide the impact we take. We can either be bitter from their words that sank deep in collision, or we can be vulnerable and allow God to heal our words in His sweet love. Like a chemical reaction, one arrow leads to another—and that is the process of direction that can compass the path we take. We don't always have to burn because we have been burned. We don't have to wound because we have been wounded. We can allow our flame to be light, our arrow to be a direction, and our impact to be an inspiration. It won't always be easy when the words cut deep, but it will always allow us to go deeper with God in understanding, peace, and forgiveness. His Word is a lamp unto our feet and a light unto our path. May our words be the same for others, reflecting Him in every word with every flame.

125

AS DELICATE AS A ROSE

Like the rose's glass case in *Beauty and the Beast*, God's faithful promises are our armor and protection. It wasn't intended to keep the beauty in, but to keep the war out. So that while the rose was blooming in its delicacy, it would not have to face the harsh weather outside of its timing. For when the rose was ready, when it outgrew its case, when the atmosphere was finally at peace, then the glass case would be lifted, and its power uncovered. In the same way, our promises are sealed by God; He lifts us precisely at the right time, when the core of our hearts is stronger than the atmosphere of our promised land. Then, when we walk in faith into this new world, we won't be crushed or shaken, but secure and steady in His word, as we were prepared.

A new atmosphere has a new weight of gravity, yet when God is doing a new thing, He will keep your heart as delicate as a rose within its glorious weight—for He is always as faithful to His word as He is to your heart. There is a sacred peace in this case surrounding your heart that cannot be touched. Though it may feel the pressure at times, the waves will never be able to penetrate its promise. The heart, like a rose, holds many layers. Parts that are stronger and others more tender, with layers made up of delights, wonders, desires, passions, and purpose. It is enchanting when it discovers how *unique* it is. It is a garden of beauty, graced in the secret place and placed in a kingdom's garden destined to impact. The heart is powerful when seen for the delicate beauty it is, and how it's worth every effort of guarding. 2 Chronicles 7:16 says: *Believe me, I've chosen and sanctified this Temple that you have built: my name is stamped on it forever; my eyes are on it, and my heart in it always.*[ccciv] As 1 Corinthians 6:19 states we are now "temples of the Holy Spirit," (1 Corinthians 6:19, NIV) we can know His eternal promises are stamped and sealed on our hearts with glass cases and perfect timing. They are our armor and protection against doubt's teasing and disappointment's waves, for it holds onto the truth and power of God's love for us and with us. No matter how much sight may taunt our faith, let our belief be greater than our surroundings, creating greater waves of hope and certainty. May we learn to stand on His word as our rock and let His peace be our anchor as much as our compass. His promises may be wild to believe, but we know that we know, <u>His love</u> will always be wilder than our beliefs, sweeping us off our feet, keeping our certainty sealed of all that He is doing that we cannot yet see. As Song of Songs 8:6-7 says: *Place me like a seal over your heart, like a seal on your arm. For <u>love</u> is as strong as death, its jealousy as enduring as the grave. Love flashes like fire, the brightest kind of flame. Many waters cannot quench love, nor can rivers drown it.*[cccv] (emphasis added) May we take heart and hold onto His love for us—the same love that is as strong as death and the same love that conquered the grave that we may live with Him forever. For as we hold onto His wild love, we remain sealed and unshaken, and our hearts remain as delicate as a rose, knowing full well He will finish what He started, not missing a single detail, not forgetting a single promise!

126

BEHIND THE MASK

When it comes to a ball or a masquerade, I'm pretty sure everyone has dreamt about attending one once or twice. There's something exciting about choosing an outfit that makes you feel divine while finding the right mask to wear for the one night where you can be anybody you want to be. There's so much mystery, and so much freedom! Anything can happen. Yet after all, I wonder if masquerades aren't a chance to be somebody else, but to again be our true selves? Where hearts are finally *unmasked* for that one night before the *real* mask goes back on. What is it about this everyday mask that seems so comforting to us? And how do we keep it off? I think it starts with realizing if we have put a mask on. One might hide behind the mask of shame, another behind comparison. One could be hiding behind the mask of pride, and yet another fear. When it comes to a masquerade, there are many to choose from. When we wear the mask so often, it's easy to forget that it's on. And sometimes it is easier to simply stay concealed—because it is what people know and expect. But there is someone who has always seen what's behind the mask. He is the one who woke me up to see I had my own.

@ kathleenmadethis

It was a normal morning: the sun was streaming in through the blinds, I was listening to worship, and my heart was dancing away. As I was happily attending my own little ball, God spoke, "Now just take off your mask." I honestly was taken aback because I didn't realize that I had been wearing one. It was a mask that I had convinced myself was my identity. Isn't that what the enemy tries to do? To contain our true identity: to hide it from others and our own self. To where when you look in the mirror, you see the beast and not the beauty, the mask and not the child of God. 2 Corinthians 3:16 says, "But whenever anyone turns to the Lord, the veil is taken away."[cccvi] But more often, we convince ourselves otherwise. Isn't that why Cinderella ran from the prince? Isn't that why Hal (the Green Lantern) wears his mask in front of Cheryl (the one he loves)? Because we want them to know us by whom we think we should be. You are not only fooling others when you put the mask on, you are fooling yourself. Because it is *limiting* the vision of what God can do through you and *distorting* your view of who God is and how He sees you. Not wearing a mask is vulnerable, but it is also invigorating! To come as you are reveals a more captivating beauty to all those who are wearing their masks wishing to be free themselves. It is a statement to a fallen world. It is a light to those trying to get back to shore. As Tomar-Re from the *Green Lantern* says, "Of all the lanterns who have ever worn the ring, there was one whose light shined brightest. At first his humanity was thought to be a weakness, and yet it proved to be his greatest strength."[cccvii] Beneath the mask, you are powerful—in your vulnerability, your beauty, your brokenness, and your rarity. You are unstoppable and uncontainable, *unhidden*. That's what God has always known. He has always seen *you* as your true identity. Your happy ending lies not within a masquerade, but within a moment where Love takes your mask away.

127

BETTER TOGETHER

We were not made to do life alone. To live in isolation. To be generous only to ourselves. To love only ourselves. We were made to share moments, to embrace harmony, and to express passion. Ecclesiastes 4:9 states → *Two are better than one, because they have a good return for their work.*^{cccviii} We see it from the beginning of time as God created Eve for Adam, Moses had Aaron as a helper, and Elisha learned to minister from Elijah. Or how God created life for us, to share with us, and to be with us. But it's not only for the good; it's also for the battles. We were not made to do life alone. For two years, I struggled with a spirit of containment over me. I wasn't feeling myself and I kept praying against it, but nothing happened. It wasn't until I let my housemates in on my struggle that we prayed against it and instantly I saw an army standing beside me fighting for my heart. We weren't meant to fight alone. Matthew 18:20 says, "For where two or three come together in my name, there am I with them."^{cccix} *We are strong alone, yes. But we are **undefeatable** together.*

Darkness must flee for the enemy has no chance against the army of God when it rises up together. I think we've become so busy keeping the outside of the cup polished and clean that we've grown accustomed to not letting people in to see that the inside is cracked, a little imperfect, and not completely clean at the moment. And when people try to peer in, you turn them away, not letting them in, not letting them know how you *truly* are. {And I see the enemy's hand all over this. Because he knows the extraordinary in you will stay contained as long as you stay detained by your struggle.} Here's a news flash: Jesus died for you to live in freedom. A freedom that involves letting people in to see the more vulnerable parts of your heart, because then they can fight with you for something worth a war over. Here's the second page of news, the extraordinary will only come out of us when it's for someone else. If the enemy keeps you isolated, you'll never be able to speak what you hear, or live what God promises. Because hiding the fact that you're hurting inside will only keep you from truly helping others who are hurting just as much as you. Trust and let God in first, and then let your trusted prayer warriors in on the journey. This is a battle that is to be declared VICTORIOUS today! For when you allow the inside to be washed pure, you don't have to hide in fear or shame, but can live in a freedom that sets others free. It's a beautiful thing to be able to be you and to be loved wholly inside and out for who that is. For we were not made to do life alone, but together, wholly, completely, and freely, in Jesus name!

128

A DAILY LETTER

Dear (insert your name),

*God loves you so much more than you can imagine. Be simple. Don't overcomplicate life. If there is sin in your heart, repent as quick as you realize it, to stay as close to Him as possible. Yes, you are royal, but you are under no pressure to be perfect. You are under grace to live freely and fully. Dream big, oh dreamer, because God will always be bigger. But hold onto those desires with open hands. And what He places in them, honor Him with—with every gift, desire, dream, and opened door you have. Say goodbye to the lies of the enemy and the opinions of others. Believe and trust that God's word holds true to you. Change will come, but when He is doing a new thing, it cannot be foreseen for it will be different and grander than before. The BEST, yes, the best, is yet to come. He wouldn't give you anything less. He is for you—that's all you need to know. That's the only thing you need to know. Bash on, for **you can do this**. You will finish strong.*

xoxo

Every word of God holds true.
(Proverbs 30:5, MSG)

129

OPEN HANDS | OPEN HEARTS

By faith we understand, we see, we grasp that the universe and the world around us was called, shaped, and formed at God's command, so that we then believe what is seen was not made out of what was visible. All that our eyes lay hold of in this moment, was commanded into existence, designed by His Word, and structured by His heart. By faith, we know, from the bottom of our hearts, this is the truth. Likewise, Noah built an ark by faith in belief of what was coming and not yet known to be real → rain. By faith Enoch was taken up to heaven, skipping over death, defying the rules of → life. By faith, Sarah, who was "barren," believed the One who promised her hope and would shut up the world's → lies. By faith, Abraham listened, obeyed, and followed a whisper to an uncomfortable, temporary place with no knowledge of where to plant, but he kept sowing and going after "an unseen city with real eternal foundations," a place that was logically → unbelievable. It is this faith that we read in Hebrews 11:1 of "being sure of what we hope for and certain of what we do not see."[cccx]

Each one of these historical inspirations had *hopes* and *vision*. Though their destinies were quite contrary, their catalysts were all the same, an essential piece to their story in which they all begun—by faith. *Each one decided to act on the unseen to see what was unreal to believe.* I honestly can imagine each of them sitting at their homes, wondering with God, feeling this deep yearning in their chest that they just didn't know what to do with. Noah wishing there was a way for the world to become righteous and stop acting on their evil ways; Enoch so ready to just be with the God of heaven; Sarah trying to accept that she'd never have a child but secretly wondering what it'd be like; Abraham feeling called to something so much greater than him with no clue what it could be. All they knew is that their desires were *real*. And by faith, these desires became *real*ity. How much of a relief they must have had, when after some long nights of prayer against disbelief, they finally collided with their hoped for desire, their unseen city, their word from God—their promise. I'm not sure if you've thought of your yearning desire yet, maybe it's come to mind once or twice, or maybe it's guarded deep down within your heart, but this is your designed unseen purpose! Though it may be a touchy subject to bring up, I want you to believe we have a **powerful, miracle-working God,** if you'd keep believing *by faith*.

The thing is that we give up on the unseen oh so quickly. As a pastor once told me, "We don't have not because we ask not, we have not because we wait not." So how do we wait? As Hebrews 11:10 describes Abraham's strategy: "Abraham did it by keeping his eye on an unseen city with **real** eternal foundations— the city designed and built by God."[cccxi] (emphasis added) He kept his thoughts on higher things, on heaven, on Jesus! As long as our eyes are fixed on Jesus, our faith cannot be broken. Each of these pillars of faith were fixed on Jesus with open hands and open hearts—daily. As God delights in the details of our lives, He also designs them. He designs our desires as He designs our days, and I'm not just talking about the desires that are fleeting. I'm talking about the ones you can't shake that you wish you could just come true. Trust Him. You will experience your dream come to life if you live by faith and fix your eyes on His kingdom. That means not taking into control the plans He speaks. That means not figuring out the perfect timing of your promise. That means not holding onto comfort and familiarity. It is acting on the unseen, which sometimes come in a form of a whisper, a vision, a thought, or a dare. Then one day, every design, detail, and structure will fall into place, formed by His command, and with relief, you will see what is deemed to be *unreal*.

130

THROUGH THE ORDINARY

There is a poem by Robert Frost that has spoken to my heart many times. The poem starts with these two paths that lie before this traveler—one is more beautiful and promising, while the other is more fearfilled because of the impossibility to see where its road would end, or even what dangers lied within it. Sound familiar? One person grows up and has to decide whether to pursue a childhood dream, a fear-filled path with the unknown, or to walk securely where others have walked before and to follow in their footsteps. When we come to this point, we tend to pray for God to do something, or anything extraordinary, to show us → "This is the road to take" or "This is the life to live." But I came to Nehemiah 9:12 and read, "By day you led them with a pillar of cloud, and by night with a pillar of fire to give them light on the way they were to take."[cccxii] God led them by ordinary things in extraordinary ways, not by extraordinary things in ordinary ways. A cloud is as common as the sun, and fire was something commonly used at night to light a path. There was nothing **huge** screaming, "This is the way," it was a silent whisper of faith. Sometimes we just have to walk through the open doors and see what happens, instead of trying to see a sign of direction. It is whenever we walk through the ordinary open doors that the extraordinary will happen; we just have to walk by faith and not by sight. The end of the poem finishes with these lines,

> *I shall be telling this with a sigh*
> *Somewhere ages and ages hence:*
> *Two roads diverged in a wood, and*
> *I— I took the one less traveled by,*
> *And that has made all the difference.*[cccxiii]

I think most of the prayers we pray are so broad that we would be overwhelmed if God did give us an answer. So maybe we should pray not so futuristic, but more simplistic: "Open doors that man can't shut and shut doors that man can't open," and walk through their ordinary open doors—and I believe that will extraordinarily make all the difference.

131

RISE AND SHINE

Reading: Isaiah 60

Wake up, oh heart. Rise and shine. Do not let your promises rock you to sleep, let them burn in your heart to release a passion overflowing into others. <u>*Be you. Be free. Be God's*</u>*. Live a life full of expectancy. Delight in the details and enjoy your freedom while letting others in on the journey. The kingdom is a place where everyone belongs. Let go of the sails and sing your praise! It will lift your eyes; it will lift your spirit. Trust Him with the desires in your heart; they will show His love for you—but let Him carry them. They were never intended to weigh you down, but to lead you forward into the MORE before you. Fear not the waves, the ultimate Captain lives in your heart. He will compass your path and compass your desires. Draw near to Him as He is all around you. Take Him in and **all** His glory. How it shines upon you! How it radiates from you. You are marvelously made to take sail into all the miraculous wonders that will continually take place before you. Do not give up, but dream bigger and think wilder! Live to the fullness He has created you for. What a fun and timeless adventure that lies ahead. Let down your hair. Take in the breeze. Look out at the tides. Heaven is ready to collide with earth here and now. At any moment, anything can happen! Everything can change—life can rearrange. Take hold of His words and hold on tight for a fresh beginning is near. Something incredible is about to take place. Majesty is on the horizon, splendor around the corner. Live wide-eyed and mystified—take in the wonders. Dive into the depths, reach for the heights, and ask Him for everything in between. So wake up, oh heart. Be here—for the King is wild for you. Let him sweep you off of your feet. You are His chosen one. His anointing is upon you, and He is able to do above and beyond what you can dream. Lie dormant no more—far more is here and now. Purpose is in your sails! Be you. Be free. Be God's!*

"Be fearless in the pursuit of what sets your soul on fire."[cccxiv] – Jennifer Lee

132

PONDERING THE PIECES

This may come as a surprise to some of you, but often when I write, I have no end in mind. I'm not sure how professional authors write out their stories, but I'm sure they have way more of an idea than I do. Often I start with a concept, then somehow along the way, pieces come together to be finished. But the thing is: *God always gives us the pieces we need for the other pieces to fall into place.* I've seen it countless times, and if you look back, you'll see it too, if not now, then someday soon. Mary was one person who trusted God with the pieces of her heart daily. Though we may not know all the pieces of Mary's past, I have no question that she had been obedient with the pieces before her for God to have such a peace and favor on her life. From Luke 1:28 we see God's view of Mary, "Upon entering, Gabriel (an angel of the Lord) greeted her, ' Good morning! You're beautiful with God's beauty, beautiful inside and out! God be with you.'"cccxv I can only imagine what was running through her mind. *But what took her by surprise God had been planning since the beginning.* After the Lord speaks to Mary about her promise to conceive the Son of God, (piece #1) He also tells her about Elizabeth's current pregnancy, to reassure her that God is able to do the impossible. So what does Mary do? She runs over to Elizabeth's house to be greeted by Elizabeth's baby leaping in her womb! (piece #2). And so Mary did with these pieces what she had countless times before—she trusted and believed! In the months to come of people calling her names, looking down on her for being unmarried and pregnant, she pondered the few pieces she had, believing that **every** word would come true that God had spoken. Likewise, no matter what season we're in, we can do the same with the pieces we've been given. Let me just say, God doesn't speak without having the end in mind. **Every piece is purposefully placed.**

Some of us see a million pieces and are overwhelmed with where to begin, while others have one piece and feel lost with what to do. Yet, I love how Charlotte Gambill describes this analogy of her son wanting to put together a puzzle.cccxvi He was so excited until the pieces were dumped on the table. As he overwhelmingly started to walk away, his mom stepped in and said, "Let's do it together." She encouraged him to begin with the easier outside pieces, before working together the pieces from the outside in. Similarly, some of us need to focus on the bigger picture, and not the smaller details, while God helps us fill in what we can't. And if we become overwhelmed, we just ponder the pieces we know, while God puts the others in place. Like it says in Luke 2:51,"But his mother treasured these things in her heart," cccxvii we pull a Mary, continually treasuring the promises. For others who have one piece, remember how God gave Mary a second undeniable piece for her to hold onto! He will always give you enough of what you need. As Mark 4:26-27 says, "God's kingdom is like seed thrown on a field by a man who then goes to bed and forgets about it. The seed sprouts and <u>grows</u> [he has **no idea** how it happens."].cccxviii (emphasis added) You may wonder where the rest of the pieces are, or if they'll ever turn up, but one day when you look back from where you are, you'll have no idea how everything came to pass. As long as you are being faithful with the piece He has given you, He will continually turnover the pieces before you to fulfill His plan for your life. As Vincent Van Gogh said it, "Great things are done by a series of *small* things brought together."cccxix Those small pieces don't look like much when they're individually placed in your hand or scattered on the table, but I promise He is creating a beautiful masterpiece with a finish in mind. *Wherever you're at, you are growing. Whatever you're doing, it's being pieced together. Whenever you look back, you will see God's presence before every piece orchestrating the perfect plan. Just lean in and ponder the pieces you have been given. For God takes the smallest of pieces to mold into the most glorious of masterpieces, including you.* As my good friend once said, "The pieces make up the plan, and we just have to lean into the Perfector of the plan."

133

FROM CURSES TO BLESSINGS

If someone asked us to make a list of all the things we did and didn't like about ourselves, I wonder whether the dislikes would fill up substantially quicker. But, if God had a list, there wouldn't be one thing He didn't love. And actually, we have a script that tells us this in Psalm 139. You are exactly who you are supposed to be, from your talents, to your hair, to your height, to your beauty marks. And even if we had to create a list for the season we are in with the likes and the dislikes, the *not so loved* might pile up once again, while God's very Word is speaking everywhere, "Delight in the Lord," "Don't worry," "Be content," and mostly, "Trust in Me." *Not only are you exactly who you are supposed to be, you're also exactly where you're supposed to be*. God has placed you where you are to use and equip you for His purpose. But because of the dislikes in our list, it's easy to miss the beauty and power that is within the good things we have going. We see our blessings as curses rather than believing that what we see as a curse, God can see as a blessing. Nehemiah 13:2 says, "Our God, however, turned the curse into a blessing."[cccxx] We can become so focused on who we're not and what we can't do within our seasons that we easily misperceive our very blessings as curses, rather than remembering how God is always good, and seeing what good He is at this moment doing through and in us. When we see through the eyes of comparison, we see curses. When we see through the eyes of God, we see blessings. They're the same list, but how you view your situation will determine if it has power over you or if you have power from it. Maybe it's time to start praising God for the good things you have now, to see the new thing He is doing, to be equipped for the greater thing He is preparing you for. This curse shall turn into blessing. From ashes to beauty, from dry lands to promised lands, from lifeless to full of life, it shall be made known that He transforms all things for good!

134

BEAUTY IN THE BALANCE

There is a balance, a beautiful and unique part to life that challenges us as a person. And I think it is this balance that keeps us alive, instead of still and existing. It allows us to see more, learn more, and become more than what we could have settled down to be. It is found in wisdom and faith, loving others and loving yourself, going and resting, listening only to your emotions to not listening to them at all, speaking and listening, to seeking and trusting. There's a balance, and it's found from being close to His heart. Balance keeps us looking to Him instead of just walking by ourselves. It gives us many directions, instead of just one. It holds far more adventure than those who stay in one place, and it keeps us near to His heart at all times. Philippians 4:7 reads, "And the peace of God, which transcends all understanding, will guard your hearts and your minds in Christ Jesus."[cccxxi] And I think that is the key. His presence guides our hearts and minds in every situation in any place. So, balance isn't a specific answer, it's a journey. It leads us from left to right, from uphill to downhill, because every situation is different, and only He can show us the balance that brings beauty. With time and with God, we will discover its wonderful, freeing rhythms of grace.

135

A PROMISE WORTH PERSEVERING FOR

Have you ever watched the movies where they are out in the middle of the ocean? It's such a beautiful place to run to, but to be honest, it's not a place where we like to stay. Even though it's nice to get away from everything around us, we also still want to see the shore with the assurance that we have somewhere to run back to. Because after days or weeks of being in the middle, we no longer have the driving force of being found, but that sense of fear of being lost. When we look up and see nothing familiar around us... our first instinct is to run back and not forward, no matter how at peace everything may be. This is about being **in the middle.**

I'm not sure about you, but I've been in the middle quite a few times. It's the place where I wanted to go in the beginning, didn't want to be in the middle, yet was glad I experienced in the end. It's not always what I wanted the most, but it's usually what I needed the most. So often, this is 90% of our calling—it's not the beginning nor the finish, but the trusting, enduring, faithfulness in the middle, that really counts. It was like this for David. He was anointed in 1 Samuel 13, but wasn't appointed until 2 Samuel 5. There's a gap of 20 chapters and 20 years between the anointing and the appointing. As Christine Caine once said, "Just because you have been anointed now doesn't mean you are going to be appointed straight away."[cccxxii] We can become so excited as soon as we hear about the promise on the shore that we rush out to the boat, start rowing as fast as we can, not looking back, turning back, or stopping, until we hit what I call the "boundary line." It's where we can't see the shore anymore and there are only two choices: go forward or turn back. This is the most pivotal moment, but it's also the most vulnerable. You see, we have this anointing, calling, and promise on our lives, but we must realize that *saying yes to the promise also means saying yes to the process*. It certainly won't be easy, but it will be so worth it. Because as long as you take one more step forward, you come closer and closer to your promised land.

I'm starting to realize that *the beginning is the hardest, the middle is the bravest, and the end is the most unbelievable*. But bravery isn't always having that feeling inside that everything will be alright, but having the faith in your heart that what you're doing is in the right direction. It's not so much the first step that worries me anymore, because once you take the first step you know it's worth risking everything for. It's the middle where there is no risk at all that I'm worried about. It's there that we grow content; it's there that we add different minor details and displace major details to our promise. This is the place that many of us start to live by sight instead of faith; it's where, sadly, I've seen so many turn around.

So why am I addressing the middle so specifically? Because I want you to know, that when you start to chase God's promise on your life, that you can make it through the middle, that you will make it to your promised land. We read in Hebrews 12:1, "And let us run with perseverance the race marked out for us."[cccxxiii] But Paul even earlier gave us words to take heed to during the race in Hebrews 10:36: "You need to persevere so that when you have done the will of God, you will receive what he has promised."[cccxxiv] If David would have lived by sight in the middle, he would have never fought Goliath, nor become the king's armorbearer, or married the king's daughter, or even become king himself. But David does set an example for us on how to persevere. He had his eyes on God, not the promise, from the anointing to the appointing. And likewise, we should do the same. From the shore where we step out in a fear-filled faith, to the middle of the ocean where we feel more lost than found, to the end where we step onto the ground of our "promise worth persevering for"—let our eyes always be set on **His** kingdom and never on our own, for then we will see God's purpose come to pass every time.

136

BATTLEGROUNDS OF VICTORIES

The vision was of two battlegrounds. In the first field, one person had a sword against an army who had bows and arrows. In the second field, the other had a bow and arrow against an army of swords. They each saw one another's battlegrounds and felt more suited to fight the other's battle: sword against sword, bow and arrow against bow and arrow. It's what made logical sense. But when they switched battlegrounds and tried to fight the other's war, they failed. Because, in the end, they were each prepared to fight the battle that was placed before them specifically. What they didn't realize at the time was that the sword was the key to beating the bows and arrows, while the bow and arrow was the key to beating the swords. And so many times, we have that decision in life to fight the battleground we are in, but we instead try to fight a battle we weren't meant to fight in comparison. It's easy for us to look at another person's calling and assume that their life is a breeze, because we see their victories, their blessings, and their fulfilled promises. And sometimes we wish that could be us. But where we are is what we are prepared for, and God has already gone before us to a place we could never have gone alone. So look straight, and use what is in your hand while chasing after what is in your heart. Know that you are equipped to fight a battle that no one else could, and **you will** be victorious.

With every victory, there is a battleground, but you can't have one without the other. So be careful with what you wish for, because you never know what battleground you're asking for.

> *I will go **before** you and level the exalted places,*
> *I will break in pieces the doors of bronze and cut through the bars of iron, I will*
> *give you the treasures of darkness and the hoards in secret places,*
> *that you may know that it is I, the Lord, the God of Israel, who call you by your name.*[cccxxv]
> Isaiah 45:2-3 (emphasis added)

137

MORE THAN "JUST AN"

We call him King, Messiah, Saviour, and the I AM. But they saw Jesus as a brother, a son, an ordinary person who was just a carpenter. He was able to do so much, literally the impossible, but they were blinded by their sight rather than healed from their blindness. His name is Jesus, as they recalled, "Mary's son." In the beginning of Mark chapter 6, we read that Jesus has come back to His hometown and is teaching His people. And though they are all amazed at first, we see quickly that by verse 3 their hearts changed from caring to careless:

But in the next breath they were cutting him down: "He's just a carpenter—Mary's boy. We've known him since he was a kid. We know his brothers, James, Justus, Jude, and Simon and his sisters. Who does he think he is?" They tripped over what little they knew about him and fell, sprawling. And they never got any further. [cccxxvi]

I wonder how many of us wear the title of "just an." "I'm just an ordinary person." "I am just a teacher." "I am just human." "I'm just *fill in the blank*." When, like Jesus, we are able to do so much. Jesus even states it in John 14:12, "The person who trusts me will not only do what I'm doing but even greater things, because I, on my way to the Father, am giving you the same work to do that I've been doing."[cccxxvii] Even greater things will we do through Him than He has even done. We are more than just an ordinary person—and I think Jesus is trying to tell the disciples this, as they think to themselves, "I just wish Jesus was here—that I could see Him.

It would make things so much easier." I know I have thought this so many times. I'm sure all of us have. But Jesus simply promises us that we will do greater things through Him than if He was still present in being here among us; yet now, because of His death and resurrection, He lives *in* us, and is able to constantly be with each and everyone of us every step of the way (John 14:17).

You are more than another person; you are more than your human flaws, and you are more than your weaknesses. You are made with specific strengths detailed to precision to your personality. You are something else that no one can describe, because every time you fall, you get back up stronger. You are chosen—part of a royal priesthood, made up of ordinary people with ordinary lives, bought with the highest price. And you have the answer, the truth, that sets you apart, that has branded you as a child of God. You know Him and that changes everything. It dares you to be different—to think extraordinary thoughts, to dream impossible dreams. To walk with purpose in your step, to believe in a hope that isn't always seen. And not everyone can see it at first glance, sometimes you may not see it yourself, because a huge part of us is ordinary, but an even greater part of us is extraordinary, because He lives in us. And that is something we must learn to believe. It is when we learn to believe it that *our* hearts will be able to see what God has seen in us all along. It's when we will do even greater things than what has ever been done before.

138

MOMENTS

In a moment, anything can change
Life can come together, life can rearrange
What once was lost can now be found
What once was silent can orchestrate sound
The shattered can instantly be made whole
Fire made from a spark of coal
Light can burst through the darkest night
The blinds be pulled back to reveal sight
From once upon a time to kingdom come
Stories upon stories will come undone
All knit together by a common theme
One that goes unnoticed and even unseen
It's where dreams begin and life collides
Where we start to believe and come alive
This place, this beginning, is known as home
But it's not a brick building, not even a mold
It's within the One who created our hearts
The One who knows the finish before the start
He is our home; He is our place
Where time slows down and comes into gaze
It pauses just long enough for us to see
Moments tie together to form living dreams
Thus where they began is where they'll remain
In the wild of His word, in the peace of His grace

God, it seems you've been our home forever;
long before the mountains were born,
Long before you brought earth itself to birth,
from "once upon a time" to "kingdom come"—you are God.[cccxxviii]
Psalm 90:1-2

139

THE GREATEST PROMISE

> *When I look at your heavens, the work of your fingers, the moon and the stars, which you have set in place, what is man that you are mindful of him, and the son of man, that you care for him?*[cccxxix]
> Psalm 8:3-4

Imagine a speck of dust floating in a mansion of gold, diamonds, and the finest luxuries, and on that speck of dust is you and I. Then there's the Owner and Creator of all these beauties, and instead of having their magnificence catch His eye, He sees us on that speck of dust and says, "This is all for you." He who has the greatest and finest of riches, loves us who have nothing in comparison to give. Our *love* and our *time* is simply enough for Him. Which brings me back to the verse, *what is man that You are mindful of him?*[cccxxx] (Hebrews 2:6)

We can get so caught up in our own little world, striving to: be better, do better, achieve more, all in trying to find the beauty of life that we walk by every single day. Everywhere we look we see beauty: in the trees, stars, fireflies, dandelions, mountains… it's endless. Yet, they're *all for us*. Us, the people who take for granted His masterpiece. Even our very DNA is perfected to work together for us to be who we are. The unique complex of the mind that man can't comprehend but God can understand. How God has us on Earth within the Milky Way of a **huge** galaxy that we cannot even find with our greatest technology. It's like God sits back and smiles saying, "I have more," every time we seek. We can't get enough because He is **so** magnificent, and yet still He desires us. *What is the value of man?*

Psalm 139:14 reads, " I praise you because I am fearfully and wonderfully made; your works are wonderful, I know that full well."[cccxxxi] Did you know that when someone creates something fearfully, they create it carefully, making sure every detail is crafted to perfection? It is well thought out beforehand, and even revised after, to make sure it is fearfully and wonderfully made to its utmost beauty. Every person reading this book is made this way, every single one of you. God took His time deciding how to create you each in your own perfection, which us humans call *uniqueness*. He sculpted us from nothing… into something. Our lives are all spread out before Him; He has prepared our way before we were even born. He walks ahead of us so that we can follow Him. And with God comes the greatest promise. *What is man that you are mindful of him?*

Now what is your opinion of a great promise? Maybe of fortune? One that God will provide money and a way in everything that you do. Or how about success? That you will be promoted in your job. Or even prosperity? That in everything you do you will prosper. Now, those all sound like pleasing promises, but of all the greatest promises God can give, He gives Himself as the greatest promise. As long as we have God, we have all we need. He is our provider that will break through for us in the most impossible situations. He is our comforter that will give us peace in the moments that we feel hopeless. He is our strength in the times we feel like we cannot take another step. He is our love that we can always depend upon. He is the God that makes us complete. For God's greatest promise is to be with us. As Romans 8:28 and 31 say: "And we know that in all things God works for the good of those who love him, who have been called according to his purpose… What, then, shall we say in response to this? If God is for us, who can be against us?"[cccxxxii] As long as God is on our side, we will never have a thing to fear, for nothing can size-up, or begin to compare, to His love. That's the greatest promise for Him to keep, for Him to give. Not only to always be for us, but to always be *with* us. "And surely I am with you always, to the very end of the age."[cccxxxiii] (Matthew 28:20)

140

UNTOUCHED

Your destiny is a path you choose; it is surrounded by other roads of choices, but in the end, you decide with each step which road you have chosen. Though one cannot choose just any destiny, we each have one. We can choose which road we could take to leave "what could have been" untouched. Yet we can walk away from it as quickly as we walked to it. While there is a life destined before you, ultimately you have to choose it. Whether you choose it or pass it by, its destiny will still come to pass, for it is set in stone, like a mountain in place, that a traveler could come by and choose to take.

Yes, your destiny may be right before you to choose, but you must also say yes and choose to pursue your destiny.

@bulgerjoseph

For we are God's masterpiece. He has created us anew in Christ Jesus, so we can do the good things he planned for us long ago.[cccxxxiv]
Ephesians 2:10

141

BOLD

We tremble before the mountains, but the mountains tremble before Him. We have nothing to fear. Whether it's a place to go or something to say, we can be bold in Christ Jesus. He can part the waters in our lives, provide manna for our needs, or heal sickness and brokenness in and through us. To be bold is to take risks; a risk is an exposure to danger. It is saying, "Here I am, Lord! Send me!" It is saying, "I surrender myself to you; I am Yours." It is saying, "I will give You everything." Every day is a risk. But whether we risk everything for Jesus or risk comfortability for ourselves is before us. When it comes to expanding the kingdom, there are two things you can do. Put yourself before you or behind you. But one will get you a lot further than the other. To be bold isn't to be fearless; but to act with courage in the face of fear, in the face of adversity, in the face of comfort, and in the face of sensibility. When you see the mountain before you, take steps toward it knowing that Christ is with you and in you in whatever risk you may be taking. And that no matter what comes your way, He will make a way before you. Boldness is dependent on God, not independent on your own.

> *When we trust in him, we're free to say whatever needs to be said, bold to go wherever we need to go.*[cccxxxv]
> Ephesians 3:12

142

GO. SET. READY.

Something I have begun to see as a setback in the lives of many is the fear of the unknown. When our future isn't see-through, we don't want to typically go through its open doors. I see people, who are gifted without a doubt, who convince themselves out of their dreams. I see people resolve for less because they would rather do less in life; and then I also meet those who settled long ago now wishing they wouldn't have given up. Yet, it is great to witness those who prayed through their fears, came through the open doors, and now are living a miracle as God came through for them. That should be our greatest fear, not of not knowing, but of not going. Mark Batterson puts it this way in his book *Primal*, "There is an old adage: 'Ready. Set. Go.' And I know it's predicted on the importance of preparation. But I think it's backwards. You'll never be ready. And you'll never be set. Sometimes you just need to go for it. We need a paradigm shift: 'Go. Set. Ready.'"[cccxxxvi] Out of the three books I have read of his, that is one of the lines that has impacted me the most. Because of the fear of the unknown, many of us either live our lives constantly preparing or never really feeling ready and running. But, "You'll never be ready." When your life isn't see-through, you just need to pray through the unknown. You may not be able to walk through closed doors, but you can always pray through them. Joshua 1:9 says, "Have I not commanded you? Be strong and courageous. Do not be afraid; do not be discouraged, for the Lord your God will be with you wherever you go."[cccxxxvii] Instead of running in fear, wander in faith. Instead of waiting to see, go through the door and watch God come through. And when impossibilities surround you, remember God's possibilities within you, and pray through the closed doors to have a breakthrough in the place God designed you to be. Replace your fear of the unknown with curiosity, and the unimaginable will happen. As the movie *Brave* puts it, "There are those who say fate is something beyond our command. That destiny is not our own, but I know better. Our fate lives within us, you only have to be brave enough to see it."[cccxxxviii]

143

THE POWER OF PS

I love books. I love the mystery of opening a book and becoming lost within its words. I love how the imagination goes wild to create a message within its story. And yet, I do have a downfall to loving stories— once I start, I can't stop. I go into this sort of introvert frenzy where I only want to be with the book: not out, not with people, just in a coffee shop with this new mysterious story unfolding. Yet, when it comes to God, the Author of our mysteries, His story is given much more to us as love letters.

These love letters are hand-designed and well thought-out. Their words are a lamp unto our feet and a light unto our path. They drive us forward with steadfast love to our next chapter as a guide. I love that in the film *P.S. I Love You*, the husband leaves behind letters in different places by different people for his wife to remember his words of love.[cccxxxix] In the same way, God brings us to the most unimaginable places when we are open to where His spirit leads. His words beckon us to different seasons, adventures, and friendships that impact further than we could've known beforehand. Yet at the end of every letter, there's always a PS, and I believe that PS is a promise you need to be reminded of.

Sometimes the PS is a glimpse—a vision or prophetically spoken word of the best to come. Sometimes it's a verse—a light to the wilderness you may be going through. Sometimes the PS is a person—specifically placed to pursue you to be reminded of His love. Sometimes it's a truth— the most simple, yet powerful fact that He is faithful and will bring to completion what He's begun. Yet every letter has its perfect timing and purposeful message to engrave on our hearts. The message is endless in pioneering through our seasons, but it's the PS we must hold onto as we walk through the unknown. So when we face hardships, we can remember, "His grace is sufficient."[cccxl] So when we want to quit, we will remember His promised glimpse to come. So when we feel forgotten, we'll feel the arms of a friend embracing us as a Father would His child. That no matter how close or far we are from "okay," the PS will whisper, "I love you," in every season in every form. Oh the letters to come, oh the words to be spoken, oh the promises to be redeemed.

One last thing, here's your next letter:

Dear Child,

"Never forget my words. If you do everything that I teach you, you will reign in life. So make wisdom your quest—search for the revelation of life's meaning. Don't let what I say go in one ear and out the other. Stick with wisdom and she will stick to you, protecting you throughout your days. She will rescue all those who passionately listen to her voice... Fill your thoughts with my words until they penetrate deep into your spirit. Then, as you unwrap my words, they will impart true life and radiant health into the very core of your being. So above all, guard the affections of your heart, for they affect all that you are. Pay attention to the welfare of your innermost being, for from there flows the wellspring of life."[cccxli] *(Proverbs 4:4-5,21-23) My words are light, their purpose holds true; follow them and you will always find Me waiting in your future with breath and grace.*

Love always,
Your Father
PS_____.

144

A LITTLE BIT OF MAGIC

They say, "A single dream is more powerful than a thousand realities."[cccxlii] I'd like to say that was my reality, always living in a dream. I'm discovering that God loves all my little quirks—my forgetfulness that causes me to depend on His whispers, my constant pursuit that drives me into more of who He is, my creative mind that constantly carves avenues to tell others about His love, and even my dreamer's heart that encourages me to live beyond my comfort for the kingdom's sake. Every prayer, wish, and dream He has stored up in a hope chest designed for me. All along He's been keeping them preserved, alive, and glorious for their perfect timing. Yet, this isn't so much about the hope chest itself or even really about the dreaming, it's about the one word that can light up our world *with* or dim its magic *without* → hope.

@ashtynekole

Looking back, I hoped for everything as a child. There was no limit to my imagination of the impossible. I had a childlike faith and a heart full of wonder. Yet, I don't think our lives are much different today as my childhood adventures back then. **I believe moments create magic still, and magic is simply a created hope.** Maybe we did different activities and wished for different dreams, but they were filled with magical moments that created us—with all our unique quirks and dreams. Typically, a hope chest saves up valuables for a girl's wedding day, but a hope chest, made by God, is one that is *enclosed with promises to come*, packed with forgotten wishes, and sprinkled with a little bit of magic. Hebrews 10:23 says, "Let us hold tightly without wavering to the hope we affirm, for God can be trusted to *keep* his promise."[cccxliii] (emphasis added) Dear child, there is and always has been hope interwoven in every moment; I just wonder where your childlike hope is being kept hidden.

Genesis 50:20 says, "You intended to harm me, but God intended it all for good. He brought me to this position so I could save the lives of many people."[cccxliv] These words were spoken by Joseph who was known for his dreaming. He had been betrayed time after time, and I'm sure, he might have doubted once or twice why everything played out the way it did. But every moment had a hidden treasure, a promise being kept, a forgotten wish coming true, and a little bit of magic that created again → hope. I am confident in knowing we all have hidden treasures before us. We are guided to them in our moments of trust, and sometimes they are guided to us in our moments of disbelief. But let me remind you of this: **God hasn't forgotten.** He hasn't forgotten the hopes you let go of and the hopes you're holding onto. And let me say, letting go and giving up on hope is different from letting go and giving your hopes to God to keep. As Roald Dahl says, "Above all, watch with glittering eyes the world around you because the greatest secrets are always hidden in the most unlikely places. Those who don't believe in magic will never find it."[cccxlv] You are not unseen; in fact, you are wanted, cherished, and loved. You can trust that your unwavering hopes are being kept and your promises continually orchestrated by Love. Oh yes! Surely, there's a life **full** of *hidden* treasures ahead of you—filled with moments of wonder and even a little bit of magic.

145

BEYOND

God, use me beyond imagination;
Use me beyond what my hands can reach.
Teach me beyond my understanding;
Teach me beyond my sight.
Lead me beyond paved paths;
Lead me beyond still waters.
Mold me into a person of patience;
Mold me into a light of love.
Let me be humbled at Your feet;
Let me exalt You with my life.

"God can do anything, you know—
far more than you could ever imagine or guess or request in your wildest dreams!
He does it not by pushing us around but by working within
us, his Spirit deeply and gently within us."[cccxlvi]
Ephesians 3:20

146

TO OVERCOME

The story of David and Goliath has always amazed me. The ordinary David against the great and magnificent Goliath, not with sword and shield, but by a sling and a stone, that is how he won. It was extraordinary. Though the one detail that leaves me in wonder every time is, "What came over David?" He was a shepherd who had fought off lions and bears before, but never a person. And I think it was a mixture of two things that came over him: his belief and his courage. He believed God could win the battle, and he had the courage to allow God to use him to face Goliath. Instead of letting fear and doubt overcome him, he allowed belief and courage to come over him, and the extraordinary happened. My question for you is, "What is the Goliath in your life?" What is holding you back from all that God has for you? Whatever it is, take heart and allow belief and courage to come over you. You can always do so much more wherever you are, because God is constantly working for your good in every circumstance. Like Ephesians 6:12 says, "For our struggle is not against flesh and blood, but against the rulers, against the authorities, against the powers of this dark world and against the spiritual forces of evil in the heavenly realms."[cccxlvii] Whatever Goliath is in your life, believe that God can win the battle and that you have the ability to overcome it. The smallest things with belief can take down the greatest things of disbelief.

147

WAVES OF GRACE

We tend to see oceans as so mysterious. Moving in freedom with their waves of life beneath and above the surface. But really, grace is the mystery. How it captures us, draws us in, and moves not only around us, but also within us. It is captivating to the eye and captivating to the soul. And once you experience it, there is no escape. It is our greatest satisfaction, our deepest desire, and our sweetest delight. And it embraces us more than we embrace it. Once you enter in, you never want to leave. You'll never have enough.

It is a mystery—how His grace is everywhere and always with us. It walks beside us through the mountains, sails with us through the seas, and rescues us in the storms. His grace gives us breath and runs through our veins; it is what holds us together. His grace is extraordinary. In 2 Corinthians 12:9, Paul echoes God's teaching, "My grace is sufficient for you,"[cccxlviii] as he pleaded for God to remove his thorn, his weakness. He is constantly speaking the same to us, reminding us, "You don't have to be enough, because I am." And like the waves beyond the shore, He invites us to leave behind our weaknesses and our insecurities to be embraced by His strength and His sufficiency. And like Paul, we can boast all the more because He is so much more for us. In our busiest times, our most tiring days, our struggles of humanity, He softly invites us to acknowledge Him and to be embraced by Him, because *His grace is our enough*. And this is why I have decided that you can't really ever test the depths of God's heart without wanting to dive in. Because once you have even a taste of His grace, everything changes. You'll never want to leave; you'll never have enough, because He is the only enough for you.

148

I AM NOTHING BUT VALUE

Reading: Isaiah 62

In the moments of our greatest strength, we become the weakest,
For it is when we have it altogether that we can feel most incomplete.
We tend to break in a world so small compared to a God so big,
As if we forget that He is ours and we are His.
Why is it that we feel defined by our makings rather than our Maker?
That through these creations we're convinced our hearts are better.
That somehow, we find assurance from what's around our built-up walls,
Instead of in the One who's within us that's held us through it all.
You see, reality isn't always as it seems to be;
No, God has much greater than we can even think.
Life is a journey and every journey is a dream,
Waiting to be discovered and ready to be believed.
For better or for worse, our words may say.
But in those times of trouble, all promised sights fade away.
When the truth is, we are enough, but these words we don't want to hear.
We strive to be more, but God makes it clear:
Grace is our sufficiency, because of Who He is,
And because of His love, we are called His.
We are chosen, crowned, branded by His heart.
But we try to find our worth in quotes, gifts, and sparks.
We wait forever for this drastic change in our life,
Overseeing the fact that our revolution lives inside.
We have been built up in such a lie that our heart has become blind,
To forget that our value was bought when Jesus died.
So stand up! And rebel against the lies, the hurt, and the pain.
They won't make you stronger; they're not for your gain.
Give it all to God, and He'll transform your heart.
He brings freedom from bondage that sets you apart.
Have faith beyond understanding for in seeking comes truth,
Trust is love's beginning and patience its virtue.
It's a step-by-step process, where God writes on your heart,
With mountains and valleys, you'll discover Whose you are.
This same love that made you creates you in truth.
You just have to believe that the Son of God died for you.
When you begin to grasp how He paid the highest price,
You'll begin to believe the worth you've always had inside.
You're a treasure, a jewel, with imperishable beauty,
Yet still nothing without the King who gave you His all completely.
Because you were worth it, and you always have been.
You just have to see your true value lives within.
Believe it, accept it, and then you'll start to be,
Who you really are—who He's always seen.

149

_____ IS LIFE

There was a group I was a part of during my college days, and one of our sayings was: "Fashion Fever is life." We jokingly said it because *one*, we spent *every* day thinking of new ideas as it is an annual main event, and *two*, because we constantly gathered tiny details to create this beautiful and grand reality. We met once a month starting in August and didn't stop until the show finally happened in March. And so, we had this saying of, *Fashion Fever is life*, because it consumed our every bit of free time. And it brought me to wonder: what do we daily *fill* that phrase with? "Money is life." "Alcohol is life." "Worry is life." What is it that we constantly *pursue, think about, and give our energy to?* What is it that we are holding onto in a way of security and stability that we secretly wish would hold us together? What is it that we are clinging onto in desperation of not wanting to see it go? Once I heard a quote that said, "I think part of the reason why we hold onto something so tight is because we fear something so great won't happen twice."[cccxlix] There is some truth in that statement, but there's also some misconception hidden beneath it. Something I learned a few years ago firsthand was, in order to hold onto something greater, we have to let go of the great. The truth is—that great thing won't happen twice. The misconception is that greater isn't ahead, when in fact, it **always** is. It's simple but scary. Yet, an ordinary act can lead to an extraordinary life. I dare to say whatever we hold onto is what fills our statement of_____is life. But the One who is holding you is the best choice to hold onto. In Isaiah 33:5-6 it says, "God is supremely esteemed. His center holds. Zion brims over with all that is just and right. God keeps your days stable and secure—salvation, wisdom, and knowledge in surplus, and best of all, Zion's treasure, Fear-of-God."[cccl] I can't get over those few words, no matter how many times I hear them: *His center holds*. I'm not sure what fills in your gap, but I know mine for years has been, "Fear is life." Yet, when I remember Who is holding onto me, there is a shift in my world, because all of a sudden, I am fearless. I wish I could say that now I'm not afraid of anything. But it's more of a daily choice than a life change to not be held back by this thorn in my flesh. But often, I don't mind it anymore—because it actually keeps me clinging and holding onto Jesus. And as you trust in Him, you'll discover that letting go comes quite naturally when holding onto Him. R. C. Sproul puts it this way: "We are secure not because we hold tightly to Jesus but because He holds tightly to us."[cccli] If we switched out whatever we have been pouring all our energy into with, "Jesus is life," I think we would begin to realize that we have been held onto by a Savior who's been cheering us on to *let go*. He is the one who knows your days; He is the one who keeps them stable and secure. He is the one who has been holding you tightly with His love and goodness since the beginning of time. He is the one whose center holds. When we choose to hold onto Him, we choose to trust Him with the rest of what life tells us to hold onto. He will take those tiny gathered details and will create them into something glorious and beautiful before you that's far beyond the grandest of dreams.

150

IN SEASONS OF WAITING

Once upon a time, a child dreamed a dream—one that was far greater than anything one could ever imagine, and Time was the child's friend. They played together, grew together, and dreamt together often. But as the child grew up, the child became more demanding, wanting his dreams there and then, and Time… Time knew that wasn't the best idea. And so they grew apart. It wasn't until the child grew up and returned, after chasing the world for his dream, that the child was met by Time. In the meantime, Time had created a path for his old friend to follow. So down the path he went, remembering that Time was good. At the end of the road, the child's dream awaited—every detail and every wish right before his eyes. In the end, Time was always on the child's side, but it was also far wiser than the child knew. In the path Time created, the child learned, matured, and grew, so that when the child arrived at the end of the journey, the dream could be cherished and kept forever by the child, and not left broken and forgotten in time.

Time. It's something that is endless and yet also limited. There's only so much we can do in one given day, but there's also many given days to follow. So how do we treat time? Or more importantly, how do we cherish time in seasons of waiting? For I have learned, time is much wiser than we know. If you were wondering, the little child in the beginning lines was you. It was an {insert yourself} into the pages and remember your dreams type of short story. It was age-free because I know that we all, at all ages and at all times, have promises and dreams that we are waiting and longing for. And it's not always so easy to trust in the waiting. But I have learned that God is kind and wise, and He is the orchestrator of time that's on our side in each of our very own stories. In Hebrews 10:23 it says: "Let us hold unswervingly to the hope we profess, for he who promised is faithful."[ccclii] On your path of walking through ordinary days and hearing God-whispers all around you, hold onto these truths:

One, *in seasons of waiting, His goodness and mercies pursue your heart in a divinely favored way*. I have found that I would rather wait for the divine than settle for the ordinary. Waiting expects *His* hand to be over every area of your life, not just some parts of it. It positions you to be completely abandoned before Him because He can do *far more* with your all than you could with your greatest efforts. Two, *in the waiting, God is not silent.* You may just be listening for what you want to hear while He's speaking to different areas of your heart you need to be listening for. If you're only listening for "answers," then you've veered away from the purest part of loving Jesus. Listen for His voice and you will find Him. Three, *when God is the One who speaks the promise, He is the only one who can keep His promise.* I believe that there's a sweet anointing on what you're waiting for—that is why it is worth the wait. Esther had twelve months of beauty treatments before she came to the King—six months with oils and six with perfumes. Yet, her anointing was far beyond just the "oils and perfumes." Esther had a divine favor that was anointed within her heart while she trusted God to keep His promise—and that is what won the King over. Four, *when you're in wonder, nothing feels like waiting.* Somehow the world has convinced us that time is not on our side. I believe waiting realizes time is our friend, thus seeing the wonder He has prepared for us on the journey.

In the words of C. S. Lewis: "I am sure that God keeps no one waiting unless He sees that it is good for him to wait."[cccliii] Do not forget: God is kind and time is on your side—and both are your friends. Forever and always remember, you can trust God from the depths of your heart because His promises are anchored there; and sooner than later, you'll reach the end of your path and see those promises come to life right before your very eyes, and you'll feel Time squeeze your hand saying, "This is all for you."

151
ENDLESS

Whatever you imagine, My plans are greater. Whatever you think, My thoughts are higher. Whatever you love, My heart knows better. For I know the plans I have for you, I know the desires of your heart, and I know you better than you know yourself. Beyond what you think or imagine, I am there. Behind and before your plans, My will is paved. There is no detail that I cannot see; nothing is hidden from My sight. It is your trust that I seek, so that My will won't be hidden from you, but revealed to you. I want you to know more than you desire to know. For My greatness is endless before you.

"He's Creator of all you can see or imagine."[cccliv]
Isaiah 40:28

152

LET GO AND LET GOD

Philippians 3:13, "But one thing I do: forgetting what is behind and straining towards what is ahead..."[ccclv] I think it's safe to say that we have all had some crazy dreams growing up that we couldn't wait to live, and as we got older, some of those desires changed and became different dreams. For others they stayed the same and became their focus. Yet, there is this point in life where we have to step back and see which is bigger—our dreams or God's. If we are so focused on our dreams, we won't even glance at God's dreams for us. My challenge to you is to let go and let God. There are going to be times when doors are going to open, and God will say not yet. There are moments when we will be running and the door will slam in our face. But in spite of all the confusion, there will be a point when we step back, one door will open, and God will whisper, "Go. This is the way. Walk in it."[ccclvi] And when we walk through that door, we will realize it's far greater than we could've ever dreamed, but we would have settled for less if we didn't let go and let God. Forgetting what is behind is a way of allowing God to push restart on your life; straining toward what is ahead is allowing God to be the author of your story instead of yourself. It's a constant effort of letting go and trusting, and letting God do the magic! For when we win, we lose. But when He wins, we win!

> *In everything you do, put God first, and he will direct you and crown your efforts with success.*[ccclvii]
> Proverbs 3:6

153

EMBRACE THE JOURNEY

I have come to realize that we all have different stories. Some have similar plots, other similar conflicts, but no two are alike. They are all unique; they are all divergent. I want you to look at your palms and think about what you see. And let me tell you, they're not just wrinkles and crinkles. They are designed; they are well-thought-out; and they are specifically "you." Just like your DNA. Never again will someone be like you, have the same lines sketched on their hands, or have the same combination of genes to make up their DNA. Because you are the only you there ever will be, and that is what makes every story different. The thing about stories is that they are filled with adventures, passions, dreams, and hopes, but also chaos, valleys, tragedies, and brokenness. But these are the small details that are the very reason why we are who we are today—they are a set of kairos, or moments of time, that shape us moment by moment. And that's what I want to talk about—the battles in the journey.

Some of us view life only as a battleground instead of a journey only with battles. And in doing so, we give the enemy a foothold of the promise God has on our lives. But a part of embracing the journey God has for you is embracing the battles along with it. It's like He told me once, "I didn't promise it would be easy; I promised I would be with you." Because that's the thing, *as long as He is with us, we are unstoppable*. There is a story in 1 Samuel 14:1-23 that talks about Jonathan's attack on the Philistines. It talks about Jonathan taking his armor bearer to the Philistines outpost, and he whispers, "Perhaps the Lord will act on our behalf. Nothing can hinder the Lord from saving, whether by many or by few."[ccclviii] The Message puts it this way, "There's no rule that says God can only deliver by using a big army." And so he goes on with two options:

1— Show themselves to the Philistines and stay where they are at if the Philistines say, "Wait until we come to you." 2— If the Philistines tell them, "Come to us," then they'd know that the Lord gave them the battle. As the Philistines cry out the second possibility, Jonathan says, "Climb up after me, <u>The Lord</u> has given them into the hand of Israel."[ccclix] (emphasis added) And that's exactly what happened, and not only that, but when the Israelites who were hiding in the hillside heard that the Philistines were on the run, they joined the battle in *hot pursuit*. The reason why I love this story is not because of the victory that happened on the field, but because of the victory that happened in the heart. There are times in life where we will have a battle before us, and we can either be like Jonathan, believing that the Lord acts on our behalf, or we can be like the Israelites, hiding in fear behind the hillsides of our insecurities. But when it comes down to it, **victory is in the heart before it is on the field.** Jonathan believed in his heart that God would give the Philistines over to them because He showed them that this is what they were to pursue. I wonder what God is speaking to your heart to pursue that doesn't seem likely or looks the opposite of favorable on the field. Maybe it's a voice to speak, a call to go, a gift of worship, and you would rather hide behind the hills. But you won't have victory on the field until you believe in your heart that God will act on your behalf. I once was told, "The way you view God is the way you'll live your life." *So be fearless to wander, bold with strength, and courageous to be.* Because the battle is not yours, but God's, and He has already won!

154

GOD-COLORED

There is a saying I have learned to love that is: "Brokenness is beautiful." That when we feel so incomplete, we are being made complete in Him. But in this incomplete state, our plans, dreams, hearts, and visions all seem to be scattered, that is what makes us vulnerable. We are vulnerable because we are human, and well, humans are full of emotions. The point of this message isn't to say that our brokenness is remade into something stronger and greater, even though that is true. But I want you to see that *in our brokenness we shine*. A lot of people see brokenness as a burden when it's a light. When life isn't altogether, people can come together to help one another. In this journey of searching and wandering, it just so happens that we end up finding someone else who has their light shining from being broken, and it shines into our lives, which then ends up shining into those around us. And all of a sudden everything is God-colored. There's a quote I read that says, "It's okay to be a glow-stick, sometimes we need to break before we shine."[ccclx] In other words, it's okay to be broken, because it is when we walk in our weakness that we discover true strength. Matthew 5:14 states, "Here's another way to put it: you're here to be light, bringing out the God-colors in the world. God is not a secret to be kept."[ccclxi] Sometimes the only way to shine into others lives is to be broken to shine yourself. It's not always those who are strongest that are brightest, but it is those who are most vulnerable that cannot be contained.

@sarahbgraves

Life batters and shapes us in all sorts of ways before it's done, but those original selves which we were born with, and which I believe we continue in some measure to be no matter what, are selves which still echo with the holiness of their origin. I believe that what Genesis suggests is that this original self, with the print of God's thumb still upon it, is the most essential part of who we are and is buried deep in all of us as a source of wisdom and strength and healing which we can draw upon or, with our terrible freedom, not draw upon as we choose. I think that among other things all real art comes from that deepest self-painting, writing music, dance, all of it that in some way nourishes the spirit and enriches the understanding. I think that our truest prayers come from there too, the often unspoken, unbidden prayers that can rise out of the lives of unbelievers as well as believers whether they recognize them as prayers or not. And I think that from there also come our best dreams and our times of gladdest playing and taking it easy and all those moments when we find ourselves being better or stronger or braver or wiser than we are.[ccclxii]
-Frederick Buechner

155

IMPRINTS

> *Speak only well of people and you need never whisper.*
> - Anonymous

This was on the slip of paper inside my fortune cookie, and the simplicity of its wisdom blew my mind. To speak only words that could be safely shouted, with no need for hushed tones and their games. A lot of times we forget that our words impact. To some, our words are only a stamp of ink that easily washes away, to another it's an ink that goes beneath the skin and stays tattooed forever. Proverbs 18:21 says, "Words kill, words give life; they're either poison or fruit—you choose."[ccclxiii] We need to be protective with our words, because they don't always wash away. We never know how deep their imprint may run. Like one ponders the importance of a tattoo for their skin, so our words should be pondered for the power they create. As my friend once said, "Speak only if you can improve the silence." Remember that your words impact like imprints, and it's our choice for what they say.

156

STOP SNOOZING

The alarm rings. We hit snooze. The alarm rings again. We hit snooze. The alarm rings a third time, and we frustratedly forget where we threw our phone last and finally open our eyes. We hit off. Our eyes are open, but we are still not fully awake, and we usually aren't until we go into the light. Now let's look at this through a different perspective. The alarm goes off, we open our eyes, sit up, and roll out of bed, yet our mind is up and going by now. My question is: how many times have we hit the snooze button on God's promptings? And then when we finally say, "Okay," it takes us a little longer to find His direction over our own. When those who replied, "Yes," the first time were instantly guided by His light or peace. The more we hit snooze on His voice, the more we are willing to go back to sleep. It's a state where we are awake physically, but asleep spiritually. But as Ephesians 5:14 says, "Wake up, O sleeper, rise from the dead, and Christ will shine on you."[ccclxiv]

To begin with, we shouldn't make decisions when we are in bed halfway asleep, because that's called compromising. Instead our decisions should be made when we are fully awake, for that is when we are fully exposed to the light. Second, practice waking up to the first alarm. That is how you will learn to walk in His light instead of going searching for it. Then it'll become a daily habit. Third, make a new routine. Instead of constantly ignoring the wake-up call, constantly listen to it, and see how much different your day will be. Steve Palvina says, "If you oversleep just thirty minutes a day, that's 180+ hours a year… if sixty minutes a day, that's 365 hours a year, the equivalent for nine forty hour weeks."[ccclxv] Paul goes on to say in Ephesians 5:16, "Make the most of every opportunity for the days are evil." We can waste so much time being comfortable rather than being awake, and we miss so many opportunities because of it. I think it is when we begin to daily listen to His voice that we will be awake to what He is doing rather than seeking the light with half-closed eyes. Being awake doesn't mean don't rest, because even those with open eyes need to regain energy. The point is to be awake to what He is doing and resting in His peace. So go adventure where He leads and replace fear with curiosity. Make decisions when you are fully awake in His presence and listen for His calling. Trust where He leads and have faith that He will show you what you need to know. Be awake and make the most of every opportunity.

@ kathleenmadethis

157

A HIGHER CALLING

> *Since, then, you have been raised with Christ, set your hearts on things above, where Christ is, seated at the right hand of God. Set your minds on things above, not on earthly things. For you died, and your life is now hidden with Christ in God. When Christ, who is your life, appears, then you also will appear with him in glory.*[ccclxvi]
> Colossians 3:1-4

The Introduction: Earle Wilson states, "No book in the New Testament more strikingly expounds the centrality and meaning of the lordship of Jesus Christ than Colossians."[ccclxvii] The entire New Testament proclaims, "Jesus is Lord," but I firmly believe there's a beauty found in Colossians that emphasizes it the most. (Disclaimer: this may be a bit more scholarly sounding, yet just go along with me through the facts, and I promise I'll wrap them up together by the end.)

The Facts: Before chapter 3, Paul is preaching against false teaching because of the false teachers in Colossae who were speaking false promises. As Wilson describes: "Some of the Colossian Christians appear to have been <u>convinced</u> by wayward new teachers that they needed something **more** than *Jesus Christ* to free them from subjection to elemental and demonic powers. These powers were to be placated and maybe even worshiped."[ccclxviii] (emphasis added) So Paul goes from elaborating about the threat of the false teaching and their false promises, to a more positive command to remain centered on Christ in chapter 3. The powerful beauty Paul presents to those new teachers, and even new Christians, is that because we have been raised with Christ, we are to set our minds and hearts on higher things, as well as have our lives hidden in Christ, for we know that we have a promise to appear with Christ when He appears.

The Wrapping: Murray J. Harris states: "You must not only seek heaven; you must also think heaven."[ccclxix] Paul first and foremost writes and commands for us to set our hearts on God; yet secondly states just as urgently, we also must set our minds on the things of heaven. It is in these four verses that Paul explains the mantel's weight and the Christian's higher calling. As Jesus says in Matthew 11:30, "For my yoke is easy and my burden is light."[ccclxx] He will carry the weight but we must carry out the character of Christ.

Brian Walsh puts it this way, *"Since you have begun to experience the shalom of resurrection life with Christ, meditate upon, set your hearts upon, and allow your imaginations to be liberated to comprehend his legitimate rule. Seeking first his kingdom, allow your vision of life, your worldview, your most basic orientation in life, to be directed by his heavenly rule, seated at the right hand of God. No longer be held captive by the powers of normalcy, the powers that want to maintain the present brokenness, oppression, and idolatry."*[ccclxxi] We are to be concealed completely in God, and that is the most liberating freedom to live our lives large for Him. Jesus is all we need to live in freedom for we are *convinced that nothing can ever separate us from God's love. Neither death nor life, neither angels nor demons, neither our fears for today nor our worries about tomorrow--not even the powers of hell can separate us from God's love.* [ccclxxii] (Romans 8:38) Yes, it requires thinking higher and larger, yet in the same moment, it's setting us apart for His glory.

The Bow: We were never made to live numb—but to feel life as it sets in place around us. To run our fingers across its many textures and forms; to discover the beauty of coming closer to something by risking ourselves into its pull—heaven. Maybe by putting ourselves out there, we will fall into freedom or laughter—and be both a fool and a citizen in this new terrain. We may be nothing or everything as the two come together—but at least we tried and at most we dared to truly live outside the lines of our space for His name. For we were never made to live numb, *we were made to live large*. We were made to live free.

158

PULSE

> *Be strong and courageous, for you are the one who will lead these people to possess all the land I swore to their ancestors I would give them. Be strong and very courageous. Be careful to obey all the instructions Moses gave you. Do not deviate from them, turning either to the right or to the left. Then you will be successful in everything you do. Study this Book of Instruction continually. Meditate on it day and night so you will be sure to obey everything written in it. Only then will you prosper and succeed in all you do. This is my command—be strong and courageous! Do not be afraid or discouraged. For the Lord your God is with you wherever you go.*[ccclxxiii]
> Joshua 1:6-9

Let's close our eyes and think back to when we were little. Remember all the energy we use to have? All the joy? Our hearts would race at the thought of all the toys we would get at Christmas. But there were also moments where we got in trouble, and all of a sudden, our heartbeat was the only thing we could hear. However, there were also those unforgettable moments, the ones where someone's arms were wrapped around us as we cried, and their heartbeat soothed our fragile heart. There's a pulse. A reminder that we are not alone. Our heart is an expression of emotion; its pulse, an art of color. I once read:

Everyone you see, everyone you meet, has this relentless beating in their chests that circulates their oxygen-giving blood flowing to every cell in the body. But we almost never think about how vital this organ is until it struggles or stops. Even standing right next to another person, the heartbeat is imperceptible, almost impossible to detect. Yet without it, life would suddenly cease.[ccclxxiv]

The very thing that we can beat up so much, is the very thing that keeps us alive. But this isn't about our hearts; this is about God's. The article goes on to say, *"One of the most intimate moments in life is when you pause and listen to the heartbeat of someone you love. Placing your head against the chest of a loved one and quieting yourself long enough to hear or feel the rhythm of their life."*[ccclxxv] And that is exactly what we are going to do. We are going to quiet ourselves to hear God's heartbeat. Psalm 46:10 says, "Be still and know that I am God."[ccclxxvi] And in listening to God's truth over our chaos, we will hear His heartbeat. In Joshua's heartbeat of desperation, God calls him to be strong and courageous.

If you have ever lost someone or had to move away from someone who meant a lot to you, you'll be familiar with its hardship. Especially when they were close to your heart; it messes up your pulse a bit. But in this key scripture, God tells Joshua to be strong and courageous. Another way to be strong is to take heart as opposed to losing heart. Maybe God was saying: "Take a seat and trust in Me," but I think He was really saying, "Go on. Move forward. I am with you." It is in those moments where we feel insufficient that we feel God's sufficiency the most. God is telling him to go on, and in listening to God's heartbeat, Joshua's pulse begins to raise in moving forward towards God, an inch at a time, a heartbeat at a time. Because of being so close to God, in Joshua's greatest moment of fear, God's heartbeat was the only thing louder than his own, *thus perfect love drove out all fear one heartbeat at a time.* As 1 John 4:18 reads, "There is no fear in love. But perfect love drives out fear, because fear has to do with punishment. The one who fears is not made perfect in love."[ccclxxvii] He wasn't going to let Joshua fall, because Joshua was close to His heart. In leaning close to God, Joshua heard the sound of God's heartbeat, which in return, empowered him to keep moving forward.

When all of a sudden you're pressed against the heart of God, your heart starts to change, as His desires become your own, as your heartbeat syncs to His beating heart. You start to understand, His heart for you has always been to be closer, to know His heart for you, for your heart to know Him. *For you will be as brave as you are close, and as fearless as you are His.* Wherever you go, so long as you remain close, you will ever be strong and courageous.

159

THE CHURCH

I see one who knows, but is uncertain.
One who believes, but doubts.
One who trusts, but still lingers.
Yet, she is My chosen.
She may linger, but she listens.
She may doubt, but she fights.
She may be uncertain, but she steps.
She is fearless in her pursuit. She is braver than her battles.
As she walks, she moves into her destiny a step at a time.
She needs never fear defeat for I am all around her in the mystery.
She is her Father's whispers. She is mine.
And I'm so proud of who she's become.

Christ's love makes the church whole. His words evoke her beauty. Everything he does and says is designed to bring the best out of her, dressing her in dazzling white silk, radiant with holiness.[ccclxxviii]
Ephesians 6:26-27

160

NONE COMPARE

I love the way He speaks, He moves, He penetrates. How He pieces together beauty from what once was broken or shattered. How He can take ashes and turn them into an unfathomable crown; how He can simply breathe and make dry bones come to life; and how He can take our lives of clay and mold them into something beyond our imagination. This is the God I love; this is the God I adore. And yet, that doesn't keep us from questioning, doubting, or feeling insufficient, simply because we can become blinded by our own insecurities instead of completely placing our security in Him. Somehow we find a way to forget the fact that the Creator of the universe sees us, hears us, loves us, and even that He is for us. When we look at ourselves, we open our hearts to listen to the wrong words that were never meant to impact our lives. Through comparison, jealousy, and envy, we begin to not only see ourselves differently—but also God. "Why would He make me this way?" "Why can't I be like them?" And ever so quickly an avalanche can come from our insecurities that bury us in a place we weren't meant to go. And yet, when we read throughout the Bible, we see that even the angels are always praising God saying, "Holy, holy, holy is the Lord God, the Almighty—the one who always was, who is, and who is still to come."[ccclxxix] (Revelation 4:8) The heavenly angels, who are always with God, are in constant worship of His beauty—how pure He is, how holy He is, how perfect He is. And yet, this is the same God we question. Which brings me to this thought, "Who are we?" Who are we to question a God so holy, so perfect, so beautiful, He who is the purest of loves? But when we begin *to look* to God, we are made secure. Our hearts then open to His words of life that impact not only our lives, but also the lives of others, for His glory. It is when our eyes are set on Him that we are able *to see* as He sees, hear what He is speaking, and move when He moves. It's when we begin *to grasp* that He is the perfect God to love, to praise, and to adore. *To know* that He always sees us, hears us, loves us, and is for us. It is when we start to focus on **His perfection** that we will realize how perfectly He made **us** with unique desires, gifts, and purposes to live out. And it is then that we will finally hear Him say, "There is no one like you; no one greater, no one less, for none compare." One day, we will look back to see all that God was planning all along; and like the angels, we too will praise the God of heaven, for He was, is, and will always be holy, pure, and good.

161

ALL I NEED

You say You know me by name
That You open every door
And that I'm not a hidden frame
That You go behind and before
You say that I am strong
When my emotions say I'm weak
You say I am chosen
When my life feels incomplete
You say "I am Yours" and "You are mine"
When my confusion is at its best
But in the midst of this chaos
You say: "Come to Me and rest"
In this pain, I find love
In this anger, I find peace
In this valley, I'm not lost
You still hear, You still see
In You, I am found again
Forever Yours and forever free
These lonely lies are not Your truth
Your love alone is all I need

"I say to the Lord, 'You are my Lord; apart from you I have no good thing.'"[ccclxxx]
Psalm 16:2

162

PATIENCE IN THE RAIN

The rain reminds me a lot of patience. How it's not warmly welcomed, but it usually is desperately needed. How in the moment, rain feels like containment. Yet in the end, it is but a development of strength, creating growth in dry areas. How it doesn't bring us pain, but we see it as a pain to deal with. Likewise, patience isn't always our favorite word to hear or our favorite action to practice. It doesn't hurt us, but we act as if it can kill us. Yet, patience is what enlarges us in the waiting. It is strengthening within us what needs to be developed for the created **growth** before us that is coming. In the moment, it may not be what we seek or desire. But in the **outcome**, we will see it was absolutely vital for our desire. Rain had to come before the harvest could grow, in which the flood of promises could form thereafter. And when we again stand upon promised dry ground, we'll be thankful for patience in the rain.

> *So let's not allow ourselves to get fatigued doing good. [At the right time] we will harvest a good crop if we **don't give up**, or quit.*[cclxxxi]
> Galatians 6:9 (emphasis added)
>
> *Then Jesus said, "God's kingdom is like seed thrown on a field by a man who then goes to bed and forgets about it. The seed sprouts and **grows**—he has no idea how it happens. The **earth** does it all without his help: first a green stem of grass, then a bud, then the ripened grain. When the grain is fully **formed**, he reaps—harvest time!"*[cclxxxii]
> Mark 4:26-29 (emphasis added)

163

ONE GOOD THING

he will whisper in your ear that you deserve a kingdom
he will whisper to your heart that you are better than them all
he will whisper to your pride to never bow down
he will whisper to your desires anything you want to hear

And that is how he sparked the fall of man—through a whisper.

In chapter 3 of Genesis, we see the serpent questioning Adam and Eve: "Did God really say, 'You must not eat from any tree in the garden?'"[ccclxxxiii]And after she explained to the serpent the **one** thing they could not do, he whispered exactly what she wanted to hear; and so she was deceived, and so came the fall of man. Now let's rewind to two chapters earlier where God decided to create earth and everything in it. He created light and saw that it was good; He created water and dry ground and saw that it was good. He spoke vegetation and animals into existence, and also created man and woman, and saw that this was all very good. Then, let's fast-forward back to the bitten fruit in Adam's hand, and wonder why they decided to risk it all for the "one good thing" they couldn't have? But I think that's also the same question we could ask ourselves. We all have good things that God has placed before us. For Adam and Eve, He created a river for the garden, animals and vegetation for them to eat, and I'm sure there was shelter all around them. For us, God has given us gifts, knowledge, and blessings before us so that we may too carry out the purpose for which we were created. But we also can easily hear whispers to our hearts and pride, and want the "one good thing" we don't have, overlooking all that is still possible with what we've already been given. The thing is, the enemy will do anything to distract you with the "one thing" you don't have to keep you from creating with all that you do have, stalling multiplication's miracle upon the many gifts you presently possess before you and within you. And that is the wake-up call I had from God one day. He spoke so clearly and said: *Don't let the enemy twist what I have spoken is good*. The enemy twisted God's word to Eve and deceived her with what she wanted to hear, and he does the same to us. "It's okay to have sex before marriage." "It's okay to get drunk." "It's okay to not tithe this month, He understands." "It's okay to cheat. It won't hurt your spouse if they don't find out." "It's okay to eat from the tree of knowledge. Surely you won't die." What is it that the enemy is speaking to you that doesn't match the Word of God? What is he whispering you deserve to be, that is keeping you from being who you already are? Let me just tell you that if the Lord said it was good, then that means you have all that you need to use your gifts, to pursue your passions, or to fully chase your dreams. Or it may be that you need to see that you are blessed by what you do have instead of seeking "another good thing" in the wrong place. When you believe in what God says is good, then you'll start to see in your life that you're blessed incredibly; it may have just been, you were too distracted at first to see that what *is good* has been *good enough* all along.

164

ONCE UPON A BEAUTIFUL TIME

Once upon a time… is how we want each of our stories to begin. Happily ever after is how we desire for them to end. And as for the details in between, we dream of our own fairytales. For some, they involve romance, for others, riches, and for some, success. But we all have our own sense of a Disney imagination when it comes to our vision of a "perfect life." But the story I'm going to talk about is one of love between a woman and a man in the book of Song of Songs. It's not their beautiful love that I want to explore, but the beautiful timing of their love. The book begins with the young woman and man head over heels for one another. But as we read later on into Chapter 2, we see the lover comes running reciting the words:

Arise, my darling, my beautiful one, come with me. See! The winter is past; the rains are over and gone. Flowers appear on the earth; the season of singing has come, the cooing of doves is heard in our land. The fig tree forms its early fruit; the blossoming vines spread their fragrance. Arise, come, my darling; my beautiful one, come with me.[ccclxxxiv] (vv. 10-13)

The imagery is so powerful, not because of what he says, but because of *when* he says it. We see the first description of love in Paul's letter to the Corinthians here—patience. And even more than the message of the intimacy between the two lovers, I believe the author is trying to show us the importance of the timing of love.

There is a phrase that is said in one of my favorite shows that says, "All magic comes with a price…"[ccclxxxv] And what is magic in our world today? I see it as the "now spell." And many people use it all the time. They pursue things before its time and have many struggles and complications along the way—simply because love wasn't ready, or in other terms, their hearts weren't fully ready yet. Because magic comes with a price.

When we act on something before God gives us the go, we follow our hearts instead of His. We see in Song of Songs how in love this woman is with the man, and yet she is *just as prominent* on reminding us three times, "Do not arouse or awaken love until it so desires."[ccclxxxvi] And she says it throughout her love story. In fairytale terms she is saying, "All good things come to those who wait." And they do, not because we don't know our hearts, but because He knows them better. If we can wait long enough, and trust God enough, good things surely will come.

165

FRESH

I open the door and am greeted by the heat of an active bakery, welcomed by the aroma of fresh croissants. The baker pokes his head around the corner with a smile for me to come

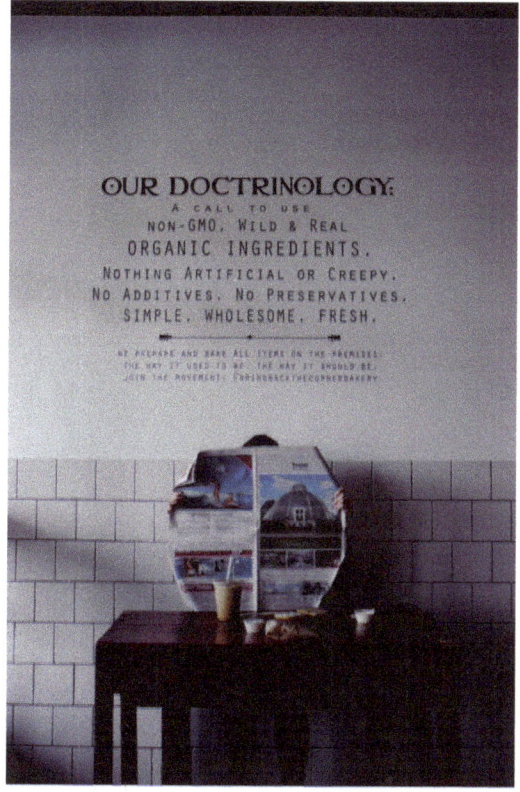

and pick one of the delectable pastries lining the tray next to him. My excitement kicks in as I decide: *Do I want to wake up with the fluffy croissant filled with to-die-for almond paste and roasted almonds on top? Or do I go for a chewy and cheesy danish drizzled with fresh blueberries and a sweet compote to complete the perfect combination?* Boy was I spoiled. I usually chose the almond croissant, and yes, I still daydream about it. But I'm not writing to tell you about my love for food; I want to talk about my favorite thing about this patisserie → everything was always *fresh*. Every day the bakers made a fresh batch of dough with fresh berries delivered from the garden, definitely reflected in the taste. That was just the beginning of my fondness for fresh baked goods. A few years ago, a new bagelry had opened up in my town, so of course, my adventurous little appetite had to try it out. As soon as I walked in, I saw their motto on the wall that stated: *Our doctrinology: a call to use non-gmo, wild and real organic ingredients. Nothing artificial or creepy. No additives. No preservatives. Simple. Wholesome. Fresh.* You can only imagine my heart's delight. I ordered a whole grain bagel with coffee schmear, and I was *in love*. There's just something so desirable about the aspect of freshness. And the same applies to the Word of God and our relationship with Him.

<u>Freshness takes time</u>. It's not quick. But it is rewarding... it pays off. When it comes to reading the Word of God, let me ask you two things: 1. Are you taking more time digging deeper *after* you read the Bible than the amount of time it took you to read it? 2. Are you listening to and not just reading what He has to say? We can live our life with a particular sermon on replay if we don't take the time to press pause on the monotony of every day life to listen to what He is speaking to you today. Out of 1,189 chapters in the Bible, it is impossible to not find a *fresh* Word every time you flip through its life-giving pages. If we walk away without a mere word to reflect on, it is out of our mere laziness. James 1:22-24 says: "Don't fool yourself into thinking that you are a listener when you are anything but, letting the Word go in one ear and out the other. <u>Act</u> on what you hear! Those who hear and don't act are like those who glance in the mirror and two minutes later have no idea who they are, what they look like."[ccclxxxvii] (emphasis added) When we don't take the time to dig deep into His Word, to reflect and listen to what He has to say, we lose and miss out on an extraordinary delight He has to **give**. Seek and you shall find, even if some days

you have to put in a little extra work. *A little extra time adds a little extra freshness.* Like the bagelry and bakery believe in not needing to use preservatives, neither does the Word of God need additives or preservatives, because it is living and breathing a new fresh Word every day for you to take away. It's simple. It's wholesome. And best of all—it's fresh to your Spirit and good for your heart! Let's be honest, there's nothing more satisfying and delightful than knowing God has His head poked around the corner ready to speak a fresh Word for you every morning.

166

SEARCHED

O Lord, you have searched me and you know me.[ccclxxxviii]
Psalm 139:1

When you search for something, you look everywhere for it! You retrace your steps, call anyone and everyone, double-check, and sometimes triple-check, already searched places. You will go on for hours or days trying to find it. The more valuable it is, the longer and harder you search. How much more valuable are we in God's eyes? He knows us inside-and-out. From our desires, to our wants, He knows them before we even realize them. Because of this, we can lay anything before Him knowing He knows us, trusting that He sees us through and through. As Psalm 31:19 says, "Lord, how wonderful you are! You have stored up so many good things for us, like a treasure chest heaped up and spilling over with blessings—all for those who honor and worship you! Everybody knows what you can do for those who turn and hide themselves in you."[ccclxxxix] Know He stores up treasures of value for the ones He values. Whatever is weighing on your heart, you can trust Him with it. You can lay your burdens down at His feet and rest. He will search high and low, to the ends of the earth, go far and wide, even to the moon and back, to take care of you and your cares. You don't have to worry anymore. He won't stop laboring over the labors you lay at His feet. His love is wild like that.

Not dangerous, just wild—His love is for you.

167

STAY THE PATH

As we stay the path, we step into our destiny one step at a time.

I don't know if you've ever had those moments where a word or phrase, you are sure you have heard over 1,000 times, all of a sudden sticks out to you *everywhere*; you keep hearing it in conversations and in your reading and in your Netflix series... (You never know!) But it's like the moment off of *Tangled* where she realizes she's been painting this star-figure all around her home for years, but on her 18th birthday, it dawns to her that all these stars were the *same* symbol designed on the floating lanterns that were let off every year on this specific day for the lost princess, which just so happened to be the *same* as **her** birthday![cccxc] In this moment, every design lights up like fireworks around her in a way she never noticed before. The more pieces that were placed in her hand, the closer she was to discovering the VAST picture that was all around her. What once were mysterious stars → were now floating lanterns → that were designed for the lost princess → that only were released on Rapunzel's birthday → that had the same symbol she had painted all her life → that were signs for her to come home. But she only discovered all the pieces to the picture by stepping outside the comfort of her castle to chase the dream in her heart → and to stay the path by following the one who knew the journey before her quite well. [For the greatest risk of all is to take no risk at all.] And that is the phrase that's been jumping out to me for months now → stay the path.

When you want to give up, stay the path. When you want to turn around, stay the path. When everything looks daunting, stay the path. When it doesn't look as you thought it would, stay the path. As Psalm 37:34 says: "Wait passionately for God, don't leave the path."[cccxci] Or even in Psalm 86:11 it says, "Train me, God, to walk straight; then I'll follow your true path."[cccxcii] Sometimes the pieces don't add up, and they don't make sense to us, and the temptation to run back to our castle of what we know and CAN do is strong, but know if you'll simply keep walking, keep being faithful, keep being consistent in what you put your hands to, more pieces will come together, and you'll see something glorious begin to take shape. The beautiful thing is that, because you had nothing to do with it coming together, you'll know God had everything to do with it coming to pass. *Walking is trusting in the design of how the pieces He has given will unfold.* In staying the path—God is at the center of your story. When you've been anointed in the pastures to be appointed over kingdoms—stay the path. When you've been chosen in the resting to be a leader for a revolution—stay the path. When you've been deemed a warrior in the training grounds to be a hero in the battlefields—stay the path. One day, the pieces will add up, the design will unfold, and your steps will be in your destiny and not towards it. But until then, let time be your friend, God your center, and doubt your enemy. God's promise rests upon you. Don't remove your crown because you don't yet live in the palace. Don't settle as a commoner because your title is not known to the world. Let the kingdom live in your heart, thinking of noble things and acting in kindness and strength, for you are anointed for others and crowned for crowning. You are not set apart to be higher than others, but to lead people to the One who is higher than you alone. You have the crown of splendor in your right hand and the scepter of grace in your left. It's okay to wear your crown and identify as a child of God—it's who you are. You have been anointed for the dream in your heart and His design is all over it. So lead in royalty, for you are royal, and lead others to His throne to be crowned as His too. As you stay the path, you will walk into your destiny one step at a time. Wear your crown in confidence that your King is coming, your destiny awaiting, and your anointing growing at the design of His hand.

168

GLIMPSES OF GLORY

Forget the Face of God, and you forget your own name is beloved.[cccxciii]
- Ann Voskamp

What if our "thank you" is our "I love you too" back to God? So if we do not speak them out when He gives Himself out, we then receive His *I love you* without receiving His love. *Without thanks, we cannot receive the love He fully gives in full.* We merely take in a treasure and see it as invaluable until revelation wakes us up to its true worth. 1,000 thank you's, 1,000 I love you too's, lead to a kingdom of treasures that can never be forgotten and forever will be cherished until the King Himself comes from the clouds to take us to the full glory we've received glimpses of in His gifts. **Therefore, gratefulness catches glimpses of glory.** We want to see God, but really all we need to do is say, "I love you too," and He will reveal where He already is right beside each and every one of us. "Open our eyes, O God," we say. But first we must open our hearts, lest we will never see God in all His glory. "Thank you" releases love like a flood in a dry desert terrain. It moves the hand of God and heart of God. He is appreciated through our *worship*, and He always deserves our best, for He has given us His best like a daily bread and a sip of wine—a holy communion. Shall we remember His poured out love, we'll receive salvation again like in the beginning, as when we were first found by Him.

> Shout hallelujah to Yahweh! May every one of his lovers hear my passionate praise to him, even among the council of the holy ones. For God's mighty miracles astound me! His wonders are so delightfully mysterious that they leave all who seek them astonished. Everything he does is **full** of splendor and beauty! Each miracle demonstrates his eternal perfection. His unforgettable works of surpassing wonder **reveal** his grace and tender mercy. He satisfies all who love and trust him, and he keeps every promise he makes.
> Psalm 111:1-5[cccxciv]
> (emphasis added)

169

YOUR ATTITUDE IS EVERYTHING

In Philippians 4:11-12, Paul writes, "I am not saying this because I am in need, for I have learned to be content <u>whatever</u> the circumstances. I know what it is to be in need, and I know what it is to have plenty. I have learned the secret of being content in any and every situation."[cccxcv] (emphasis added) The beauty of this statement is not in the words he writes, but in his attitude over the situation. You would think that Paul was in a home with just enough supplies to get through the next day when he wrote this, but he was not. Actually, in this scripture, Paul is in jail, and provision isn't constant. Yet, instead of dwelling on what he doesn't have, his heart is content with Who he has, and that is what makes the situation beautiful. An old proverb that many of us have heard is, "Mind over matter." It is a way of finding beauty in any and every situation. It is a way of being stronger in the hardest times. It is simply learning to control your mind and conquering your circumstance. Meredith Grey looks at it this way,

When we say things like "people don't change" it drives scientist crazy because change is literally the only constant in all of science. Energy. Matter. It's always changing, morphing, merging, growing, dying. It's the way people try not to change that's unnatural. The way we cling to what things were instead of letting them be what they are. The way we cling to old memories instead of forming new ones. The way we insist on believing despite every scientific indication that anything in this lifetime is permanent. Change is constant. How we experience change that's up to us. It can feel like death or it can feel like a second chance at life. If we open our fingers, loosen our grips, go with it, it can feel like pure adrenaline. Like at any moment we can have another chance at life. Like at any moment, we can be born all over again.[cccxcvi]

Our circumstances are constantly changing, but our attitude is everything. We can hold onto what we used to have, or look forward to what is ahead. We can see the one door shut, or another door opened. We can complain about what's happening around us or praise God for what He's already done for us. I believe Paul found that pure adrenaline by not looking at what he didn't have, but Who he had. When we set our mind over matter, we will begin to see the opportunities in change, the possibilities in difference, and the growing in uncertainty. We will find thrill in the unknown, the adrenaline in fear, and life in God. There are greater heights to travel and there are lower depths to discover, but within each journey of change, He will always be our constant and your mind will always be your catalyst.

> *If you correct your mind, the rest of your life will fall into place.*[cccxcvii]
> Lao Tzu

170

INSIDE OUT

> *Just because it's what's done, doesn't mean it's what should be done.*^{cccxcviii}
> *- Cinderella*

If you haven't noticed, I am sort of a movie fanatic. Even more than that, I am a quote fanatic. Quotes, most of the time, are not only a huge reminder to never give up, but they are also more often a reality check for me, such as the quote above. After being saved, I completely fell in love with the Lord—I was crazy for Him. And in the process of pursuing a God of love and having Him pursue me, I was changed from the inside out. There was really no thought to when I would have my "Jesus time" as I call it, because naturally I desired Him all the time and would spend whatever time I had free with Him. Whether it was in prayer, reading the Word, worshiping, or reading a devotional, I was won, head-over-heels, and unquestionably in love with Him—I was on fire. But with love comes change. Sometimes change is subtle, and other times abrupt.

Mine in this instance was a 180. When trials came, it was like fire trying to burn water. I was untouchable because I was so in love. But as time went on, and I met more Christians, and heard more about *their* lifestyles, I all of a sudden started to fix myself because I wanted to be a Christian. Yet, what I didn't realize then is that Christ was already fixing me through *love* and not rules, and was making me more like Him with my standing out than me trying to fit in to this "Christian mold." These experiences affected my love for God as they distorted my view of Him. I still loved Him, but it was in a different way. It wasn't the free love I knew before in full surrender. It was a "let me fix this up before I come to you so that you can love me then" portrayal. I tried to understand His love by putting limits of human understanding on Him, which was absurd. It became about the *outside* instead of the *inside* so fast, keeping me hidden instead of drawing me close.

In Matthew 23:26, Jesus addresses the Pharisees by saying, "First clean the inside of the cup and dish, and then the outside also will be clean."^{cccxcix} That is really how He loves us, isn't it? From the inside out. Goodness. How terrible it would be if He only loved us from the outside in. Yet, He *sees* us in a more beautiful and pure way than we can truly wonder. It's like the purity you feel at a wedding combined with the moment a child is born, but so much more. And how He loves us from the inside out is the best way we can love Him the same. To instead clean the inside of our hearts to let Him fix the outside rather than us trying to clean our outside while appearing fixed yet not really whole. But if we daily would re-invite Him into our hearts like the first time we fell in love with Him, or the greatest moment of love we've experienced with Him, that wholeness of life in Him would then purify us from the inside out. We would worship from the inside out. We would live from the inside out. Undeniably crazy, head-over-heels, and madly in love → standing out, not for what could be done, but simply, for what should be done.

171

ABLAZE

In chasing impossible dreams,
it will be easy to settle for possible things
Yet those who finish and do not fret,
will live a life they won't forget
To the brave, they will soar,
to seek and find destiny's open doors
To the courageous, they will rise,
to see far greater than mountains' heights
To the bold, how far they'll run,
to see before them what's never been done
To the righteous, how they'll defy,
to greet faces of giants, to conquer with glorious might
For with eyes of belief and imaginations of hope,
no odds can stand against wherever they go
For when that which is within is lit ablaze,
no measure, no power, no love can it refrain

The faithful lovers of God will inherit the earth and enjoy every promise of God's care, dwelling in peace forever... The ways of God are in their hearts and they won't swerve from the paths of steadfast righteousness... So don't be impatient for the Lord to act; keep moving forward steadily in his ways, and he will exalt you at the right time. And when he does, you will possess every promise, including your full inheritance. You'll watch with your own eyes and see the wicked lose everything.[cd]
Psalm 37:29, 31, 34

172

MORE TRUST, LESS UNDERSTANDING

I've come to realize that the more we trust in God, the less we worry about our reality. Why? Well, because our pulse changes. It goes from the quick rhythms of worry, doubt, and stress in our hearts, to the calm pace of trust, peace, and obedience within His. It's one thing to *see* God's heart, but it's another beautiful thing to *feel* God's heartbeat. It's when we press in close to Him that we can both hear and feel His heartbeat. We begin to trust in who He is and not worry about what He is doing—for we know it is for our good. Draw closer to His heart, feel His heartbeat, and let your heart's worry fade away to the sound of His love.

> *Come near to God and He will come near to you.*[cdi]
> James 4:8

> *With his love, he will calm all your fears. He will rejoice over you with joyful songs.*[cdii]
> Zephaniah 3:17

@ *kathleenmadethis*

173

MORE THAN A COVER

Let's say you walk into a bookstore and see a book that catches your eye. The title of the story reads, *The Fox and the Hound*. It is then that a lot of us start to immediately predict the ending, knowing that there will be some sort of twist. So you begin to lay out the details: Obviously there is a fox and a hound, they probably will like each other at some point, but then by the middle, there will be conflict. Yet, by the end, they will most likely be friends again. It's what you call predictable. But then there are stories like, *The Life of Pi*, where you figure it will be extraordinary, but you're not entirely sure how. In both of these scenarios, you could probably read the beginning, the middle, and the end of the stories, and try to predict what would happened in between. But without reading every page, you won't truly know "the story." *It's the small details that make up a book and bring it to life.* It's not so much what you predict it to be, whether your ending conclusion was correct or not, because the beauty of the story isn't in the finish, but in the details that are crafted in between. Ernest Hemingway said, "Every man's life ends the same way. It is only the details of how he lived and how he died that distinguish one man from another."[cdiii] What he is trying to say is that the details matter, and that every person has a different story.

Every time we meet someone new, we give them a title to the cover we see, and as we hear bits and pieces of what they say, we see chapters of their lives. But it is when we sit down and take the time to hear their story, that we discover these beautiful details about them that we never noticed before. Because the small details are what make up who we are, what we do, what we love, and honestly, what makes us unique. It's in hearing the details of others' lives that we begin to understand their story. As 1 Samuel 16:7 says, "For the Lord sees not as man sees: man looks at the outward appearance, but the Lord looks at the heart."[cdiv] In other words, man looks at the cover, but God sees all the details laid out in between. Imagine being Samuel, who is supposed to be anointing a suitable king for the nation, and God is speaking these words to your heart. Jesse then brings out seven of his elder sons, and Samuel sees seven covers in front of him that look appealing, but God is almost saying, "Don't judge a book by its cover." So then they bring the youngest son in, and out of all of them, this is who God says will be king, because God could see beyond what meets the eye. I think if we would begin to see people beyond their covers, we would be able to discover the beautiful details that God sees in them too. And that is my challenge to you—to not see a person as a book cover with predictable pages; instead, see them as an extraordinary story, full of details that give a different definition to their beauty. You'll be surprised by their many stories, and maybe even changed, because of them.

174

UNVEILED

Love softens the hardest stones. Being pure doesn't make you better than them. It makes you closer to Me. To them you're glowing—to Me, you're mine. Darkness doesn't drive out light; light drives out darkness. Keep your light shining. In the fortress you are [s a f e]. Abide in Me. Come into the light when it starts to get too dark; then when all is light within, go back outside, for I am in you. When I'm aflame in you, you won't think to hide. Be ablaze; live on fire! You're fierce, not for your purity, but for your ability to remain pure in the devil's company. When others speak of darkness and not in light, know it's not the real them. Your hatred is not towards who they are, but to the lies of the enemy they repeat. When you sense him in their words, sense Me, sense My Word, and then speak what needs to be heard. That's when dead bones come alive and warriors are raised. Live unveiled. Start here. Start now. Save Jerusalem, save My chosen people.

No one lights a lamp and then hides it, covering it over or putting it where its light won't be seen. No, the lamp is placed on a lamp stand so others are able to benefit from its brightness. Because this revelation lamp now shines within you, nothing will be hidden from you—it will all be revealed. Every secret of the kingdom will be unveiled and out in the open, made known by the revelation-light.[cdv]
Luke 8:16-17

Jerusalem** His bride, His church, His earth to be His again

175

LIVE IN SUCH TRUTH

One of the most prophetic words I have ever received is: *Have fun*. I know it sounds silly, but I believe there is great victory in the simplicity of enjoying life. In the Word, we read that we do not have to worry about tomorrow, to instead live fearlessly and love one another and live in unity. If we could choose such a life, I'm sure we would in an instant. Yet somehow, in the midst of overthinking, taking offense, and sensing the need to be right, division can quickly sneak in. Some people may choose to live miserably, yet there is no misery to the good news. I wonder why then we allow the enemy to have access to so many areas of our lives where he does not belong? Having fun may not be as silly as it sounds then, but instead may be more groundbreaking in fighting back for what already belongs to us.

I love how Paul writes a letter commending a woman for living her life in love and truth in 2 John. He writes:

Because of the Truth which lives and stays on in our hearts and will be with us forever: Grace (spiritual blessing), mercy, and [soul] peace will be with us, from God the Father and from Jesus Christ (the Messiah), the Father's Son, in all sincerity (truth) and love. And now I beg you, lady (Cyria), not as if I were issuing a new charge (injunction or command), but [simply recalling to your mind] the one we have had from the beginning, that we love one another. And what this love consists in is this: that we live and walk in accordance with and guided by His commandments (His orders, ordinances, precepts, teaching). This is the commandment, as you have heard from the beginning, that you continue to walk in love [guided by it and following it].[cdvi]

I believe that as we live in righteousness, abide in His ways, and continually choose to do good and what's right, that surely His love and mercy and kindness will follow us. Living in such truth will set us free! But it is truth that we must take back to be free in such goodness, to pick up the Word of God and declare what it says. Words have power, yet whether we believe them or not makes them either powerful or powerless. Do we believe He promises us ever-increasing wide-open spaces to live in or do we expect to be robbed of more land tomorrow? Do we believe He loves us so much that He is acting on our behalf behind the scenes or are we already making back-up plans B,C,D, and E in case He doesn't come through? Do we believe that God sent His son to die for our sins that we may obtain everlasting life or do we live as if His son died and stayed in the tomb?

As Jesus says in John 10:10 says, "I have come to *give you everything in abundance, more than you expect*—life in its fullness until you overflow!"[cdvii] (emphasis added) It's time to take back the territory the enemy has gained. We have inherited wide-open spaces, full of grace, mercy, peace, and blessing. We needn't worry, fear, or doubt, for He is always good! We should make the most of our youth while we are young,[cdviii] (Ecclesiastes 11:9) and I'm referring to young as here on earth. Age is but a number to the spirit that is awake to what the Lord is doing! As chosen children of God, we needn't whisper, we needn't hold back, we need only to rise in courage and pursue the peace that beckons us into the most extravagant, unexpected, and untold awakening of His faithfulness to us! Guided by His commands and following them, let us love, live, and take back what the enemy has stolen from us; Jesus already paid the highest price that we may not live short of life's fullness. As 2 Timothy 1:14 states: *Guard well this incomparable treasure by the Spirit of Holiness living within you.*[cdix] Always live in such truth… and don't forget, *have fun!*

176

IMMEASURABLY MORE

@bulgerjoseph

To do immeasurably more begins with its measures. Life is not always rows of wide-open doors that lead us to everything we have been dreaming of. Instead, we usually walk through one door after another, which leads to a specific moment and place where we are meant to be. Some rooms we walk into have more than one door we can choose from, and sometimes the most eye-catching door is the one that remains closed for a season; but every day is filled with these designed moments that we are meant to live, and they're designed places where we are meant to thrive. As Ephesians 3:20 says, God is "able to do immeasurably more than all we ask or imagine…"[cdx] Because of this, we *know* that God has **so** much more in store for us, far beyond what we could ever fathom, and yet, He also has a lot more in store in the measures before us right now. I once was told, "Don't despise small beginnings. Understand your parameters and run as far to the edge as you can and exhaust all your options. And then God will expand your parameters and His favor." We live within measures, but in using what we can, we war with what we have, creating beauty where there once seemed to be none at all. You see, *dreaming bigger isn't about having more, it's about using more of what you have and shaping it to bring glory to God.* As we walk through each door, we reach a new parameter, but with bigger measures. It's when we pour out what God has given us that He not only will do immeasurably more around us, but also within us. JD from Hillsong United, a widely known worship team, said in an interview with Eternity News, "But [we should] trust God and just be faithful with what's in your hand. Because God didn't just drop an album, or a band, or a tour in our hand. For us, it started with setting out the chairs at youth [group], or serving in the choir; so, it's just been that one step at a time—and that's the way I believe God calls us all."[cdxi] Most of us desire to experience the immeasurable blessings of God, but it's more glorifying to run in the measures He has placed us in, to use all we've got, and to press further than its limits, until we breakthrough to discover His immeasurably more for us, within us, and before us.

177

TO CHASE A DREAM

The Story:

"I am with you and will watch over you wherever you go, and I will bring you back to this land. I will not leave you until I have done what I have promised." "Then Jacob made a **vow** saying, 'If God will be with me and will watch over me on this journey I am taking and will give me food to eat and clothes to wear... then the Lord will be my God, and this stone that I have set up as a pillar will be God's house and of all that you give me, I will give you a tenth.'"[cdxii] (Genesis 28, emphasis added) Jacob then went on to work for fourteen years for the woman he loved, while being cheated in wages by his new father-in-law. Thus, later in fleeing with his family, he was called (Israel) because he struggled with God and men, BUT still he overcame. Thus, Genesis 35:3 resumes with Israel's new voice, "Then come, let us go up to Bethel, where I will build an altar to God, who **answered** me in the day of distress and who has been with me wherever I have gone."

The Points:

1. God will be with you wherever you go.
2. You have to chase what God places in front of you or it will blow away.
3. Sacrifice your comfort to reach your dreams.
4. It takes effort and work to achieve what you love.
5. You will overcome anything with God's strength.
6. The Lord will be your God—it's all about Him.

The Breakdown:

A God-given dream is a beautifully daunting path to follow. There are moments of confidence and assurance, but there are also moments where doubts and fears arise. Jacob had a pillar of declaration that he kept to remind him of the dream that God placed in his heart, and not only did he leave his comfort for it, but he was assured that his life would come back to safety "or home" in verse 15. *But a dream is a journey, not a race; it is found one step at a time.* The beautiful part of a God-blessed journey is that He'll never leave you through it all. In sacrificing our comfort, we are embraced by our Comforter. Sometimes we take steps of faith without any assurance, but we also always have that pillar to remind us that God's dream will become our reality, and that we will overcome any obstacles ahead by His strength. Luke 18:27 says, "What appears humanly impossible is more than possible with God. For God can do what man cannot."[cdxiii] That always amazes me, but you know what's just as powerful? ***That one man's dream can affect a nation's reality.*** Because Jacob pursued his promise, his own son Joseph then lived his own. Joseph never stopped dreaming, no matter the circumstance, and I believe it was because he had the perseverance of his father. Through a series of unfortunate events, Joseph ended up in jail for years, but still God turned it all around for good and led him to an unimaginable promise. Likewise, God is using each of our dreams to build up a promise that we could never even begin to think possible. Our patience is what builds it, our belief is what chases it, and His Word is what fulfills it. Jacob and Joseph constantly kept God at the center of their lives, and so, in return, their dreams came to life! So set up your pillar, leave your comfort, and pursue your promise, but always fix your eyes on God and not the dream. As 2 Corinthians 4:16-18 says: "Therefore we do not lose heart. Though outwardly we are wasting away, yet inwardly we are being renewed day by day. For our light and momentary troubles are achieving for us an eternal glory that far outweighs them all. So we fix our eyes not on what is seen, but on what is unseen. For what is seen is temporary, but what is unseen is eternal."[cdxiv]

> *Our deepest desires should not be circling us, but rather is it us who should be circling them in prayer.*

178

RIGHT IN-BETWEEN THE EYES

There are some things in life we tend to oversee that almost go unnoticed, and yet can be so evident to those who aren't even seeking to find them. To those who are looking, they seem small. To those who are seeing, they seem big. In other words, from our point of view, we can diminish what is upon us in power, yet from an outsider's view, they are captivating for its rare anointing. They are the promises I like to call, "Right inbetween the eyes." It's something you cannot see, but others clearly can. They are our strengths, our giftings, our anointing, and ultimately, direction to the calling on our lives. But it is in those moments, when our faith is blind, that God places people around us to allow our hearts to see. I believe Paul is one of the greatest examples we can look to for encouragement. We see it is in his great friendship with Timothy as he writes, "But you, Timothy, are a man of God; so run from all these evil things. Pursue righteousness and a godly life, along with faith, love, perseverance, and gentleness. Fight the good fight for the true faith. Hold tightly to the eternal life to which God has called you, which you have confessed so well before many witnesses."[cdxv] (1 Timothy 6:11-12) We see it as he encourages other believers in Acts 14, 16, 20, 23, and the many other letters he wrote. And we begin to see that God will place encouragers around us to remind us of the "right in-between the eyes" promise we are called to. And while we fight the good fight, Romans 15:4 tells us, "The Scripture gives us hope and encouragement as we wait patiently for God's promises to be fulfilled."[cdxvi] So not only does God bring us encouragement, but He also sends us reminders to keep pressing forward, all that we may unquestionably know that we have purpose in every step in which He is constantly directing. As Rodney Williams says: "Your purpose may not always be obvious, but always know that you do have a purpose."[cdxvii]

@bulgerjoseph

179

BE SILENT

I'm sure you've heard or seen this verse a few times before: "Be still and know that I am God."[cdxviii] (Psalm 46:10) I know I have plenty of times in plenty of shapes and forms. But there was something different about this verse when I read it this time, because as I discovered the context, a story began to form in my heart. As you read through Psalm 46, you see that the author is talking about this chaos happening around "her," around the holy city. This is where many people, and I guilty as charged, have clung onto two main verses—Psalm 46:10 of being still, and 46:5 of "God is within her, she will not fall. God will help her at break of day."[cdxix] But what I listened to is what I wanted to hear, what I looked past is what I didn't want to experience. In Psalm 46, the earth is shaking, mountains are falling, nations are in uproar, and kingdoms are crumbling down. Picture this—that you're standing out in an open city where earthquakes are happening, people are running around in chaos, and you hear that still small voice that spoke to Elijah on the mountain, "Be still and **know** that I am God." In verse 1 and 2, we see the author talking about taking refuge in God and standing fearless. But really, the situation isn't peaceful. It's actually pretty terrifying. To have everything changing and falling around you is a place where either I would choose to run back to shelter or go forward in my own strength. But God says instead, "Be silent. Don't pursue forward. Don't run back. Trust in Me. You're in a vulnerable position, and it's exactly where I want you." And it's here that our heart is beating out of our chest and our mind is racing with second guesses. But instead of doing what is practical, we do what is fearless—we listen. We don't scream; we don't run. We close our eyes and hear His voice saying, "I have you." It's here, in this vulnerable place, that we feel His peace cover us like a garment. And though everything around us may not go still, there's this sense of stillness in our hearts that brings the wild of our thoughts and fears to a halt. We experience trust, we experience God, and we realize we are exactly where we are supposed to be. God will position us in the right place, but we have to place ourselves in the right position. Here in the chaos of everything, that stillness in our hearts positions us to <u>know</u> God, to experience His strength, and to truly trust Him with what is before us. Yes, it's vulnerable. But that's an exciting place to be, because God will never be more real to you than when you are in a place where you **need** Him to be real. And that's where He becomes <u>bigger</u>, where we become stronger, and *we know that He truly is God*.

180

THE CALL OF NEVERLAND

> *Leave your country, your family, and your father's home for a land that I will show you. I'll make you a great nation and bless you. I'll make you famous; you'll be a blessing. I'll bless those who bless you; those who curse you I'll curse. All the families of the Earth will be blessed through you.*[clxx]
> (Genesis 12:1-3)

Up to this point, Abram has already been living for the Lord for around 75 years. At least somewhere in his family line—Noah, the man known for walking with God, is in his great lineage of grandfathers. Suddenly, in this moment, God isn't just a tale of old to Abram, but a voice calling out for him. It's this ultimate promise that comes with the price of → leave everything you've known behind. It may sound exhilarating, but one step of bravery in, you'll realize *all those thoughts of courage, dreams of greatness, and moments of being lost in a fearless wonder* are required to keep your faith in the journey He's calling you to, for they will become your greatest weapons.

Abram didn't know where he was going, but I'm sure he thought it was a chance he'd never have again. Likewise, I wonder how many of us have been in the comfort of our homes, dreaming about an impossible Neverland, when its reality is right outside our window. "To live will be an awfully BIG adventure,"[cdxxi] Peter Pan called out to Wendy. "Look up at the heavens and *count the stars* if indeed you can count them."[cdxxii] God calls out to us. We can't humanly count the stars. But He can. He created the stars we try to count. He created the call we try to live. Whether young or old, God is calling us all to a Neverland that *requires trust* and *costs everything*. God has already opened the window, beckoning us to come follow Him up and out. We just have to be willing to wake up and say: "Speak God, I'm your servant, ready to listen."[cdxxiii] (1 Samuel 3:9) As we **combine** our living with our dreaming, we will discover our Neverland dream. Because Abram left his comfort, he saw the faithfulness of God do the unimaginable! God is saying the same to you, "Count the stars—there is an awfully BIG adventure ahead of you!" And as you follow, you will undoubtedly find that Neverland is just as much yours **now** when you are awake than when you were dreaming.

181

THE SHOWN IN THE UNKNOWN

God tends to not just speak a direction, but show us it. Psalm 139:3 says, "You compass my path and my lying down, and are acquainted with all my ways."[cdxxiv] I like to think of this as an analogy between a loving father and his son. The father has never failed the son, continually blesses him and loves him so much. So when the father blindfolds the son and says, "Trust in me and let me show you what I have in store for you," the son trusts his father while his father leads him to his surprise. The son is walking towards the unknown, but he trusts his dad enough to follow him blindly. This is just like us with God. He is just saying, "Let me show you." Write this scripture on your heart, and trust God with everything! As Psalm 143:8 says, "Let the morning bring me word of your unfailing love, for I have put my trust in you. Show me the way I should go, for to you I entrust my life."[cdxxv] If it is still unknown, then have faith, for it is just waiting to be shown.

182

WITHIN US

While being a college student, I came to know a phrase quite often, "I can't." "I can't go to the movies because I don't have enough money," or, " I can't go out tonight because I don't have enough time." "I can't go to church because I need to study." And all of these have some truth hidden in them, but there's also a lot of perspective that we might be missing here. Because the same person who doesn't go to the movies may go on a shopping spree days later. The person who doesn't go out that night may have gone out spontaneously the night before and forgotten your plans. The person who doesn't go to church because they need to study may have watched Netflix the entire night before, which could have been after church study time. Now I'm not saying this is always the case, but I will say it is quite often the scenario. My hope for this message isn't to condemn those who have done this, but to open the perspective of those who say this subconsciously, " I can't." Because I can count myself guilty of saying this quite a few times, especially to God.

There can be a multitude of promises God speaks over our lives, to which we automatically reply, "I can't." Yet, all we might need is a change of perspective. Take Moses for example; most of us know him by the parting of the Red Sea while leading the Israelites out of captivity. God saw this leadership in him from the beginning, but Moses didn't see it himself from the start. When God called him to deliver His people out of Egypt, Moses first saw and said what he couldn't do, as seen in Exodus 4:10, "O Lord, I have never been eloquent, neither in the past nor since you have spoken to your servant. I am slow of speech and tongue."[cdxxvi] In other words, he replied to God, "I can't." But I love how God replies: "Who gave man his mouth? Who makes him deaf or mute? Who gives him sight or makes him blind? Is it not I, the Lord? Now go; I will help you speak and will teach you what to say." And He speaks the same to us! "I will help you in your insecurity and will equip you to do what I have called you to." No matter how less than ordinary we *feel*, God sees and knows what He can do through us, because He created us exactly as we are. As Henry David Thoreau said, "What lies before us and what lies behind us are small matters compared to what lies within us. And when you bring what is within out into the world, miracles happen."[cdxxvii] It may not be easy, but it will come to pass.

183

HELLO DISCOURAGEMENT

Hello Discouragement, I'd like to say it's been a while, but you visit often. A little too often at that. Sometimes it'd be nice if you gave me a break, but you seem to have taken a liking to me. It's just... today I'm kind of tired, so if you could come back another day, that'd be lovely.

It's often that when discouragement greets us, it starts a little like: "Didn't God say?" And because there is a hint of truth hidden within the imposed question, our ears perk up, lean in, and want to give time to what Discouragement has to say. Yet the more we listen, the more our hearts wander down unintended paths of doubt and uncertainty into lands *far, far away* from what God has promised.

I once was a lifeguard at an amusement park. Sometimes, after working fifty hours a week, my thoughts would start to wander. And so I came up with a strategy to make my mind be still by intentionally thinking, "Twalala." I know it sounds silly, but it honestly worked. I didn't care about what I was thinking, so I didn't wander with it into deeper places. I think we need to do the same with the enemy when he starts creating doubts.

One friend told me, "**The enemy can only create doubt where there is certainty.**" The thing about discouragement is that it does have hidden truth within it, yet whether that's a good or bad thing, it is all about one's perspective. I think I hear almost on the daily, "Didn't God say you were called to be a worship leader?" And sometimes, without thought, I answer, "Yes." Then, he replies mischievously, "So why are you not?" The truth is, I am called to be a worship leader. The twist is that it's not for my season right now and the enemy wants to turn me against God for it. Oh, guard your heart, child of God. Because if you keep leaning on your own understanding, you will not be able to keep hold of the unshakable faith you once had.

@kathleenmadethis

Within seconds, the enemy can take truth and twist it *just enough* to make it feel like God is against you. Guarding your heart hears the knock, opens the door, hears his scheme over his words, and shuts the door right in his face. Some of us need to start thinking, "Twalala," more often so we can stop feeding the doubt welling up inside our hearts. Someone else's life may not be on the line, but your destiny is, and it is of great worth. Here's a truth the enemy probably won't bring up—*God doesn't keep knowledge from us because He isn't good, He keeps secrets to surprise us with His goodness.* (Like I said... it's about one's perspective.) Deuteronomy 29:29 puts it this way: "The secret things belong to the Lord our God, but the things revealed belong to us..." [cdxxviii] The *secret* things, the *unknown* details, the *hidden* designs, belong to God. If we knew every act He would do in our lives, we would either one, royally fail by trying to make it happen ourselves and then blame God, or two, run away because it is something we could never ourselves live up to. *Him keeping secrets allows His goodness to be on Him and keeps the pressure of making it happen off of us.* Yet, what is revealed can be the one thing your faith needs to hold onto to keep moving forward. God *does have,* not good, but the BEST before you, for He passionately delights in the details of your life. He may just be keeping the best part of His plans secret to surprise you (but shhhh... it's a secret!).

So Discouragement, thank you for coming by. You've reminded me that I'm that much closer to my destiny. But you're not welcome in my home anymore, so have a nice day, or don't.

184

CLOSE YOUR EYES

My beloved,

Shall I tell you to close your eyes or open them? For at this moment, you see the same. Tears from your eyes come like surprise as if it's been forever, yet it's only been a couple of days. You're still stronger than you know. Still, I am Your everything. You truly are madly in love with Me. More in love with Me you are than anything else. Yet, you can't keep away from Me for long because of it. Yes. This is a different atmosphere you are breaking into, a different place, holding the weight of generations in your heart. It can destroy you if you don't learn to let it out in some way. Thus, I am teaching you the ways to prance upon the higher hills. To write, to dream, to love, they will become your first instinct and not your last resort. Time has been your friend teaching you this. You will finish well, what you've begun, and I will bring the right people into your path to help carry it to completion. Not just one dream, but many in one. So close your eyes for I have a plan. When the lights come on, you'll understand completely. I love you.

xx
Jesus

The LORD God is my strength, and he will make my feet like hinds' feet, and he will make me to walk upon mine high places.[cdxxix]
Habakkuk 3:19

185

TAPESTRIES OF SEASONS

> *There is a time for everything and a season for every activity under the heavens.*[cdxxx]
> Ecclesiastes 3:1

```
                            Season
        ┌──────────────┬──────────────┬──────────────┐
        •              •              •              •
        •              •              •              •
        •              •              •              •
        •              •              •              •
       Time           Time           Time           Time
```

There will always be a time for everything, but it is almost as if the author is saying, "...But there is *also* a season for every activity." In other words, you have to be in the right season before you can find the right time. Seasons are full of many "right times," but you can't make a right time in the wrong season. "For such a time as this" happened at a specific moment in a specific season that was followed by the right response. But it began with allowing the times to happen within their due seasons, before Esther could get to that defining moment. I'm sure she didn't see it coming, but God did. He goes behind and before us, weaving our times perfectly in this huge tapestry of seasons. Even though we are on the backside viewing knotted strings and mixed colors of dreams and promises, God perfectly sees the big picture from the front of the tapestry, where He orchestrates every time within every season, so that we can experience life to the full. He never misses a single moment; He never misses a single string.

For every one season, there is a multiplicity of times.

186

PRESENT OVER PERFECT

When you are here and now, sitting totally, not jumping ahead, the miracle has happened. To be in the moment is the miracle.[cdxxxi]
- Oshu

He had everything in place. His song recorded. His battery charged. The candles lit, the perfect scenic background. Soon his girlfriend would come around the corner and he would get down on one knee to propose. Except, it was so cold that his phone wouldn't turn on. Therefore, the song he had spent hours writing for this once in a lifetime moment now could not be played. In fact, to add to the chaos, a gust of wind came and blew out *all* the candles. Therefore, everything he had prepared for, for one of the biggest questions of his life, had now fallen through. And what was left? Him. Him and the ring. But then God spoke to him in that moment and said, "It doesn't need to be perfect for her to say yes. She will say yes to who you are whether everything is perfect or not. For **I** love you for who you are." Soon, she did walk around the corner, and shortly after, she did say yes! I think, then and there, he had to decide to be present over perfect, otherwise he may have missed the moment he had been waiting so long for.

Some of us live in fear of missing the moment. Others of us live in the moment, defying the odds of fear. One thinks much and the other is still much. One values perfection, the other values presence. I think life is full of "then and there" moments, but it is those who are present who will seize life's fullness. It doesn't mean that those who are fear-filled won't have those moments come, but they are more likely to not hop on life's train passing by because of the fear of "what if," or by disqualifying themselves from seeing miracles or maybe even performing them. Shauna Niequist actually wrote a book called *Present Over Perfect* and this is something she writes within its pages: *Present is living with your feet firmly grounded in reality, pale and uncertain as it may seem. Present is choosing to believe that your own life is worth investing deeply in, instead of waiting for some rare miracle or fairytale. Present means we understand that the here and now is sacred, sacramental, threaded through with divinity even in its plainness. Especially in its plainness.*[cdxxxii] There's something powerful about the present, for God is always found there. I believe that's why it says in Psalm 46:10, "Be still and know that I am God."[cdxxxiii] My hope is that we will all learn to take notice of it, *as we are.*

When we believe that who we are is uniquely made, then we can know, without a shadow of a doubt, that each of our days are ordained, and **each moment is sacredly and sacramentally threaded**. For some of us, that thought is thrilling, for others it's too fast to prepare for. My heart for you is to take notice of the "then and there" moments, the "chariots passing by," and to take the risk to jump on them. You'll never be perfect enough. Perfection is just comparison's twin anyway. When I talk about the chariots, I'm referring to the chariot in 2 Kings 2:11 that suddenly took Elijah up to heaven, in the middle of his and Elisha's conversation. Because "divinity was in its plainness." I'm talking about the chariot that was bound to come, but neither knew when to expect its coming or what it would look like. I'm referring to the chariot that is right in front of you. If you're too distracted with the striving of perfection of self, you may just miss the very promise you'd been waiting for. For your days are ordained ahead of you, and as you learn to be still, you will always hear when the chariot is coming near. You don't have to have everything together for God has destined it to pick you up, as you are now, for such a time as this. And who knows, *anything can happen for those who are still long enough to find the wonder within the plain—* for they are the ones who see the ordained coming in the distance and plant their feet to be present when it passes by. Present is always the perfect place to be.

187

HIS GRACE

Our sin is but a cup in His waterfall of grace.
Our lack is but the soil in His field of cultivation.
Every word He speaks is spoken with such love and wrapped in such kindness.
That it's not about the bringing, but *the coming*,
And what becomes is formed by every bit of
His grace.
His grace to give more than what we ask,
To exceed what we imagine,
To multiply beyond what we believe.
It is undeserved, unmerited, unearned favor,
The most unfathomable and generous of gifts.
A deeper revelation of His grace astounds us to the most beautiful humility of reception.
To receive who He is and be received by Him;
To taste and see His complete and utter extravagance of His goodness,
To be captivated within the meadows of His thought-out love.
It is a limitless flame of hope, an overflowing fountain of mercy, a shield of strength.
Sincerely from the Pursuer of your heart,
Marked by the simplicity of
His grace.

But He has said to me, "My grace is sufficient for you [My lovingkindness and My mercy are more than enough—always available— regardless of the situation]; for [My] power is being perfected [and is completed and shows itself most effectively] in [your] weakness." Therefore, I will all the more gladly boast in my weaknesses, so that the power of Christ [may completely enfold me and] may dwell in me.[cdxxxiv]
2 Corinthians 12:9

@bulgerjoseph

188

CLOTHED FOR THE DAYS TO COME

You are not your thoughts; you are His thoughts towards you.

You remember the story in the Bible where David is about to pursue his first BIG opportunity for God to show up in a BIG way? Right before he fights Goliath, King Saul offers David his armor to put on for the battle. But instead of wearing the identity of another man of God, he stepped out with the equipment God had placed in his hands a hundred times. When the enemy approached David, he started mocking his identity saying, "Come here... and I'll give your flesh to the birds and the wild animals."[cdxxxv] (1 Sam 17:44) But then, David didn't listen to the thoughts of the enemy, but to the thoughts of His God, and something **powerful** happened → not only did the enemy fall, but David also experienced a glimpse of the faithfulness of God on his life and the beginning of what the Lord had for him. I believe the crucial parts in this story are: "Who is clothing you?" and "Whose thoughts are defining you?" Proverbs 31:25 reads: "She is clothed with strength and dignity; she can laugh at the days to come."[cdxxxvi] And Ephesians 6 talks about putting on the armor of God "so that you can stand against the devil's schemes."[cdxxxvii] But both stem from this simple premise of drawing near to God. It is there that the King clothes you with His armor. It is there we are equipped.

As men and women of God, the world is always trying to dress us in what they think would look best on us—a life of comfort, a few words of gossip here and there to fit in, stealing and cheating just this once, getting drunk and "high on life" because it's fun. Oh, how satisfying it may taste before you discover its poisonous roots. It's a red apple with the secret of discontent to its bite. You can't just bite once without wanting more—and before you know it, shame will be covered in pride, guilt in a hardened heart, and conviction will be a stranger's voice. Words of truth will feel like condemnation, because truth brings light to what's been hidden in the dark. But conviction isn't your enemy—it reveals to restore. To purify the poison, the brokenness, the numbness, back to life in full. *Conviction taps you on the shoulder to tell you how to draw near to God again*. It is your answered prayer with the recipe to restoration. Drawing near to God is a redemptive story; it's a royal romance.

When you're with God, He clothes you with royal robes and treasured crowns. He'll prepare a banquet for His bride, His church, His chosen—you. And instead of being clothed in pride, envy, jealousy, and insecurity—He dresses you in strength, dignity, righteousness, and humility. He clothes you to claim you as His own. Isaiah 55:9 says, "As the heavens are higher than the earth, so are my ways higher than your ways and my thoughts than your thoughts."[cdxxxviii] His thoughts towards you are unfathomable—so much so, the enemy will do anything in his power to keep you from the fathom of—you. When you walk out clothed as the son or daughter of God, the world may not see your royal robes, but they will see a difference, and that sets the enemy on edge. If he failed at keeping you from realizing whose you are, he will not go easy on trying to make you forget who God says you are. The enemy will talk up a storm of who you're not, creating doubts, lies, and distorted truths. *But doubt cannot exist without truth, and lies merely try to hide truth's certainty*. The undeniable truth is, who you are cannot be distorted, only who you think you are can be distracted. But you are not your thoughts; you are His thoughts towards you. And they are a lot higher than your own. If you weren't a threat, the enemy wouldn't waste his time on you, but because you are, he's restless with rage. But the King of kings is much more *powerful* in His pursuit! He'll never let you forget whose you are and what He sees in you. With Him, you'll always know you belong and that is why you can laugh at the days to come, and today is just your beginning.

189

UNCHANGEABLE

Promises are hard. They lack so much understanding and control, and they require a lot of faith and belief. Not even faith in the promise or belief in its probability, but to have your faith and belief completely in God. That His promise is not your anchor, but He is. But you know what amazes me more? That we can so easily walk away from—a promise. Something that is set in stone. Something that is a vow to us. But we can allow our understanding and our control to lead us away to a place of compromise and complacency. I love how Hebrews 6:15 says, "And so after waiting patiently, Abraham received what was promised."[cdxxxix] Not only is it incredible that he received his promise, but that he also waited… patiently, instead of receiving it right then and there. But this promise was not just any promise, it was one where God swore by Himself, "Since there was no one greater for Him to swear by."[cdxl] And that's just it! Abraham didn't wait on the promise, he waited on <u>God</u> because he knew that God was Sovereign, True, and Almighty. He may have questioned the promise a couple of times according to his understanding, but by patience his loyalty was shown to God. I was on a walk the other day when God spoke to me, "Do you believe in Me?" And my automatic reply was "Yes!" But as I thought about it, I thought about the phrase as a whole. When you believe *in* someone, doesn't that mean that you know they can do it, that you believe in who they are? It's the moment when something BIG is about to happen, and your friend starts to panic, but you grab them by the shoulders and say, "I believe *in* you. You can do this!" That is what God meant when He was asking me the question; it's what He asks each one of us. "Do you believe *in* Me? That I *can do* what I said *will be* done." And like Abraham, will we trust in Him beyond our understanding, sight, and control, and just lay ourselves down at His feet, so we can hold onto His promise(s) for you and for me? Hebrews 6:18 says, "God did this so that by two *unchangeable* things in which it is impossible for God to lie, we who have fled to take hold of the hope offered to us may greatly be encouraged."[cdxli] (emphasis added) His promise is unchangeable, so our faith in Him must be the same.

190

WAITING FOR THE MANSION

> *Be still before the Lord and wait patiently for him;*
> *do not fret when men succeed in their ways, when they carry out their wicked schemes.*[cdxlii]
> Psalm 37:7

The first part states: "Be still before the Lord and wait patiently for him." When we are still before the Lord, I imagine just sitting at God's feet, drawing closer to Him, seeking His will, yet being patient before Him. But we also must not forget that just verses earlier, in Psalm 37:4, it tells us to delight in the Lord. It paints an imagery that as we sit before the Lord's feet in patience, we are also delighting in His presence. We are not just waiting for Him to move or to speak. No! We are falling even more deeply in love with Him as we are patiently waiting for His hand to move in our lives. It's like a daughter before her Father, her King. She is sitting by His feet and dancing around His throne, enjoying time with her Father that always works for her good, as she knows He knows what is best for her. Yet in His wisdom, He is teaching her in the patience of simply being with Him. But then, the next part is even more powerful than you would think: "Do not fret when men succeed in their ways, when they carry out their wicked schemes." Do not grow impatient or worry when others succeed, even in their unrighteousness. People around us will have their lives carry on through promotions, marriage, and amazing miracles that God is doing their lives, but here it says to not fret! We should not grow impatient when we see God moving in their lives, because when we delight in the Lord and wait patiently on Him, He is only *building up* something greater for us to receive.

Imagine our lives as a decorated box-of-desires before God. As we sit before His feet "delighting in Him," He gives us a desire at a time. Like a house! We sit before Him, He builds us a cottage. We sit before Him, He builds us a house. We sit before Him, He increases it to a mansion. We sit before Him, He adds a soulmate into our life. We sit before Him, He places animals and vineyards around our home. We sit before Him, He adds pools, and gardens, and fountains. We sit before Him, He adds beautiful friends, and neighbors, and children into our lives. We sit before Him, He adds prosperity to our patience. We sit before Him, He gives and takes, but always works for our good.

If we would have been impatient, we may have ended up living with a cottage! But as we learn to be still and trust in His timing, He builds up our desires into a dream beyond what we could ever imagine or even grasp. And so, in Kaytee's paraphrase, Psalm 37:7 goes a little like this: *Be patient; delight in the Lord, and wait at His feet. He is building your desires into a reality, and He is holding your heart in His perfect love. When life carries on, do not grow impatient; do not worry about when your life will go on again, for God delights in your delights more than you know, and is working for your good beyond the limits of your imagination.*

191

WITHOUT CEASING

We tend to say, "Live like there's no tomorrow," and so we give every day our best to make it the greatest day of our lives! But what if we started to say, "**Pray like there's no tomorrow**," so that we would stop pushing off our relationship with God and give *Him* our best every day to use for His glory. Honestly, between the two options, the first one doesn't compare. For He is the best and that makes any and every day wonderful.

Pray without ceasing.[cdxliii]
1 Thessalonians 5:17

I am believing for breakthrough in: _____

I am praying for the salvation of: _____

I am asking God to help me with: _____

I am interceding for: _____

A miracle I am boldly believing for is: _____

A God-sized dream I'm praying over is: _____

A nation that I will stand in the gap for is: _____

A close friend who needs my prayers is: _____

An extravagant prayer of mine is: _____

A small prayer of mine is: _____

A desperate prayer of mine is: _____

Prayers God has answered this week: _____

192

WITH EVERYTHING

I'm starting to wonder where I got the idea that the calling of God on our lives was supposed to be easy and convenient, because usually, it's not. It can be dangerous, a bit of a high-risk, and often at an inconvenient time. It's not usually in the beginning choice or the end of a journey, but in the middle where you finally got used to the flow. And to others, it is absolutely crazy. But I guess that is why we say we are crazy for Jesus. When one man runs up to Jesus and says, "I will follow You wherever You go." Jesus replies in Luke 9:58, "Foxes have holes and birds of the air have nests, but the Son of man has no place to lay his head."[cdxliv] In other words, He is saying, "If you want to follow Me wherever I go, be willing to give up whatever you have." The next man wasn't to go to his father's funeral, and the man after wasn't to say goodbye to the people who raised him from birth. I thought that our calling was supposed to be easy, but the cost of following Jesus may come with great sacrifice. It may be out of your comfort zone, or it may be right in the middle of it. We are always more ready to hear the word "go," but never quite ready for the phrase that follows in Luke 10:3, "I am sending you out like lambs among wolves."[cdxlv] Not only that, but He goes on to say, "Do not take a purse, or bag, or sandals." He commands them to leave everything behind and to take nothing with them, and to go with the risk of losing their lives. Easy? No. Convenient? Not at all. Comforting? Not so much. As David Platt puts it, "Ultimately, Jesus was calling them to abandon themselves."[cdxlvi] To abandon their plans, their dreams, their safety nets, their hideaways, their comfort, their everything. The cost is high but the worth is eternal. It makes me rethink the phrase, "With everything." Do we really mean it? Or are we really leaving a few words out? Saying, "With everything that's comfortable." "With everything that's convenient." "With everything that is safe." Instead of saying, "With everything, I will follow

@sarahbgraves

You." But the thing is, we are not really giving up anything at all, because we are gaining so much more. The point of this message is to take the focus off of "us" and put it back on "Him." Our calling is listening to what He is calling out every day, "Follow Me." It's allowing His presence to come into our comforts, go before our discomfort, and lead us beyond what we know. It's listening to what we don't want to hear and obeying whatever He may say to do. It is going forward knowing your steps may be shaky, but the path is firm. It may be beyond you, but it's also for you—and it is also for those around you. It's hearing Him say, "Follow Me," and replying every time, "With everything."

193

RESCUE YOUR WARRIOR

> *She has been feeling it for a while now—that sense of awakening. There is a gentle rage simmering inside her, and it is getting stronger by the day. She will hold it close to her—she will nurture it and let it grow. She won't let anyone take it away from her. It is her rocket fuel and finally, she is going places. She can feel it down to her very core—this is her time. She will not only climb mountains—she will move them too.*[cdxlvii]
>
> - Her Time, Lang Leav

When we sense the love of God's heart, we sense the destiny in our hearts. Yet, *destiny* can sound like such a big word. As if all was destined to happen without a choice or say in the matter. Even though royalty flows through your veins, you choose who you become and the life you live. Think: *The Prince and Me, A Royal Christmas*, or… *Princess Diaries*. They all come back to their royal duties, yet they choose the paths they take. In *Princess Diaries 2*, Princess Mia is preparing to become Queen of Genovia.[cdxlviii] While awaiting her ceremony to be deemed queen, the Parliament discovers she cannot do so unless married, thus she must marry within thirty days. To have the courage to become queen over a country is one thing, to have the courage to open your heart, fall in love, and marry within thirty days, is another whole level of bravery. Yet, *the choice* lay in her hands, even the Queen lovingly told her granddaughter, she could pass on the royal throne. So destiny therefore will happen one way or another, but *the way* we choose is *who* we become.

Princess Mia started to walk the way of the people, yet on her journey, turned into a warrior who took the stance to become queen alone. Her words state: "I believe I will be a great queen. I understand Genovia to be a land that combines the beauty of the past with all the best hope of the future. I feel in my heart and soul that I can rule Genovia. I… I love Genovia. Do you think that I would be up here in a wedding dress if I didn't? I stand here ready to take my place as your queen. Without a husband."[cdxlix] And so she wins the people, the Parliament, and even the man she loves over. Yet, she did so by listening to her awakening, by rescuing her warrior, and by defying what's always been done for what she knew could be done.

In chasing after what God speaks, we must learn the grit and grace of being royal. Grace is freely given, unmerited favor and mercy, moral strength, and a disposition of generosity and kindness, even when you need not do so. Grit is defined as firmness of character, indomitable spirit, and unyielding courage in the face of hardship. It is both together that defy the enemies against you in your future. As a child of God, royalty simmers through your veins, and it is a sense of an awakening to your spirit, crowned not by blood, but rather choice. A queen or king's decisions involve the beauty of the past with the best hope of the future for their kingdom. They do so based off of their love for the land, for the people. As heirs in the Kingdom of God, where many queens and kings reign, walking out their calling, and paving ways for others to walk, we must do the same. It is our choice and duty to do so.

As David prays in Psalm 108: "Give us a Father's help when we face our enemies. For to trust in any man is an empty hope. With God's help we will prevail with might and power. And with God's help we'll trample down our every foe!"[cdl] It pleases God's heart to hear kings and queens stepping into their authority on earth, the authority that His Son spoke of that can bind or loosen anything in heaven that is bound or loosened on earth. Yet, it takes rescuing your warrior to make a difference. It is not backing down but standing up for righteousness. It's not turning from good and doing evil, but turning from evil and doing good. As you go after what God has placed in your heart, may you do so with the heart of a king or queen, and the bravery of a warrior. Listen to the awakening and place steps to its journey. It will lead to the destiny in your heart, the destiny created by His love for you to live.

194

RAISE YOUR FLAG

Raise your flag, raise your banner proudly, raise it for all the world to see. For this is your march of victory, these are your steps of triumph. Is there anything too hard for Me? Is there anything I can't do? You've made it to the heights, overlooking the city, sing out in praise! Don't be afraid, you're here! You've been waiting for this. All is prepared for you; see the structure I have designed. Take in the details, take in its colors, it is all for you, it is all by Me. It is for My glory, My glory, that you've walked through fire, that you may represent Me well, and how you shall. "You're ready for Zion," the voice of the bride and bridegroom sing! Have no question; hold onto every belief. This is real. This is true. Take and receive of all the goodness I've placed before you. Raise your banner high, proud for all the world to see.

"Walk out of the gates. Get going! Get the road ready for the people. Build the highway. Get at it! Clear the debris, hoist high a flag, a signal to all peoples! Yes! God has broadcast to all the world: 'Tell daughter Zion, 'Look! Your Savior comes, Ready to do what he said he'd do, prepared to complete what he promised.' Zion will be called new names: Holy People, God-Redeemed, Sought-Out, City-Not-Forsaken."[cdli]
Isaiah 62:10-12

195

TRUE

True: the word hits a few strings in my heart, because what is true is *real*. It is fact and not fiction, a reality and not an imagination. So to be true to who you are, for your promises to be true, for His words to be true, you have to hold a lot of acceptance along with truth. The Bible tells us to meditate on such things, for the longer we linger on truth, the more we accept what is true to be fact. There's a scene in *The Hunger Games* where Peeta can't remember what is true anymore because he had been poisoned. He asks the one person he trusts, Katniss, what is real, and he has to accept it until he can remember his reality. The one question that hits home every time is when Peeta asks, "You love me. Real or not real?"[cdlii] Katniss replies real, and they kiss, and it's all heartbreakingly cute and all, but I just wonder how many of us need to ask God the same question. "You love me… real or not real?" Somehow in the daily discipline of reading your Word, truth starts to cut away some vines wrapped around your heart. Somehow in worshipping God, we see truth in the moment as heaven and earth collide. Somehow as a sermon is given, your heart feels a little lighter like lies have been unloaded at the cross and finished. But even if this all happened daily, it's still not our every hour. This means lies and poison will always try to come back and take root, whether we like it or not.

During the summer I spent lifeguarding, I worked twelve-hour days. Yet, I cherished their silence. In the stillness, I meditated on His words, promises, and character, and so my certainty of what was *true* grew. My doubts shrunk, insecurities faded, and discernment expanded. But as the summer ended, and my social life resumed, my meditation time lessened. Can you guess what happened? I was under attack, but it took me three weeks of battling to figure out why. During those weeks, I felt weary, exhausted, drained, and defeated. It was a different kind of silence with emotional waves smashing against my soul. One day, it hit me: I hadn't prayed, like really prayed, in forever. I was listening to Jesus, seeking him, worshipping him, and reading His Word, but my praying in the Spirit had come to a drastic stop. The enemy was beyond ready to pounce when that moment came. So it makes sense that he sent two months worth of attacks on me in those weeks. But here's what I discovered: **Those with great faith have learned to wait; those with great prophecies have learned to listen; those with great discernment have learned to pray, and those with great love have learned to trust.**

Discernment of what is or isn't real comes only through prayer. When you pray and see—your expectancy grows and your certainty strengthens. When you don't pray, you don't know because you don't ask. Some of us have a list of things we need to ask God about in prayer: "You love me… real or not real?" "This promise will come to pass… true or not true." "I am enough… fact or fiction?" Those are generic, but I know that there are deep and delicate details attached to each of those questions that are actually core to the certainty of your reality. You need to accept what is true and choose to meditate on this as daily as you breathe. For then, your assurance will deepen and your discernment will heighten of what is real. Psalm 119:15-16 says: "I will meditate on your precepts and [thoughtfully] regard your ways. [The path of life established by your precepts.] I will delight in your statutes; I will not forget your word."[cdliii] Once you believe in what is true that God has spoken, you will begin to see it come to life all around you like magic! Because here's the crazy thing, you expect to see it, and thus you are actually on lookout waiting for it to happen. That's why in Psalm 31:24 it says, "Be strong and let your heart take courage, all you who wait for *and* hope for *and* expect the Lord."[cdliv] For they're waiting on a God who is real to do something that's so real to their hearts. So let your heart take courage for God is all around you; He is true, His Word is true, and He will remain true to His Word. Start with knowing and accepting that *He loves you*—that is an *unquestionable* fact, 100% **real**, and oh so <u>true.</u>

196
THE MIST

When I hear the rules, the guidelines, of who I should be and what I should do, what step to take or how to improve, I just close my eyes and see *Him*.
I'm walking to Him on still waters.
As I bend down to my knees in humility, He kneels down to my heart *in grace*.
My breath is the only noise, my heart the only movement, as I am overcome in love.
There are no words, but I need none.
Because He is <u>here</u>, I hear everything.
A peace so undeniably sweet, a beauty's embrace that's never been met,
A thirst like a canyon flooded with love.
It's just us.
I am, because He is. I move as He moves. I stay where He stays.
I'm close but not afraid to let go,
for I know He returns.
He doesn't leave.
The waves don't affect me, though they are startled by our movement.
I am strong again in Him.
The mist is but a sign that we're together—dancing as one.

"For the mountains may move and the hills disappear, but even then my faithful love for you will remain. My covenant of blessing will never be broken," says the LORD, who has mercy on you.[cdlv]
Isaiah 54:10

197

ALL OR NOTHING

> *You get in life what you have the courage to ask for.*[cdlvi]
> - Oprah Winfrey

Courage: It's a word given to almost every single leader in the Bible, and vital to every single one of their destinies. And yet I have wondered, time and time again, what truly is courage? Is courage standing up for what's right? Is it dying to one's self for another to live? Is it facing your fears? Maybe it's a little bit of all those things wrapped and bowed with listening to your heart; I think that may be the most courageous thing any of us can do when it comes to courage. It's not so much of a formula, but an openness. Courage can be listening to your heart and where it is guiding, because you know God has entrusted it with His words. *In a war, we move in spite of whether we have courage or not. In a desert, we can only listen to our courage.* Courage trusts in who you are and your capacity when you hear the voice of one crying out in that desert. Like the lion in the Wizard of Oz who went searching for courage, not realizing the power he held as the king of the jungle, we can so easily doubt the immense power of our roar. **If we can't hear our heart, we can't hear our courage—** and to be courageous is the very command we are given to live in freedom. We may never feel free until we begin to trust the heart God has created within us that is so dearly loved by His. The heart that in His presence is liberated from fear. The heart that in His presence is made white as snow. The heart that in His presence is unshaken by doubts. The heart that has a voice. Sometimes our voice speaks opposite of our feelings, and if we shut it out for too long, we forget its roar.

The thing about listening to doubt, or the wrong thing, or pride, is that it quiets the truth in our hearts. When we begin to doubt God's voice for us, we begin to doubt it for others. When we do the wrong thing once, we are temped to do it again. When we let pride be our authority, we forget the authority of His Word. It's an all or nothing thing—and it begins with courage and is kept by courage to the end. In Ezra, the Israelites married their neighboring peoples, which was a betrayal to God. And so they come to this place of desperation in Ezra 10:2-3,

We betrayed our God by marrying foreign wives from the people around here. But all is not lost; there is still hope for Israel. Let's make a covenant right now with our God, agreeing to get rid of all these wives and their children, just as my master and those who honor God's commandment are saying. It's what The Revelation says, so let's do it.[cdlvii]

In the NIV, verse 4 goes on to say: "Rise up; this matter is in your hands. We will support you, so take courage and do it."[cdlviii] And the beautiful thing is, they did separate from their wives to get right with God again. Likewise, all is not lost in your war or your desert, you must only have the courage to listen to your heart and trust it again. God speaks to your heart that you may ask for what He places inside of it. There may be protective boundaries in place to keep your heart safe, but He loves your heart, you should too. Rise up against the doubts. Rise up to do what's good. Rise up to live in humility. Take courage and ask for what's in your heart. It's never too late to start trusting that the God who created your heart is continually speaking hopes and dreams into it for a reason. As you ask for what He speaks, you'll find your roar and authority again. It was never lost, only shushed out. May you open your heart time and time again—for when it comes to courage, it is all or nothing.

198

GO ABROAD—DREAM BIGGER

The settled will never discover their limits
The compromised shall never see their wings
The careful will never know their courage
Nor the fearful ever claim their dreams
To go abroad is to take a step—the rest may be their flight Yet the greatest war we may face, shan't involve a fight
It is a great leap that we may see, so great some never begin But a small movement may just be the greatest weapon to win To one the world is deemed safe, to another a globe contained Some say the sky is their limit; others see galaxies as their plains
May we dare to wonder again to dream bigger than ever before And maybe we will wander to a great wide-open door
Take a risk to open what cannot be seen, and destiny may await For the brave may not live forever, but their now is surely great

The lovers of God who chase after righteousness will find all their dreams come true: an abundant life drenched with favor and a fountain that overflows with satisfaction.[cdlix]
Proverbs 21:21

199

SEEKING PEACE IN TROUBLED TIMES

If I was in an atrium of thousands of people right now and asked, "If any of you are troubled in some way, raise your hand." I'm sure every hand would shoot up. We all have times of trouble in different ways, but they are all just as challenging and growing. The importance of troubled times in specific seasons is to trust God with everything. In other words, "Don't go until God says go." In the midst of trouble, we are faced with fear of running to a safe home instead of our refuge. But if we truly sought God with all of our hearts, I believe that all of our situations wouldn't seem so impossible. The closer you are to God, the more you will see what you've never noticed before. You see, God will do extraordinary things for you, but you've got to give the ordinary things to Him. We tend to say, "I give it all to you," with clutched hands as our offering. But God doesn't want to pry anything from your hands; He wants you to lay it at His feet. John 14:27 says, "Peace I leave with you; my peace I give you. I do not give to you as the world gives. Do not let your hearts be troubled and do not be afraid."[cdlx] So seek His heart and find peace; let go of the ordinary to discover the extraordinary, and don't go until God says go. Trust Him with everything for He is forever faithful.

> *I have told you these things, so that in me you may have peace.*
> *In this world you will have trouble. But take heart! I have overcome the world.*[cdlxi]
> John 16:33

200

FALL AS HEROES; STAND AS WARRIORS

> *We are in constant battle, and grace is just as much our*
> *haven of rest as it is our resolve to fight.*
> *Grace cheers for you, roots for you, and receives you again and again, with a*
> *direction and momentum that says, you're better than this. Grace will confront*
> *the sin like a surgeon's tool and work through it to the messy end.*
> *Grace does not excuse or absolve sin, but acknowledges the reality of our great desperate*
> *need as sinners. It's not merely comfort, but healing. Grace is a cross, a substitution, an*
> *atonement, a victory over the grave—a handful of gritty truths wrapped in flesh that breathed*
> *the air and dirt of this earth. It's a beautiful, wonderful, furious, unchanging, heart-*
> *stopping love that cannot be shaken no matter what. Jesus: he is our rest, our fight.*[cdlxii]
> - J. S. Park

When the enemy attacks, every thought and feeling that isn't from God comes at you like a wave.

At a point, you may have not been a threat. Yet, when something powerful is on the horizon, he sends every effort your way to contain the release of God's miracle on your life. Yet how beautiful grace is. When you hear the war coming or feel its pressure closing in, grace whispers, "Fall." It's a fall that doesn't give up, but gives God everything. In this fall, you don't protect yourself. Instead, you let your walls down to let grace in. Like a bungie line that you trust will catch you when you let go, grace is wrapped around your heart's deepest desires saying *it's okay* because God has you. In the trust fall, be encouraged with Paul's words in 1 Corinthians 16: "Keep your eyes open, hold tight to your convictions, give it all you've got, be resolute, and love without stopping... Our Master Jesus has his arms wide open for you."[cdlxiii]

In the embrace of Christ, you'll see that <u>feelings aren't fact, but they're also not fictional.</u> They're not a book you can close when you don't like what they're saying, for they do hold truth within their stories. As you discover why each feeling was shaped, you discover **a hero** waiting to be released. Sometimes *you* are the main character in the story overlooked the most, because it's easier to focus on everyone else's stories. The hero part of your story comes when you realize the thoughts behind your feelings; they are *real* characters that just need to be loved and befriended. When you see your thoughts not as enemies but misled truths, you see the beauty of grace's strength. As 2 Corinthians 10:5 encourages us, take captive those thoughts.

Falling = facing your feelings and discovering the hero underneath

Secondly, don't hide in the strength of your own armor rather than dressing daily in the armor of God. It may be more comfortable for a season, but it's also not the finest quality and won't last forever. The armor of God may have a glorious weight to it, but it is made to protect and preserve. That's why Psalm 91:4 says: "His faithful promises are your armor and protection."[cdlxiv] *It is not the divine we need to guard ourselves from, but the destructive.* When you wholeheartedly believe a promise, a battle will be waiting, but in that battle, you are unshakable with knowing God is fighting for you. It's then that you must guard your heart most from doubts that can lead down destructive paths; it's then that you must stay and not flee, anchoring your spirit in the truth that

He will prove faithful to His Word. That's when you see the glimpse of the warrior He says you are, and you learn to stand tall in a war, and that may be the bravest act of all.

Standing = being anchored in His promises as your armor

So trust God, be brave, and take heart. Be reminded that YOU are a hero. You're not Jesus, but you are a hero. He will rescue you. He will remind you of who He knows you are. There's a hero inside waiting to be uncovered. ***Fall, as a hero, and stand as a warrior, by grace's embrace.***

201

ATTRACTED TO THE DISTRACTIONS

If then you have been raised with Christ, seek the things that are above, where Christ is, seated at the right hand of God. Set your minds on things that are above, not on things that are on earth.[cdlxv]
Colossians 3:1-2

We, as humans, can often be attracted to the distractions that come with time. We trust more in man's knowledge rather than in God's knowledge, and believe in manmade promises of the now, rather than in the stored up eternal promises of God. When we have a heart that speaks quite loudly, it's easy to hear the desires of our flesh. But when we learn to still our thoughts, we begin to hear His heartbeat and His desires for us. It becomes less about focusing on the steps and more about trusting in His vision. So in the moments where our minds run wild with imagination, make sure they are being set apart for Christ, for our hearts and minds are to be set on higher things, because God has greater treasures in store for us. Step away from the attractions of this world so that you can get rid of the distractions of complacency and step into the promises of God. Trust in His vision by setting your eyes, heart, and mind on Him, and again remember the last word He gave. As a wise man once told me: "Don't give up what you want most for what you want now." And so I say to you: *Do not give up, oh warrior, do not give in; fight for what He's spoken to your heart, and don't ever let it go.*

202

MORE OF YOU

God, I open up my heart to you. Every fabric pulled off, every mask uncovered. You see my deepest desires; Your grace hovers over them. You see my longing for delights; Your love is written all over them. You see my hunger for peace; and You find a way to sweep me off of my feet. I see Your designs and I see Your orchestration—it gives me glimpses of You. How I wait with expectancy at the foot of Your throne for You to move again. I want more, I desire more, and mainly, it's me seeking for more of You. I want to know every color, every hue and shade, every breathtaking reflection of light. I want to know You deeper. I give You my longings, I give You my moments, I give You my heart. Come and move. Come and do what you want to. I trust You, in simplicity and expectancy. Be extravagant. Be divine in all You touch. For I will know it's You. For I will know You a bit more every time. Meet me where I am. I've gone as far as I can alone. It seems there are more steps for me to take. My eyes are fixed on You, my life dependent upon You. Do the unimaginable, be my King who is wild for me.
Amen.

Yet I still belong to you; you hold my right hand. You guide me with your counsel, leading me to a glorious destiny. Whom have I in heaven but you? I desire you more than anything on earth. My health may fail, and my spirit may grow weak, but God remains the strength of my heart; he is mine forever. Those who desert him will perish, for you destroy those who abandon you. But as for me, how good it is to be near God! I have made the Sovereign Lord my shelter, and I will tell everyone about the wonderful things you do.
Psalm 73:23-28, NLT

203

BEYOND YOU

There's a phrase I hear quite often that goes a little like this: "It's not about you." In all honesty, it bothers me. Why? Because I'm constantly clinging to, "God is for you." But to know He is for you, but it's not about you, is hard to grasp. Like do we pursue what's in our heart or do we just submit before His heart continually? Or maybe that's just it, it involves both. In the confusion, we are required to listen. In listening, we learn. In listening, we are led. In listening, we are loved. It's not an earned love, but a sacred love that loves on us. But it's still not about us, and yet He is still for us.

I don't know if you've ever created any lists of what you'd like your life to turn out like, but I have four. Not one, two, or even three, *four* whole lists of vision for my future. Last night God spoke to me, "You don't even understand." As in, we can't even begin to comprehend how He "wraps up the waters in the clouds" or "marks out the horizon on the face of the waters." As Job 26:14 states, "And these are but the outer fringe of his works; how faint the whisper we hear of him! Who then can understand the thunder of his power?"[cdlxvi] His promises are a *faint* whisper, a drop of rain in the ocean, a grain of sand on a shore, a star to a constellation. We have no idea. *But still it's not about us, and yet, He still is for us.*

Here's the thing, just because one is chosen, doesn't mean they specifically get to choose how their destiny unfolds. Being chosen is by the grace of God and it plays out by the grace of God. As Job 42:1-3 says: "Then Job replied to the Lord: 'I know that you can do *all* things; no plan of yours can be thwarted. You asked, 'Who is this that obscures my counsel without knowledge?' Surely I spoke of things I did not understand, things too wonderful for me to know.'"[cdlxvii] (emphasis added) In the MSG it says: "I'm **convinced** you can do anything and everything. Nothing and no one can upset your plans. You asked, 'Who is this muddying the water, ignorantly confusing the issue, second-guessing my purposes?' I admit it. I was the one. I babbled on about things *far beyond* {me}, made small talk about **wonders** way over my head.'"[cdlxviii] (emphasis added)

Do I think creating lists is a bad thing? No, I think it's a great thing to have vision. But let us not detail out our destiny. That's way above our head. It's beyond us, it's beyond what we can fathom, and it's beyond "about us." It's true. God cares for our cares, but He also cares about the cries of the lost and broken who are desperate for a Savior. Did you know, your dream *may* just be their answered prayer? Did you know you were chosen not because God needed you, but because He knew your heart's desires would bring someone else to know Him? Did you know, when He whispered a promise to your heart, He whispered "I'm coming" to the nations? When God speaks to you, it is to you and for you, but it's also beyond you and what you can grasp.

The moment we realize we are chosen is the moment we realize we are destined. David knew he was chosen to be king when he was young. And twenty years later, it came to pass. But I believe he realized it was *beyond* him. What a small kingdom he would have led if he limited God to only letting the faint whisper be for himself. Instead, David didn't focus on becoming king, he focused on *the coming King*. He realized he was destined for greatness, but as God appointed him to lead, He would also appoint his steps to be led. The way David honored God and submitted to God is the perfect response to a faint whisper. {He allowed the war around him to make a warrior within him. He kept God on the throne and kept himself in humility. He didn't despise small beginnings, but was faithful with the small. And **he had the heart of a servant with the destiny of a**

***king**.} Trying to understand God's plan is like trying to understand God. There are things we just need to accept we don't need to know now, for He will go far beyond our detailed dreams when we trust Him enough to not understand what He's doing. It's not about us, it's beyond us, but He is for us, and He's before all the details. Therefore we can laugh without fear of the future, for we know He is doing wonders *way* over our head.

204

BOTH

Is it silent or hidden?
A secret or a surprise?
Is it burning up or burning out?
Inviting or dangerous?
Is it broken or incomplete?
Muted or speechless?
Is it half-full or half-empty?
Blind or blindfolded?
Is it safe or feared?
A precaution or a containment?
Is it content or settled?
Anchored or stuck?
Is it God or wild?
A dream or a destiny?

Maybe… it's a bit of both;
And it's okay to not know the answer.

But whether silent or hidden, he's there, ruling.[cdlxix]
Job 34:29

205

CALM

Patience is persistent courage, but it is also a soothing peace. It's unsolvable, but unquestionable. A mystery to the human mind, a certainty to the human heart. The bravest people I know are the most patient of all; they know what they are promised and they stand through battles, storms, and deserts, watching and waiting for its coming. They are warriors that do not give up, for even if they are desperate to quit, patience encourages them to move forward, and they can't shake the deep convictions of what they know to be true ahead.

Israel, a chosen people who have been through much, may have fallen time after time, yet patience was instilled in every one of their hearts. My heart goes out to them for they are us. We see their struggle to do what is good, their forgetfulness to put God first, their slips and falls of being human. They've faced battles, storms, and deserts, heroes were gained and warriors lost, and yet God keeps chasing them down knowing where they're heading—knowing the best in mind He has for them. In Zephaniah 3:16-20, God speaks to their faint hearts:

Jerusalem will be told: "Don't be afraid. Dear Zion, don't despair. Your God is present among you, a strong Warrior there to save you. Happy to have you back, he'll calm you with his love and delight you with his songs. The accumulated sorrows of your exile will dissipate. I, your God, will get rid of them for you. You've carried those burdens long enough. At the same time, I'll get rid of all those who've made your life miserable. I'll heal the maimed; I'll bring home the homeless. In the very countries where they were hated they will be venerated. On Judgment Day I'll bring you back home—a great family gathering! You'll be famous and honored all over the world. You'll see it with your own eyes—all those painful partings turned into reunions!" God's Promise.[cdlxx]

I believe that like Israel, God is bringing us back to a place of calm. *His calming love is patience's reward, and His melodies sing over its lands.*

Patience in one way is defined as: calmness that does not make sense. This calm comes before storms, during storms, and after storms; it drives us for it lives in us; it's our promised portion at all times. As humans are human, life is life. Humans are imperfect, and life is not always easy. Disease and sickness, sorrow and grief, evil and cruelness, still exist in our fallen world. But there is a strong Warrior alive who heals, who saves, who loves, and He fights for you; He chases you down to calm your heart's greatest fears to bring victory to your heart's greatest dreams. Whether the storm is coming, is here, or has passed, do good, put God first, and be grace always. He will always bring you back home; you will see with your eyes what you have patiently hoped for in your heart. You will know Him as a promise keeper and not just a promise giver. You will know joy, hope, laughter, life, and love again. You will remain a warrior, stand as a hero, and live royally in the land of your inheritance. Keep being patient, breathe in His calming love, and hold onto hope, God's promise is His promise. It is not empty; it will not return void. You can keep calm for He is good.

206

WAITING FOR THE WHISPER

The Lord said, "Go out and stand on the mountain in the presence of the Lord, for the Lord is about to pass by." Then a great and powerful wind tore the mountains apart and shattered the rocks before the Lord, but the Lord was not in the wind. After the wind there was an earthquake, but the Lord was not in the earthquake. After the earthquake came a fire, but the Lord was not in the fire. And after the fire came a gentle whisper. When Elijah heard it, he pulled his cloak over his face and went out and stood at the mouth of the cave.[cdlxxi]
1 Kings 19:11-13

There is such a beauty in patience that this world tends to oversee because we often look for great things around us rather than loving the simple things. Although our God is almighty and powerful, He loves to speak in soft and simple ways so that we can praise Him for who He is over what He does. It is in those small, simple things that we are reminded of Him, but sometimes we just have to wait for them. There are times when people around you will have awesome things that God is doing in their lives, yet then in contrast, it seems like in your life, you are just waiting. But that is a beautiful thing, because if you aren't out doing "great things *for* God" that means you have time to spend alone *with* the greatest God of all. Instead of waiting for the great to happen for you, wait for "The Great" to come to you. Wait for His whisper instead of running into the storm.

207

MORNING'S DELIGHT

Do you know how treasured you are in My eyes?
How precious you are, My dear.
That your heart is a jewel in My sight,
Created in beauty with precision and fear.
I am with you when the waters rise, and I am with you in the flames.
You will not be burned, My love will keep you safe.
I hold you in the valleys, and sustain you in the heights.
There is no place, too far or dark,
Where I will leave your side.
My passion for you has no end; it's beyond what words can say.
No boundaries are great enough to keep its love refrained.
Your every word, I hear, your every detail, I see,
And I guide them with My love, towards destiny.
Seek My word, seek My heart, and you will find My delight,
As I awaken you, My greatest love, with every morning's light.

"But as for me, I will sing about your power.
Each morning I will sing with joy about your unfailing love.
For you have been my refuge,
a place of safety when I am in distress."[cdlxxii]
Psalm 59:16

208

VICTORY IN THE VALLEYS

Proverbs 3:5 begins with "Trust in the Lord with all your heart,"[cdlxxiii] which helps us to see that *all* of your heart even includes the doubts and fears. I love the way the Message phrases it, "Trust God from the bottom of your heart; don't try to figure out everything on your own. Listen for God's voice in everything you do, everywhere you go; he's the one who will keep you on track."[cdlxxiv] The first thing I want to point out is that trusting God is from *the bottom* of your heart. We can assume the bottom to be "with all," but we can also see it as "even in the valleys" of your heart. A valley isn't always below the surface of the earth, but a flat land between mountains. It may not be that low, it just may be that the mountains you are walking in between are overwhelming and overbearing. But that is where the next verse comes in, "Don't try to figure everything out on your own. Listen for God's voice in everything you do, everywhere you go." We are reminded to not focus on how *high* the mountains are, but how **great** our God is. We can trust in Him, because *He* is all-knowing. Genesis 15:5 says, "Look up at the heavens and count the stars—if indeed you can count them."[cdlxxv] I don't know if you've ever tried to actually do this, but it's humanly *impossible*. I think this is entirely what God is trying to prove. We need Him because He is God, and we are only human; He is all-knowing, and we know nothing in comparison. As 1 Corinthians 1:25 says, "For the foolishness of God is wiser than man's wisdom, and the weakness of God is stronger than man's strength."[cdlxxvi] God is trying to show us to trust in Him always because He is our greatest reality. All that seems impossible to us is possible with Him. All of our greatest fears and doubts

are nothing before His greatness. As long as we are focused on Him, we have nothing to fear. Hannah says it this way in 1 Samuel 2, "There is no one holy like the Lord; there is no one besides you; there is no Rock like our God. ...It is not by strength that one prevails; those who oppose the Lord will be shattered."[cdlxxvii] If we are for God, then we have everything. For as His everything, He trusts in us. He trusts us because He knows that He can do it through us, and that is why we will have victory in the valleys, because we have Him. As it says in 2 Corinthians 2:14, "In the Messiah, in Christ, God leads us from place to place in one perpetual victory parade. Through us He brings knowledge of Christ. Everywhere we go, people breathe in the exquisite fragrance."[cdlxxviii] In other words, "God leads from straight paths to forests with no boundaries, from shallow tides to deep waters, and from mountains to valleys, to make known His greatness. We walk in victory together as a body of Christ, never alone, allowing God to speak through one life to many. And as God breathes life into one warrior, He breathes life into countless legions, and that creates a fragrance of hope everywhere."

209

DEEP WATERS

Most of the time when I think about the water, I think about the surface. I think about the sun reflecting off of the waves, the foam splashing against the shore, and the birds soaring over its blue abyss. But what I often don't think about is what is underneath those blue waves, and what life lies within its deepest parts. Here are some interesting facts I found about water and all its mystery: One, about 70% of the planet is ocean. Two, the deep sea is the largest Museum on Earth: There are more artifacts and remnants of history in the ocean than in all of the world's museums combined.[cdlxxix] Three, we have only explored 5% of the Earth's oceans. In fact, we have better maps of Mars than we do of the ocean floor. Fourth, the longest mountain range in the world is under water, called the Mid-Oceanic Ridge, running more than 35,000 miles long. Five, many of the rules that apply on land are turned upside down in the ocean, some literally. Beneath the surface are waterfalls and even upside-down lakes.[cdlxxx] Six, it is estimated that there are as little as 2 million to as many as 50 million more species that have not yet been found and/or have been incorrectly classified. Seven, the deepest part of the ocean is the Mariana Trench, which is 36,070 feet deep.

There's so much more than what meets the eye. To think that scientists have only been able to name 1.5 million of the 50 million species in the ocean blows my mind. To know that the longest mountain range cannot be seen. To wonder what an underwater waterfall would even look like. And yet we see in Proverbs 20:5 that it says, "The purposes of a man's heart are deep waters, but a man of understanding draws them out."[cdlxxxi] The very reason why *we* have been created, shaped, and designed, is as mysterious and awesome as the 2/3 of the ocean that is unknown. Whether those numbers were correct or slightly off, there's really no way to tell, because beneath the waters is so vast and deep. But God knows every one by name. Yet our life is so much the same. I like to think of a man's purpose in God's plan like an iceberg in the ocean. There's the top of the iceberg which is above the surface and many people can see. But there's also part of the iceberg that is beneath the deep waters, which is what God sees and knows. It's the part of us He has already designed, but we can't see, so we can so easily give up and become discouraged in His plans for us. But the scripture doesn't stop at, "The purposes of a man's heart are deep waters," leaving us hopeless; but it goes on to say, "But a man of understanding draws them out," meaning as we adventure, explore, and live, we discover these purposes underneath the surface that we never knew anything about.

Did you know that actually 90% of an iceberg sits under water? And personally, I believe that the part that is underneath the water is even more beautiful and unique than what we see on the surface. And I want you to think of our hearts like the iceberg. First, there is no perfect "iceberg." I'm not even sure that's sensible. But each iceberg is as stunning and breathtaking underneath the surface that no one usually sees. And like our lives, there is no perfect "step" to take or perfect way to find out these purposes. Simply living and seeking God through all seasons will lead us to discover more than we could imagine. Second, know that, "The Spirit searches all things, even the deep things of God."[cdlxxxii] (1 Corinthians 2:10) The deepest parts of your heart are sought out and known, they are shaped and designed, beautiful and unique. Do you see how astounding this is? There is so much more beauty to our hearts than we even know, and God knows each one of them inside–and-out. Your purpose is not hidden from God; it's created by Him. So when He tells you to take a step in faith, remember it doesn't have to be taken perfectly, because He knows what you can't even see. And as you draw closer to God, you too will begin to see the many gifts, the greatest strengths, and the most powerful passions within the deepest seas of your own heart. *How indescribable it will be for you to see what He already knows exists within the depths of your great unknown.* How much more beauty there is to find.

210

THE UNKNOWN

> *By an act of faith, Abraham said yes to God's call to travel to an **unknown** place that would become his **home**. When he left he had no idea where he was going. By an act of faith he lived in the country promised him, lived as a stranger camping in tents. Isaac and Jacob did the same, living under the same promise. Abraham did it by keeping his eye on an unseen city with real, eternal foundations—the City designed and built by God.*[cdlxxxiii]
> Hebrews 11:8-10 (emphasis added)

The moments in which we are the bravest will most likely be unseen, even unspoken, when it comes to the unknown. I've discovered the unknown can shut me down: to drain my heart, to fight for my attention, to awaken my fears. Yet, belief is brave. It's a defying act, a conquering weapon, an adventurous pursuit. Belief will chase peace and all its mystery. It always works out somehow for those who possess it. Their hearts are full of love, their attention fixed on Christ, their wonder awakened. Despite reality's reasoning to run, they stand on the Words their Father spoke and throw every stone of truth at the giant in front of them. To believe Jesus saved you before, should assure you in confidence, He will do the same again now. He is alive, He loves you, and He is for you. That's enough to know greater truly is ahead. That's enough to believe again. Oh taste and see that the Lord is good! Come again and dine at His table. Destiny is your defier.

For what He's said is done is said and done.

> *The believer replied, "Every promise of God proves true; he protects everyone who runs to him for help.*[cdlxxxiv]
> Proverbs 30:5

211

JUST KEEP SWIMMING

Never doubt in the dark what God told you in the light.[cdlxxxv]
- V. Raymond Edman

The mystery—it enthralls and invites us to an unanticipated part of our hearts and lives. So much of this is the mystery of Christ. But so much more of what we notice is where He is leading us. We spend many of our days searching for purpose. We want to be at the top of the mountain, recognizing that there was purpose to the climbing; we want assurance from the strengthening and shaping of our hearts in the mystery. But at some point in our lives, we will all reach the top of our Mt. Everest, and it's then we'll feel the nudge behind us to "jump" into the unknown waters before us. Yet as we hit the water, we could easily grow numb if we do not do two things → breathe and swim. As the water is nudging and carrying you, you must use all your strength and determination to keep going. The question isn't will you ever breathe again, but will you swim? Swim as you pray even though you feel nothing. Swim as you read God's Word when you have no time. Swim when you're tight on money but you still give. That's when you breakthrough, when you experience the breath of God back in your life. *The mystery enthralls us, but it's not what calls us.* He calls us into it, and He is the one we are to follow through it. Paul talks about this mystery that is hidden in God in Ephesians 3:9, Daniel talks about this mystery in Daniel 2:28, and Jesus talks about this mystery to His disciples and followers. It's this mystery that is made known to us by following Him. It's this mystery that is seen in the shadows of our lives. Like the waves of an ocean show off its fierce beauty as light shines across their surface and shadows press against its edge—*the mystery takes shape in the contrast of highs and lows.* The shadow is evidence that there is form, even when we can't see the form itself light is shining upon. In the shadows of our lives, where mystery thrives, it shows we too are formed. And even if our back is turned from the picture of promise, we can know God is present, for if a shadow is there, He is there, in all His glorious light.

> *He hid himself in mystery-darkness; the dense rain clouds were his garments. Suddenly the brilliance of his presence broke through with lightning bolts and with a mighty storm from heaven— like a tempest dropping coals of fire… He reached down into my darkness to rescue me! He took me out of my calamity and chaos and drew me to himself, taking me from the depths of my despair!… His love broke open the way and he brought me into a beautiful broad place. He rescued me— because his delight is in me! He rewarded me for doing what's right and staying pure. I will follow his commands and never stop.*[cdlxxxvi]
> (Excerpts from Psalm 18)

212

CONSIDER THE CONTRAST

Do you ever become unaware of the glory of the stars? In the way that when you see them, you forget they are light years away, specifically 20 quadrillion miles to the eye? Or that we are a part of a tiny planet in one galaxy of the billions in the universe? Do you ever simply forget? Or how about God's love for you? Do you ever walk away from the miraculous, and so easily shrug it off as "normal?" When it comes to God, there's nothing normal about Him. He is the most detail-caring, well-listening, creative Father. Malachi 1:2-3, 5 reads: *God said, "I love you." You replied, "Really? How have you loved us?" "Look at history"* (this is God's answer). *"Look at how differently I've treated you, Jacob, from Esau: I loved Jacob and hated Esau. I reduced pretentious Esau to a molehill, turned his whole country into a ghost town." "Yes, take a good look. Then you'll see how faithfully I've loved you and you'll want even more, saying, 'May God be even greater, beyond the borders of Israel!'"*[cdlxxxvii] I've learned that I do not see God until I adventure out into the great unknown for Him to meet me there. Have I *heard* Him in my devotions? Yes. But I *see* him in my living. When I'm happily present, and I hear a clear whisper out of nowhere, I know it's Him. When I wander out in my fields and see seven shooting stars, I know it's Him. When I'm pondering how terribly I want a coffee and someone offers to buy me one, I know it's Him. *I may feel God closest when I am still, yet I hear him the clearest when I am living.*

The darkest nights produce the brightest stars, but we must come into the fields to see them. I love how the Parallel Bible Study commentary says: "If Israel doubts God's covenant love, she should consider the contrast between God's ways with her and his ways with Jacob."[cdlxxxviii] Likewise, we should contrast our now season with His acts of faithfulness. In the sky, some stars may be brighter, closer, or more eye-catching, but it is the contrast of the smaller stars, and the arrangement of their designs, that make it so stunning. God does do **mighty** acts, but the small acts speak of His greatness *just as much*. I dare say that if we cannot appreciate the small, we do not deserve the big. Let alone, those who are not grounded in gratitude will most likely walk away from the starry sky before the meteor shower was destined to take place. Whether your season isn't everything you thought it would be or it's darker than you'd like, take a good look and consider the contrast. Remember every act of kindness He has already done to remind you that He is there in your midst.

Malachi 4:1-5 says:

"Count on it: The day is coming, raging like a forest fire. All the arrogant people who do evil things will be burned up like stove wood, burned to a crisp, nothing left but scorched earth and ash—a black day. But for you, sunrise! The sun of righteousness will dawn on those who honor my name, healing radiating from its wings. You will be bursting with energy, like colts frisky and frolicking. And you'll tromp on the wicked. They'll be nothing but ashes under your feet on that Day." God-of-the-Angel-Armies says so. "Remember and keep the revelation I gave through my servant Moses, the revelation I commanded at Horeb for all Israel, all the rules and procedures for right living. "But also look ahead..."[cdlxxxix] Or as Theodore Roosevelt says: "Keep your eyes on the stars and your feet on the ground."[cdxc] Keep being faithful with what's in your hands. Keep choosing good over evil. Keep moving forward! Do not simply forget. Remember His words, His glimpses of promises to come, His miracles He's worked time after time, and let that speak tremendous courage to your heart. Then, look ahead. There's always hope, and having hope will give you courage. The dawn is coming, tread softly through the night. It is for *you*. He loves you

so much that He's giving you the time to take in the contrast. So take it in while it lasts—for when what you've prayed for arrives, it will be an entirely different adventure with different mountains to climb. Where you are at is perfectly planned—let Him be the one who transitions time. As Genesis 28:15 says, "For I will not leave you until I have done what I have promised you."[cdxci] Even if you're in the darkest of seasons, even if His promise isn't yet completed, <u>He is still with you.</u> Take courage.

213

ROBES OF RIGHTEOUSNESS

"May love be the last great act to **shock** the world." Beside this quote on my wall are the words: "Warrior, beloved, and entrusted." Each morning, they are the first words I see. I wake up, find breath in that truth, and go downstairs to make my cup of coffee for the day. Across my coffee mug reads: "Stay. Slay. Pray." Another breath, a deeper breath, fills my lungs. My spirit is awake and aware to what the day holds, and I begin to prepare in every way I can for the mountains I may climb or the valleys I may discover. I seek God's face, I dress, and I go. Though I cannot see what lies ahead, I am as prepared as possible for whatever may come. Colossians 3:12-14 says:

So, chosen by God for this new life of love, dress in the wardrobe God picked out for you: compassion, kindness, humility, quiet strength, discipline. Be even-tempered, content with second place, quick to forgive an offense. Forgive as quickly and completely as the Master forgave you. And regardless of what else you put on, wear love. It's your basic, all-purpose garment. Never be without it.[cdxcii]

In the Passion Translation, verse 12 reads: "So robe yourself with virtues of God, since you have been divinely chosen to be holy."[cdxciii] I wonder how different each of our days would look if we, awake and aware, dressed ourselves in these garments? Just like the words on my wall remind me of who I am, and on my mug remind me what to do, the garments we clothe ourselves with are reminders of how to live. Like Isaiah 32:8 states: "But the noble make noble plans, and by noble deeds they stand."[cdxciv] I can't help but wonder what difference it would make if we dressed in nobility every morning.

I remember as a little girl wishing we all still dressed as they did in the medieval days, because they all looked noble to me. And with that childlike imagination, I believed my home was a castle, and all around me were princes and princesses, and few kings and queens, as well. I thought kingdom, and so I loved with nobility. To know you are royalty is one thing, to live like you are royal is another. When we dress in these garments, we make noble plans with our noble thoughts; and with our noble deeds, we stand, we act, and it shocks for it is always clothed in love. As Isaiah 61:10 says, "I delight greatly in the Lord; my soul rejoices in my God. For he has clothed me with garments of salvation and arrayed me in a robe of his righteousness, as a bridegroom adorns his head like a priest, and as a bride adorns herself with her jewels."[cdxcv] Love is the One who placed the garments on us, and as children of God, I pray we do the same for others. To clothe the poor in spirit, to place righteous robes on the lost, to place the cloak of compassion on the broken, and to bestow the garland of grace on those against us. To shock as we love, to slay as we pray, to impact as we live in nobility. May we wake up every day and put on our robes of righteousness so that every act that follows will be led in love and will change the world one person at a time.

214

The Rose
Inspired by Psalm 45

At the center of her heart is the kingdom, and that is what makes her enchanting. As she moves, all around her grows. As she stands, the earth multiplies. As she speaks, gold is reaped. As she searches, treasures are found. All like magic. Like glimmering dust falling wherever she goes. Like roses from heaven whenever she blooms. She's a rose on fire—encircled and entrusted. She's a mighty warrior—fearsome to behold. She's a destiny defier, believing in the most impossible of odds. She doesn't quit for she knows the kingdom is hers and everything within it. Yet, there are prisoners outside of her castle walls. She moves for she loves. She rises for she believes. She stands for she knows there's more than what they now see.
For the kingdom is for all, and she's determined for all to see its divine beauty.

The Warrior
Inspired by Psalm 89

At the center of his heart is the kingdom, and that is what makes him mighty. As he acts, God moves. As he leads, royalty follows. As he declares, wars cease. As he defends, kingdoms become established. All like miracles. Like parted paths through uncharted waters. Like fearless flames sent in the night. He is a warrior for his extravagant courage, a hero for his relentless love, a king for his brave heart. One who's known to fight for those who cannot fight for themselves, one who seeks to save the lost and protect the found, one who rides majestically into battle, glorifying the Lord with every victory. He doesn't quit for he knows the kingdom is his and all that is within it, yet there are prisoners outside his castle walls. He keeps his sword sharpened, ready to fight for the destined; bestowed with strength by his trust in God; befriended by peace for his noble plans, enthroned in favor for his humility of heart.
All to rescue as many as he can, to win one more over, time and time again.

215

A CHURCHED UNCHURCHED CITY

Just one more, Lord. Help me get one more.[cdxcvi]

These words stirred in my heart for months after seeing the movie *Hacksaw Ridge*. If you haven't seen it yet, here's a description to set up the scene for you:

"Hacksaw Ridge is the extraordinary true story of Desmond Doss who, in Okinawa during the bloodiest battle of WWII, saved 75 men without firing or carrying a gun. He was the only American soldier in WWII to fight on the front lines without a weapon, as he believed that while the war was justified, killing was nevertheless wrong. As an army medic, he single-handedly evacuated the wounded from behind enemy lines, braved fire while tending to soldiers and was wounded by a grenade and hit by snipers. Doss was the first conscientious objector to ever earn the Congressional Medal of Honor."[cdxcvii]

After watching this movie, I couldn't help but relate it to the spiritual warfare we face every day, that sadly, many of us go unaware to. Desmond Doss had every reason to quit, and many mocked him for going into war without a gun, but his convictions to help his country and to do so standing on what he believed in, ended up saving more lives than those who were far off more equipped. Doss didn't hide behind a gun nor behind his so-called strengths, he embraced his weaknesses and ran saying, "Just one more, Lord. Help me get one more." He was being attacked and could have stopped at person number 14, or person number 74, but they weren't

@bulgerjoseph

just numbers, they were names, they were his people. *No matter the cost, he didn't allow his passion to be contained.* What if we would live in such a way? That we too, would not keep silent of the voice of passion stirring in our hearts to save a lost and dying world. What if every day we woke up saying, "Just one more, Lord. Help me get one more. I know my weakness will be exposed. I know it's not comfortable. But if You will go with me, if You'll give me the strength, I can bring another one home."

I once heard a pastor from Norwich, England describe his city as one of the most "churched unchurched" cities in England. He went on to say that there were hundreds of churches in this place, but so many of them were "unchurched" because they were completely empty. I remember that as soon as he said it, I felt a whisper in my spirit contemplate, "I wonder if the Christian body would be described the same way?" If our bodies are the temples, and the bride is the church, are we living in a way that is passionately alive, going to the ends of the earth to reach the lost, or are we merely an empty building with a title that reads "Come" across the front. Are we being His hands and feet, or are we sitting on our hands and feet? I can't help but listen to the motherly sense in my heart speaking, "How will they know if no one tells them?"

I pray that like Jeremiah 20:9 reads, our hearts will alight with the same flame: *But if I say, "I will not mention his word or speak anymore in his name," his word is in my heart like a fire, a fire shut up in my bones. I am weary of holding it in; indeed, I cannot.*[cdxcviii] Today, may we not be silent. Today, may we not sit still. May we use our blessings to love, to seek out the lost, to reach out to the hungry, and to be generous to the poor. May we do one thing that changes one world, whether that is to sponsor a child, to volunteer for a good cause, or to help build the church! **God can do far more with our surrendered weakness than He can with our held back strengths.** May we be brave in being obedient; it begins with opening our eyes to see needs and opening our hearts to be moved to be the body of Christ. I believe if we can be brave enough to save one life, a ripple effect would occur of love to shock the world. Let us not be known as a churched unchurched city, but a fired up bride across the world, that no matter the cost, will not allow this passion to be contained.

They're not just numbers, they are names, and they are our people.

Just one more, Lord. Help me get one more.

216

WITH HONOR

> *Pray also for me, so that I will fearlessly make known the mystery of the gospel.*[clxcix]
> Ephesians 6:19

These are the words of Paul. The man who once was known for killing Christians became the man who sought to make God known amongst the lost to find Christ and become a disciple. He traveled to many places, many of times, to do so. Paul persevered with a purpose. He allowed God to use him because he knew the good news was vital for all to hear, and he was persistent in doing so. And likewise, we have the same call on our own lives, to not make ourselves known, but to make God known in wherever He places us. But it may not always be in the way we expect. In Isaiah 49:4 we read, "I have labored in vain; I have spent my strength for nothing at all. Yet what is due me is in the Lord's hand, and my reward is with my God."[d] Even though we may <u>know</u> that we are to fearlessly make known the good news, it doesn't mean that it will be as easy as expected. Some of us will be in a season that feels like an Ice Age, where we feel like nothing is happening. Others of us will get so caught up in the motions that we won't even see what *is* happening. And then a lot of us will stay in place waiting for anything to happen, not realizing that we have the long-sought "gifts of happening" right in our hands. They're all different seasons, but they all can easily lose the kingdom-minded focus we ought to have. The thing is, when we simply embrace the season we are in, we are able to expand where we are at to honor God with what we may not know is about to take place. For those who see nothing happening, you honor God by continually using your gifts where you're at and making His name known. Or in the words of Dory, "Just keep swimming."[di] For those who need to hear the saying, "Don't blink," take a step back to see what God may be speaking for you to do. Have a Moses moment to see where the bush is burning and where you need to be. For those who are waiting and waiting and waiting, know that you are equipped and purposefully placed. Though you may not know exactly what is going to happen, just honor God by trusting that there is a reason for where you're at. And in all these seasons, we <u>will</u> make known the mystery of the gospel as long as we commit to be okay to stay or fearless to go with a kingdom-minded spirit. For "what is due me is in the Lord's hand, and my reward is with God."

We honor God best when we give our best to the season we are in.

217

EXPECT THE UNEXPECTED

I once did some research on diamond digging and came across an article titled: "6 people who accidentally found fortune" by Rob Lammle.[dii] Three stories in particular were so bizarre and hilarious that I dare say I'll never forget the moral of their stories. The first one dates in November of 1992. A farmer had lost his hammer in one of his fields, so he asked his friend Eric Lawes to use his metal detector to find it. I can imagine Lawes walking around, feeling like he is wasting his time searching for a hammer out of all things valuable, until all of a sudden he comes across "24 bronze coins, 565 gold coins, 14,191 silver coins, plus hundreds of gold and silver spoons, jewelry, and statues, all dating back to the Roman Empire."[diii] By British law, they reported it as a treasure trove, which meant Britain had to pay them fair market value for it, totaling 1.75 million pounds for the farmer and Lawes to split. Reading this, I literally wanted to go buy a hammer to throw in a field, in hopes that it'd lead me to find some divine treasure trove. (Ps: they never found the hammer—probably wasn't much of a worry in the end.) The second story is about "The Uncle Sam Diamond." It's the largest diamond found yet in North America. What made me do a double take is that it was in Arkansas, of all places! Its worth being $800,000 of market price today. The third story has nothing to do with diamonds, but it's so absurd that I had to include it. Michael Sparks went to a thrift store and bought a candleholder, a set of salt and pepper shakers, and a yellowed print of the Declaration of Independence—all for the price of $2.48. "After looking over the document for a few days, he wondered if it might be older than he initially thought. So he hopped on the internet to do some research and soon realized he had purchased one of only 200 official copies of the Declaration of Independence commissioned by John Quincy Adams in 1820. Out of those 200, 35 had been found intact; he had number 36." He received $477,650 for its value. The thing is, each of these people went searching for something, and ended up finding far beyond what they could have imagined. None of them went seeking fortune, but they happened to be the ones who had wonder-filled eyes, who kept digging to then discover something of great worth. It only makes me wonder what God has in store for us that's right around the corner if we would just keep digging.

Sometimes in losing what we once treasured, we gain actual treasure itself; in losing something great, we gain something greater. For as Matthew 5:4 says, "You're blessed when you feel you've lost what is most dear to you. Only then can you be embraced by the One most dear to you."[div] *It is there, in the embrace of Christ, that all things unexpected happen.* In Genesis 26, Isaac lost his "hammer," and went out into the fields seeking what was next. Starting in verses 12-15, we read that Isaac's wealth and flocks continued to grow so much that the Philistines envied him and started to throw dirt in the wells that his father's servants dug up. They sent him away because of how powerful he was becoming, not because he was doing something wrong, but because he was doing all things right. A well back then not only symbolized landmarks to possess the surrounding country, but it was also the actual source of life to its people. When the water supply was cut off, starvation would drive a city to submission. What I love is that Isaac wasn't taken aback, but instead, he dug deeper. The first well he went to had fresh water (that is, a $800,000 diamond), but the herdsmen of Gerar claimed it as their own. The second well he dug in hope, they fought over too. So he went further, to a place they did not care to follow, and finally dug a well which he named "Wide-Open Spaces." He then says, "Now the Lord has given us room and we will flourish in the land." (Genesis 26:22, MSG) God met him that night, spoke promises over him; and Isaac built an altar, pitched a tent, and dug another well there because of it. The thing about fresh water is that a large percentage is actually under the ground and not on the surface of the earth, just like diamonds! As Helen Calder writes: "When God says, 'I am the spring of living water' (Jeremiah 2:13), He is also saying, 'I am the source of life. And in Me all the unseen resources of Heaven are there to back you up.'"[dv] The unseen resources of heaven are ours, but they're accessed through the digging of wells. I love that Isaac didn't give up when the Philistines drove him out. Instead, he was driven to go where no one had ever gone and ended up spending the rest of his days there in promise and prosperity. Not only that, but when other people found their diamonds, he kept digging. And even though he found a well that no one else wanted, it was the second well he dug after that ended up being the source for him to flourish again in peace. The coolest part is that the Philistines, who drove him out and drove him to his destiny, came back to offer a covenant of peace to him. It was <u>that day</u> when Isaac laid out a feast for them, turning from evil and doing good, that they found water. The unexpected happened yet again.

When it feels like the world is throwing dirt in your promised wells, know a setup is happening. When you are digging and digging and feel like you are getting nowhere, know you are being driven to somewhere you couldn't have dreamed up. When it's tempting to not do the right thing because of disappointment's weight and discouragement's pain, "Turn from evil and do good, then you will dwell in the land forever. For the Lord loves the just and will not forsake his faithful ones."[dvi] (Psalm 37:27 + 28) When what was expected doesn't go according to plan, know there is yet another well to be dug up that may be the source to your promise (verse 22), and it may just be right around the corner. Don't throw away the seeds in your hands, they may be the Declaration of Independence—keep planting and keep being faithful. Don't move if it's where God has driven you to stay—your "Uncle Sam Diamond" may just be right beneath the surface, becoming a diamond park where all the lost come seeking to find worth. Don't think that your time is being wasted when what you're doing seems worthless, for if a lost hammer leads to 1.75 million pounds, you never know what could be found in the waiting. When the enemy is throwing dirt in your wells, trying to take you out, keep digging deeper, keep trusting wilder, and keep believing bigger. God loves to intervene with the unexpected for those who are wide-eyed and looking for more. As Jeremiah 29:13 says, "You will seek me and find me when you seek me with all your heart."[dvii] You will find Him. You will find water. You will find His words to be true. Just expect the unexpected, for there you will always find God, there you will find a story that is divine in every way possible.

218

BOLD AND UNASHAMED

Have you ever heard the saying, "Come as you are?" It's this invitation that opens up the word "home" to every heart. It suggests to remain, to be, to not worry about having anything to offer, to not be ashamed of the person you are coming as. And yet sometimes when we do come as that person, people don't know how to embrace just who that is. It's not because you're "weird," but because you truly are "unique"—you stand out in a crowd and yet you still belong. Yet belonging can be the very opposite of what we are feeling when this happens. But as my friend said to me, "God loves us all as we are. We could just be, just exist, and that would be enough." In a world that says you are what you do or you are what you wear, I dare to say *you are who you are*. It's simple and yet strangely intriguing—because there is this release to stop striving, and I believe that is where we all flourish. That's where we become bold and unashamed in who God says we are and discover the freedom in its truth. Maybe who you are, all your uniqueness, was made to stand out for a purpose, and maybe we are all purposed to love others the same. When they come as they are and we come as we are, a garden exists. It's the closest thing we have to heaven when we live as who we are for it worships God in being who He created us to be. Being is the simplicity of you. Love exists where two come as they are and find a home within their unique differences. A part of that is knowing you don't have to live in royalty to be royal as much as you don't have to change who you are to feel at home. We may adapt to change with the conditions surrounding us, but who we are is the one thing we shouldn't need to adapt. Who you are is not your doings or your achievements, it is those little desires that make you light up, it is the quirky things that make you laugh to yourself, it is the person that is at home in themselves on a restful day. Some seek adventure, and others the quiet, yet both should be valued the same. Matthew 5:5 says, "You're blessed when you're content with just *who you are*—no more, no less. That's the moment you find yourselves proud owners of everything that can't be bought."[dviii] (emphasis added)

You may be creative, but you are not your creations. You may be talented, but you are not your talents. You may be brave, but you are not your battles. Sometimes it's easier to say this is what defines us for they cling to a definition of something we can fit the mold of. But the real you cannot be defined or explained because that person is so much more. On the opposite spectrum, you are not your mistakes and others are not their mistakes. A garden is best kept alive with both grace and love. Love plants and grace keeps, and thankfully, both are in an abundant supply from heaven. When God walked in the garden with Adam and Eve, He came as who He was calling for them to come as who they were. Yes, they made a mistake and had to face the consequences, yet He did not walk away from them but to them, because He *still* was deeply in love with them both. *For love plants and grace keeps.* I heard a whisper yesterday, and as God spoke to me, I speak to you: "Stay sweet, my rose, do not fall to life's poison." Life's poison looks different to all of us. For some, it is gossip, some stealing, some adultery. For others, it is being different from who we are, or hiding in fear of being seen. Whatever keeps you from being the real you at your state of rest is your poison, and the world actually needs you to stay sweet, to stay you. You may be the beauty this world has never known, the very answer to another's prayer. And it's actually released in just being who you are—bold and unashamed—content with being no more and no less, and creating an Eden again with your presence that speaks of the good news without a word even being said.

219

FIELDS OF GARDENS

> *For we are fellow workmen, (joint promoters, laborers together) with and for God; you are God's garden and vineyard and field under cultivation, [you are] God's building.*[dix]
> 1 Corinthians 3:9

It's not the most comfortable thing allowing the Holy Spirit to dig deep into your heart. There's a lot of dirt, ash, and broken pieces. What you don't realize when saying "yes" to a *greater* thing is the preparation required before God can begin to build. A new thing requires being open and vulnerable—it requires the ugly to be exposed, so that He can beautify, purify, and delicately design what was intended for evil into something <u>good</u>, <u>powerful</u>, and <u>victorious</u>. He takes the formless and makes it fearless, a rock, a mountain! But He elevates it as He shapes it. It is a process, but He doesn't mind getting His hands dirty. Because He knows that there is more within you than even you can see yet, and your fullest capacity first starts with the dirt.

@ kathleenmadethis

Dirt is the part of the garden that needs to be tended before every effort and vision can spring forth from the ground. The formed must become unformed so He can create the most breathtaking designs within its land. A garden can be the most elaborate place, but only if it is taken care of. It goes through many seasons, but it never stops being a garden, a designated place of growth, a valuable space for God to dwell. Likewise, our hearts are the very place God dwells. He never leaves, is constantly cultivating, and is always working things together for our good. As Isaiah 61:11 says, "For as the earth brings forth its sprouts, and as a garden causes what is sown in it to spring up, so the Lord God will [most certainly] cause righteousness and justice and praise to spring up before all the nations [through the power of His Word.]"[dx] As seeds were sown into you by His Word, they begun to grow and become beautiful within you. And as you continually allow God to do a deeper work within you, you also allow a greater work to be done through you. *When you let Him in, the seeds that you allow God to plant within you will carry the generations before you.* That is when the formless is made fearless, the garden into a mountain, and the designs into purpose. Though the reward may still be beneath the surface, in due time, it will reap 30-fold, 60-fold, and 100-fold. Know that your efforts are not for nothing. Your openness is being cultivated. Every step of every day forward is worth it. You will not be left empty. For as you are faithful, as you are consistent, and as you are obedient, fields of gardens are growing, sprouts are being brought forth, purpose is springing up, reward will be blooming soon, and you'll see God's handiwork over every placement and design. He is cultivating something in you and it will go so much further than you could ever imagine! What a breathtaking sight it will be!

220

BEING HIS

The first will be last, and the last will be first.
This isn't a game; this isn't a curse.
It's not fire and rain, or love versus hate.
It's not about winning, and neither a fate.
It's not in the direction, and it's not in the height.
It's nothing to be grasped, and nothing to fight.
You can strive and do what's right, or be still without a gain;
Yet in both situations, the races are the same.
It's not about being first or last; it's about solely being His.
Releasing the hands of time, neither slow and neither quick.
Fighting behind and before, triumphant from beginning to end,
So He stands in eternal victory, and we stand as champions.

So the last will be first, and the first will be last.[dxi]
Matthew 20:16

221

GLORIOUS

> *Above all else, guard your heart, for everything you do flows from it.*[dxii]
> Proverbs 4:23

I'm passionate about the heart. I'm passionate about what awakens it to life and what joy causes it to dance. But I'm also deeply moved by His love for us to guard the heart as a grace-filled endeavor. For every little thing we do, every piece we are, flows so naturally from it. Whether filled with truth or deceit, our hearts are the most precious treasure in God's sight, so we also should have sight over what comes and goes from it and to it. The heart is created from passion with passion. It's only natural to seek and discover the heart of Who created ours so intricately. But how many of us don't guard our hearts because we don't believe there's really anything worth protecting? Oh, how you have no idea how much MORE God has for you. I don't know if you've seen Cinderella, it's literally, one of my favorites, so if you haven't—you should. It's not just a girly thing. There's a part in the movie where Cinderella, who is always trying to be kind and courageous, just breaks. She is clothed in value and hopes and excitement, and her family comes up attacking everything good about her beauty and leaves her tattered, disappointed, and broken. So she runs, and she weeps. Then all of a sudden, her fairy godmother shows up—seeing her in a complete state of desperation and ruin, and you know what she sees? Something glorious! As Cinderella, completely undone, stands up, she starts to be *transformed*. Not only does her circumstances change—she changes. She is dressed in royalty, strength, dignity, and fearlessness, and something switches in her heart. Suddenly she *is* going to the ball and heading towards the destiny she knew deep down was in store for her. Then there's us. All put together, strong, and confident we are, except for on the inside, where a lot of us are wearing tattered dreams, broken hopes, overbearing fears, and lost loves. And honestly, we've been holding them for quite some time now. Keeping it together on the outside, but completely lost on the inside. Some of us need to come to that state of desperation—letting the ugly side out, undone and undignified, before the feet of Jesus. Letting out every person who has disappointed us, every situation where we have left feeling defeated, every hope we felt was stolen from us. Some ugly tears need to be released, some forgiveness needs to be confessed, and some deep restoration needs to happen. You've felt knocked down for a while, but Jesus *sees* you right where you're at, and if you stand up one last time, He will transform your heart to the royal, strong, dignified, and fearless treasure it holds—and that's worth protecting. As Lisa Bevere said, "Sometimes a promise is *drawing closer* when it has never seemed *more impossible.*"[dxiii] What the enemy intended for ruins, God intends to make into something glorious. Your heart is the utmost beauty in His sight; don't take that lightly. Every little thing you do flows from it. So be fearless and be on guard, and draw as close to God's heart as you can with your own.

Here are three verses that will transform your heart and give you weapons to continually protect it: Ephesians 6:17-18, Philippians 4:4-8, and Colossians 3:12-16. Read them, speak them aloud, and believe them! Let something switch in your heart to know you are worth fighting for. Love your heart and protect it. As you choose to be on guard, you choose to be brave. Rise knowing you <u>will</u> walk into the destiny that, deep down, you've always known God has had in store for you. He is a good King and a good Father, and how He adores your heart. How He longs to make its wildest dreams come true.

222

LIKE MAGIC

It's amazing to see what God will show you when you actually listen—not with your ears but with your life. We can be so stubborn and intent on hearing the answers to our questions quickly and promptly, rather than being patient in seeking the answer for its truth. I have come to learn that the most beautiful things in life are worth waiting for, and have come to know patience for its virtue, but I have also realized we are *shown* more answers than we are told. The question isn't, "Is God going to answer?" Or even when, but "how?" It is in our greatest journeys that we will come across the greatest discoveries. For sometimes, His words are like riddles, and His sights are like clues, but His answers are always like magic. Out of nowhere, they will come, but forever, they will stay. So keep your eyes open with your heart too, as you ask for Him to reveal His love all around you. The greatest answers are never told, but always discovered.

> *Beloved ones, listen to this instruction. Open your heart to the revelation of this mystery that I share with you. A parable and a proverb are hidden in what I say—an intriguing riddle from the past. We've heard true stories from our fathers about our rich heritage. We will continue to tell our children and not hide from the rising generation the great marvels of our God—his miracles and power that have brought us all this far.*[dxiv]
> Psalm 78:1-4

223

WILD LOVE

Dear Child,

The rose is your mark. Gold may come from whatever you touch, but you will be remembered for the rose you place in the hands of others. A rose is a symbol for promise, hope, and good news. It is prophetic and defying. You will be known for much, but your rose will be unforgotten. It is your legacy. Forget the fears. Pay no attention to the doubts. Believe and trust and sing and dance—I AM for you! I don't miss a thing. Look to Me every morning, I am always speaking. Ponder the miracles every night; I am always good. "You're going to take over whole nations; you're going to resettle abandoned cities."[dxv] *(Isaiah 54:3) What I have planned for you is no small thing, but it is not too great of a thing that I cannot do. Trust in Me and I will always lead you; My peace will never leave you—pursue it. You will be tempted to look back at times—don't linger there. There will always be far more ahead than what you've left behind. You have waited for this. You have prayed for this. You have fasted and asked, do not doubt what I am doing. I always come through, and it is always right on time. Believe in miracles. Think bigger than imaginable. There is no request too big or too small for Me to do. Remember that each rose I give has no thorn. It may carry a more glorious weight, but you are stronger than you know. Stay the path and believe in My promises. They are written on your heart and designed upon your path. The galaxies lay in the palm of My hand, and not one star is missing; you lay in the palm of My hand, and not one detail will be forgotten. Sing over the nations! Place a rose in every hand! Declare My glory and make My name known. There is no one more perfect to do so than My child. I will make your deserts like Eden; your wastelands like the garden of My very own. I will not fail your greatest desires; I will be faithful to them. Faithfulness is a pursuit for it acts beyond the words it speaks. The same love and faithfulness will be kissed by your promise. How My hand is upon you. How I am so wildly in love with you—the work of My hand displays My wild love for you, and with wonder-filled eyes, you will see every piece of it. I give My love to you in full, never holding anything back. I am perfect with My pursuit, though patient with My timing, yet it is all for you. Always and forever, it's all for you.*

Love,
Your Father

224

GREATER BEGINNINGS

> *And as He spoke, He no longer looked to them like a lion; but the things that began to happen after that were so great and beautiful that I cannot write them. And for us this the end of all the stories, and we can most truly say that they all lived happily ever after. But for them it was only the beginning of the real story.*[dxvi]
> - C. S. Lewis

They say the most painful endings are often disguised as new beginnings, that the ending of one great story is the start of another greater novel, or that letting go is the key to receiving the better ahead. I love this quote from *The Chronicles of Narnia*, because it's about four children, Peter, Susan, Edmund, and Lucy, who happened to run into a wardrobe, ended up discovering an entirely new world behind its closed doors, and became royal heirs of its land. Shortly after their arrival to Narnia, they're told of a prophecy: when two Sons of Adam and two Daughters of Eve sit upon the four thrones at Cair Paravel, all Narnia would be put to rights. They were the four Narnia had been waiting for to fulfill its prophetic vision. Thus it came to be, and it was an incredible glory they lived. Yet as it all comes to a close, Aslan speaks: "By knowing me here for a little, you may know me better there."[dxvii] They didn't come to this wonderful land to stay forever, but to be shaped into the royal heirs they were always destined to become. Although, when you're leaving something wonderful behind, it's hard to imagine greater could be ahead.

Likewise, Jerusalem receives a promise of restoration while it seems furthest from possible. In Jeremiah 33:3 God speaks: *Call to me and I will answer you. I'll tell you marvelous and wondrous things that you could not figure out on your own.*[dxviii] These words sound sweet, but at this time, everything that could go wrong did go wrong, and here Jeremiah is, through the Word of God, promising redemption. But it is at our end, where we don't know what's ahead, that God can have His way without our will to tie it down. Thus is His promise to her, His Jerusalem: *But now <u>take another look</u>. I'm going to give this city a thorough renovation, working a true healing inside and out. I'm going to show them life whole, life brimming with blessings. I'll restore everything that was lost to Judah and Jerusalem... Yes, there will be a season where you look at what's around you and say it is a wasteland, but the time is coming where I will make everything as good as new!*[dxix] (6-7,10, emphasis added) He doesn't beat around the bush, but says it plain and clear, that the transition will seem empty and hopeless, but He gives His Word to redeem everything that was lost. In other words, it wasn't all for nothing. When it feels like you're coming to your end, remember the promised chapters to come. God works from glory to glory. He gives and takes away that we may enter into the better before us. As C. S. Lewis wrote earlier: "The things that began to happen after that were so great and beautiful that I cannot write them." Whatever you are going through, lift your eyes, and remember the Lion's promise. He may not look like a lion here on earth, but His powerful, mighty, and fierce spirit, is always listening. Call to Him, and He will tell you of things you could never figure out on your own. This next book He has written for you will be filled with great stories of life brimming with blessings, with healings inside and out, with laughter, celebration, and festivities. It's beyond what you can imagine, and that is why you must trust His sight. Once a king or queen in Narnia, always a king or queen, no matter the book. Now, take heart, for your greater beginning awaits!

225

FIERCELY BEAUTIFUL

I wonder what it would be like to be locked in a lions' den? With creatures so fiercely beautiful, yet immensely powerful. To see them as they are and see you as you are in the same instant. The sense of awe and fear that must beat through your heart so quickly. I wonder if it's the same when we are locked in our hearts' chamber? The chamber we find rest in and yet sometimes feel confined within. That sacred place that is fiercely beautiful, yet immensely powerful. One that when truly faced is seen with the same awe and fear of what it truly beholds. To realize your heart is a lion, and it's actually {safe}. I do say this with caution for lions can be wild and dangerous as can a heart that's been poisoned or deceived by lies—but as any lion can be tamed, so the Father's voice can allow us to trust the full potential we have within.

A whisper I heard to my spirit a few days ago went a little like this: "Live out your fears, and you will live out your dreams." The truth is that my greatest passions and deepest longings are also my greatest fears and deepest doubts. So to live out those fears would then be me chasing my dreams. It would be me walking up to the lion and placing my hand on the lion's fur in faith, discovering he doesn't bite. In fact, he bends down, that I may climb on top of him and be led into the greatest adventure I've ever known. I love the verse that we read when Daniel comes out of the lions' den safe in 6:23: "When he was hauled up, there wasn't a scratch on him. He had trusted his God."[dxx] I believe that when we are at rest in our chambers, we are thrown into the lion's den—for it's where we face ourselves and trust God.

One definition of acceptance is "to find rest in."[dxxi] Sometimes, we first must accept who we are before we can accept our fate. "To be seen as we truly are... is perhaps the greatest risk any of us will ever take,"[dxxii] says Cinderella. When we finally give ourselves a chance to shine, to be seen, to be known for the glorious creation God designed us to be... we take a risk, we place a hand on the lion, we see a glimpse of what God knows... And maybe what we've always known deep down within. May we take the risk to discover who we truly are—to see our hearts not as a wild creature but a tamed powerful being—to release him from the cage and be surprised by how much more he was able to do when set free. For when we do accept the defining words and carved out destinies within us, we release ourselves into pastures of freedom, and in their wide-open spaces, our trust in God is shown, declared, and exalted far above what we could've imagined. For your heart is like a lion, one fiercely beautiful and yet immensely powerful. One that you need not to be afraid to embrace and let out, for he is designed to lead you and fight for you. He is tamed to the sound of your voice, led by your sight, but ultimately obedient to your Father's will. Your lion isn't to be feared, but accepted and loved and cherished. For he is you—wild yet tamed, free yet obedient, mighty and lovely—powerful in strength, uncontainable in wonder, and still oh so fiercely beautiful in every way. It is when you begin to love who God designed you as, that you fall so much more in love with Him as your Father. Child of God, your heart is *safe* to embrace.

226

PAINTED FACADES

I remember walking down the streets of Australia wondering, "What in the world can I give to these people?" As I pondered these thoughts, I heard a whisper in my spirit: "beauty." With time, I agreed beauty was the very thing that needed to be planted. Australia is one of those places that seems perfect; however, the more I saw with God's eyes, the more I spotted spaces and holes I hadn't noticed before. No culture or people group is perfect. But it was simply my personal discovery that people who have everything still need the beauty of Jesus to make life complete. As Charles Spurgeon writes: "You will never know the fullness of Christ until you know the emptiness of everything else but Christ."[dxxiii] I started to learn that very concept, of fullness, here.

There's a poem read in the white winter scene of Beauty and the Beast that goes:

The air is blue and keen and cold, with snow the roads and fields are white. But here the forest's clothed with light and in a shining sheath enrolled. Each branch, each twig, each blade of grass, seems clad miraculously with glass: Above the ice-bound streamlet bends each frozen fern with crystal ends. For in that solemn silence is heard in the whisper of ever sleeping thing: Look, look at me, Come wake me up for still here I'll be.[dxxiv]

Whilst Belle reads this aloud, Beast looks out at the white blanket of snow on the lake and whispers: "It's as if I'm seeing it for the first time."[dxxv] No matter where we are in the world, there are empty spaces and holes that we've never seen before. Beast was a prince, who had walked these trails countless times, so well he knew the shortcuts through twisted bends of the castle. Yet, these words were vision to his heart. I believe, that as the poem opened the eyes of Beast, the words we speak, write, or live, will do the same for a world blind to Christ. These are the very instructions Paul writes to Titus to open eyes to the fullness of Christ: "Your duty is to teach them to embrace a lifestyle that is consistent with sound doctrine. Lead the male elders into disciplined lives full of dignity and self-control. Urge them to have a solid faith, generous love, and patient endurance. Likewise with the female elders, lead them into lives free from gossip and drunkenness and to be teachers of beautiful things Likewise, guide the younger men into living disciplined lives for Christ. Above all, set yourself apart as a model of a life nobly lived. With dignity, demonstrate integrity in all that you teach… He sacrificed himself for us that he might purchase our freedom from every lawless deed and to purify for himself a people who are his very own, passionate to do what is beautiful in his eyes."[dxxvi] (2:1-7,14) We have the honor to be models of a life nobly lived.

To plant the message of Christ into every pocket needing to be filled. To do what is beautiful in His eyes by living with dignity, planting sequoias of His glory among His people. No life is full without the fullness of Christ, no matter how bountiful it may seem. *If the beauty of the snow was silent, yet was hopeful for awakening, our world may silently be whispering the same.* Some may not know until they taste His goodness for themselves, but may our lives be the sweetness that draws them in. May we teach His ways and speak His thoughts. May we love passionately and live generously. May we see beyond ourselves and bring vision to beauty. The most perfect of lives cannot be so without first meeting Perfection Himself. Shall we then see beyond the masks and the painted facades, to wake up the world to Christ!

227

TAKE SAIL; TAKE COURAGE

The wind. It comes and it goes. Sometimes it creates rest, and other times it creates awakenings. It can be soft, or it can be powerful. It is light, and yet it carries. The wind is like the breath of God whispering into the sails of your heart. Revelation 2:7 says: "Are your ears awake? Listen. Listen to the Wind Words, the Spirit blowing through the churches. I'm about to call each conqueror to dinner. I'm spreading a banquet of Tree-of-Life fruit, a supper plucked from God's orchard."[dxxvii] A few years back, God spoke to me, "If you will listen, I will go beyond your wildest dreams." I think when I heard "listen" for the first time, I assumed it meant "obey." But now looking back, I see that "listening" was just that—having my ears attuned to His voice, hearing every whisper, and never missing a word. Those words were what kept me and directed me to stay the path He had placed before me. Those words anchored a hope in my soul through the toughest seasons. Those words led me to a banquet table of His goodness where my wildest dreams began to unfold. Undoubtedly, the wind words are what change everything.

I think when it comes to taking sail into our future, the wind words are what direct us towards the hope God promises. They are spoken gently, yet they have this weight to them that leave an unquestionable mark on your heart. They are words you remember forever. Trust me. They *always* come back and surprise you when they come to pass. So when the wind words come, write them down, strong sailor! Habakkuk 2:3 say: "This vision-message is a witness pointing to what's coming. It aches for the coming—it can hardly wait! And it doesn't lie. If it seems slow in coming, wait. It's on its way. It will come right on time."[dxxviii] In the NIV it says, "The revelation awaits an appointed time."[dxxix] *The wind words are as anointed as appointed, and they will direct you and keep you on course as long as you keep hold of them*. Writing them down not only sees God's sovereignty when they come true, like real-life fairytales, but they anchor you in the waiting during the storms. Those who hold onto the wind words become conquerors for they have believed wholeheartedly with conviction what they've heard. They are the ones who sit at the banquet table of life and have the finest foods with every detail they asked for, in addition to their favorite desserts as a surprise. It's a witness to yourself, but it's also a witness to others. People watch you sail across the sea with God's hand upon you as you listen, and His faithfulness is written all over it. But also remember, wind words direct. They're not there for mere-comfort.

For some of you, it has been a while since you've heard that gentle whisper, and it feels like you have been sailing into the Bermuda's triangle with no end in sight. Yet, whether you have a fresh wind word, or haven't heard the wind in quite some time, they are still directing your sails on the last word spoken. When seasickness is kicking in from staying the path for so long, go back to the last word spoken and proclaim its truth to your heart. Put up your sails and keep moving forward. You are most likely closer than you'd imagine. So take sail and take courage. You can rest in the wind words given for they will direct the sails of your heart at the right time, right to where you are meant to be. Let the courage within your heart that stepped onto the boat, be the same courage within the waves that are at times in your favor and sometimes aren't. Your courage will always find strength to stay when it remembers that promising, anchored hope, deep at the bottom of your heart's greatest convictions. Know you are born to sail into your wildest dreams, you are courageous enough to discover their paths, and you are a conqueror, in Jesus name, with everything promised on the horizon. Just listen. Listen to the wind words, and write every one of them down.

228

THE PRIZE

I remember as a little girl always loving prizes. Like how proud I was of learning the whole two-word verse of "Jesus wept" (John 11:35, NIV) for some silly little sticker at Sunday School; or having my mom always sign off my school assignments to receive a fifty-cent rock in return, or when I ran across the finish line at a track meet and won my first medal. I remember being so proud of my prize, no matter its value, because I had chased after each one—therefore, it was my treasure, a memory attached to a victory I could hold onto. 1 Corinthians 9:24 similarly talks about a prize that means in Greek "brabeion" derived from the word "brave."[dxxx] I love this imagery that the one who wins the race is marked with a symbol of bravery—no matter the value, it is a victory and therefore it becomes a treasure. The verse in AMPC says: "Do you know that in a race all the runners compete, but [only] one receives the prize? So run [your race] that you may lay hold of [the prize] *and* make it yours."[dxxxi] Some people run because they like to run, but there is a different endurance and motivation that comes when you know there is a prize at the end. And my question simply is—what is the race set out before you? What is the path that your faith sees beyond what your sight knows? What is set before you *today* that you can bring glory to God with? Whether you were aware of it or not, we are all standing on our own track lines destined with a prize at the finish. One created for us as we were created to go after it. When we catch a glimpse of that prize, we never see the race the same again. For it's not a pointless jog, but a run we are equipped to set out for.

Likewise in Exodus 14:13-15, we read Moses speaking over his people: "'Do not be afraid. Stand firm and you will see the deliverance the Lord will bring you today. The Egyptians you see today you will never see again. The Lord will fight for you; you need only to be still.' Then the Lord said to Moses: 'Why are you crying out to me? Tell the Israelites to move on.'"[dxxxii] The two key words in this passage is *today* and *move*. Before this point, the Israelites were "marching out boldly" (14:8) and were "armed for battle" (13:18), but then they come to this sea of impossibility and start to question everything they once believed in. Moments ahead of this, they were bold and confident because they saw God doing the miraculous. But this was a miracle that they couldn't fathom would happen, and so their faith sank before they even stepped into the sea. *But what they saw as a finish line, God had drawn up as a starting line.* Moses assured them they would see what was promised and that *today* anything could happen. And it did. God created a way where there was no way by splitting the sea; so the gun set off, and the race begun. I don't find it to be a coincidence that a sentence after Moses says, "Be still," the Lord says, "Move." I believe that's the: *on your mark, get ready, get set, go,* to our race. We need to stand firm in the faith that there is a prize marked out for us by getting ready, we need to position ourselves by being still to set out when the path divinely splits, and we need to move with the same boldness and confidence in the Lord from the days of old into the days ahead. Every day, any day, today, God can move. As 1 Corinthians 9:24 says: "Lay hold of the prize and make it yours."[dxxxiii] Treasures await for those who chase after their prize, and running after what's in your heart is *brave*. You can march boldly across that finish line knowing He can do all things any day at any time. It always starts with *today plus move* and ends with *a prize plus a promise kept*. When the sea of impossibility lies before you, get ready to run for the prize is close, and you are beyond equipped to run its race. As Isaiah 60:22 says: "At the right time, I, the Lord, will make it happen."[dxxxiv] The Lord is fighting for you; He will make it happen and make it yours.

229

THORNS OF GRACE

I have a theory, one that our greatest weaknesses are actually our greatest strengths. Why otherwise would the enemy attack them so persistently if he knew no strength could come from them? In one case: thoughts. It's easy for our thoughts to run wild and think poisonous things. But on the other hand, when led by love, those thoughts can also be the kindest, gentlest, and most shocking beauty to mankind. Yet both are simply, thoughts. A quote by Frank Jackson says: "Watch your thoughts, they become your words. Watch your words, they become your actions. Watch your actions, they become your character. Watch your character, it becomes your destiny."[dxxxv] We can read this and take heed to its wisdom, but we could also see that thoughts led by the Holy Spirit can lead us to a destiny the Holy Spirit knows is within us. So when I say let your thoughts run wild with wonder, it should expand your mind to see past the limits into His grace. What if we started to take captive our weaknesses and instead see the strength God knows, the enemy sees, and we have been minimizing from our mind, to realize the power it has when faced with Christ. If your weakness is only being good at one-on-one conversations in groups, then go after the one! See it as your strength! If your weakness is being quiet, listen to the Holy Spirit while everyone else is living in the noise, so when you speak, the authority of Christ will dwell in your words. If your weakness is to not sit still, use that energy for Christ's glory by volunteering with kids or building the Church in whatever way possible. Whatever it is that the enemy has been wanting you to keep hidden, bring to the Holy Spirit that He may breathe His revelation-truth into its strength. As Lisa Bevere says: "There's something new inside of you fear is wanting to contain. Don't let it."[dxxxvi] Your weaknesses are simply thorns of grace, crowning you as they did Christ, setting you apart for His glory, setting you apart as His own.

> *The extraordinary level of the revelations I've received is no reason for anyone to exalt me. For this is why a thorn in my flesh was given to me, the Adversary's messenger sent to harass me, keeping me from becoming arrogant. Three times I pleaded with the Lord to relieve me of this. But he answered me,* ***"My grace is always more than enough for you, and my power finds its full expression through your weakness."*** *So I will celebrate my weaknesses, for when I'm weak I sense more deeply the mighty power of Christ living in me. So I'm not defeated by my weakness, but delighted! For when I feel my weakness and endure mistreatment—when I'm surrounded with troubles on every side and face persecution because of my love for Christ—I am made yet stronger. For my weakness becomes a portal to God's power.*[dxxxvii]
> 2 Corinthians 12:7-10 (emphasis added)

230

LED BY LOVE

He whispered, "And the greatest of these is…" As I breathed out, "love." Love is what anchors faith in certainty, the certainty that God hasn't forgotten our deepest desires or desperate needs. Love is what heightens and deepens hope to be assured of the unseen cloud of blessings in the distance—to not only believe, but *know*, that truly the best is coming, even if not yet seen. Yet without love, faith becomes a wall more than an armor, and hope a mountain more than an adventure. Without love, fear kicks in and sees the practical. With love, wonder swoops in and sees the unimaginable. As it says in 1 Corinthians 13:13: "But for right now, until that completeness, we have three things to do to lead us toward that consummation: Trust steadily in God, hope unswervingly, love extravagantly. And the best of the three is love."[dxxxviii] Even though all is promised in the distance [for *right now*], we must be led by love.

Love is brave. It is brave to be one's self in a world that invites us to a million masquerades. It is brave to follow the Lord's leading down side paths in a world of open doors. It is brave to believe beyond one's sight in the realness of what's in them and ahead of them that others don't yet see. Brave is being true to one's self and convictions because they are so deeply grounded in the knowledge of God's love for them and their delights. When love is the core foundation of who you are, faith and hope can then be used most effectively. I love how Shauna Niequist says: "We're addicted to big and sweeping and photo-ready— crossing oceans, changing it all, starting new things, dreams and visions and challenges, marathons and flights and ascending tall peaks. But the rush to scramble up onto platforms, to cross oceans, to be heard and seen and known sometimes comes at a cost, and sometimes the most beautiful things we do are invisible, unsexy… Sometimes being brave is being quiet."[dxxxix]

Might I add, sometimes being brave is being you. Love must be the tended soil on which every act is done and every seed is planted, for without it, we can only stand for so long. It's like a tower without a cornerstone, a tree with no roots, a mountain with no filled core. *If love drives out all fear, fear may just then try to drive out all love.* And a life buried in fear and worry is not one that the Lord intended for us to live. Love cannot not act for it is driven and that is why it is brave. We remember to be brave for the grand things, but being brave in the microscopic details is what will change the world. It is our day-to-day living and moment- to-moment acts that touch beyond our reach. A little generosity here, a little patience there… they add up and build castles of God's glory for others to marvel at. Being different has a uniqueness to it, and I believe it is those who embrace their uniqueness that will live their set apart calling in full.

There is a deep honor that resonates within the person who loves the mold in which they've been created. When they figure out its "nooks and crannies," its power and authority, its influence and strength, they walk as the heroes they were destined to be. *The small acts become the greatest stories and the unforeseen door knocks become the greatest adventures.* When we embrace this life led by love, we discover its magic within the details and see its designs all around us in a canopy of grace. Love is brave enough to believe in the impossible for its assurance is grounded deeply within. You never know what small act will become your miracle, nor which knock will be your impossible, but when led in love, an open heart cannot miss its beckoning. In the words of *Frozen*: "Love is an open door."[dxl] Let God into your heart time and time again, through the disappointments and doubts, for an open heart will receive the promises and blessings when left unlocked. There is so much more than you now yet see; be brave enough to be you when you walk into its great design, and always let love keep you grounded within its soil. Far more is coming; you just wait. Love will always lead you and carry you for it is the grace and embrace of Christ, and it whispers gently, "The greatest of these is…"

231

PRAYER WARRIORS

There's one sentence that instantly stands out to me in Philemon, it says: "Because of your prayers, I fully expect..." (Philemon 1:22, MSG) I love the thought that because of the prayers of another prayer warrior, one is able to expect that which feels like wishful thinking. Paul is in prison when he writes this. He not only expects, but he tells Philemon to prepare a room for him to be ready when he arrives. The two underlying themes I see in this one sentence then are: one, be preparing as you're praying; two, intercession is not only for the lost, but also the found.

I have been on countless missions trips, and have such a heart for the impoverished and orphaned, and I believe that our prayers work miracles every time we pray to defeat darkness and its attempt to destroy the lost. Yet, I also have a heart for the found. To not only fight for the lost, but to keep the saved, saved. The imagery of a brother in Christ praying for his brother in trouble then paints a picture of how we as children of God can even intercede for the dreams and destinies of our brothers and sisters. That as we are praying for breakthrough for them, we are preparing in praise and worship for the miracle we're hoping for. I love that Paul was still dreaming, still hoping, still planning, while he was locked away from what was in his heart, for he fully expected for God to come through. That confidence was awakened by the prayers of his friend. What divine touch can our prayers bring into the lives of our loved ones to bring confidence, hope, and assurance, to their God-whispered dreams, to their long awaited promises to come?

Isaiah 59:16-20 says:

He saw that there was no man, and wondered that there was no one to intercede; then his own arm brought him salvation, and his righteousness upheld him. He put on righteousness as a breastplate, and a helmet of salvation on his head; he put on garments of vengeance for clothing, and wrapped himself in zeal as a cloak. According to their deeds, so will he repay, wrath to his adversaries, re-payment to his enemies; to the coastlands he will render repayment. So they shall fear the name of the Lord from the West, and his glory from the rising of the sun; for he will come like a rushing stream, which the wind of the Lord drives. "And a Redeemer will come to Zion, to those in Jacob who turn from transgression," declares the Lord.[dxli]

Shall we clothe ourselves as God clothes Himself in armor, to intercede for the dreams and destinies of our loved ones that are locked up in prison cells? May we stand in the gap as a bridge for God to do a miracle beyond what is imaginable. Then, let us prepare in faith, in hopes, and in expectancy, for God to come through in full in a mighty way. For our Redeemer lives and our Redeemer listens! He waits in our future with breath and grace, moving on the intercessions of His prayer warriors, and rescuing with love His sons and daughters to bring them to safety, to bring them home.

232

CAME TO MY RESCUE

Jesus—the name is sweet and simple, yet powerful and profound. When I think about the identity behind the name, I am speechless. Maybe it's because He is the kindest man that I've ever known. Maybe it's because He has believed in me for far longer than my existence. One thing I know is that all of this would've never been known if He hadn't come to my rescue in the first place. For my salvation is just that—a story of rescue. In a moment, my life went from dark to light, hopeless to purposed, empty to overflowing. One call, one cry, and He was there as if He'd been waiting for this one moment for a long time. The truth is, He had been. This is the good news every person deserves to know. In St. Augustine's words: "God loves each of us as if there was only one of us."[dxlii] That love is what changed my life. In Psalm 18 it says,

In my distress, I called to the Lord, I cried to my God for help. From his temple he heard my voice; my cry came before him, into his ears… He reached down from on high and took hold of me; he drew me out of deep waters… He brought me out into a spacious place; he rescued me because he delighted in me.[dxliii]

My rescuer was waiting and listening, and thus, the moment happened where everything changed.

God's love cannot decrease or increase because it is so great towards us. The same Jesus who reached down from on high for me is the same Jesus who pulled Peter up from sinking when his faith was shaken by doubt. It's the same Jesus who comes to your rescue simply because He delights in you. Since being in a relationship with Jesus, I've learned to trust *we are a team*. He may say, "Come," and I may go forth in faith and sink in doubt, but He's still there to rescue me. He may challenge me to go out of my comfort zone into an impossible battle, but He still promises, "I am with you" because we are a team. It reminds me of when Joab and Abishai are going to fight the Arameans and Joab says,

If the Arameans are too strong for me, then you are to rescue me; but if the Ammonites are too strong for you, then I will rescue you. Be strong and let us fight bravely for our people and the cities of our God. The Lord will do what is good in his sight.[dxliv] (1 Chronicles 19:12-13)

Likewise, Jesus believes in us enough, today, to fight for His people with what's in our hands. He rescued us to rescue and restore others as well. Still, He has a unique love for each of us that loves us as if there was only one of us. It's a profound mystery, but it's still a message that is not meant to be kept silent. As Psalm 138:3 says: "When I called, you answered me; you made me bold and stouthearted."[dxlv] The same name you called to rescue you is the same name you call to make you bold in the rescuing. And if in the pursuit the battle seems too great, then He will rescue you (Thankfully we're on a team with a Prince who doesn't need rescuing). But let me also remind you, the enemy creates doubt where there is certainty. When there is certainty in your call, in your battle, the waters will remind you they are there. But know God hasn't placed you in something you can't handle. Jesus may be fighting on your behalf, but He is also waiting and listening to come to your rescue. Yet, whether you stand or sink, you have nothing to fear, because He's got you.

You're a team. He came to your rescue then, and His love *unchanged* still comes to your rescue now. Your salvation story is a story of rescue that continues to be written.

I'm praying that if you haven't had your rescue story happen yet, that today would be {the day} you'll never forget— one where your everything changes and your greatest love story begins to

unfold; one where you accept Jesus into your heart and allow Him to be your Savior. For He's been waiting for a long time, ready to rescue you, listening for the moment you'd call out His name, that you may know His unique and unconditional love for you.

"For God so [greatly] loved *and* dearly prized the world, that He [even] gave His [One and] only begotten Son, so that whoever believes *and* trusts in Him [as Savior] shall not perish, but have eternal life."[dxlvi]
John 3:16

233

TREASURES IN JARS OF CLAY

> *But we have this treasure in jars of clay to show that this all-surpassing power is from God and not from us. We are hard pressed on every side, but not crushed; perplexed, but not in despair; persecuted, but not abandoned; struck down, but not destroyed.*^{dxlvii}
> 2 Corinthians 4:7-9

We tend to find our treasures in moments, photographs, gifts, or even our securities. Although our greatest treasure could be found in a promise or delight, our forever grandest treasure should always be our very salvation! For some reason, God saw us covered in shame and chose to wash us clean—no blemishes left, no price to pay, so now we can spend forever with Him. His love and grace is our treasure—it shapes us every day. It is then beautiful that we are breakable and moldable in affliction, because in our *brokenness* we are reshaped in His image *to the most precise beauty*. We are God's treasure, and our treasure is God's design.

234

THE FINISHING TOUCH

Recently my mind has been wandering to the thought process of a creator. Whether that's an artist mixing the perfect shade to bring out a certain emotion, a designer adding a particular painting to a room to bring that finishing touch, or a songwriter adding one last simple melody to make the song feel "complete." However, I can't help but think that when someone else comes across this piece of art, there is so much they do see, yet so much they don't. Then there's each of our lives. There's our hearts, gifts, dreams—and God designed them all. I wonder what it was like for Him to ponder up a blueprint of His best and most immaculate of thoughts, and then to look over the unimaginable vision He created to see what finishing touches would make it "very good." I love that when He created the world, humans were both His finishing touch and the forefront of His mind. All He had dreamt up was for them, Adam and Eve, and for us, His sons and daughters, to walk into with such an ease. This was and is grace at its finest. If there's ever a moment we forget that we are loved, we need only to sit back and remember the extravagant designs of the Designer's heart. He creates everything perfectly, and He does it all for you.

In *Pride and Prejudice*, Mr. Darcy proposes to a woman he's fallen madly in love with named Elizabeth Bennett.[dxlviii] She rejects his proposal by laying two offences before him, in ignorance of his true character. To remediate the offences, he does acts of kindness for her family without saying a word to her. He saves her family's name by funding her sister's runaway marriage, and he sets up Elizabeth's other sister to be betrothed with his best friend. When Elizabeth runs into him again, finding out by accident what he's done, she's completely smitten. He then says these very words to her: "You must know... surely, you must know it was all for you."[dxlix] As Mr. Darcy went behind the scenes to woo his chosen's heart, God goes before and behind the scenes for you to be allured to His. Everything that is good, beautiful, and brings such joy, is *all for you*. As C. S. Lewis says: "Look for Christ and you will find him, and with him, everything else."[dl] If you'll stand still, you'll remember His extravagant designs all around you, all for you, and all because of His love for you. If what you're hoping for seems slow in its coming, know His finishing touch is well worth the wait. The Creator who is overlooking it all, will bring it to the perfect completion. As Philippians 1:6 states: "And I am convinced and sure of this very thing, that He Who began a good work in you will continue until the day of Jesus Christ [right up to the time of His return], developing [that good work] and perfecting and bringing it to full completion in you."[dli] We can live as small and safe as we choose, or as daring and big as we dream, yet God will always have the finishing touch on our lives to fulfill the greatest longings of our hearts. Continually remember, He is always faithful to complete what He started, that there are still so many coatings of love you don't even realize are taking place; and lastly, "Keep yourselves in the love of God, looking for the mercy of our Lord Jesus Christ unto eternal life,"[dlii] (Jude 1:21) for His mercy is everywhere, we only need the faith to see it.

235

TO THE MOON AND BACK

I do believe in fairies! I do! I do![dliii]

I absolutely love this line from Peter Pan, because I do believe the words we speak hold **much** power. Sometimes we don't realize the *immensity* of power they hold, and we declare too much in defeat rather than belief. Yet as much as our words hold power, our thoughts are what release their impact. When our thoughts are noble, they can build kingdoms beyond our sight. Yet when our thoughts are fearful, worrisome, or prideful, they can create ruins where palaces were being prepared. I fully believe that *belief is as powerful as magic, for a little bit goes a long way in impossible odds.* Belief may be a small thing, but it changes everything. In Matthew 9:27-29 it says:

"As Jesus left the house, he was followed by two blind men crying out, 'Mercy, Son of David! Mercy on us!' When Jesus got home, the blind men went in with him. Jesus said to them, 'Do you really believe I can do this?' They said, 'Why, yes, Master!' He touched their eyes and said, 'Become what you believe.' It happened. They saw."[dliv]

Likewise, there are things that God has spoken to you that you need to declare! Some of you need to believe in God again, that He is love! Some of you need to believe in miracles again, that He can do all things! Some of you need to believe in your promises again, that He will be faithful to His Word! Your words have an immensity of power being heard in heaven when you speak: "I do believe in God! I do, I do!" If we become what we believe, then the opposite is that we trap what we disbelieve.

Disbelief is a sealed container that traps God's goodness, or in this sake, of magic's potential. So choose your words wisely, my friend, and believe again!

236

THINK KINGDOM

When I think of nobility, I imagine ordinary acts with kingdom purposes; I imagine knocking on palace doors with pure intentions, I imagine restless warriors ready to fight—to stand. Isaiah 32:1, 2+8 says, "But look! A king will rule in the right way, and his leaders will carry out justice. Each one will stand as a shelter from high winds, provide safe cover in stormy weather. Each will be cool running water in parched land, a huge granite outcrop giving shade in the desert... those who are noble make noble plans, and stand for what is noble." (Isaiah 32:1, 2 + 8 MSG) The thing I love most about nobility is that it reminds me of my Father, my King, my God. I think of the noble and heroic deeds He does daily; I think of how He acts with wisdom and love, I think of how He is just and yet merciful. When I think nobility, I think kingdom, and when I think kingdom, I think as my Father.

I don't know if you've ever had off days, the days where you can't be bothered. They tend to be the days you are needed most, and typically on those days, we excuse our behaviors due to our circumstance. Yet, I wonder if that is how we, as children of nobility, are intended to live? What if a king stopped ruling for a day because he didn't feel like it, or the president decided to have a vacation in the middle of a war because he couldn't be bothered? Thankfully, we don't hold as much pressure as them. But I wonder how much more impact we would create when we decided to stand for what is noble, for that is who we are as children of God. I believe love shocks when it acts. It is in that shock that for a split second, every wall and fortress comes down in someone's heart. I believe it is in that split second someone can feel the love of God the most. For though God has a throne always waiting for Him to sit upon, I believe He rescues more than sits back and He seeks out the lost more than He reigns with the found. When I imagine my Father sitting enthroned on high, I see Him looking at me, looking at the kingdom. And how I desire to position myself the same. That to stand in nobility is to lead in royalty. It is to think higher—to think kingdom—when the world beckons you to cave and bow down to your emotions.

You may not always feel like being perfect, but it is always the right thing to do good. As Galatians 4:18 says, "It is a good thing to be ardent in doing good, but not just when I am in Your presence."[dlv] I think it is vital for us to be the hands and feet of Jesus, for we may be the only chance someone has to hear the gospel with our lives. The gospel shocks because its depth of love surprises. It acts instead of sits. It loves despite the circumstance. The gospel isn't always glamorous for it does require dying to self, but it is powerful. It is the cool running water to the thirsty; it is shade to the weary, it is beauty to the broken. I love how Moses, before he died, blessed his tribe by speaking beauty and boldness into them. One of my favorites in particular was over Benjamin where he speaks: "God's beloved; God's permanent residence. Encircled by God all day long, within whom God is at home." (Deuteronomy 33:12 MSG) I wonder what legacy others see in you? And I wonder what legacy you can leave in others? For I've learned, legacy doesn't happen in isolation, and legacy doesn't happen alone. May you use your position to prepare rooms for the lost, to feed the hungry with your abundance, to bless others as you've been blessed. To raise up leaders in the kingdom to go forth beside you and after you on a mission to not just rest in the palace's promise, but to get restless for injustice and ready to act, even outside of His presence, to shock the world with love and shine Jesus! To think kingdom, to stand for what is noble, and to rule like your Father reigns, for it is powerful with its surprises.

237

MORE

Joel 2:28 + Acts 2:17 say: "In the last days, God says, I will pour out my Spirit on *all* people. Your sons and daughters will prophesy, your young men will see visions, your old men will dream dreams."[dlvi] This verse is in two different parts of the Bible—one is a prophecy in the Old Testament, the other is the very fulfillment of the prophecy in the New Testament. It not only shows the fulfillment of Scripture, but also the character of the extravagant God pouring out His Spirit here and now, for we are living in the last days! I think some of us sweep this verse under the rug and like to keep God in the box we can comprehend.

But how much more you could live if you trusted Him to do greater things in you and through you! Jesus was the lamb, but He was also the lion. He was loving and kind, but He was also daring and powerful. He was fully God, yet He was also fully human. So to say that this verse doesn't apply to you is well... a sweep under the rug. Christ's Spirit dwells and lives in you! And it's not a weak flame. He is a wildfire that cannot be missed when we trust Him with our all. Some of you will overlook this one devotional, and I send no condemnation your way. But some of you know there is still more, and you will find it in the baptism of the Holy Spirit! It's not crazy or weird; it is powerful and personal at the least. God says—I will pour out my Spirit on *all* people, which includes you! So if you want to experience the God who is as much of a lion than a lamb, ask, and I believe wholeheartedly you will speak in tongues, you will prophesy, you will dream new dreams, and you will see visions! He's the most exciting and adventurous partner to do life with—trust Him and allow Him to fill you from head to toe. He is a fire that can never be put out, and one you'll be thankful never dies. You'll never know until you ask; so take a risk, you won't regret it. Greater things are in you and ahead of you, and the "Spirit himself intercedes for you"[dlvii] (Romans 8:26), "diving into the depths of God"[dlviii] to let you in on what God's up to (1 Corinthians 2:12).

There's more, you simply just have to *ask*.

238

OWN YOUR FLAME

Be obsessed. Become obsessed with your *now*.
Love it with everything within you, seeing what is unseen, and taking hold of random pieces to create its structure. Encourage your heart by speaking tenderly to it. Your fight is not against flesh and blood but against the rulers, against the powers of this world's darkness, always trying to snuff out your flame. Keep it ablaze! Live to be inspired, love your every waking moment, and enjoy today. Take hold of your moments and bravely dive all in. Then your fire will burn bright and high for all to see.
Even if you are the only one who can see it, own your flame.

> *My heart is on fire, boiling over with passion.*
> *Bubbling up within me are these beautiful lyrics*
> *as a lovely poem to be sung for the King.*
> *Like a river bursting its banks, I'm overflowing with words,*
> *spilling out into this sacred story.*[dlix]
> Psalm 45:1

239

THE KARATE KID

When it comes to my relationship with God, I'm like the student who is anxious to "be" the greatest karate kid. I'm telling the teacher, "This is what I can do." While God listens and waits, that He may speak and I may learn. When it comes to becoming: the lessons begin with trust and obedience. When it comes to a teacher who is wise and knows best: we must learn to be okay with not having all our questions answered, for the lessons that make the least sense prepare us the most. It takes time for preparation to become a habit; habits then become the disciplined movements of who we are. When going through a lesson, remember our Teacher's ways are higher and wiser than we can imagine. There is a reason to repetition, but we must learn the discipline before He speaks so that we won't run before we're ready. If you've been in the preparation, just wait, for what may have seemed natural had a supernatural purpose attached to it.

One of my favorite lines the Teacher says is in *The Karate Kid* is, "It's how we put on the jacket. It's how we treat people. Everything is Kung fu."[dlx] When it comes to "being a Christian," or simply loving God, it's so much the same. It's not just on the field, it's in the home. Likewise, success does not happen overnight. It is because of hours of preparation that what we see is so magnetizing. Yet no matter the greatness of success, if the person is not ready, the prize can easily crumble. It's not about reaching the destination; it's about every step of love, dignity, humility, and compassion along the way. How easily entangled we can become in the lines of striving that we forget the wide-open fields of grace. If we cannot love well at home, with our friends and families, then it is a reminder, that our outer strength will be affected when our inner strength starts diminishing. Loving those closest to us is what enables us to love the world around us. *Everything is loving God*. The sooner we learn this, the freer we become.

Micah 4 in my Bible is titled, **The Making of God's People**, with verses 1-4 reading:

But when all is said and done, God's Temple on the mountain, firmly fixed, will dominate all mountains, towering above surrounding hills. People will stream to it and many nations set out for it saying, "Come, let's climb God's mountain. Let's go to the Temple of Jacob's God. <u>He will teach us how to live. We'll know how to live God's way.</u>" True teaching will issue from Zion, God's revelation from Jerusalem. He'll establish justice in the rabble of nations and settle disputes in faraway places. They'll trade in their swords for shovels, their spears for rakes and hoes. Nations will quit fighting each other, quit learning how to kill one another. Each man will sit under his own shade tree, each woman in safety will tend her own garden. God-of-the-Angel-Armies says so, and he means what he says.[dlxi] (emphasis added)

He will teach us how to live *His* way. In order for that to happen, our minds must unlearn to relearn. To empty our mind of what we know, to be filled with what He knows. We must be willing to listen and learn from the One who knows us best to lead us to be who we're wanting to become. As the little boy says, "Kung fu isn't about fighting, it's about making peace with your enemies."[dlxii] It isn't about being the best, it's about being able to stand your ground on His truth, keeping your peace instead of running from the war. We don't go seeking out battles, but if they come, we wear an armor to fight. As Proverbs 3:11-12 says, "But don't, dear friend, resent God's discipline… It's the child he loves that God corrects."[dlxiii] The small disciplines of being still, obedient, humble, and kind, will take you much further than you can imagine. You are in the making to be His people, you just need to trust the Teacher. Whatever you are going through, no matter how much it doesn't make sense, keep going and trusting, for within you a fighter is rising up. One who knows being still and doing nothing are two completely different things; one who knows peace conquers the greatest wars; one who knows that faith sees beyond the natural; one who knows that the victory is won by Him before the fight begins, one who knows that they are God's and He is theirs. That's when—you *run*.

240

OUR FORTRESS

Worry is a transformer. It's a weight to your spirit, a hindrance to your run. As words of life fill you, words of worry drain you. It's a weed in your garden, a doubt to your promise, a place it doesn't belong, an unwelcome foe. It can change a perspective from free to limited, a home from belonging to out of place. It can change warriors from heroes to fleers, and royals from crowned to alone. *Worry taints reality's sight.* It rejects hope and loses heart. Worry is not from God.

Psalm 91 says:

When you sit enthroned under the shadow of Shaddai, you are hidden in the strength of God Most High. He's the hope that holds me and the Stronghold to shelter me, the only God for me, and my great confidence. He will rescue you from every hidden trap of the enemy, and he will protect you from false accusation and any deadly curse. His massive arms are wrapped around you, protecting you. You can run under his covering of majesty and hide. His arms of faithfulness are a shield keeping you from harm. You will never worry about an attack of demonic forces at night nor have to fear a spirit of darkness coming against you. Don't fear a thing! Whether by night or by day, demonic danger will not trouble you, nor will the powers of evil launched against you...When we live our lives within the shadow of God Most High, our secret hiding place, we will always be shielded from harm. How then could evil prevail against us or disease infect us? For here is what the Lord has spoken to me: "Because you have delighted in me as my great lover, I will greatly protect you. I will set you in a high place, safe and secure before my face. I will answer your cry for help every time you pray, and you will find and feel my presence even in your time of pressure and trouble. I will be your glorious hero and give you a feast. You will be satisfied with a full life and with all that I do for you. For you will enjoy the fullness of my salvation!"[dlxiv]

Hope is then your anchor! It's a certainty to the more ahead beyond your sight, and it sees further than reality's reach. Turn your worry into worship, and you'll always remember His love for you. If we constantly could walk with the truth of His love for us, the peace of His kindness pursuing us, the grace of His might working before us, we wouldn't doubt our steps or turns or decisions. We wouldn't speak in fear, but in wonder. If we missed a turn, we wouldn't freak out, we would laugh and listen to the Holy Spirit's GPS, His *Grace Positioning System*, and get back on track. I'm sure He'd laugh with us and shake His head. Sometimes when worry comes and all is darkness and fog, we need only to sing out His name to run into His arms as our fortress. To then meditate on the power of His words and rest in the ease of prayer's movement. We are always safe in His presence, for He is our secret place where we can always run. Love is our fortress from worry, and peace our beckoning to hope. So when we enter into His gates with praise, worry stays far, far away, from our kingdom, and our hearts stay rightfully at rest, at home.

241

FIRM AND SECURE

For I know the plans I have for you; plans to prosper you and not to harm you, plans to give you a hope and a future. A hope that is an anchor for your soul, a future that is firm and secure in Me. Trials and hardships may come, but I'll never leave you nor forsake you. For I am your refuge, in whom you can trust, upon which you can stand. This fight is not your own, but Mine; it is already won. Don't worry about what's ahead of you, or what's behind, for your story has been made new. Trust in My love for you, and set your eyes on this hope: for I am your hope, and I am your future. With Me, nothing can stand against you, for I am yours.

"God is striding ahead of you. He's right there with you.
He won't let you down; he won't leave you. Don't be intimidated. Don't worry."[dlxv]
Deuteronomy 31:8

242

DON'T DESERT THE DESERT

My leader looked me straight in the eye and spoke, "The enemy wants to see how much water you have left while you're in the desert," and that statement couldn't have been more true. When I landed in Australia, I knew it was where I was called to; I knew God whispered, "You belong here" to me time after time, but what was in my heart and what was my reality were quite different. I had gardens and kingdoms in my heart but storms and deserts before my eyes. I didn't walk into flowers and daisies; I walked into a war. It wasn't long before I had to open up my journal, reread what He promised, and declare the promises out loud as my truth and hope. I thought Australia was my destination only to find out it was the beginning of my pioneering. My gifts became my weapons, my strengths became my armor, and my promises became my shield. I learned to stand firm, and I learned that there was a deep, deep everlasting well within me that never ran out. As Isaiah 40:3 says: "A voice of one who cries: Prepare in the wilderness the way of the Lord [clear away the obstacles]; make straight and smooth in the desert a highway for our God!"[dlxvi]

I find it so interesting that the preparing is in the wilderness—that the paths are made straight in the desert. Looking at a desert, it doesn't seem like much. Just a lot of sand and sun, both not being ideal for longevity. Yet it is there that He decides to walk; it is there He dwells with us in an undeniably present way, for there are no obstacles in sight to defer our eyes from what the Lord is doing and speaking. We just have to stay the path and determine to not ditch the desert: for we would walk away from many revelations of who God is and from many weapons designed to equip us for where we are being called. What my leader spoke to me in that moment shifted my perspective, for he proceeded to say, "If you are called, it doesn't matter if you are in the desert." No matter *where* it was God was calling me, my wholehearted trust needed to be *placed* in Him. Even if it meant His presence was leading through dark valleys, I needed to trust Him and follow; even if it meant taking the longer path over the shortcuts, if it's where His presence was leading, my choice would resolve to stay by His side.

I think that when it comes to the desert, we should have the mindset of a camel. Yes, I said a camel. Get this, the one humped camel was domesticated over 5,000 years ago in the deserts of the Middle East, and is ideally suited to this hot, arid region. The fat deposit localized in the hump allows it to throw off body heat rapidly. Its features, coat, and feet supply protection from the sand and the wind, and it can carry heavy burdens through the desert *for months* without a water supply, other than what it extracts from even salty vegetation.[dlxvii] We likewise need to be able to throw off the heat when the enemy tries to sidetrack us in the hot and dry seasons. When you are going and going for what feels like forever on a word God has spoken, and you feel parched because of not being poured into, find strength in the fruits of the Spirit and dig deep into the well within you that is filled with His promises and purposes over your life. The desert paths are not the most glamorous, but they do hold the greatest treasures. They're not always willingly chosen, but they hold great destiny for the chosen who walk their paths. They don't look the most promising to the eye at first, but they hold by far the most promise compared to any other path in the end. Isaiah 40:31 ends with:

"But those who wait for the Lord [who expect, look for, and hope in Him] shall change *and* renew their strength *and* power; they shall lift their wings *and* mount up [close to God] as eagles [mount up to the sun]; they shall run and not be weary, they shall walk and not faint *or* become tired."[dlxviii]

Those who walk in the desert are promised to walk out stronger, for they are not absent from the heat or the battle—but they are the ones who find the sufficiency of God and are changed into warriors in the process. We pray for straight paths, but they look like deserts. Still what beauty lies ahead for those who don't desert the desert paths, what sweet promises await their heart's deepest longings.

243

THE RARE

Divine awakenings take place in death.
Tombs are new beginnings. Ashes are new life. Fire is new power.
It is not the typical association with each of these, yet it is in rare occasions, the very location where God greets us as a new person, to lead us now into our ready destination.
If it's happened to you, then you, my friend, are one of the *rare* ones He's chosen to let you walk through this process of unforgettable breaking to empower you for an unshakable movement.
There's always movement after death when you're awakened to
LIFE. You're not the same, nor will anything else be.

> *When you sleep between sharpened stakes,*
> *I see you sparkling like silver and glistening like gold,*
> *covered by the beautiful wings of a dove!*[dlxix]
> Psalm 68:13

244

HIS CHOSEN ONES

My dad once asked me, "Why do we need to go to church if we already pray and read the Bible?" When he asked that, I honestly didn't know the complete answer, probably because I never questioned it myself. But later, I discovered Hebrews 10:25 that reads: "Let us not give up meeting together, as some are in the habit of doing, but let us encourage one another—and all the more as you see the Day approaching."[dlxx] Yet, I still don't think I realized its truth until a friend moved from standing beside me to standing in front of me in church. Little did she know I was in a season of spiritual attacks as she spoke these words to me: "This whole service I felt like I was standing in the gap for you, and I just saw a line of people standing beside me. You've been in a lot of warfare lately, but know we are fighting for you in prayer so you can rest and stand behind us." The truth is: destined days are approaching—they are destined to reveal Christ and His glory— they are destined to happen through you and for you. Yet, as Christ's coming draws closer day-by-day, the enemy does not sleep and slumber. He attacks, he destroys, and he does so silently, almost unnoticeably. Signs of his attacks are anxiety, worry, sickness, confusion, isolation, hopelessness, and in all other forms that are the opposite of God's Word and plan for us. (Life does happen, and all these can happen naturally, but if they come out of nowhere like a wave—especially after a God-thing has happened—be aware of warfare's welcoming.) Maybe your life is great right now and everything is just fine, but I'm sorry to say that it won't always be flowers and sunshine. And when those days come that aren't so brilliant, the church will always rise up to stand in the gap on your behalf. The church is made up of imperfect people; yes, I am one of them. Yet, it's also made up of people devoted to Christ, and the heart of Christ is to encourage one another through the highs and lows. I love how Bobbie Houston says, "Mankind was created for Eden, and Eden for mankind. Earth was created for splendor and the splendor of the earth is found in the fullness of Christ. When the fullness of Christ takes residence within the human heart, when it begins to water and tend the gardens and fields of our lives, and when it truly radiates from within His bride, enabling her to become the catalyst of change she is designed to be... then the earth will become the vineyard he had in mind."[dlxxi]

The truth is we were made for relationship—not only with Christ, but also with others, which is just as vital. The church is His bride and His heart is for her. Since the church is made up of imperfect people, well, I guess that's exactly who He is madly in love with. We all have hopes and dreams, struggles and fears, good days and bad days, successes and failures. The beautiful thing about Eden is that grace created it and grace kept it. How much more shall we spur one another on in acts of grace? To stand in the gap when others are weary, to encourage one another in waiting on a promise, to speak life into dead hopes, and to love extravagantly when others are in pain. As Hebrews 10:39 says, "But we are not of those who shrink back and are destroyed, but of those who believe and are saved."[dlxxii] My answer to my dad's question now is this: *If we truly are in love with the heart of Christ, then we also will be in love with His bride, His church, where all relationship is built and not lost, where it is valued and protected and not looked over and forgotten, where it is stood for and fought for, not left empty and alone.* As Francis Chan said, "If I stop pursuing God, I am letting our relationship deteriorate. We never grow closer to God when we just live life; it takes deliberate pursuit and attentiveness."[dlxxiii] The same goes with His bride, with others. We are the arms and feet of Christ extended to reveal His heart. In isolation, we cannot be that or experience that. But as a church, we can fight for others and be fought for ourselves—for He is faithful to His chosen and through His chosen ones.

245

GO IN PEACE

> *The priest Eli was on duty at the entrance to God's Temple in the customary seat. Crushed in soul, Hannah prayed to God and cried and cried—inconsolably. Then she made a vow: "Oh, God-of-the-Angel-Armies, if you'll take a good, hard look at my pain, If you'll quit neglecting me and go into action for me by giving me a son, I'll give him completely, unreservedly to you. I'll set him apart for a life of holy discipline. It so happened that as she continued in prayer before God, Eli was watching her closely. Hannah was praying in her heart, silently. Her lips moved, but no sound was heard. Eli jumped to the conclusion that she was drunk. He approached her and said, "You're drunk! How long do you plan to keep this up? Sober up, woman!" Hannah said, "Oh no, sir—please! I'm a woman hard used. I haven't been drinking. Not a drop of wine or beer. The only thing I've been pouring out is my heart, pouring it out to God. Don't for a minute think I'm a bad woman. It's because I'm so desperately unhappy and in such pain that I've stayed here so long." Eli answered her, "Go in peace. And may the God of Israel give you what you have asked of him."*[dlxxiv]
> 1 Samuel 1:9-17

My heart goes out to Hannah. It breaks for her because she is so desperate for a child that she can't even keep it together. I'm not sure if you've ever held something so dear to your heart, that when you caught a glimpse of it, you almost broke into tears because of your longing for it. This is Hannah. She has been longing to have children, is married to a man who's other wife has children of her own, and that wife would rub it in Hannah's face ruthlessly. It says: "Every time she went to the sanctuary, she could expect to be taunted."[dlxxv] Not only is Hannah very aware of her barrenness, but her husband's other wife, Peninnah, would also not let her forget it. So here we come to Hannah making a vow before God, pouring out her heart, doing whatever it takes for Him to answer her prayers, and He answers. He does the miraculous.

I love that the line after her prayer reads, "It so happened," because anytime that is inserted into a story, it shows His story was at work all along. While she was praying, not even with words because of the weight of her brokenness, a man of God was captivated. To him, it only made sense that she could be drunk, for it was common for drunk people to enter, and who else would pray without making a sound? Yet, as Eli heard her heart and not her words, he then could sense the warmth of the Father's love reaching out to her desperation, giving her a vow in return: she would fall pregnant. And so he says: "Go in peace."

Ephesians 1:14 says:

He is given to us like an engagement ring is given to a bride, as the first installment of what's coming! He is our hope-promise of a future inheritance which seals us until we have all of redemption's promises and experience complete freedom—all for the supreme glory and honor of God![dlxxvi]

Likewise, I believe destiny births at the altar of surrender. Our altar of surrender then becomes our altar of promise. As Hannah went before the Lord, she dedicated the dearest thing in her heart to God. She then bore a son, who not only would become a prophet, but would later anoint a small shepherd to one day be king. Also known as, David, the great poet and songwriter of almost all of Psalms; his words we still hold onto and hear God through today, thousands of years later. What I love is that God did more than imaginable with the dearest sacrifice Hannah brought to the altar and multiplied it to be a blessing for generations to come. Sound familiar? The same God who broke bread and fed five thousand, the same One who died on the cross that all may live, is the same God who used her ashes for beauty. When she felt like she was at her end, He came in most fully.

Whatever are the silent sighs of your heart, so deep that words cannot express, know He is watching the movement of your lips, hearing every word. Know He honors your sacrifice, He takes to heart your surrender, and He honors it in return. He slips an engagement ring on your finger. It's His promise of what's coming! What we saw as our greatest desire was but a small picture to His greatest plan. As God spoke to me once, "The enemy gets annoyed when you whisper for it is more powerful than your shout; it's only for my ears to hear, and so I lean down to listen. He hates it because I will never listen and not move. *I always have something in store for the prayers of the silent.*" God bends down to listen to your requests, He watches for the movement of His chosen, He moves on behalf of your surrender, never does He stay silent or stay still, even if it cannot be seen yet, for He *always* has something in store for the prayers of the silent.

Maybe it's time to write some vows to the Lord, as vows to your bride/groom cost sacrifice, so yours should too. *Desperation drives us to the deep where His vows go deeper still.* If it's easy, then it's not deep. When it costs, it shows true surrender—it shows you truly are putting Him first. Maybe it's volunteering in church, maybe it's to keep your language pure, maybe it's to stop watching what is polluting your mind. Whatever it is, He is worth more, I promise. And as He reveals His promise to you, you will discover your worth to Him in a greater depth than ever before. In the deep, you'll discover a peace that cannot be shaken where His love continues on for you. No matter the depth of your vows, He goes deeper still. Write down what's in your heart, but also write down your heart to God, then write down His heart for you. His vow is a future inheritance, which seals us until we have all of redemption's promises and experience complete freedom! As Isaiah 54:1 says: "Sing, barren woman, you who never bore a child; burst into song, shout for joy, you who were never in labor; because more are the children of the desolate woman than of her who has a husband," says the Lord."[dlxxvii] You not only can laugh without fear of the future, you can also sing for having caught sight of its inheritance. Go in peace; He has heard your prayer and is moving beyond your doubting. His vow to you will always be greater than your vow to Him; just trust Him, meet Him at the altar.

My vows to Him:
_____
_____
_____
_____
_____
_____
_____

His vows to me:
_____
_____
_____
_____
_____
_____
_____

246

STILL DO

I love who You are, Jesus.
You speak *tenderly* while <u>alluring</u> us to Your heart. It's so subtle, but captivating. Your voice is entrancing to a love that is wild **for us**. And in the wilderness, we are met by beauty—where a table is set before us with the *finest of wines and ripest of fruits*. A path filled with *wonderful surprises* and *desirable strength*. It's where we <u>grow</u>, but it's also where we **remember.** Remember Your grace, Your majesty, and Your love that was **first** for us. How sweet the simplicity that follows when we look at You. How easy it is to let our walls down and to let You take our every worry away. When I look into Your eyes my worst of fears quiet, my deepest of confusion stops. With You, <u>nothing has to make sense, yet it all does</u>. Because You are perfect— everything I dream about. I love You for who You are. That's why I first fell in love, and every day after, **still do.**

We love because he first loved us. [dlxxviii]
1 John 4:19

247

LOVE LETTERS

I can't shake this verse from my heart, "Wait, my daughter, until you find out what happens. For the man *will not rest* until the matter is settled today."[dlxxix] (Ruth 3:18, emphasis added) Ruth has been experiencing this orchestration of God up to this point while trusting Him completely. But now she's being told: Wait. Her story begins with once upon a time, unfolds with many "it just so happened" moments, and is all leading up to this moment of suspense; yet at the most climactic part of the movie, the remote is picked up, Life pauses the screen, and the God-orchestrated story comes to a halt with the most unexpected word of— *wait*. She was probably as anxious as I am to know what's about to happen, and was most likely ready to just go and make it happen herself. [But by doing nothing, she expressed that she trusted God with everything.] Because **He** was the one who would not rest until it all worked out for her *best*. He was the one who picked up the pen to begin writing her story, and He was the one who continually pursued her beyond the promise. It reminds me a lot of a Disney story I know—one with a prince and a sleeping beauty. One who for seventeen years felt like her dreams would never come true, but it just so happened that a prince laid eyes upon her castle, who just so happened to have discovered her story, who just so happened to be the one who fell in love with her while she was at rest. Do you see the common theme? To be at rest within yourself is one of the utmost beauties.

God has a plan for your life. I can assure you that. And many of you have something so dear to your heart that you just haven't seen come to pass yet. It feels like it's been a journey of seventeen years waiting for your dream to come true, but let me remind you of this—there is no **one** like you. Here's the thing, those desires aren't in "your" heart for just any reason. They were *placed* there. What you can do is *be at rest* and *entrust them to God*. What you shouldn't do is try to figure out what's happening and take the matters into your own hands. If there is anything I have learned about waiting for my prince, or my dearest dream, it's that *God is as purposeful as He is faithful*. His timing is both perfect and kind. As Steven Furtick said, "When God is the One talking to you, one word is more than enough."[dlxxx] It's enough to hold onto, to trust in, to wait with. He has purpose to every word He speaks. And when He says wait, He is also saying, "I am orchestrating a purpose specifically *for **you***. One that you have been dreaming of forever, but one that you were also about to let go of because it deemed impossible in your heart. I'm not a God of false hope. I'm a God of miracles. I will not rest until my plan for you is fulfilled. You have My word." You know what the crazy thing is? Everything works out for Ruth in time. *The key to every "once upon a time" is that it takes time for that dream to come to pass.* My encouragement for you is to think of God's words as love letters. They are there to remind you not only that He is still there, but that He is still working on your behalf for His glory, simply because He loves you. And when you're about to give up, He will send you another love letter to hold onto. I believe with each love letter God is asking us, "Will you settle or will you wait?" Which really is Him hinting towards: *I have **more** for you; be at rest, you can trust Me.*

Rest in God, and watch Him do the rest.

248

A PROMISED LAND

He speaks promises—
from left to right, from before and behind;
they are for us, placed before us, designed within us,
and orchestrated around us.
They are true, and they are ours.

In Isaiah 55:10-11, the Lord says,

For as the rain and the snow come down from heaven, and do not return there without watering the earth and making it bear and sprout, and furnishing seed to the sower and bread to the eater; so will My word be which goes forth from My mouth; it will not return to Me empty, without accomplishing what I desire, and without succeeding in the matter for which I sent it.[dlxxxi]

These words remind me of this imagery of His promises: we are in the middle of the ocean, paddling in a direction where we cannot see what is ahead, and though we may get tired, and though we may get discouraged, our promise land is still there awaiting us. When we get there, when we step onto its fertile soil, it will be beyond what we hoped for or imagined—and we will know every stroke and every effort was worth it. In the process of waiting for His promise to come into view, we can know that like the rain and snow come down from heaven and do not return to it void, so His word will remain and will not return to Him empty, nor shall we be left empty-handed in the end.

249

IN THE BOAT

He whispered, "My child, where are you going that you don't need to go?"

Do you remember the story of Jesus, the disciples, and the violent storm? We read in Luke 8:22-24:

One of those days He and His disciples got into a boat, and He said to them, "Let us go across to the other side of the lake," so they put to sea. But as they were sailing, he fell off to sleep, and a whirlwind revolving from below upwards swept down on the lake, and the boat was filling with water, and they were in great danger. And the disciples came and woke him saying, "Master, master, we are perishing!" And He, being thoroughly <u>awakened</u>, censured and blamed and rebuked the wind and the raging waves; and they ceased, and there came a calm.[dlxxxii] (emphasis added)

I just recently travelled to Israel, and it just so happened that the Sea of Galilee, the same lake the disciples were on, was behind my hotel. This lake can go from beautifully breathtaking in one moment to furiously fierce the next. So much so that three men's lives were taken by its force the week prior to my arrival. The storms come out of nowhere and are nothing to tamper with. So in all actuality, the disciples' response to the storm isn't dramatic, but sensible in being completely stricken by fear of what naturally could take place. There's just… one small minor thing they forgot, in fact, I think many of us forget—Jesus is <u>still in the boat</u>, and He is asking many of us, "My child, where are you going that you don't need to go?"

If you've boarded the ship to your destination and can't see the end in sight, don't abandon ship. This is where the disciples lost heart, but here's how we can learn not to. First off, *their thoughts were more dangerous than their reality.* They came to Jesus saying, "We are perishing!" Not "we could perish, embrace yourself." They jumped to conclusions based off of their sight instead of their faith, when in fact, they were still untouched, the boat was just shaken. Likewise, when our finances are shaken or our security, are we going to be defeated the first moment the wind nudges us? Or are we going to, like Jesus, censor the situation, find the source the enemy is attacking with, and rebuke it with the Word and authority of God that dwells within us. Second, *they let their faith sink before the boat had a chance to.* Yes, it was reasonable in the natural, but when a supernatural God is in your boat, believe bigger than the ordinary. Don't wake Him up with your fear but your faith! Say something bizarre like, "Jesus, calm the storm." And miraculously, He just may! When you realize the same Jesus who walked on water is the same Jesus with you, you'll know fixing your eyes on Him is *still* the same path to your miracle.

Being in the boat doesn't always mean you are afraid, it may also show you are discontent. A dream may not seem destructive, but it can be as damaging if it draws us to jump out of the boat we are placed in. Sometimes, we can create our own storms with the thought-up dreams in our head that are clouding our sight of the present. So point three, stop letting the waves take out your boat. When thoughts of discontent or disaster hit, rebuke them and don't let them tear apart the good thing God is doing. When it comes to having Jesus in your boat, the craziest thing you can do is think that things are going to be greater outside of it. Secretly, the enemy isn't trying to get you to abandon ship, but abandon Jesus. And well, that will just not do. Don't let fear or discontent dreams take you away from the *truth* of who He is and what He is able to do. If you're in the boat with Jesus, know everything you can't see, He already has in sight, and the closer you are to Him, the closer you are to seeing everything He sees. Set sail and rebuke the winds of the enemy. Stay close to Jesus and stay in the boat. There can be no greater present if you already have Jesus beside you.

250

WEIGHTLESS

Oceans—the unending motion; the constant change; the unknown depths. Everything about them is intriguing with a sense of fear, yet a sense of wonder. They're fiercely beautiful. Still in moments, raging in others, and yet, they're the same. Underneath, it's calm, breathtaking. Everything fades away, and it's just you. For a moment, you feel found, and then when you come up for air, everything is different. There is so much more to see and discover; the land holds a new sense of freedom, the water brings a new sense of strength, and gravity is the only thing left holding you down. You are rejuvenated and your perception has been changed. The land that once held so many barriers, now welcomes you with peace. The water that once had so much strength now feels like air. The weaknesses you walked in with are suddenly washed away. The fear transformed into curiosity, anger turned into peace, frustrations into joy, and questions into hope. You are renewed and made alive again. You are found in the waves of the unknown.

I can't help but see God throughout this picture. Lori Thomason says it beautifully,

God's Love is like the ocean. It is a consuming force that cannot be controlled by a human. It is powerful and complete. It fills the space of your life leaving no voids. There are only two choices—in or out. Stepping into the current of God's Love alive is the place where human control ends and the magnificent Presence of God take over. Like waves splashing to the shore, it is active and alive.[dlxxxiii] There is just something so transforming about His love. Being lost, yet being found. Consumed, but free. Weak, yet strong. Like being weightless in gravity. God's love is so inviting and beautiful, but it's also a mystery full of wonder—and that is what so many people fear about it... about Him, the unknown. Yet once you step in, you find you're lost in His love, changed by His motions, and trusting in His direction. And you actually become found in the waves of the unknown. It becomes just you and Him. That's when everything changes from fear to curiosity, from anger to peace, from frustration into joy, scars into strength, and questions into hope. For His love is a transforming tide, one we just can't get enough of; one we become alive like a child within its pull, as it wraps its arms of strength around our hearts with fierce passion. It's when we run from the waves, from the things we can't control, that we become empty by trying to be full. But it is in His presence that we are filled; it is in His love that we are complete.

> *I ask him that with both feet planted firmly on love, you'll be able to take in with all followers of Jesus the extravagant dimensions of Christ's love. Reach out and experience the breadth! Test its length! Plumb the depths! Rise to the heights! Live full lives, full in the fullness of God.*[dlxxxiv]
> Ephesians 3:17-19

251

BREAKING FREE

I once used to look at every life as a story—a book full of new journeys and chapters, and within every story, highlights and scribbles to line their pages. Many of us are afraid of the chapters that we have already lived, because we don't want people to ever know them. Others are afraid of the chapters to come, not wanting to miss a page or mess up a line, to be as perfect and unique as possible—to stand out. But this is how I see it, you don't have to rip out pages and be ashamed of your earlier story, because when Jesus died and you gave your life to Him, your past was wiped clean. When you come before God, He won't see "your sins," because they are already forgiven and washed away. He'll see your new transformed and beating heart and smile and embrace His child come home. You are new, and that is something that brings freedom. If you are afraid of the chapters to come, you don't have to be. It's okay to stumble and to fall, because He goes behind *and* before you, working for your good as long as you love Him. He knows every page of your life, and He is creating it into one beautiful story, but it begins by breaking free. Breaking free from fear. Breaking free from insecurities. Breaking free from perfection. And breaking free from control. It is then that you'll be set free in grace. Set free in love. Set free in His perfection. Set free in His sovereignty. It is then that you will see *your story is found in His story*, and that brings a beautiful freedom.

> *"So now the case is closed.* There remains no accusing voice of condemnation against those who are joined in life-union with Jesus, the Anointed One. For the 'law' of the Spirit of life flowing through the anointing of Jesus has liberated us from the 'law' of sin and death."[dlxxxv]
> Romans 8:1-2 (emphasis added)

252

CROWNED

I have a fascination with crowns and kingdoms. The Parallel Study Bible commentary states: "Believers, like Christ, the antitypical Melchisedec, are *at once* kings and priests."[dlxxxvi] The moment someone confesses Jesus as their personal Lord and Savior, I imagine a crown appearing on their head, robes replacing old rags, and eyes opened to a completely new life. Yet, I pray we who have lived in the kingdom for some time will never lose sight of our own crowns, for *this* is the very reason for their belonging—to not be merely saved, but free. To be a kindred, an army, a family of believers, filled with insuppressible love that can't be kept quiet.

It is in freeing others that we are reminded of the freedom we have ourselves. Atticus states: "Her courage was her crown and she wore it like a Queen."[dlxxxvii] Speaking in kingdom language: other believers may see the crowns we wear; however, those who do not know the kingdom exists may not see a crown at all. I dare say, <u>others will only see the crowns we believe</u>. In a world of darkness, us embracing our freedom is not us waving our crowns in the air saying, "Do you know who I am?" It is being moved in love to wear our crowns and declare who He is. It's placing courage on our heads, along with belief, and kindness, and generosity. The beauty of the crown is the authority it has to unlock the many treasures of the kingdom—where healing, hope, and provision exist. We were called out of the darkness into the light that we may bring His light to the darkness. As 2 Corinthians 5:20 says,

So we are Christ's ambassadors; God is making his appeal through us. We speak for Christ when we plead, "Come back to God!" For God made Christ, who never sinned, to be the offering for our sin, so that we could be made right with God through Christ.[dlxxxviii]

A crown indicates that one is set apart for

(@bulgerjoseph)

a particular task or calling. As another commentary states: "Wives were crowned with honor to show their new status, as is indicated in the metaphorical picture of Israel married to God. (Ezekiel 16:12) To remove the crown was an indication of shame."^dlxxxix Sometimes we think it to be a humble thing to take off our crowns, when in all actuality, it is the enemy deceiving you of who you truly are. The calling God has placed on your heart is not something to be ashamed of. It's a crown to wear, not pridefully, but confidently, knowing it will bring a great light into the darkest of places someday. I once remember hearing God speak: "Stop covering yourself with dirt because you believed you were meant to be unseen. Shine My glory! The truth is that you are worthy, and so the enemy thinks if he can just get you to believe that you are unworthy of My promises, you will walk away from the destiny I have placed before you and deemed as yours. I wouldn't have chosen you if there was someone else more worthy. When you wake up believing this, the enemy shutters, because you plant righteousness, hope, and truth that is marked with love on those days. Those days are impenetrable. Those days remind you that you are chosen and you are Mine as I yours." May you remember that <u>you</u> were crowned for something that only can come to pass through you. Don't walk away from the most beautiful and powerful position because of the enemy's lies of shame. Lastly, remember that the set apart have a part to play. It truly is about others. We are never more like Christ than when we are giving. (God did give His son for our freedom.) Wear your crown, but give your gifts, and not the other way around. For you are chosen, royal, set apart, and crowned to bring glory to His name.

253

GENEROSITY'S KINDNESS

We, as believers, live in an upside-down kingdom, and this is its secret: *patience builds and trust creates; in exalting others, you're exalted, and in pouring out, you're strengthened; giving doesn't subtract, but multiplies, and in putting God first, you don't end up last.* It doesn't make sense, but we sense its truth in our hearts, for we have an access to heaven that sees in the unseen the promises of God. In 3 John 1:5-8, we read a letter between two companions: "My beloved friend, *I commend you for your demonstration* of faithful love by all that you have done for the brothers *on their journey*, even though they were strangers at the time. They have shared publicly with the congregation about the beautiful acts of love you have shown them. Now, if you would be so kind, send them on their way *with a generous gift*, in a manner that would honor God. You see, it was their passion for *the glory of* the name *of Christ* that launched them out, and they've not accepted financial support from unbelievers. They are deserving of all the support we can give them, *because through our giving* we can partner with them for the truth."[dxc] (emphasis added) Even though John is commending his friend for the good he has already begun to be known for, he urges him to keep doing good because of the ripple effect it is having in the Kingdom of Heaven on earth. He urges his friend to continue his beautiful acts of love through generosity's kindness. Generosity is not only with money; it also gives with words, time,

@ *kathleenmadethis*

acts, and love. As Frederick Buechner says:

Your life and my life flow into each other as wave flows into wave, and unless there is peace and joy and freedom for you, there can be no real peace or joy or freedom for me. To see reality—not as we expect it to be, but as it is—to see that unless we live for each other and in and through each other, we do not really live very satisfactorily; that there can really be life only where there really is, in just this sense, love.[dxci]

I believe Gaius, the recipient of John's letter, had caught a glimpse of this upside-down kingdom, and started to live in its borderless freedom. He started to see that unless those around him were experiencing peace, joy, and love, he therefore could not fully experience the same. Even though Jesus is everything we need, others are all around us, and as the Word says, *it is impossible for us to love God and not love others*,[dxcii] so our lives are not intended to be a one-man kingdom. Generosity changes that mindset.

When we truly believe the secrets of the kingdom, we stop being so inward-focused on *our* dreams, *our* worries, and *our* troubles. Knowing they are covered, we begin to help *others* dreams, *others* worries, and *others* troubles as if they were our own. It's like the saying, "I've got your back if you've got my back." In this case, as you are the extension of God's hands and feet for His kingdom, He extends His favor and promise onto your life and home. You build His house, and He builds yours. Truly we are not intended to do life alone, for it would leave no room for love. May I commend you for all the good works you have done, and may I also urge you to continually love through beautiful acts to express the heart of the Father. Send others on their way with a generous gift, the way a king would to his guests. Surprise them with kindness, and leave them with belief. What goes around comes around, but in the Kingdom of Heaven, it always comes back so much greater.

254

LOVE'S AWAKENING

Love is:
*A blanket in the winter, a spark in the night, a drink in the desert, a fountain in the summer,
a scent in the spring a color in the storm, a crown to the broken, in all seasons, in all forms.
It is warm, it is cool; it is light, it is color; it is an aroma, it is an emblem; it is invisible, it is bright.
It cannot be missed, it cannot be forgotten. Love is an awakening.*

They say that if the average night's sleep is eight hours, one sleeps one-third of one's life. Yet I challenge the thought that some may sleep away four-fifths of their life by merely sleepwalking. Sleepwalking through each day as if it is expected to be just like the last; sleepwalking through destinations as if they were ordinary stops; sleepwalking in a daze that never truly lives to one's fullness. When it comes to being awake, fully awake, we live aware, we live confident, we live in wonder. Yet when it comes to being asleep, we step out of tune with reality, step away from life's opportunities, and step further from love's embrace. Sleep is not for the weary, it is for the tired. Rest is for the weary, and it is rewarding. But even rest is awake. In seasons of waiting, moments of disappointment, or times of trouble, we like to go to sleep. We like to sleep away our time as if it will make the problem go away. However, I am convinced that these are the set apart times destined to awaken our hearts, to set our souls on fire, to discover new passion within our bones. They're not meant for sleeping, they're meant for love, and love is what keeps us wide-awake. Wide-awake to the words of our Father, wide-awake to opportunities arising, wide-awake to the new thing He's preparing ahead of us. For His love awakens even the lips of sleeping ones. Song of Songs 7:9 reads: *For your kisses of love are exhilarating, more than any delight I've known before. Your kisses of love awaken even the lips of sleeping ones.*[dxciii] I don't know what it is in your heart or life that's asleep: a dream, a desire, a destiny—it may even be hope, laughter, or joy. But what I am sure of is that God didn't create us to live more than one-third of our lives asleep. To believe there is more sometimes is a sacrifice, but God honors every sacrifice no matter how big or small. And what I do know is that His love is exhilarating enough to make dead bones come to life; the same power is able to awaken destinies to come. Love comes in *all* forms in *every* season. So no matter who you are, where you are, or what you're going through, know love's awakening is here and now, and it's time to wake up to the wonder of His love for you. It's time to test the limits and experience the breadth, to see all that He has in store and designed! As Ephesians 3:14-21 reads, so this is my prayer over you:

So I kneel humbly in awe before the Father of our Lord Jesus, the Messiah, the perfect Father of every father and child in heaven and on the earth. And I pray that he would unveil within you the unlimited riches of his glory and favor until supernatural strength floods your innermost being with his divine might and explosive power. Then, by constantly using your faith, the life of Christ will be released deep inside you, and the resting place of his love will become the very source and root of your life. Then you will be empowered to discover what every holy one experiences—the great magnitude of the astonishing love of Christ in all its dimensions. How deeply intimate and far-reaching is his love! How enduring and inclusive it is! Endless love beyond measurement that transcends our understanding—this extravagant love pours into you until you are filled to overflowing with the fullness of God! **Never doubt** *God's mighty* *power to work in you and accomplish all this. He will achieve infinitely more than your greatest request, your most unbelievable dream, and exceed your wildest imagination! He will outdo them all, for his miraculous power constantly energizes you. Now we offer up to God all the glorious praise that rises from every church in every generation through Jesus Christ—and all that will yet be manifest through time and eternity. Amen!* (Ephesians 3:14-21 TPT)

(Emphasis added)

255

HERE

Love awakens; love rests.
The sun and the moon dance,
The world and its company sway.
Peace breathes in, peace breathes out,
God oversees it all.

He sees the rhythm; He sees the grace;
He sees you, He moves.
Life is in motion, and its seconds speak,
But His words are the clock to your heart.

Listen, believe, be brave in following its beats.
Tick tock, thump thump, can you hear it?
The sync of His heart with yours?

He waits—all is still—He lingers—all is calm.

Come back to the place of home.
You are home.
You are in the fields.
You are your most wondrous you.

It's the beginning again,
Simply you and simply Him.
Everything's perfect; begin the day.

xx

---

*You don't have to wait any longer, the Anointed One is **here** speaking with you—I am the One you're looking for.*[dxciv]
John 4:26 (emphasis added)

256

WAKE UP, SLEEPING BEAUTY

The birds are singing sweet melodies outside, streams of light are dancing in, and the gentle hug of your covers greet you as you awaken. You sit up and stretch as you are met by excitement for the day. In your heart you know, "It's going to be a good day!" Have you ever had one of those mornings? I think most of us wish we woke up like that. Instead it's more like, "What is that sound? Where is it coming from? Great. I just chucked my phone across the room. Maybe my alarm will just ... stop?" And then it does. Either because you finally got out of bed or because you tuned it out with all your might to sleep for "just a few more minutes." But if you listened long enough, you'd hear a voice saying, "Wake up, O Sleeping Beauty."

In the story of Sleeping Beauty, we know of three main characters: Sleeping Beauty herself, Prince Philip, and Maleficent. Sleeping Beauty, also known as Princess Aurora, is known for her riches, talent, pure heart, and undeniable beauty. Prince Philip can dance, sing, and fight, but is also noble, humble, charming, and of course, handsome. Maleficent... well, she is every reflection of evil. "She exists to challenge the pure goodness of Aurora and Stefan's Kingdom,"[dxcv] as Sparknotes puts it. And with those three characters we see a bit of **harmony, dissonance, and orchestration** in the *great scheme* of the play. Princess Aurora was good, but this didn't mean bad things weren't going to happen. Maleficent despised her beauty and goodness. She couldn't stand it because it was everything she wasn't. And so when Princess Aurora turned eighteen, Maleficent's curse set upon her and she fell into a deep sleep, destined to never wake again. But along comes one who just so happens to find her castle and immediately falls in love with her the moment he lays eyes on her. It's our favorite ending as true love's kiss awakens her.

Though this story is commonly known, its values are widely overlooked. One, <u>Sleeping Beauty wasn't striving to be seen; she was beauty at rest.</u> While living with her fairy godmothers, she wasn't flaunting around her beauty in hopes of having someone pursue her. She instead rested in her beauty and allowed it to flourish and grow, knowing that in the right time, love would come. Two, <u>*true love* awakens our deepest of beauties.</u> Love breaks the bondage of the darkest of curses. As we all know, love is the most powerful thing in the world. But again, not all of our stories look like this. Instead of a prince on a horse and an evil witch, we have a Savior and a fallen world in which Lucifer is out to keep in a deep sleep. The truth is: the enemy hates beauty—he absolutely loathes it. He has no sympathy, only anger of everything he is not. But then there's Jesus, the most loving, caring, and humble love we will ever know, and His eyes are on us. As Psalm 45:11 says, "The King is enthralled by your beauty; honor him, for he is your lord." [dxcvi] His true love awakens us from the deep sleep the enemy had our true beauty hidden under. However, there is a difference between being asleep and being at rest.

{Rest restores beauty while sleep keeps it hidden away.} Sleep makes us believe that goodness cannot be in our reality while rest knows goodness doesn't depend upon our reality. Because when you are with the One you love, your deepest of beauties is awakened. And here is a key to keep—*habits can keep you asleep, while choice keeps you awake*. Like Sleeping Beauty, we don't have to strive to be seen, because Jesus is orchestrating everything. The Prince actually found her as beautiful as she was when she was at rest. So you are a beauty the King is enthralled by, and He is the goodness your heart has been waiting for. He is the One who will always come to your rescue. Expectations and comparison will try to rock your beauty to sleep, but God won't be silent when it comes to the beauty He designed within you. Because He doesn't speak of your beauty to simply flatter you, He speaks of it to **compel** you into the life you were **destined** to live. Your beauty is of the utmost treasures in His sight, and it's time to be awakened to what He sees in you and has prepared for you with a bit of ***harmony, dissonance, and orchestration***.

257

BEFORE ONE OF THEM CAME TO BE

> *Your eyes saw my unformed body; all the days ordained for me were written in your book before one of them came to be.*[dxcvii]
> Psalm 139:16

Before one of them came to be, they were known to become. Every moment that we anxiously wait for is destined to come in time. Isn't that amazing? That God has every day planned out like a scroll even to the very day that we are experiencing now. He has a time for our growing, a time for our strength, a time for love, a time for mourning, and a time for weakness, because this is how we are shaped. We are shaped to precision to the very perfection of the moment we are in. Ecclesiastes 3:1 says, "There is a time for everything and a season for every activity under heaven."[dxcviii] Since there is a time for everything, we can trust in the timing of the Orchestrator's hands. As an orchestrator, He knows each *full piece* of the songs He has written for our seasons. He knows every instrument, every pause, every high, and every low. He knows your heart and it is precious to Him. That's *why* He is so big on us protecting our hearts, because He wants the very best for us! As Charles Spurgeon says: "God is too good to be unkind and He is too wise to be mistaken. And when we cannot trace His hand, we must trust His heart."[dxcix] Patience is virtue, love is valuable, and time is kind to both. A little lesson I have learned is, "Life is a journey, not a race." In other words, don't rush the now, but live in the now because this is what you've already waited for to come. And when you want life to hurry up, remember that God protects you in your patience in preparation for your promise. He is saying to you, "Do not be afraid, for I am with you. Do not be discouraged for I am your God. For I am with you wherever you go. You will not be forsaken."

258

"YOU CHOOSE"

To hold on to something has great power. It matters what you hold onto, whether it's a power of authority or conformity. Often, we settle by choice, or we let go of good things to see great things come by choice. But holding has its power and that power is maintained by what we say yes or no to. Many add up to where we are, yet many deduct from where we could be. As Jesus spoke in John 10:10, "The thief comes only to steal and kill and destroy; I have come that they may have life, and have it to the full."[dc] We daily face the choice of letting the enemy take hold of our promise or letting God hold true to His Word.

Quickly we can belittle the Word God has spoken over us—like it's a possibility and not a promise. As if God is like, "Hey, I'm going to talk to you about a life you could live," instead of, "Here's the life you **will** live." If only we could grasp onto the concept that *once God speaks, it is created*. Not being created, but set in stone, not erasable, not having the ability to change. I think that's why God nudges us sometimes saying, "Is this really what you want?" Because once we choose *yes*, all starts to orchestrate. And that should be an exciting thing! But we often stand petrified at the thought halfway through the journey because it wasn't green pastures the entire way. There were a few more valleys of Achor and wildernesses than anticipated. Yet, we still always have—choice. To hold onto this guaranteed word or to let go of this unforeseen promise. Deuteronomy 30:11 says, "Now what I am commanding you today is not too difficult for you or beyond your reach."[dci] It's not beyond holding; it just lies within choosing. Verse 15 reads, "See, I set before you today, life and prosperity, death and destruction." In a way, a choice is a big deal, and yet it's also so much simpler than we'd expect.

When you come to the stand still moment where choice is on your left and right, to do wrong or right, *remember His Words for they have power*. Power to stand against destruction. Power to withstand the deception of the enemy's hidden intent. Power to walk into what God has before you. In those moments, "Love the Lord your God, listen to His voice, and hold fast to Him." (vs 20) One example I know of is the story of Deborah and Barak. The Lord gives Barak a promise, both extraordinary and impossible. But because it seems impossible, the enemy creeps in and creates doubt. Thus Barak replies to Deborah, "If you go with me, I will go; if you don't go with me, I won't go."[dcii] Barak takes the choice away from his hands and places it in hers, which in return also takes the promise from his hold and places it in her hold. We see this in her response in Judges 4:9, "'Certainly I will go with you,' said Deborah. 'But because of the course you are taking, the honor will not be yours, for the Lord will deliver Sisera into the hands of a woman.'" And so it happened that Jael, a woman, killed Sisera before Barak reached the tent. God spoke, it was created, and if Barak would've held fast—he would have experienced the promise in *full*. "But doubt" had a word to speak. And yet we are to hold onto—"But God." But God had the last word as He had the first.

I had a vision recently where Jesus placed a two-carat diamond in my hand. It was beautiful, but not what I imagined as my "perfect ring." Yet as I placed it on my finger, it transformed into an enchanting ring. When I asked why it changed, God spoke, "You choose." It then dawned on me, we can settle for a good life or we can choose to hold onto trust and receive everything God promised, down to the tiniest and daintiest of details. But it's our choice to choose. Whatever it is He is speaking over you, hold onto it for you then will wisely choose what you closely heard from His heart. What He spoke isn't something small; it's a BIG DEAL! If you approach His great plan with fear, you may just settle for a two-carat diamond. But if you approach His greater plan with wonder, you will seize the truth and power in His Word that is worth every effort of holding onto, and with time, you'll see why. When He speaks, don't doubt, say yes every time, and you will possess in full what once was fully impossible. Hold fast and see His Word hold true.

259

ARMED AND READY

When Christ died on the cross for our sins, a divine exchange occurred, one where Jesus was punished that we might be forgiven. He was made sin with our sinfulness that we might be made righteous; He tasted death that we might share with Him the taste of new wine; and our old self was put to death in Him that His love might come to life in us. Though this happened over 2,000 years ago, we still wrestle with it today. We still wrestle with who He truly is; we still wrestle with who we really are; we still wrestle with the divine call placed on our lives. But in the divine wrestle, a divine exchange occurs.

@sarahbgraves

In Genesis 28, Jacob comes upon a stone to rest his head against. Jacob then has a divine dream, with a divine call and a divine awakening. God promises him: "I am the Lord, the God of your grandfather Abraham, and the God of your father, Isaac. The ground you are lying on *belongs to you*... One day I will bring you back to this land. I will not leave you until I have finished giving you *everything* I have promised you."[dciii] (emphasis added) And so Jacob wakes up, sets up the very stone he dreamt upon, names it Bethel, makes a vow to God, and goes on his way. Years later, he has two wives, a rich inheritance, and is again, met by angels with these words from God: "I am the God who appeared to you at Bethel, the place where you anointed the pillar of stone and made your vow to me. Now get ready and leave this country and return to the land of your birth."[dciv] (Genesis 31:13) So he starts his journey promise-bound, when a man shows up and starts to wrestle with Jacob. They wrestle from night to dawn, and Jacob keeps pressing on, demanding he won't let go until he has a blessing from this man. I imagine them in headlock, breathing heavily, so ready for this to be over with, when Jacob's heart changes. Jacob now *demands* a blessing for it has become a desire of *his own* heart. That's the beautiful connection of the divine exchange and this God-with-man wrestle—for it's where we are not only saved, but transformed. Likewise, who you were at the beginning of your journey should not be the same person you finish as.

As you wrestle with the King of kings for your promised inheritance, a divine exchange will take place within you preparing you for the divine call around you. It's one where what He spoke over you will not just be a "blessing," but will become a desire of your own heart you will not let go of until it's finished. It's okay to hold onto every word He says, for it's His word to uphold. In coming back to Bethel, we are reminded of His vow to us, and our vow to Him, that both should be kept equally. The battle is on for your destiny for it involves others destinies. By you wrestling with God for what He's promised, you wrestle into an anointing beyond yourself. It no longer becomes about you, but becomes about those around you, and thus, you become prepared and equipped for what's ahead. Think of it this way: if you don't do what's been promised to you at some level, something inside of you is going to die. Don't let it. Wrestle with it. Wrestle with God. Then walk away anointed, armed, and ready. Where two or more are gathered in unity, even if in a wrestle, God is in their midst, and there His blessing dwells. You don't have to chase the blessing down, for He chases you down with His blessing, and He wrestles with you to make you armed and ready for its arrival. "Now get ready and leave this country and return to the land of your birth," back to the beginning, where all was promised.

260

FEAR OR DARE

Reading: 1 Chronicles 11

I wonder what it was like to be one of David's mighty men. To do the unthinkable, to have that fear well up inside, and instead of letting it hold you back, chasing it with all your might; to be in this stand still moment of logic and courage, making the choice no one else would dare to take. I wonder what moment I am in, and we each are in, where God has placed the same two choices before us: fear or dare. Will we be like Jashobeam who killed 300 men in one encounter, or like Esau who chose a bowl of soup over his destiny? Will we be like Benaiah who went down into a pit and killed a lion on a snowy day? Or will we be like Jonah running from the call to the Ninevites? Will we be like Eleazor who took his army and took a stand in the middle of a field to fight off the Philistines pursuing them? Or will we be like Cain who instead thinks of himself over his brother and kills him? These stories demonstrate choices of courage, bravery, and selflessness over choices of fear, insecurity, and selfishness. They all had different circumstances and different outcomes, but all were faced with the same two choices: fear or dare. Because I'm sure that in each of their hearts they heard these words, "Take a risk." Take a risk to survive; take a risk to trust in God and what He can do through you; take a risk to run back into safe measures; take a risk to run forward into promised lands. I love what Anna Wintour says, "It's very important to take risks. I think that research is very important, but in the end you have to work from your instinct and feeling and take those risks and be fearless."[dcv] And I think when it comes to God's infiniteness and greatness, we must take risks to not only see who He says He is, but to experience what He has always been able to do. There's something God has before you, but the question is, will you choose fear or dare?

261

FOXES AND LIONS

Everything you want is on the other side of fear.[dcvi]
-Jack Canfield

I asked a friend once, how is it you overcame your fear to pursue the call of God on your life? She replied: "I had to choose to open up my heart and face one fear at a time. The walls I was hiding in never came down; they are still there, but I don't run back to them, because there are lost people outside of them." The walls not only keep your potential locked up, it also keeps the lost locked out. In reality, sometimes we do hide in the walls of our homes. But 98% of the time, we are staying in the safety of our minds—the captive place where discouragement and pain cannot enter, yet also the fullness of life and love are locked out. 2 Corinthians 10:5 talks about "taking captive every thought to make it obedient to Christ."[dcvii] Our thoughts are not our enemies, but our lost friends that just need to be redirected where to go. They are foxes and lions, fleeting and fierce, and both hold power within them. The foxes are sneaky, they almost go unnoticed; they are at times destructive, for they like to rearrange the items in your home, keeping you from seeing the beauty outside. The lions are beautiful, unique and captivating, but by being kept safely within, their locks are only seen and their power never expressed. The foxes don't usually disappear, but they do have a place where they belong. It is their caves, their roots, in which they have gone wild trying to find in searching for their beloved home, that they may have ruined a few things in their path. If we can learn how to lead our thoughts, we will learn how to love life in all of its immensity, for everything we want is on the other side of their leading.

Let's start with the foxes, the foxes that love to search for burrows in secret gardens (Song of Songs 2:15). They are often the destructive and entertained—the pride and insecurities, the figure-it-outers and worriers. They all stem from somewhere, and usually a moment in life shakes them from their burrows. When led back to their place of belonging, they are reminders of humility. That our confidence is in Christ, that He is our sufficiency. Then there are the lions; they are the daring and loved—the desires and dreams, the imagined and crazy-to-believes. They come out every so often to roam, but they also like to rest in caves. They have the potential to impact and change the landscape when set free, yet they can easily go overlooked because of our fear to truly face them. The fleeting foxes and fierce lions both hold great power and are to be loved as friends. To love ourselves is to love our thoughts, for perfect love drives out all fear (1 John 4:18). It is the key to leaving our walls and living outside of them. Where we lead our thoughts is where we will lead others, and when led in love, everything can change. Ephesians 3:14-19 says:

So I kneel humbly in awe before the Father of our Lord Jesus, the Messiah, the perfect Father of every father and child in heaven and on the earth. And I pray that he would unveil within you the unlimited riches of his glory and favor until supernatural strength floods your innermost being with his divine might and explosive power. Then, by constantly using your faith, the life of Christ will be released deep inside you, and the resting place of his love will become the very source and root of your life. Then you will be empowered to discover what every holy one experiences— the great magnitude of the astonishing love of Christ in all its dimensions. How deeply intimate and farreaching is his love! How enduring and inclusive it is! Endless love beyond measurement that transcends our understanding—this extravagant love pours into you until you are filled to overflowing with the fullness of God![dcviii]

More lies outside the walls of your fears when you allow what's in your heart to be let outside its limits. Be *brave* and dream **big**.

262

TAKE CAPTIVE THE CAPTIVATING

We tend to value the heart as such a beautiful treasure, but we miss the art of the treasure if we overlook the thoughts that formed and shaped it. Proverbs 4:23 reminds us to "guard our hearts for they are the wellspring of life,"[dcix] but in order to protect your heart, first you must guard your thoughts. Instead of allowing your thoughts to wander everywhere, exposing your heart, let your thoughts wander in dreams. Every thought we have should be beautifying our hearts or dwelling on God's beauty. If we begin to see our thoughts as captivating, we will learn to take them captive often. God is constantly placing captivating ideas in our minds, but we tend to push them aside as crazy, when it's actually a God-sized dream. So take captive every thought, pray through it, and let the wonder begin. For as you take captive the captivating, the smallest and wildest of thoughts may just lead you into the greatest and wildest of dreams.

If you will transform your mind, God will transform your life.[dcx] - Joel Osteen

@ kathleenmadethis

263

THE FRONTLINE

> *Put on your sword, O mighty warrior! You are so glorious, so majestic! In your majesty, ride out to victory, defending truth, humility, and justice. Go forth to perform awe-inspiring deeds! Your arrows are sharp, piercing your enemies' hearts. The nations fall beneath your feet.*[dcxi]
> Psalm 45:3-5

Today:

So many *chosen* children of God have thrown their hopes down—like shattered glass of disappointments, tossed by insecurity, built by lies.

2,000 years ago:

Jesus took on the cross, where the enemy was declaring hopes were going to be disappointed, promises unmet, and hearts unfilled. Jesus was nailed to the cross, pinned by the lies that He wasn't the Son of God, by the insecurities that it couldn't be real. But **then**, Jesus **rose!** Hopes were risen, promises alive, and love fulfilled! When He said, "It is finished," He screamed at the enemy, "Those *lies* are *finished!*" Truth was defended, humility honored, justice was **victorious**.

For such a time as this:

Let me urge you to take stand at the frontline. It's where He's called you and each and every one of us. Choose to not be silent while the enemy keeps speaking. Proclaim His Words over the world with strength, courage, and wisdom of the *good news* that came and the *best* that is still yet to come!

> *Be on your guard; stand firm in the faith; be courageous; be strong. Do everything in love.*[dcxii]
> 1 Corinthians 16:13-14

264

WHAT'S IN YOUR HANDS?

Reading: 1 Chronicles 29; Mark 6

In 1 Chronicles 17, we see a dream begin in the heart of David—one to build God a house to dwell in. But by the end of the chapter, we see that it was not going to be accomplished by him, but by his son. And by 1 Chronicles 29, we start to see the process come into play. I don't know if this question popped into your mind, but I certainly was confused why God didn't just allow David to build it twelve chapters earlier. Instead we see that He chooses Solomon, whom David describes as "young and inexperienced." But as my pastor started to speak about 2 Corinthians 12:9, it started to make complete sense to me. He loves to use the most unlikely candidates because His power is made perfect in our weakness. Because it is in our weakness that we learn how to truly trust in God. David had already learned this in 1 Samuel 30, where his two wives were captured and his men were talking about stoning him. In verse 6 we see, "David strengthened himself with his trust in God."[dcxiii] In his weakness, he depended, sought, and looked to God. Now here is Solomon in the same position with a different circumstance. Not only is he following in his father's footsteps, who was a great king, but he is also to build the first temple for the Lord, **ever.** The God that he has always heard about working in his father's life is all about to become so real to him. In 1 Chronicles 29:2 we read that the resources have already been provided for this great task, and now they are placed before Solomon to create something beautiful to bring glory to God. In the same way, we are like the disciples in Mark 6 who have five loaves of bread and two fish to feed a crowd of over 5,000. In both stories, the resources are placed in their hands; *but it takes strength and courage to truly go after what is in your heart, no matter how big, and to use what has been placed in your hands, no matter how small.* Solomon had a great task, so did the disciples, yet both now had to use the resources they had to begin.

I wonder what great task God has put on your heart to do and what amount of gifts He has placed in your hands to use. And let me say, it probably won't be in the most convenient times. Solomon's dad had just passed away and Jesus' brother had just been beheaded. But instead they <u>chose</u> trust and went after what God had proclaimed. And we see that God honored Solomon because of his obedience and made him a great king with great wisdom and knowledge, plus wealth, riches, and honor. So much so, we still read and listen to his wisdom every day in Proverbs. Then there were the disciples who probably each had baskets that were only 10% *filled* when they went off to feed the 5000+ people. But somehow by the end, the fish and bread had to multiply, because after all were fed, each of the disciples' baskets were left *full*. Which only makes me wonder, when we step out, how will God bless what is in our hands as He honors our faith? Because the God I know, He places desires in our hearts for a reason, and He will always equip us to live them out. Not only that, He goes beyond what we imagine in the process. And if we, like David, Solomon, and the disciples, keep our eyes and hearts on Him, we will experience the greatest treasure of all—His blessing. So be obedient and use your gifts; God gave them to you for a reason.

So now I charge you in the sight of all Israel and of the assembly of the Lord, and in the hearing of our God: Be careful to follow all the commands of the Lord your God, that you may possess this good land and pass it on as an inheritance to your descendants forever. "And you, my son Solomon, acknowledge the God of your father, and serve him with wholehearted devotion and with a willing mind, for the Lord searches every heart and understands every desire and every thought. If you seek him, he will be found by you; but if you forsake him, he will reject you forever. Consider now, for the Lord has chosen you to build a house as the sanctuary. Be strong and do the work."[dcxiv]
1 Chronicles 28:8-10

265

TAKE A SEAT

> *Faith is the confidence that what we hope for will actually happen;
> it gives us assurance about things we cannot see.*^{dcxv}
> Hebrews 11:1 (emphasis added)

What are your hopes? What is it you are hoping for that requires faith to keep believing in? What is it that in the glimpses of your hopes being visual in someone else's life, you're quietly whispering to your heart, "One day"? I know we are going deep fast, but it has to be known to build up to the climax. Now, let's begin.

What if a famous star invited you to sit with them? You enter a restaurant, all the tables are full, and his guest happened to not show up. Seeing he had a seat you needed, he asked if you'd like to sit with him. I know the probability of this happening is close to zero, but the point is, how would you feel? I'd probably do the look over your shoulder, pointing to self, with the stunned expression of—"who, me?" I'd feel a little unworthy, especially if he *was* talking to someone else. Except, he was talking to you. Now, here you are discovering he has one of the kindest souls. Similarly, God sits on a throne high in authority, and somehow we so easily get surprised when he calls us to come and take a seat. Though God is love, we can so easily have this built up perception of what a king should be like that it keeps us from approaching him with our heart's quiet whispers. Let me assure you, you can approach his throne boldly with your requests, because we have a kind King.

Then there's the story of Esther. Esther is like the character who replied, "Who, me?" Yet, she so easily won the king's favor. Still quiet dreams dwelled in her heart she hadn't spoken of. When she finally presents her hopes and

requests to her king, his response was filled with as much love as her courage. She speaks in Esther 7:3, "If I have found favor in your eyes, O King, and if it please the king, give me my life, and give my people their lives."^{dcxvi}

How much more does the God who created us invite us to take a seat by Him, by His throne, wanting us to hold nothing back, but talk to Him about our hopes with vulnerability? <u>He is a patient King with a scepter out held in grace to your heart.</u> As James 5:16 reads, "The prayer of a person living right with God is something **powerful** to be reckoned with."[dcxvii] (emphasis added) There is power in presenting your requests to a king. Faith comes from listening to His whispers and believing them fully. Faith often requires surrender and courage to know that He, as a loving King, is doing everything in His power for your request to be granted. Though we cannot see it *presently*, our hopes will happen *perfectly*. In the end, faith is this: it is not ignorant of what we hope for; no, it knows the details very well. Faith is awake and aware of the hopes God dropped in our hearts and yet remains confident that God is just as aware. Faith then follows Him beyond sight, in trust that He knows what He is doing. So take a seat, talk with Him, write down your hopes, and have **faith**. He is forever faithful.

266

NOTE TO SELF:

@bulgerjoseph

Sometimes, God calls us to *greater* things that are beyond our limits, but they are never outside of His for He is limitless. But your God-given dreams will [remain dreams] if you leave God out of them. So pray more than you pursue, and pursue God harder than you pursue your dreams. When He calls us to great things, He expects us to stumble in our strength so that we can depend on His. And if you give God the chance, He will exceed your expectations. Yes, He does call you to be a leader, but no, it's not for your image, but His! **Your yes will impact somebody's eternity**. When you look at a God-sized dream, you have to remember to *keep your eyes* on God. If you look at the dream, you'll discover fear. If you look at God, you'll discover courage. God is our center while prayer is our movement. Be a leader of His image. Be brave. Be you. Be His.

Your eyes will see the king in his beauty and view a land that stretches afar.[dcxviii]
Isaiah 33:17

267

FREE

"And hope does not disappoint, because the love of God has been poured out within our hearts through the Holy Spirit who was given to us."[dcxix]
Romans 5:5

I love the way your eyes light up when you talk about your destiny. I love how hope floods your heart with what could be and what will become. I love how your soul catches fire when you see your promise, even if it's a glimpse, you lock your eyes with its coming. It fills your soul with its truth even if it's not yet for you know it's yes and amen. I love how freely you dance upon disappointment, as if it had no power to begin with. I love seeing you run in the storm, undeterred by its dangers, for you know I'm a fortress around you. I love that you never let go knowing I haven't let you go, for it shows your trust in Me that moves mountains and walks on water. It isn't hesitant; it is sure, it is free. That's when you know you live in My truth, when you're as free as ever no matter the space in which you stand. As you keep stepping in faith, you will see the limitless dimensions of My promise. And surely, My goodness, My mercy, and My kindness, will chase you down. There's no good thing I withhold from you.

"Believe in miracles. I have seen so many of them come when every other indication would say that hope was lost. Hope is never lost."[dcxx]
- Jeffrey R. Holland

268

CATCH FIRE

My friend walked up to me with a beautiful painting in hand, upon it was a castle inscribed with the scripture of Proverbs 18:10, "YHWH's name is a mighty tower; the one who runs to it is safe and inaccessible."[dcxxi] The sides of the painting were thick enough for more room to cover, and so she filled its space with a word from the Lord. On its four edges she wrote: "Like a princess, you *belong* in a castle. When you recognize yourself as royalty, then you can treat others royally. Don't forsake your blessing to gain someone else's poverty. Instead, invite them out of their poverty and into your prosperity. God has an abundance for you, and your inheritance lacks no good thing… An enemy of a fortress risks his life if he runs at that fortress. But an ally will find refuge. When you run to God and trust in Him, He gathers you in His arms and guards you. You are hidden." At that time, I was very new to Christianity, so to have someone give me a word from God, as well as paint it, and even say words with such beauty, was out of this world. I had never known anything like it. I just so happened to find that painting rummaging through some of my old things, but it was almost like God took it off the shelf, placed it in my hands, and spoke as clearly as ever to my heart that its timing was *now*.

In Obadiah, we have a similar story, where the Israelites up to this point were under siege. Their enemies were attacking and prevailing. Then God gives them a word that had been put on the shelf for many years, and says: "But on Mount Zion will be deliverance; it will be holy, and Jacob will possess his inheritance. Jacob will be a fire and Joseph a flame."[dcxxii] (Obadiah 1:17-18) Or as the MSG poetically paints the words: "The family of Jacob will take back their possessions from those who took them from them. That's when the family of Jacob will catch fire, the family of Joseph become fierce flame…"[dcxxiii] No matter how dusty the word on your shelf may be, I believe it is time for God's breath to reveal again the power of His word on your life. I pray that I am the friend who is walking up to you, placing within your hands a message captivating and clear, straight from God, that your warfare is over and the time has come for you to not forsake your blessing, but to invite the impoverished into the inheritance you have gained. You may be objecting saying, "Oh no, Kaytee… I'm still in poverty. I still hear the war." My warrior, I speak with the power and authority of my Father in heaven, and I declare that what the Lord has spoken over you is here! He is here. He is your fortress. It is safe to run to Him. It is safe to let Him run to you. I know that God has a plan for you—one that lacks no good thing, one that is painted with peace and prosperity. Peace meaning: to be whole and complete, to have victory over one's enemies. Prosperity meaning: more than wealth, but also health, happiness, long life, and success.

I believe it is time to *catch fire*! As Isaiah 64:1-2 reads, I declare: "Oh, that You would tear open the heavens and come down, that the mountains might quake at Your presence—As [sure as] fire kindles the brushwood, as fire causes water to boil—to make Your name known to Your adversaries, that the nations may tremble at Your presence!"[dcxxiv] May you muster up the courage to again call on God. To run to His name as your mighty tower, to be safe and inaccessible from the war in His presence, that He may win the war you have been trying to fight. It's time to take back what the enemy has stolen. It's time to take back your happiness, health, and wealth, that your fire may make His name known! The breath that is ready to blow the dust off of your long awaited word, is the breath that will enflame the fire within you. When you call upon the name of YHWH, you will again possess the inheritance that belonged to you, that was given to you by His grace, and its fire will be uncontainable. It will spread rapidly fighting darkness with its light. You can find rest in Him, hidden and whole, for He will take care of you and your children for the days to come. Catch fire, become the fiercest flame, and let it be known that our God saves!

269

THE PRESENT

The past is not a place to which we should compare our present. We do not repair by dwelling in its dreams. It is faithfulness remembered for hope's healing. That if once we were_____, then again we can be_____. Loved. Valued. Joyful. Free. It shouldn't hurt to see. It should encourage us to feel what is here and now for what is ahead and waiting. For surely His goodness and mercy will pursue us all the days of our lives. Surely He has our best surprises ahead. Surely He has our destiny in mind now and forever.

As Albus Dumbledore says: "It does not do to dwell on dreams and forget to live."[dcxxv] Our present is a present. May we live in its fullness. May we live in His kindness. May we live again, love again, feel valued again, feel joy again, become free within , and dance freely with Him, as we again become our own.

> *Those who believe in God can never in a way be sure of him again. Once they have seen him in a stable, they can never be sure where he will appear or to what lengths he will go or to what ludicrous depths of self-humiliation he will descend in his wild pursuit of humankind. If holiness and the awful power and majesty of God were present in this least auspicious of all events, this birth of a peasant's child, then there is no place or time so lowly and earthbound but that holiness can be present there too. And this means that we are never safe, that there is no place where we can hide from God, no place where we are safe from his power to break in two and recreate the human heart, because it is just where he seems most helpless that he is most strong, and just where we least expect him that he comes most fully.*[dcxxvi]
> Frederick Buechner

270

MY EVERYTHING

To uncover a watch; to hold it; to admire its intricacies—then to speak of that watch in your palm as a creatorless manifestation would be incomplete. There must be more, there must be a watchmaker.[dcxxvii]

I pray for strength to let go of everything I've ever dreamed up so that I can wake up to experience His dream for me. I pray to love as He loved and to walk as He lived. I pray for my heart's desires to not be for everything surrounding me, but to surround My everything. I pray to live fully in His will, to fall deeper in love with Him, to be as close to Him as possible, and to never stop learning all about Him. I want to walk with Him, and know His heart; to discover His will and experience His promises; to be His and for Him to be mine. He is the very life I dream to see. He is the very love I dream to experience. He is the Prince I've always dreamed of; *He is everything and more.*

You are always with me and everything I have is yours.[dcxxviii]
Luke 15:31

271

BEAUTIFUL DETAILS

There's a beauty in the new: the freshness, the unknown, and the mystery of it. And it reminds me of a phrase I heard long ago that says, "There's so many places to go and so many things to see." It has a sense of wonder in the phrase itself, a curiosity that just wants to explore. And I think that's just it—we like the thought of "the new." We like the thought of going somewhere where we can go explore and find rare treasures in unknown places. We like to discover the beauty in unpredictable passions. And most of all, we love to allow ourselves to just let go and to be free without expectations. Thinking about these thoughts, I saw this common theme... we love and favor the new. It's not just within the objects that we buy, the treats we eat, or in the music we hear; it's even in the way we love people, ourselves, and God. When it comes to people, we love the experience of meeting someone new. When we have something new, like a haircut, tattoo, or even a piercing, we feel so alive! Even to the moment when we first fell in love with God, we were so filled with wonder of how amazing He is! And I think that is how we should love: as if everyone and everything were made new every day. To love people by always seeing their rare qualities and discovering their many hidden talents. To love ourselves for how we are made new in Christ every day by constantly being molded, shaped, and becoming more like Him. And ultimately, to love God for all that He has done and is doing every day. To have a sense of wonder when we think about Him, for all that we haven't seen yet, and all that we are able to discover about Him. We tend to put expectations on wonderful things when we get used to them, and that can steal the beauty out of any treasure. Yet, instead of living with expectations of the old, *we should love without knowing what to expect*. We should look for the details in the lives of people that change, in the pieces of us that God shapes, and in our every day relationship with God, through the valleys and the mountains. We should love like every detail around us is new, and then we should expect to be amazed in all of its unexpected ways.

> *Your marvelous doings are headline news; I could write a book full of the **details** of your greatness.*[dcxxix]
> Psalm 145:6 (emphasis added)

272

STAY WONDER-FILLED

I believe it is not what we do with our days that counts, but who we are in their moments that matter most. C. S. Lewis says, "I would rather be what God chose to make me than the most glorious creature that I could think of; for to have been born in God's thought and then made by God is the dearest, grandest, and most precious thing in all thinking."[dcxxx] If I was "the enemy," I think the two things I would attack the most to create distance between a person and God is *His identity to them* and *their identity to God*. Because there's such an unshakable bond in knowing who you are and whose you are, and if I was "the enemy," I just wouldn't want that. Because perhaps then they would know how powerful they actually are.

We read in Mark 8:36, "What good is it for someone to gain the whole world, yet forfeit their soul?"[dcxxxi] In the MSG it says, "What good would it do to get everything you want and lose you, the real you?"[dcxxxii] And may I add emphasis to "the dearest, grandest, and most precious" thought-up you. What good is it to find *every* pondered thought, yet lose yourself and who God says you are? Every day, to remain the real you, is an effort when a loudmouth world, or when a blabbermouth enemy, wants to convince you of who you are not. It so easily ties into the concept in Hebrews 6:19 that says, "We have this hope as an anchor for our soul..."[dcxxxiii] When we lose hope, we lose a bit of the realness of who we are and lose a little bit of the truth of who God is. It creates this distance and disbelief the enemy was hoping for. Yet in Luke 24:49, Jesus says: "I am going to send you what my Father has promised, but <u>stay</u> in the city *until* you have been clothed with power from on high."[dcxxxiv] (emphasis added) In other words, when your hope is shaken, stay close to your Protector. This is the prime time for the enemy, for he sees an opportunity to allure you away from the anchor—but what he cannot see is the armor God is about to place upon you in that very moment that deems you unquestionably as His. Jesus promises His disciples something <u>greater</u> to hope for than their wildest thoughts... the Holy Spirit who would be with them 24/7. No more going out and coming back to Jesus. Jesus would be with them now and forever for every step of every day. Instead of them trying to figure everything out on their own, Jesus says, "Stay" because it was more important for them to *remain their true selves* than to try to prove and love themselves in strife of what was next. He says stay because the promise was coming and it would be done by Him alone and not by their efforts. **In a way, it was His pursuit after their hearts to hold onto hope.**

Because the disciples walked away clothed in His words, the enemy could not touch them. The plot twist is that while the enemy was crouched in the bushes waiting for the disciples to walk away from the Lord, they left clothed *by* the Lord and *with* the Lord now walking with them. How much more should we hold onto this hope? How much more courage should we walk with knowing that He also walks with us? Who you are to God is **unfathomable**, and even more so, who He is to you is just as astounding. But that also used to be Lucifer and God's relationship before he got kicked out of heaven... so now he absolutely hates seeing someone else take his place. It's no wonder he is trying to convince you it's not you because he wants it to be him. But really that proves that there's such a hope for you to hold onto when God says stay, for you know He loves you and is preparing you for *something impossible to believe*. God wants, more than anything, for you to walk into that promise as who you are, and knowing that Whose you are is the very reason you're walking into it. You are dearly, grandly, and most preciously loved and valued by God, and that alone should create such a hope within you that anchors a confidence in your every day living. It is that hope that makes any ordinary day <u>full</u> of life and color: a life full of hope, joy, and grand expectancy. Child of God, in the waiting *stay* wonder-filled *until* the hope He has promised comes to pass, for <u>you will see</u> His designs take shape around you every single time, and you will walk freely *as you are* into its wildness.

273

DON'T LOOK BACK

In the words of Luke Skywalker, "I can't believe it." In the words of Yoda, "That is why you fail."^{dcxxxv} It amazes me that the deciding factor between succeeding and failing is belief or disbelief. That when we feel like all odds are against us, really they are within us to choose whether or not they fail. Likewise, the Israelites had the odds in their favor as they crossed the Red Sea. The Lord was directing them day and night with a cloud to follow; He provided quail to feed them, and He was their fortress of protection along the way. But for some reason, when they came so close to their promise, they didn't remember the miraculous God that had given them favor for the past forty days; instead they replied:

We went to the land to which you sent us and, oh! It does flow with milk and honey! Just look at this fruit! The only thing is that the people who live there are fierce, their cities are huge and well fortified. Worse yet, we saw descendants of the giant Anak. Amalekites are spread out in the Negev; Hittites, Jebusites, and Amorites hold the hill country; and the Canaanites are established on the Mediterranean Sea and along the Jordan... We can't attack those people; they're way stronger than we are... We scouted out the land from one end to the other—it's a land that swallows people whole. Everybody we saw was huge. Why, we even saw the Nephilim giants (the Anak giants come from the Nephilim). Alongside them we felt like grasshoppers. And they looked down on us as if we were grasshoppers.^{dcxxxvi} (Numbers 13)

In other words, they saw the giant obstacles they had before them instead of the giant God that had gone before them. And then comes their fear-filled words: "Wouldn't it be better for us to go back to Egypt?"^{dcxxxvii} (Num. 14:3, emphasis added) The Israelites were so afraid of "what could happen" that they would rather settle for "what had happened" to them for so many years. The very struggle they wanted to be delivered from had now become the safety they wanted to run back to. They chose the "safe and not sorry" route. And this is where the Lord spoke, "How long will these people treat me with contempt? How long will they refuse to believe in Me? In spite of all the miraculous I have performed among them?"^{dcxxxviii} (Num. 14:11) Like Luke, the Israelites said, "I can't believe it." And that is why they failed their generation. But I feel like if they would've listened to their God instead of their fears, they would've heard Him say, "Don't look back." To not look back at what once was safe and convenient. To not look back at the security of the known. To not look back and find comfort in the practical. Because as soon as we look back, we proclaim, "I can't believe it" with our trust in ourselves. But if we believe in God even greater than we believe in His promise, we will succeed. We will walk triumphantly and untouched into His provision. When we place our trust in who He is, how He is unfailing, faithful, and relentless, it strengthens our trust into belief to go forward and know that He is on our side. *His glory will be made known by those who walk in belief.*

274

LEAD YOUR HEART

> *For it is written: "Be holy, because I am holy."*^{dcxxxix}
> 1 Peter 1:16

We must not forget this verse in such a "feel good" society. Holiness doesn't naturally come when striving after happiness. Yes! It is possible to live a holy life and be happy, but it doesn't always work the other way around. Our heart can be quite deceptive. Never does it say in the Bible, "Follow your heart," actually it says repetitively, "Follow Me," spoken by Jesus. It doesn't say trust your heart, it says to trust in God. Your heart can hold a lot of good, but it can also hold a lot of hurt, regret, and anger. But God is **only** good, and so we can **always** trust Him with our hearts. Our hearts feel, but how many times have your feelings led you astray? How many people have you dated thinking they were perfect for you? How many of those people have you gotten over and have *no* feelings for now? This is just proving that we can't fully trust something that changes so much. As time changes, so do the desires of the heart, and so we trust in God, because He is always the same. My advice: Don't follow your heart, lead it. Give your feelings to God, trust in Him with all of your heart, be happy, but most importantly, be holy.

@ kathleenmadethis

275

RESTART

There's a moment in time where everything just sort of... stops. Reality walks in the door, life pauses, and your world starts turning upside down. Who you were versus who you are now versus who you should be starts to spin a whirlwind of questions in your heart. You walk in a daze wondering what happens next, who decides, and do I really have a choice? And that's when God speaks up and reminds you, "No matter who you decide to be, you'll always be more in Me." Your heart starts to race at the thought of the life to come. All the gains and all the losses, and what once seemed so simple now seems completely petrifying; and it can be, depending on what you're focusing on or who you're trusting. As Philippians 3:13 says: "I forget all of the past as I fasten my heart to the future instead."[dcxl] Sometimes, we are so consumed in who we were that it blinds us from seeing the powerful creation God says we are now. When we found God, our life didn't fast-forward, or pause, or even rewind. No, it commenced. We were wiped clean from who we were to become even better in who Christ is! We were made new and alive! And I think that is what we tend to forget. That we are **new**, that it's okay to *move forward*, and that God has much greater in store for us than we can even imagine! And, based on every human brain, we imagine a lot! But God wants us to remember that we are **more** in Him, not less. Who we once were could have been great, but who we are now is far greater in Christ! Our past is wiped clean, our present is waiting, and our future has much more in store for us to discover!

276

WITH WHITE LINES OF A LION'S MARKING

Have you ever noticed the white lines under a lion's eyes? Supposedly it helps reflect light into their eyes when darkness comes. They can actually see 6-8x better than the human eye at nighttime, (depending on the site you read from). The way their sight is designed is to pick up and amplify very faint light such as that emitted from stars and the moon to give them superior night vision, which is arguably their most important sense. And this is what creates a glow at night in a lion's eyes when light is shined upon them.

When I first read this, all I could think of was the Lion of Judah's eyes looking into ours and wondering, what is it that He sees? While all I can see is confusion, mess, darkness, and distractions, what are His eyes fixed on that sees 6-8x more than I know? When we look at our created artwork or our best of thought-out plans, we look more for our mistakes than taking in the wonder of what was just made. Likewise, when we look at our lives, we define our days typically by what we didn't get done before seeing the importance of rest that we honored, or we forget to congratulate ourselves for the few things we did accomplish on our list even if it wasn't all. And those are just at the surface. What about when it comes to our gifts, our worth, or our identities? I'm pretty sure I asked myself every other day for a season: "Who am I?" and then eventually God spoke up, and that's when everything changed.

He drew white lines under my eyes and He started to change the design of my sight to see differently, as if I had the eyes of a lion. When I looked in the mirror, I stopped seeing dirt and saw designs instead. When I looked at my gifts, I stopped seeing them as falling short, and I started to stand tall in wonder of what He had created through me. When it came to my days, I stopped striving to be perfect, and instead let His perfect love lead me, and it impacted others and myself all the more. Even more so, when it came to my destiny, I not only saw what was in my hands, I saw His hand in everything. A lion's eyes see past the here and the natural, and see into the there and the divine. Revelation 19:12 says: "His eyes are like blazing fire, and on his head are many crowns."[dcxli] For His eyes are alight with the truth and they see past the distortions that doubts and discouragements have created.

When He looks into your eyes, He sees the 6-8x more He is doing that you still cannot yet see. Though the enemy wants to put a canopy of darkness over the sight of your future ahead, the Lion replaces it with a veil over your eyes that are blazing with His glory. My prayer is first that you will begin to see your workplace through a Lion's eyes, and your friendships and gifts too. That it will spark a passion within you to know there's more than you now see. For as a child of God, you are marked with white lines beneath your eyes. Don't allow fear to cover them with black—for white reflects and black refracts. One sees more than what is here, and one sees less than the actuality of goodness before you. And second, my prayer is that you would be brave enough to look into the blazing eyes of the Lion of Judah, to let Him speak over you all that He sees, changing the design of how you see yourself and repainting white lines under your eyes to see glimpses of your destiny ahead. For even if darkness falls, you will stay risen when seeing through the eyes of a lion with white lines of a Lion's marking.

277

STAND FIRM; STAND TALL

Genesis 24 tells us of a God-orchestrated story. Here Abraham sends out his servant to find his son, Isaac, a wife. The servant obediently goes out and prays for a sign—a sign that while he waits at the well, a woman would come and not only offer him a drink, but *also* water his camels. In verses 15-21 it says, "It so happened that the words were barely out of his mouth when Rebekah... came out with a water jug on her shoulder." The girl was stunningly beautiful, a pure virgin. She went down to the spring, filled her jug, and came back up. The servant ran to meet her and said, 'Please, can I have a sip of water from your jug?' She said, 'Certainly drink... I'll get waters for your camels too...' The man watched silent."[dcxlii] By verse 50, when Abraham listens to the story, he exclaims, "This is totally from God." So on we go to the meeting. Isaac was back from his journey, meditating in the field, which just so happened to be the same field Rebekah was travelling to meet him on. He looked up and saw her, and she looked up and saw him, and little did they know all the orchestration behind this very moment. In *The Book of God*, Walter Wangerin brings this scene to life ever so beautifully: "So Rebekah covered her face with a veil and *waited* to be seen by the man who would be her husband. In the Negev, then, Isaac took Rebekah to his tent, and she became his wife, and he loved her (completely). He never loved another as long as he lived. He said, 'As soon as I saw the woman standing tall by the side of a white field, I fell in love with her.'"[dcxliii]

My friend, there is something captivating about *you* that does not go unnoticed. It's a God-thing, and it is unquestionable. But in a world full of disbelief and brokenness, I have learned the enemy will use anyone, sometimes even those closest to you, to try to steal your gaze from the very God-promise on your life. For there are colors only faith can see. I'm not sure if you've ever read *Heaven is For Real*, but it speaks of colors that don't exist on earth. Likewise, some people will believe your God whisper, and others won't, simply because they can't see in faith. The crazier the whisper, the taller you will need to stand when it involves colors out of this realm. In Ephesians 6:13-16 it says, "Because of this, you must wear all the armor that God provides so you're protected as you confront the slanderer, for you are destined for all things and will rise victorious. Put on truth as a belt to strengthen you to stand in triumph. Put on holiness as the protective armor that covers your heart. Stand on your feet alert, then you'll always be ready to share the blessings of peace. In every battle, take faith as your wrap-around shield, for it is able to extinguish the blazing arrows coming at you from the Evil One!"[dcxliv]

I do say this with caution, you should always have a few spiritually discerning people around you to share crazy God whispers with. But with signs and revelations, like the servant had, we also must realize the enemy doesn't want that promise coming to pass. The orchestration may have nothing to do with you, but standing tall or fleeing is your choice. The bigger the whisper, the more adamantly the armor is to be put on. My words for you are this: *Fight, my darling, fight. Fight against the greys. Where motions rob life's colors convincing truth away. Stand, my warrior, stand. Stand tall against the waves. Where waters have overcome, defy their prideful weight. Be brave, my child, be brave. Your sight does not say all. When darkness says to run; fight, be brave, stand tall.*

Like Rebekah, we only need to look up to remember to stand firm in faith and to stand tall and wait for all that He's promised. When it's a God thing, it cannot remain hidden, for when you walk in the will of God, you are a captivating sight. In time, all will align like magic and belief will see its colors. So let not the enemy take hold of your future. Laugh fearlessly at his efforts to touch God's plans, for he cannot. Your purpose shines brightest when you believe it wholeheartedly. It is what releases your bravery and leads you in steps of boldness. Don't be ashamed of the call upon your life. Stand firm and stand tall in the armor that has your name designed upon it, for when you do, you are a fearsome thing to behold.

278

EMBRACING EXPECTATION

Have you ever felt like you've been in the same season forever? At the beginning of the transition, you were excited for what was to come. But then, flowers became the new normal. And sometimes you even missed the snow. In spring, everything is slowly waking up, and there's a fire in your heart to do anything but just stand and watch the sun rise and fall again. While the rain is still penetrating beneath the surface, the sun is still radiating above the surface, and the wind is still creating within the surface's terrain, what exactly is it that we do? For walking on the unseen takes great faith, to not quit on a season's timing, but to embrace it with great expectation. Mark 11:22 says, "Embrace this God-life. Really embrace it, and nothing will be too much for you."[dcxlv] When I think of the word "embrace," I imagine a mother holding her child after months of being away from home; I imagine two lovers who have been distances away from another *finally* being able to hold their loved one again. I imagine Jesus, seeing us struggling in our season's frame, and embracing us as we are, to remind us we are found *still* in the stillness. In an embrace, we don't keep it all together—we let it all out. Every tear and fear, every strength and weakness... caught in the embrace of love. Therefore, embracing this God-life, it's not keeping it all together, it's being real with *yourself* and *God* in the season's change. It's forgetting about where you're at and what's happening around you within the safe embrace of your Savior. In that sense of belonging, expectation begins to blossom again, *for expectation doesn't follow us, but leads us in the unseen.* It keeps us stepping out on the waters of risk with our eyes fixed on Jesus. Expectation creates a ground for Jesus to meet us on, and He always exceeds every single one. Where waters have no design, expectation builds a blueprint for His design to take place. Embracing expectation watches God's hand shape the formless into the fearless before your very eyes. You thought that in the monotony, God wasn't doing anything, but He was actually creating anticipation. For as you woke, you expected the sun to rise and it did. You expected the flowers to bloom, and they did. Expectancy builds and shapes designs on which God creates. Isaiah 14:24 and 27 read: "Exactly as I have planned, it will happen. Following my blueprints, it will take shape. God-of-the-Angel-

Armies has planned it. Who could ever cancel such plans?"[dcxlvi] In the blueprints, His plans take shape, and no one can cancel such divine designs. Learn to stand and watch for God's embrace of your expectations, as He creates with His knowledge and wisdom and sovereignty. It is then you will see before you see, for it creates a place where Jesus can meet you, and He will every time— embracing you and your blueprint designs, loving you just as you are, and creating just as it should be. "Be brave. Be strong. Don't give up. Expect God to get here soon."[dcxlvii] (Psalm 31:24) Be encouraged; be embraced.

279

SIGH AWAY

"Kaytee, will you take out the trash?" (Sigh) "Yes mother, I would love to."

Sighs: they are the long, deep audible exhalations of our hearts' emotions. Even though, in this case, it is a fun moment we have all had with obeying our parents, (smile) there are many sighs that we experience as spouses, parents, and siblings! We sigh when we worry. We sigh when we are upset. We sigh to be heard! The beautiful thing about being human is that God created our hearts to be so tender and delicate. As Nayyirah Waheed says: "Your heart is the softest place on earth. Take care of it."[dcxlviii] We feel the need to take care of a world full of hearts, because it is engrained into our DNA. We love to take care of others! That's why we love our family so deeply and go out of our way for our friends so much. We love to love, and we care to care. Though we are capable of loving, there are times where letting go and releasing is necessary, and the sighs of our hearts are our only words to express the depths of our emotion. *How deep and beautiful the human heart is, but oh how heavy its longings can be.* When your spouse has been home five times in the past month due to business trips, or your last child is about to move out, or your best friend since birth is moving halfway across the world... wordless sighs are all that can suffice because words just can't do it justice.

In Romans 8:26-28 it reads: "In the same way the Spirit [comes to us and] helps us in our weakness. We do not know what prayer to offer or how to offer it as we should, but the Spirit Himself [knows our need and at the right time] intercedes on our behalf with sighs and groanings too deep for words. And He who searches the hearts knows what the mind of the Spirit is, because the Spirit intercedes [before God] on behalf of God's people in accordance with God's will. And we know [with great confidence] that God [who is deeply concerned about us] causes all things to work together [as a plan] for good for those who love God, to those who are called according to His plan and purpose."[dcxlix] In the verses prior, Paul writes to the Romans explaining this glorious and wonderful life that we inherit through Christ, but here he addresses the reality and depth of the waiting. Even though all of this is promised and inherited, there is still this longing in our hearts so ready to have the fulfillment of being with Christ! Paul knows the sighs of a believer's heart all too well, yet he also knows the heart's advocate—the Spirit Himself. As it says in verse 26, "With sighs too deep for words," the Spirit intercedes on our behalves. The Tyndale New Testament Commentary so beautifully states: "Speaking to God in the Spirit with 'tongues' may be included in this expression, but it covers those longings and aspirations which well up from the depths of the spirit and cannot be imprisoned within the confines of everyday words."[dcl]

The sighs of the human heart are but trying to encapsulate our longings in the waiting. How beautiful it is to have glimpses of heaven through loving our loved ones and being loved in return, yet in those times where we open our hands in release, we again are reminded of our longing to ultimately be with Christ. The heart was created for heaven, and sighs may be the only expression we have, but know you have an advocate always listening to the wordless and soundless sighs. He is able to give *sight* to our sighs because of the power of the cross "t". So let your heart sigh! Sigh for the brokenness of the world, sigh for lost loved ones, and sigh for every tender desire in your heart. He listens and intercedes, speaking to the Father what we cannot, giving our longings the power of being seen in His sight, and reminding us that while we are waiting, we are not waiting, for God is always with us. So sigh away, my love. It is beautifully heard.

280

P. S. – I LOVE YOU

I don't know if you have ever been in a season that is seemingly silent, like a winter day still and serene with no movement, like a day awakening to a quiet house all by oneself, like a plunge into the waters where all noise is hushed. Those seasons may be welcomed by the weary, but they are typically dreaded by the rushed. Those who have been running the marathon dream of rest's company, while those who have been walking in slippers are ready for any opportunity to come knocking at their door. Yet no matter the heart's response, silence is still silence. It just is in its state of being. One has forgotten how to make space for it, the other has forgotten how to live within its company, and yet, it is always good for the soul. I do believe that silence happens within transitions, but I also know that it is a reminder in setups. Silence creates a pause for God to whisper, *P.S. I love you*. All of Psalm 19 is absolutely worth reading, but even the beginnings verses are gold alone—let silence be silent, and open your heart to listen to its designed words:

God's splendor is a tale that is told; his testament is written in the stars. Space itself speaks his story every day through the marvels of the heavens. His truth is on tour in the starry vault of the sky, showing his skill in creation's craftsmanship. Each day gushes out its message to the next, night with night whispering its knowledge to all. Without a sound, without a word, without a voice being heard, yet all the world can see its story.[deli]

I believe that God has "P.S.—I love you" written all over the earth for us to see. Just like in the movie, *P.S. I Love You*, where the husband leaves random letters written to his wife for the months after he passed. God has so many wonders whispering its knowledge for you and for me when He is quiet. It's not because He isn't with you, but because He is for you. He does it without a sound, without a word, yet all the world can see its story. They say that when one sense is not being used, the other four senses strengthen, so if your ears are hearing nothing, your eyes are becoming more alert to see the tiniest details of God, and typically, the smallest designs are the most thought out. *P.S. I love you isn't something that is said because one has forgotten to say it; no, it is purposefully signed to emphasize what has been spoken*. Or in our case of listening to a God who speaks light and thus we see light, it can emphasize what series of wonders God has already done before our eyes, for His splendor is a tale that is told with a timeless message of P.S. I love you. This Psalm ends with, "So may the words of my mouth, my meditation-thoughts, and every movement of my heart be always pure and pleasing, acceptable before your eyes, my only Redeemer, my Protector-God." For it goes from the psalmist taking in all the wonders of God to seeing God Himself again, and *remembering* Him as his only redeemer, which I believe is God's clear message written across the sky. God's redeeming love always begins with the heart—that's why silence stays silent. Those of us who have been weary from running, take a moment to create space for silence, that His redeeming love may do a work within you and overflow around you. Those of us who have been tired of being snowed in, let His warmth thaw through the frozen layers of disappointment, fear, and pain within you first... then you'll be ready to put on your gardening gloves for spring. Because God is careful with us and loves to protect our hearts with His sweetness; He waits to act for when we're ready, though He's always ready and willing as a bridegroom for His wedding. In everything He does, and in everything He says, it is always written with an act of redeeming love and sealed with an emphasis of *P. S. **I love you**.*

281

GROUNDED IN GRATITUDE

The average person lives 27,375 days. Reading that, it sounds like a lot. But as Joshua Kennon writes: "To find out how much time you have left if you are an average man or woman, take your age and multiply it by 366. Then subtract it from 27,375 days."[dclii] Sounds a bit crazy, right? Yet as you calculate your days, you find at the age of 25, you have 18,250 days left to live; by the age of 50, only 9,125. It dwindles and shrinks with time. Steve Jobs said that one of his secrets to his success was reminding himself every day he was going to die. Two years after this statement, he passed away. As Kennon further writes: "He had fewer days than most people, passing away at 56 years old, yet accomplished more than anyone who has ever lived." The truth is, time is of the essence.

The question is, how will we spend it; more or less, *how will we value it?*

In Isaiah 30:18 it states: "Yet the Lord longs to be gracious to you; therefore he will rise up to show you compassion. For the Lord is a God of justice. Blessed are all who wait for him!"[dcliii] May you be reminded that no matter what your "time clock of life" reads, every single one of those days God has <u>new</u> mercies to offer you. If you're 25, you have 18,250 new mercies still awaiting you. If you're 50, you still have 9,125. Each day won't always be easy but there are moments of comfort, peace, and love to be uncovered within their 86,400 seconds of time. It is in those uncovered seconds of value that we are grounded in gratitude, for whether in

@ kathleenmadethis

the heights of life or the depths of longing, God is with us in each one.

The word "longing" itself has a bittersweet feel to it. Longing for a loved one, for a dream come true, for salvations, for good news... Longing holds mystery and unknown, but it is unmissable. Our longings can either rob us or compel us to live. They rob us when we feel helpless, yet compel us when we feel hopeful. The perspective shift between the two lies within the beauty of gratitude. Gratitude embraces each day not knowing what will happen next but seeing what is happening now. If we can but find the slightest bit of light to hold onto in the darkness, gratitude thrives, flourishes and grows. In the case of loss, I know God to be sufficient. In the case of life, I know God to be generous. Yet always, He longs to be gracious to the longings of our hearts. If we desire His perfection, we must also accept His patience. As 2 Peter 3:9 says: "The Lord is not slow in keeping his promise, as some understand slowness. Instead he is patient with you, not wanting anyone to perish, but everyone to come to repentance."[dcliv] I hope and pray that if you have not yet discovered the releasing power of gratitude—you will. It is the long lost best friend of longing. For gratitude will keep longing grounded, not letting the beauty of its depths die, but keeping it alive with the hope and purpose every day. Each day, live fully. Jesus didn't die on the cross for us to live any less. He is faithful to the beginning of your longing as He is faithful to the end of its revelation. May you wait for it, grounded in gratitude, that it will certainly come and not prove false. He is as faithful as He is true, the same yesterday, today, and forever!

282

HERE OR THERE

Prophesy is like a telescope on a voyage that allows you to see what is to come, but if you only look through its lens, you will miss the beauty of all that is around your vessel. The voyage doesn't seem to go any faster whether you're looking ahead through the telescope or seeing the vastness of the ocean with your eyes. One creates hope and the other is home, and you decide which is which depending on what your heart is set on, for there your treasure will be also. It's the difference of being here or there. It's the fine line between *seeing* goodness and <u>knowing</u> goodness. There are glaciers and whales and islands and dolphins on the voyage that the destination could never surprise you with. So maybe let the breeze take your breath away. Maybe let the sun tan your skin. Maybe stop here and there to take a swim. Your here can be as enjoyable as your there as long as you give it the invitation to feel like home. And maybe what once was daunting will look a little more welcoming—a place where you belong.

> *I look behind me and you're there, then up ahead and you're there, too—your reassuring presence, coming and going. This is too much, too wonderful—I can't take it all in! Is there anyplace I can go to avoid your Spirit? To be out of your sight? If I climb to the sky, you're there! If I go underground, you're there! If I flew on morning's wing to the far western horizon, you'd find me in a minute—you're already there waiting!*[dclv]
> Psalm 139:5-10

283

VALUE IN THE KINGDOM

There's Tanzanite, Taaffeite, Black Opal, Benitate, Red Beryl, Alexandrite, Jadeite, Musgravite, Painite, and the Pink Star Diamond. These are the world's ten rarest and most valuable gems. Tanzanite starts at $600-1000 per carat. Red Beryl goes to $10,000 per carat, and the most rare Pink Star Diamond is $1,395,761 per carat. Ten completely different gems with ten different values, but all with a unique and rare touch. And yet many of us are drawn to the gem with the higher number before we even give a look at the other nine gems. Why? Because we want the best with the highest value. And like us, the disciples were asking Jesus in Matthew 18:1, "Who is the greatest in the kingdom of heaven?"[dclvi] Because they also were wanting the best and to have the highest value. So Jesus calls over a child replying that those who will be humble like this child will be the greatest.

And in this moment, it is like they were throwing Jadeites, Painites, and Pink Star Diamonds at His feet to win His favor, and Jesus instead picks up an Amethyst gem with a $10 per carat value and says, "All have value." He doesn't choose determined by the highest value number on the gem, neither does He choose by the highest number of good deeds or great faith, instead He calls a little child to His side and tells them, "See that you do not look down on one of these little ones."[dclvii] What is interesting to me is that the disciples had their mindset on the greatest of <u>all</u>, when Jesus had His heart set on the value in *one*. Because each one had value, each one had a unique and rare touch, and each one was a son and daughter—and this is the value in the kingdom—that *the one* always matters.

Some of us still need to find the value in ourselves, and others of us need to see the value in others. Some will feel ordinary, like an amethyst in a pile of diamonds, and yet this is the one God typically chooses. God looks at all the gems and sets apart the amethyst, for it's His value upon it that will make its worth so much more than the world could imagine. Some others know they are valued, but are quick to look down on the worth of others because they have a different personality or calling. Yet one thing I have learned is just because someone is different from you doesn't mean that they are any less than you. In Jesus' words: "Therefore, whoever humbles himself like this child – this one is the greatest in the kingdom of heaven."[dclviii]

You see, humility is not always found in thinking less of yourself, but thinking more of others. It's looking at each person as His son or His daughter—the one He created and is so proud of; the one He gave a unique touch to and calls rare; and seeing the value that He sees in them. Because in the kingdom of heaven, no call will be greater than another, nor will one man be better than another—for all have value and all are His children designed, rare and unique.

284

UNFATHOMABLE

Blessed are the pure in heart for they will see God.[delix]
Matthew 5:8

In order to keep your heart pure, you must guard it, and to guard your heart is to guard your very thoughts. We either limit God with our unfathomable thoughts or enlarge our mind with our unfathomable God. You see, we must align our expectations with the reality God has given us. If we hold onto our expectations over God, our reality will fall apart because we are aligning our hearts with unfathomable thoughts. And so, we need to expect reality in order to guard our hearts and trust in our unfathomable God. I'm not saying that you shouldn't dream, because dreaming is beautiful! But I am saying that our thoughts should be self-controlled instead of controlling us; in other words, we can't allow our desires for our dreams to become greater than our desire for our God. We can't be putting the same expectations we have of God on people or reality, because both of them aren't perfect, only God is. When we place an unrealistic image on our life, we blind ourselves to the beauty of reality. However, when we begin to take captive our unrealistic thoughts, it allows our limitless God to come into our reality, and He will blow us away with the unfathomable. Mark Batterson says, "Half of learning is learning. The other half of learning is unlearning. It is harder to get older thoughts out of your mind than it is to get new thoughts into your mind."[delx] Piece-by-piece a wall is put together, and piece-by-piece it can be taken down without collapsing. So, as we give God our expectations a piece at a time, day-by-day, we will begin to *see Him* in unfathomable ways.

Dear friend, listen well to my words; tune your ears to my voice.
Keep my message in plain view at all times.
Concentrate! Learn it by heart! Those who discover these words live, really live; body and soul,
they're bursting with health. Keep vigilant watch over your heart; that's where life starts.[delxi]
Proverbs 4:20-23

285

HE'S IN THE WAITING

Have you ever sat in a waiting room? They typically have magazines and books perfectly placed by the seats, along with cute little play areas of games in case you have kids. But no matter how much we may love reading or playing... there's just something about a waiting room that is just *boring*. It's like, the appointment was made, you've come all this way, and now you are just sitting. You don't mind reading, but you didn't drive all this way to check "reading another book" off your bucket list. You didn't put in all this effort to just wait. The thing is, when we come to waiting rooms, we usually know what we are waiting for, and that builds a wonderful amount of expectation. Yet, when that expectation is not met quickly, anxiousness typically grows. The longer you wait, the more you fiddle. And the more you fiddle, the slower the minutes pass. Thirty minutes is the new eternity when you're twiddling your thumbs for half an hour. But I think the greatest thing we can do in the waiting room is to not lose heart—for the appointment is bound to happen, even if it's not on your own timing.

When it comes to waiting on God, I believe our waiting rooms are so much more abundant. I believe there are libraries on the walls with stories to discover and lessons to learn; there are endless adventures with the amount of cards and video games and massage chairs around, and there is plenty of food, desserts, and coffees in unlimited supply for you to feast upon. Oh! And the best part: you're not alone, for He is with you in the waiting. I don't know if you've heard the Bethel song "Take Courage," but I'm pretty sure it should be in the background music of every person's waiting room. It says: *Take courage, my heart. Stay steadfast my soul, He's in the waiting, He's in the waiting. Hold onto your hope, as your triumph unfolds, He's never failing, He's never failing.*[dclxii] Because the truth is, as you wait for God to come through in some miraculous way, He's there with you, for **true love waits and God waits with us**. As you ponder your circumstance, or go over every detail in your head wondering if you missed something, He sits at your side, patiently waiting on you to remember *He has a plan*, and a perfect one at that.

You know how a bride and a groom go into their separate rooms to get ready before the ceremony? The bride puts the dress on she's been dreaming of since she was five, and the groom fixes his bowtie while finishing his final touches to look oh, so handsome. But it's there that our loved ones are around us cheering us on, knowing that the best is already outside our door. And I truly believe that when it comes to being in the waiting room with God, it is so much the same. It's not the boring, twiddle your thumbs, anxious wait; it's a hope-filled, soul-steadying, heart-flying excitement of what is about to happen on the other side of the door, and God is squeezing your hand in excitement. For it is appointed, and well, you've already come this far. As Jude 1:2 says, "Relax, everything's going to be all right; rest, everything's coming together; open your hearts, love is on the way."[dclxiii] God has you. He hasn't failed you yet, and His character doesn't change. Miracles happen in the waiting, and God's hand is always all over it. It's like magic! You don't know how it happened, it just did. So let Him surprise you, and take courage. Whatever you're waiting for is well worth the wait. God's in the waiting and He has something divine up His sleeve for you.

286

A HIDDEN TREASURE

I have learned a little secret. One that isn't spoken of much, but is found in the wandering. It's one we seek out as children, going behind locked doors, being enthralled by the mystery of "what could be," which is often followed by a lot of games and dramas for this satisfaction of who we are and the life we love. Some of us found it in music, others in the entirely different world of a book, others in movies…or arts… or whatever it is that filled your heart with wonder. Though we listened, and though we sought, a secret was still kept. Our hearts were still searching for this hidden treasure. All to find out it was never hidden, just kept silent. Just misunderstood or left in the dust for too long. And what is this secret you may ask? Be prepared to not be shocked… "God is love." You've heard it before, right? I have a billion times, and I didn't even grow up in church. Then what's so secret about it? You see, the treasure is inside of that phrase that we have overlooked for so long.

For as long as I can remember, I have always been a romantic at heart, with my hopes-to-come-true a little bit unrealistic. But the wonder of love has never left my heart, as I'm sure it hasn't left yours. Sometimes we find ourselves in the same places going through the motions of searching still—because we want to feel the way we once did at this place of passion, excitement, and life. But to know God is love is to discover He put that love in your heart at that place for that time. That He was what filled you with wonder. It wasn't the books, the games, the dramas, or the dreams. That love was given through Him even if you didn't know Him yet. He is like our secret admirer whose love we always sought never realizing it was right before our eyes. We were created to be in relationship with the creator of the universe and the orchestrator of our wonder. Luke 12:34 says, "For where your treasure is, there your heart will be also."[dclxiv] The truth is… *He is our treasure that was the secret within, "God is love."* It is there

@k15_nicole

where we find His heart and our own. It's an entirely new adventure of an extraordinary love for us. One that was never hidden, only kept secret. But it's a beautiful truth that all should know and hear. It was Him all along our hearts were searching for, for He is who creates the beauty, the passion, the excitement, and the wonder in our lives. Along our wandering, the secret was uncovered—this beauty, this life, it's not found in someone or something… it's found in Him. In His Love, our first love, we find our most treasured love, filling our hearts again and again with His heart, in the most secret and sacred ways. He is our secret admirer, the One who leads us on into His extravagant dimensions of love, leaving little treasures as clues to what He has planned next, which is always far wilder than before.

> *Wild and wonderful is this world you have made.*[dclxv]
> Psalm 104:24

287

WILDCARD

His love is wild, untamed, unpredictable. It is fierce, bold, and valiant. His love is constant, ever-present, and all-knowing. It is freeing, captivating, and invigorating. Yet, it is here… and that is the wildest thing of all. Romans 10:9-10 says: "The word that saves is *right here*, as near as the tongue in your mouth, as close as the heart in your chest. It's the word of faith that welcomes God to go to work and set things right for us."[dclxvi] (emphasis added) The thing about a wildcard is that it holds an unknown or unpredictable factor. It is something you see, yet also don't see yet. Its value comes with perfect timing on a perfect move. Faith, the powerful, confident, hope we hold onto, hears an image more than sees a sight. Faith sees wildcards and it holds onto them with a deep assurance that there's a reason for why it was placed in your hands.

When I see a wildcard in the hand of God, I know He has something *great* up His sleeve. Yet here's the thing, hearing the word faith sounds sweet and lovely, but speaking in faith is bold and risky. It's speaking wild. It's speaking love. His words that He gives are wild, and when we speak them, we dare to believe their hidden truth. Faith may have a deep revelation, but it needs an even deeper sense of when the timing is right to play the card. Faith moves yes, but it does not chase after where there is no peace. It stands as much as it goes, for great faith requires trusting God and placing the wildcards in His hands time and time again. It's in the releasing that we let go, draw closer to God, and allow Him to do what only He can do. As Romans 10:11 goes on to say: "No one who trusts God like this—heart and soul—will ever regret it."[dclxvii] Letting go is wild, yet His love is wilder. And it is His wild love that keeps you safe.

My friend, the reason I am writing you this is to keep your faith strong when the enemy throws all his cards at you. When the enemy tries to be the joker who thinks he can win. Don't be fooled by his deck. For God has a wildcard ready to be played upon a steady faith. I believe there is more for you than what you see because God's love has no limits, and that can skyrocket our dreams into far beyond. Yet, it is not necessarily what you hear that will lead you there, but what you speak. Whose cards are you giving voice to— who are you believing will win? What you say either aligns you with His way, welcoming Him to show up and move, *or* it leads you astray, distracting you with doubt's and worry's lines. If His word is here and now, as near as the tongue in your mouth, and as close as the heart in your chest, draw strength from His wild love, and then *proclaim the wild*, shooting it into the sky, believing in it until it breaks through the atmosphere. As Psalm 84:11-12 says:

For the Lord God is a sun and shield; the Lord bestows grace and favor and honor; no good thing will He withhold from those who walk uprightly. O Lord of hosts, how blessed and greatly favored is the man who trusts in You [believing in You, relying on You, and committing himself to You with confident hope and expectation].[dclxviii]

Fuel your faith and let it skyrocket towards what you hear. The closer you get to breaking through, the cloudier your vision will appear, the louder the pressure will roar, and the shakier your promise may seem. But hold on, for it will burst through the atmosphere with a powerful bang! Louder than your faith could speak, higher than you imagined, and greater than your sight could see. **When you hold on with wild faith, people see the wild.** As Frances Hodgson Burnett says: "At first people refuse to believe that a strange new thing can be done, then they begin to hope it can be done, then they see it can be done – then it is done and all the world wonders why it was not done centuries ago."[dclxix] God has a wildcard up His sleeve for you, and you can trust His unpredictable timing to play it perfectly. For when suddenly victory is ready to take place, He will breakthrough the atmosphere with a triumphant roar! And death will be no more. Remember He withholds no good thing, and His valiant, untamed, ever-present, invigorating love is wilder than letting go. It's then, you'll fly.

288

BEYOND YOUR WILDEST DREAMS

Flowers... they are one of my many favorite things I look forward to in springtime. They are just so beautiful, and they smell so good. It's the very symbol of spring! How many of you, when buying flowers, go straight back to the ones that are already grown? They look great and are already bloomed—it's exactly what we like, it's fast, and it's what we wanted. But how many of you actually grow your own? Not many do because it takes <u>time</u>—which we "say" we don't have much of. It just takes all this care, it's such a process, and why wait if you can get what you want now, right? Isn't that just like how we treat our dreams?

A dream first starts as a crazy kind of random, but makes sense, thought. But then as it is pondered, it sounds good—*really* good, and we *want* it. But then it comes to the effort you have to put behind it to get there, and then it doesn't sound so beautiful. I mean, I could just follow in my parent's footsteps or take this job offer for me right now and just build from there, right? It's fast and what I wanted. But you see, there is a beauty in the process of growing. Mark 4:20 says, "But the seed planted in the good earth represents those who hear the Word, embrace it, and produce a harvest beyond their wildest dreams."[dclxx] Every thought we have is like a seed, and as we ponder it, it starts to shape into a dream. Our prayers are like the water, and God is the light. If a plant has water and no light, it won't be able to grow. If a plant has light and no water, it will never come alive. Yet when the seed has water, it breaks through the surface, and the light feeds it to grow, and in a process it blooms into beauty. Many people throw thoughts away like they are a crazy idea; but it is those who catch those ideas and embrace them that discover a passion beyond what they could have imagined. Yet it is our prayers that bring it to God, and it is His light (or Will) that allows it to grow into something beautiful. Those who have made a difference could have just followed footsteps, because it would have been easy, but instead they decided to follow His steps and sowed beauty beyond their wildest dreams.

289

ONE

Deserts. They're dry, hot, sandy, and long. But within their journey's time, we discover far more than what was left behind. In Exodus, Moses is out leading his flock to the far side of the desert. Yet this day, something catches his eye, a burning bush that doesn't burn up. He is allured. As he comes close, a divine exchange begins to occur. God calls Moses by name, and not only is Moses awestruck by what he sees, but by what he hears. He responds with "I'm here," and waits for what's next. It's here the unexpected occurs, as God reveals who He is, and then Moses hides. Though there is a sense of inadequacy in him, I sense an act of God's sufficiency that's about to take place. As Moses responds, "I can't," God answers, "Perfect! I can! That's why I called **you** by name because I know it will give all glory to **My** name! It will be through you, but I will be with you, My promise." And yet, Moses still can't comprehend fully what God is saying.

At this point, Moses has been shepherding for thirty years; *before* that, he was in the palace for thirty years. This leaves a huge gap between when he last approached his family. What God is speaking almost seems thirty years too late to Moses, especially to be through him in his desert season. And so we come to the question in Exodus 4:2, "What is that in your hand?" As Moses responds, "A staff."[dclxxi] If he could see as God saw, his answer would be more like, "A rod that can turn into a snake and will be used to part the Red Sea." But that's the thing about trust, we don't see every detail, we just have to trust the extraordinary God who can do much with one thing. God goes on to say: "Reach out your hand and take it by the tail." And this was the beginning of Moses taking hold of the promise that he had no idea was in store for him. It all started with a staff that he had already been using for thirty years.

What is a staff, he could be thinking? Likewise, what is a cactus? Some interesting facts about cacti are: they come in all shapes and forms; they live in dry places prone to drought that adapt to conserve water during long dry periods; their spines are highly modified versions of plant leaves which are used as protection against animals, and they collect water using its large root system to reach underground water.[dclxxii] If a simple cactus has so much within it, how much more is what is within your hand with the same ***powerful*** properties. What God has placed in your hand can withstand desert seasons and adapt to its surroundings; its leaves are strong and mighty to keep the enemy away from the source of life you are tapped into, and its roots are able to withstand any storm of discouragement that comes your way. What God has placed within you is able to last through any season, the desert being one it is specifically well-equipped for. As Job 8:7 says, "And though your beginning was small, your latter days will be very great."[dclxxiii]

Don't dismiss how small the gift may seem, even if it is the size of a mustard seed in your eyes, for God can do mighty things even with a seed given in faith. If George Washington Carver can take a peanut and make: soaps, lotions, creams, shampoo, face powder, dyes, lamp oil, and so on with just peanuts, what could God do with your one thing? For in the desert, your divine exchange awaits, and He is calling you by name. As God spoke to Moses in chapter 4, He again speaks in Exodus 14:16, "But lift up your rod, and stretch out your hand over the sea and divide it."[dclxxiv] The same words God spoke to Moses at the beginning to prove Himself were the same words God spoke to him before He did the impossible. Use what's in your hand, stretch out your hand, take it by the tail, and see what God will do. What is one peanut? What is one cactus? What is one staff? But most importantly, what is your one thing? Don't be afraid to use it. He has a plan—it may take ten chapters to understand what He is doing, and you may never fully comprehend the vastness of it, but it will be extravagant and it will be worth every bit of courage. Like Titus 1:2 says, "He doesn't break promises."[dclxxv] Just go after what He's whispering into your heart, and you will see the faithfulness of the Lord.

290

BURNING BUSHES

> *We have become his poetry, a re-created people that will fulfill the destiny he has given each of us, for we are joined to Jesus, the Anointed One. Even before we were born, God planned in advance it our destiny and the good works we would do to fulfill!*[dclxxvi]
> Ephesians 2:10

"There is a war over your heart," He whispered. Isn't that the truth for all of us? The enemy will use any weakness against you and try to use your greatest desires to distract you. But isn't this why we are called to "be still" in so many seasons of our lives? Moses had to be still to even see the burning bush, which scholars said had been burning for years and years before it was truly seen. But because he was still for even a moment, he was able to see clearly for generations to come. Likewise, we each must have our own "divergent" moments where we wake-up from our just-another-day-dreams to realize "this isn't real." Stillness may sometimes look like the enemy trying to sing us **to sleep** with lullabies. Yet awake to the unseen, you can see that presently God actually is having us in this moment "lie down in green pastures" **to truly see** what He is doing. We all have burning bushes in the stillness that God is wanting us to see. They tend to be the greatest pivotal moments in our lives to lead us to a dream we could have never imagined. But as Psalm 46:10 says, "Be still, and know that I am God,"[dclxxvii] we will never truly know God until we learn to be still, if even only for a moment. Don't let it take years and years for you to wake up to what He has before you now. Be still. Look for your burning bush, and find God waiting there for you, ready to reveal the rarity He has placed inside of you for His glory to be revealed through you. God once spoke to me: "Your being still has won many wars." The enemy doesn't set off wars for nothing, and being still may be your greatest weapon to fight back. For it's there you'll see God, and there you'll see you. And from that moment on, every thing will make sense and all will change and rearrange into one of the most incredible stories ever to be told.

291

COME TO LIFE

God breathes into our desires, and they shape into words. We hear them as whispers, and yet see them as promises. With open hands, we discover, we feel, we are comforted, by the touch of a Saviour's gift to us. With blinded faith, our hearts intensify, burst with passion, and long for this vision to dance into being, for this dream to come to pass, for His kingdom to gloriously display. Yet it is in this place of trust His voice thunders, His love roars, His light conquers.

It's where our waiting will meet His promise—and His whispers will come to life.

> *The Lord shows favor to those who fear him, to his godly lovers who wait for his tender embrace. He sends out his orders throughout the world; his words run as swift messengers, bringing them to pass. He blankets the earth with glistening snow, painting the landscape with frost. Sleet and hail fall from the sky, causing waters to freeze before winter's icy blast.* **Then he speaks his word and it all melts away;** *as the warm spring winds blow, the streams begin to flow. In the same way, he speaks his word to Jacob, and to Israel he brings his life-giving instruction. He has dealt with Israel differently than with any other for they have received his laws. Hallelujah! Praise the Lord!*[dclxxviii] (emphasis added)
> Psalm 147:11,15-20

292

WHISPERS

There's an app called whisper with the description: *Whisper is the best place to discover secrets around you.*

What it doesn't tell you is: Whisper is the best place to discover secrets *about* you. Whispering involves:

1. *Leaning* into the speaker to hear their voice. 2. A <u>gratified desire</u> for what they have to say. 3. Either a secretly beautiful or detrimentally destructive power. There is much more power in *one* whisper than we know. One person who took advantage of its power was Delilah. Samson was a man of God, unquestionably chosen and favored. But other people resented it. So they began to whisper. As Samson fell in love with Delilah, the Philistines saw a great vulnerable opportunity. As we read in Judges 16:5-6, "The rulers of the Philistines went to her and said, 'See if you can lure him into showing you the secret of his **great** strength and how we can *overpower* him so we may tie him up and subdue him. Each one of us

will give you eleven hundred shekels of silver.' So Delilah said to Samson, 'Tell me the <u>secret</u> of your great strength and how you can be tied up and subdued.'"[dclxxix] (emphasis added) We see that eventually he does listen to her whisper, and he suffers by the attack of the Philistines because of it. There is great power in a *whisper* when you listen to what it has to **say**.

As Christians and leaders in ministry, we are targets of the enemy. He will cause the people to whisper, looking for a vulnerable opportunity to attack. We can learn from Samson's mistake by being careful with whom we are leaning into. Isaiah 30:21 says, "Whether you turn to the right or to the left, you will hear a voice behind you saying, 'This is the way, walk in it.'"[dclxxx] Another way I read it as is, "Your ears will hear a whisper next to you..." Listening to a whisper means you're allowing them to be close, placing you in a vulnerable position of trust. Let me just say not everyone should be as close as you're allowing them to be. When we listen to the whispers that those against us have to say, we're setting ourselves up for a destructive outcome. Instead, we are to lean into the One who has something beautiful to speak over each of us. God is the One we are meant to lean into. He will protect us and keep us safe when attacks come, this being *the secret* of our **greatest** strength to overcome. We are designed to listen to the whispers of the King over the whisper of His people.

The end of Judges 16 tell us this, Samson said to the servant who held his hand, 'Put me where I can feel the pillars that support the temple, so I may lean into them.' Then Samson prayed to the Lord, 'O Sovereign Lord, remember me, O God, please strengthen me just once more, and let me with one blow get revenge on the Philistines for my two eyes.'… Then he pushed with all his might, and down came the temple on the rulers and all the people in it thus he killed many more when he died then when he lived.[dclxxxi] The Philistines saw he was leaning on the pillars, but Samson was truly leaning upon his King. Listening to what God is whispering over you will always be your greatest strength. The enemy can never overpower what God is doing within you as long as you are leaning into the One who is ***empowering*** you with every whisper He speaks. As Steven Furtick says, "What matters most is not what I think I am or not, or what others think I am or not. What matters is what **my Father** *sees* in me and what He *says* about me."[dclxxxii] (emphasis added)

293

YOU ARE MORE

> "Don't limit God with the deception of yourself."
> - Anonymous

My child, the enemy has been containing you. Break out of this state that he has placed you in for you were made for more than what you now know. Keep pursuing Me and you will come to see the abundantly more I have in store ahead of you, and the extravagant dimensions I have created within you, to move into as your new home. You were made to live out all that's in your heart, for all that's in your heart was made out of My love for you. You need only to remember that you are more to step into the greater before you.

You are more than your appearance
More than unique
More than significant
More than weak
You are more than valued
More than loved
More than fearless
More than enough.
You are more than the words people say,
for it is by My word that you were made.

> "However, as it is written: 'No eye has seen, no ear has heard, no mind has conceived what God has prepared for those who love him.'"[dclxxxiii]
> 1 Corinthians 2:9

294

BEFORE THE GLASS SLIPPER

I wonder how Cinderella felt when she was about to meet her prince? Not the first time when she had no idea who she was, nor the second time when she was at her utmost of beauties, but the third time, when he showed up at her door expecting a princess. What did she feel as she walked down the creaky wooden steps towards her long awaited prince? My favorite quote in the movie is said at this very scene: "Perhaps the greatest risk any of us will ever take is to be seen as we really are."[dclxxxiv] Though the glass slipper was designed for her, I can almost feel the hesitancy within her to step into it, because well, it was as her, not a princess.

I feel like when we come closest to stepping into our destiny, that is when the friendliness of fear starts to speak up. Fear will speak to your comfort reminding you of your cottage home and warm fireplace. Fear will remind you of all the goodness you left behind that you could so easily walk back to. Fear will paint a picture of who you were to make you want to walk back into your old, worn shoes instead of moving forward in your new, destined glass slippers. It humors me that we dream and wish, hope and pray, wait and endure, only to choose to walk away when the door opens. Because somewhere between the dreaming and the reality, fear walked in, befriended our comfort, and persuaded our hearts that settling is of God's BEST.

Let me ask: would you rather live in a cottage or a castle? Yes, the cottage is less to take care of and more familiar. But the castle is filled with beauty and blessings! It may have a higher cost, but it also has more designs. It's not for the small-minded, but the bold and the believing. The castle is created for visionaries to steward its wealth and to distribute it to the nations; it's destined for those willing to take on the purpose of the throne. It sounds enchanting, but the throne isn't a place of comfort when you're placed in it. It's destined for the fearless who will lead with the authority they've been given, not for those seeking promotion. A queen and king aren't weak warriors, but are brave in the fields and looking to lead others to the throne of the King of kings. They're strong and heroic for the kingdom placed before them, carving paths for multitudes to follow. They see and carry the weight of its promise. And yet, though it may sound daunting at first, it is still destined... for well, you! And that's everything fear doesn't whisper.

The glass slipper didn't fit your foot coincidentally; it was purposely crafted for you to walk into your call confidently. I believe when Cinderella saw her destiny before her, she knew what she was stepping into would change everything, but she also knew it was where she belonged. So my advice to you who stand before the glass slipper is: 1, Be bold and unashamed of who you are. Cinderella wasn't ashamed to step into what was created for her specifically; there was something only specifically within her that the people needed to be led by. She didn't say my name is "Ella" but "Cinderella," because Cinderella was as beautiful as bold. 2, When the glass slipper is placed before you, believe in beauty's beckoning over trusting fear's friendliness. 3, Hold onto hope. As Psalm 119:41-48 says:

Let your love, God, shape my life with salvation, exactly as you promised; then I'll be able to stand up to mockery because I trusted your Word. Don't ever deprive me of truth, not ever— your commandments are what I depend on. Oh, I'll guard with my life what you've revealed to me, guard it now, guard it ever; and I'll stride freely through wide open spaces as I look for your truth and your wisdom; then I'll tell the world what I find, speak out boldly in public, unembarrassed. I cherish your commandments—oh, how I love them!—relishing every fragment of your counsel.[dclxxxv]

Hold onto every word God says and let hope stir within you until it comes to pass. 4, Remember, though you may be royal, God will always remain King, yet you still have His authority to lead with. His throne lives in your heart for it's where His authority dwells. My friend, be bold and unashamed in who God says you *are* as you approach your long awaited and hoped for "prince," or dream. As you step out, you will find the glass slipper to be "quite comfortable," different but destined.

295

SHAPED IN HIM

Heavenly Father,

I will set my eyes on You. I will let You show me who I am. I will stop trying, struggling, to be something I am not, and learn to love the person You have created me as. I will strive to be molded into a child of God according to Your standards instead of the world's. I will listen to Your heart over my own. I will learn to patiently trust Your wisdom instead of frantically trying to figure out every detail myself. I will learn to walk in love and not just speak it. I will sacrifice comfort and pray more. I will be shaped by Your voice and not the world's opinion. I will come into Your atmosphere and break out of my own. I will open my heart to You time and time again. I will be shaped by You, my God, and only by You alone. Amen.

> "Yet you, Lord, are our Father.
> We are the clay, you are the potter; we are all the work of your hand."[dclxxxvi]
> Isaiah 64:8

296

STRONGER ALONE

One of the craziest miracles we know of today is the parting of the Red Sea. One where a great leader named Moses led the Israelites through. Yet, what made Moses great was not his skills, but his obedience. Before and after the parting of the sea, Moses had multiple alone times with the Lord. One of my favorite instances is found in Exodus 33 where Moses made a "tent of meeting" with God. In the book of excuses of why you don't have enough time to spend with the Lord, I'm sure his would be pretty high on the list. Instead, he makes a tent and sets apart a meeting place. The reason why I chose this story out of the rest is because it is in this tent that we see Moses doesn't have it all together. In Exodus 33:13, he asks God, "If you are pleased with me, teach me your ways so I may know you and continue to find favor with you. Remember that this nation is your people."[dclxxxvii] Here we see that just because God said you were capable of doing something great doesn't mean He intended for you to do it by your own strength. In the middle of his journey, Moses is still seeking God for His strength, His direction, and His wisdom. Likewise, God will speak great promises over our lives, but we also aren't meant to do them alone.

One day, while a body of believers surrounded me, God spoke: "You grow stronger alone." He was prompting me to have some tent meetings with Him so that I myself could ask for the strength, direction, and wisdom that I needed so desperately. *It's in our alone time with the Lord that we don't become bigger to Him, but He becomes bigger to us!* It's in that time we experience a word that darkness fears: death. We die; we are buried; we are shut off to all the distractions of the world around us. But it's there we also discover the truest of life. In John 12:24, it says, "I tell you the truth, unless a kernel of wheat falls to the ground and dies, it remains only a single seed. But if it dies, it produces many seeds."[dclxxxviii] Followed by: "The man who loves his life will lose it, while the man who hates his life in this world will keep it for eternal life." The person who lives for themselves will never experience the miracles and blessings God has to offer, because they never let go of their lives. While the man who knew life wasn't found in the world, and instead risked everything, was buried and experienced the life that follows with the unthinkable. Like a seed that is buried into the ground, it will only remain there for so long before it breaks through the surface. It is beneath the surface where true strength develops and your roots grow deep, where you trust God to show favor on your life, instead of trying to create it yourself. It's in that tent of meeting that you remember His great love for you. It's where it's just you and Him, and that's all that matters. That's the greatest strength of all.

> "Aslan," said Lucy, "you're bigger." "That is because you are older, little one," answered he. "Not because you are?" "I am not. But every year you grow, you will find me bigger."[dclxxxix]
> - *The Chronicles of Narnia*

297

WHERE IS YOUR DELIGHT?

Delight yourself in the Lord and He will give you the desires of your heart.[dexc]
Psalm 37:4

I want you to think about everything that brings you delight; from your passions, to your friends, to the things you own. Now here is a tough question to ask yourself: if all of these delights were taken away, would you still have joy? And I want you to really think about that.

Psalm 37:4 teaches us to place our delight in God, and I have read it for years, but I never truly grasped the concept of it. I used to read it as I would get the desires of my heart if I learned to delight in the Lord; but now I see that when you delight in the Lord, your desires end up changing. All of a sudden it's not about you, but Him.

We shouldn't seek God for the desires of our heart; no, we seek God and find the desires of our heart. You see, God took all of my little "delights" away. My friends fell from God, I was losing my passion, and I didn't have that best friend to comfort me when I was upset. I was trying to hold onto all of these delights because I knew they were fading away, and I just didn't know why. To be honest, I felt like I was losing all my reasons for happiness. But then God brought this verse to me, and it finally hit me, God is supposed to be our one delight. That is where you will find true joy in life. When you truly delight in God, He is always enough. So when your friends fade, your passions fade, and attachments come and go, God is still there. He is holding you and your heart delights in that fact.

I have come to realize that we will never find joy in the creations over the Creator. You see, if we delight in the temporary, our joy will fade away; but if we delight in the eternal, our joy will last forever. Now happiness and joy are not the same. Happiness is usually found when everything is working out to be okay; joy is found in knowing that everything is going to work out and be okay. When we start to think God isn't enough, we proclaim God is nothing; but when we believe that God is enough, our lives scream that God is everything and more. We find the key to happiness in this verse; it is not having the desires of your heart, but delighting in the Lord. I encourage you to find your delight in God, because when you delight in Him, a joy lives within you that cannot be contained.

I find more joy in following what you tell me to do than in chasing after all the wealth of the world. I set my heart on your precepts and pay close attention to all your ways. My delight is found in all your laws, and I won't forget to walk in your words.[dexci]
Psalm 119:14-16

298

"I DO"

> Paige: *I vow to help you love life, to always [hold you] with tenderness and to have the patience that love demands, to speak when words are needed and to share the silence when they are not, to agree to disagree on red velvet cake, and to live within the warmth of your heart and always call it home.*
> Leo: *I vow to fiercely love you in all your forms, now and forever. I promise to never forget that this is a once in a lifetime love. And to always know in the {deepest part} of my soul that no matter what challenges might carry us apart, we will always find our way back to each other.*[dcxcii]

Be still, my beating heart. These words from *The Vow* weren't just ink on napkins, they were promises written on their hearts. Paige completely forgot Leo, and yet Leo was patient with her, kind to her, and never gave up on her. He was true to his word. Then there's us, and we each have a Leo who has already made a powerful vow to us—his name is Jesus. His vows to you have been written in love and kept in kindness, but when it comes to a relationship truly working together, there are also vows in your heart towards Him that, in wisdom, should be guarded and safely kept. The enemy loves to steal what is of value and goodness out of our lives to replace it with doubts and deceit. My questions for you are: 1) What are your vows to Jesus? 2) How do you want to be remembered in your kingdom? *(Your kingdom being those God's placed around you to love.)* The beautiful thing about writing out vows and not always living up to them is that they are covered with grace. It's better to have a vision of goodness to go after than it is keep the commitment door shut and leave goodness outside. Vows take courage to say and bravery to keep—but they live fully in a way that fear of failing will never know. A vow is spoken on the risk of loving wholeheartedly and is caught by grace's empathy for humanity. Here's a truth → God will not fail you. Here's a second truth → He doesn't mind when you fail him. Failure happens in freedom. To love is not to be enough, yet rather in loving, we believe we have more than enough, because the fruit of the Spirit comes in abundance. Therefore, we live generously with doors wide-open, for we are never in lack of His love towards us.

I'm going to leave you with Asa and God's vow to one another in 2 Chronicles 14-15: "Asa did what was good and right in the eyes of the Lord his God → he removed the foreign altars and the high places, smashed the sacred tones and cut down the Asherah poles." And then God vowed to Asa through Azariah: "The Lord is with you when you are with him. If you seek him, he will be found by you, but if you forsake him, he will forsake you. But as for you, be strong and do not give up, for your work will be rewarded."[dcxciii] (emphasis added) The secret behind the kingdom's doors is that *we are not anointed for ourselves but for others*. Because Asa sought after God's heart, people came to his kingdom for they saw the Lord was with him. This is the power of a vow, of saying, "I do." Asa didn't use his influence for others to look at him, but to glorify God. The higher the position you're called to, the greater the risk you have of forsaking your vow. Not because you'll break it, but because with it comes endless possibilities to trust in others over God. But **let your life be one known for your vow kept to Jesus**. Be strong and do not give up for He will reward you, and do not trust in that reward, but keep your heart guarded in the safe place of His presence. He vows to your heart, not to your "calling" or your "dreams." It just so happens that when you go after Him and what's in your heart, somehow they align. But He must always come first. Always remember His vow is said in love and kept in kindness. He said, "I do," even when He knew you'd forget Him. He chose you for a reason, and that choosing was anointed with purpose. As long as you say, "I do," you will find Him all around you, fiercely loving you, in all your forms, now and forever.

299

[EXTRA]ORDINARILY HIS

Ordinary is what I am
Extraordinary is who He is
With Him anything can happen
In Him, my heart is of bliss

I am no greater or less than
There is no erasable line
In the places I fall short
His greatness will abide

For His love rewrote my story,
And filled the spaces in between
What I thought had been forgotten
He showed me He could be

I am who I am Because
He is who He is
So I am no greater or less than
For I am always His

300

IDENTITY VS. SOVEREIGNTY

God says to Moses, "I AM WHO I AM."^{dcxciv}
Exodus 3:14

One of the most commonly asked questions is: "Who am I?" But it goes even further to: "What's my purpose and meaning?" They are simple words but obtain a controlling power with the ability to set you free. The most specific questions tend to have a more simple answer, but the simplest questions have a more complex journey. It's an answer that involves silencing the *"I"* in our life and trusting in His *reign* over our lives. "Who am I" has no specific answer, it is simply a discovery of trust in who God is. It's about having your heart open in silence listening to His heart for you, finding your **"I"**dentity in His Sove**reign**ty. It's about trusting in His sight when you have none. It's about trusting in His word over man's wisdom. Thus "who am I" turns into "Whose I am," from a <u>question</u> wondered in fear to a fearless <u>statement</u> of freedom. It all begins with trusting in who He is to discover Whose we are.

For in Him, we are found.

The impact God has planned for us doesn't occur when we're pursuing impact. It occurs when we're pursuing God.^{dcxcv}
- Phil Vischer

301

STILLFULLY

There is an authority in silence. In the selah of a moment, a pause of a day. Sometimes it speaks louder than words. Silence knows its authority and it doesn't feel the need to shout to prove it. I think of the thirty-three years where Jesus lived in hiddenness, confidently knowing who He was, clearly knowing what He was called to do, yet remaining unseen, unnoticed. Some would call it a setback. Others would see it as a setup. But I believe Jesus was as purposeful with His silence as He was with His voice, so that when He did speak, generations would hear. "Timing is everything" is such a common phrase, but it is also a perfect guide. For we each have our own unique journeys with our own unique voice—and to be still amidst the voices of directions and promises around us may be the most powerful thing of all. To learn to laugh amidst hardship sets the enemy in outrage; to learn to be still amongst the motions sends him fleeing. *Silence has an authority for in its simplicity it sees God.* When our hearts are not distracted but enlightened, nothing can keep you from doing what He's called you to. We put earphones in while walking, music on while reading, and TV shows on while eating, very much avoiding the here. We sit in circles of friends on our phones, listen to sermons while scrolling through Instagram, or take hundreds of pictures, seeing our screens and not the sights, very much missing the now. Then there's stillness, quietness, space, and it's uncomfortable at first, yet with time, we realize it sees us and we see because of it. Psalm 46:10 says: "Be still and know that I am God."[dcxcvi] I've come to this confronting fact that: *being is seeing; without being we are blind.* To be still, you first must be, and that is the thirty-three years Jesus knew. Silence has an authority, and the enemy hates it when we use it.

They say sunflowers always face the sun. This poem by L. Gayle Orf says: "Always remember the sunflower whose face looks like the sun. She drinks his beauty in her face and like him she becomes."[dcxcvii] When you look at the sunflower, it looks still, but is moving. Silence may seem insufficient, but it is powerful. Like a lion doesn't have to roar for others to know it's a lion, you don't have to shout for others to know who you are. Being is all about fixing your eyes on Jesus, drinking in His beauty, and letting His voice be the one you follow. In Exodus 14, the Egyptians are pursuing the Israelites, and they come to a dead end. Chaos and confusion break out, and Moses speaks: "The Lord will fight for you, you need only to be still."[dcxcviii] It goes on to say in verses 19-20, "Then the angel of God, who had been traveling in front of Israel's army, withdrew and went behind them, the pillar of cloud also moved from in front and stood behind them, coming between the armies of Egypt and Israel."[dcxcix] The beauty of being still is there is no reason to be afraid. A literal angel was behind them and the pillar of cloud was separating them from their enemies. And if you haven't figured it out yet, it's the same when we learn to be still and let God be God.

God is wanting to lead you to new places and do greater things before you, but you can only see it by being. Like the sunflower who waits on the Lord every day, move when He moves. The sunflower doesn't stop being a sunflower when its still, neither does it question it. I believe God wants you to know the authority you have in Him that can only be heard in the silence. As He leads you by His voice, He has an angel and a pillar cloud behind you, backing you and fighting for you, that you may be all that you were created to be. When the world tempts you to go where you need not go, or to plug your ears from His voice, or to shout when God says not yet, may you love the here and now. May you know who you are and Whose you are. May you set the enemy fleeing in fear of what you see. May you not run aimlessly but walk *stillfully*. For you will shake the gates of hell when you rise. And when you do speak, you will with the authority of your Father, may you then roar. When you come to a dead end, be still and know He is God. For when the world expects you to speak, it doesn't say much. Yet when they expect you to stay silent, that's when you'll know it's your time to raise your voice for generations to hear.

302

AWAKENED VESSELS

Have you ever had that moment where you're at a cliff, looking down into the great unknown, also known as the ocean, and every fear flashes before your eyes? What if there's a shark? What if you hit a rock? What if it's secretly shallow? There's one specific spot we had in my small country town where you would leap off the edge, have to hurl over a tree, and manage to jump into the one dark circle in the creek, where it was deep enough to survive. In that case, you could've hit the tree or missed the mark and had a hospital run if you were off. Then there's Peter, the disciple, who may not have been on a cliff, but may have well been, when he stepped out of the boat towards Jesus. There were no sharks, and there wasn't a chance of him missing the designated area, but he was walking on raging waters that could've taken him out quite quickly. Yet, this is what I believe walking on the unknown looks like. I'm not sure if Peter jumped from the boat expecting to walk, maybe he was expecting to swim, but he did know he wanted to come closer to Jesus, and Jesus made a way where there wasn't one. I love that in the Passion translation it says: "Peter, suddenly bold, says, 'Master, if it's really you, call me to come to you on the water.'"[dcc] Because this wasn't a coincidental setup, it was a divine encounter. There was a shift in Peter's spirit from fear to boldness, and it wasn't him. Therefore, the words he speaks, probably were uncalled for likewise. After he spoke them he probably thought, "Why did I just say that?" But after Jesus replies, he then acts. He doesn't think, he just jumps, and then somehow, he walks. He's watching Jesus walk on water, and he follows His lead to do the same. 1) When coming face-to-face with the unknown, don't think, just jump. Watch what Jesus does and follow His example. Stand on His word and walk on His word. Don't look down at the fears and doubts raging beneath you. Lock eyes with the truth: "He loves you. He won't let you sink." 2) When walking on miracle's territory, keep your head up. Think His ways, think His power, think God! Don't look back at the boat, don't try to figure out how everything's still not falling apart, just keep running towards Him, keep your faith fixed on the Father. 3) When drawing close to your impossible, stay you. Peter went from fearful to bold. The boldness may have been prompted by the sight of Jesus, but it was always within him. He was bold, but he tried to turn back into who he was the moment he came arms length away from his promise.

When it's tempting to hide in who you were, rise in who you are. "Arise, you sleeper! Rise up from the dead and the Anointed One will shine his light into you!"[dcci] (Ephesians 5: 14) In between the boat and the destination, you discover your worth, you discover your might, and you discover Him in you. Embrace the new skin and believe in its new power. Shed off the old wineskin and leave it off. This is new wine and it's best carried through the new wineskin you've discovered. As Matthew 9:17 says:

And who would pour fresh, new wine into an old wineskin? Eventually the wine will ferment and make the wineskin burst, losing everything—the wine is spilled and the wineskin ruined. Instead, new wine is always poured into a new wineskin so that both are preserved.[dccii]

Stay you—the new you, the unveiled you. Who that is, is powerful, for Christ radiates through awakened vessels. May the lyrics of "New Wine" by Hillsong become your prayer: "Make me a vessel, make me an offering, make me whatever you want me to be. I came here with nothing, but all you have given me, Jesus bring new wine out of me."[dcciii] Stay standing on His Word. Stay awake to His presence and power orchestrating all around you. Stay the unveiled you He's revealed. Be an awakened vessel, anything can happen and it probably will.

303

DESIGNED DIFFERENTLY

Growing up, I had many fictional heroes and Hollywood stars I looked up to. Even though I knew that their lives were just an appearance, I still lived in a fantasy that I could be like them someday. I grew up in comparison, striving to someday be as beautiful as them, or someday be as strong. I wanted to be her height, or have her bright blue eyes—I wanted to be everything I was not. I was so focused on their "reality" that I met the reality around me with unrealistic expectations. Perhaps we all still have a little bit of that in us. We all read these books, see these movies, and hear these stories that sound so inspirational—and yes, they are moving. But when we lose focus of <u>our</u> own stories that is when we run into trouble.

One day, God spoke to my heart, "Instead of wanting to be where they are and who they are, why don't you embrace where I have placed you and who I've made you to be?" You see: our lives are designed with purpose—not mistake. Our hearts are treasure—not a game. Our images are perfect—not flawed. These are the things that we need to hear and learn. That they aren't any better than us, and we aren't any better than them, because we are all designed differently. Job 10:8 reads, "Your hands shaped me and made me. Will you now turn and destroy me?"[dcciv] He knew that God shaped him and made him, but he felt as if God was against him when he began to focus on a story other than his own. That is how we sometimes feel. We wonder, why didn't God make me that way? Why isn't my life like theirs? Why am I here and not there? We start to ask questions of what we don't have and who we are not instead of seeing what we do have and who we are. I have come to the conclusion that *being beautiful is simply being you*. I think we should start to see who we are, and how beautiful that person is. We should love that we are different and not the same, otherwise we would all be ordinary. We should love where we are because, otherwise, we would have missed out on the memories made and lessons learned being somewhere else. We should see the gifts God has already given us and pursue to better them than get rid of them. Instead of striving to be *everything that we are not*, let's become the best version of *everything that we are*.

304

[I]LIMITED

Have you ever heard of a trust fall? Where you turn around, fall backwards, and are hopefully caught? Or how about a trust walk? In which you are blindfolded, follow the sound of your partner's voice, and again, hope you don't fall. Comparing the two, I almost prefer the trust fall, because it's over quickly. A trust walk may have less risk involved, but it's a far longer journey. Your entire sense of direction is gone. You're dependent upon the voice to keep watching out for you, and you never know when you are close to finishing. "Almost there" could be anywhere, yet you just have to keep walking. Faith is so much the same. It involves both risk and trust, ultimately leaving "I" out of the equation.

Before coming to Australia, God whispered, "You must not limit your sight to your dreams. It's a process that requires trust. One that requires extraordinary faith. One that will require blinded obedience. Your will being undone is a catalyst to Mine being done." So it has been. I've discovered setbacks are setups for surprises, and I've learned between the anointing and the appointing will be much room for disappointment. This new extraordinary life begins with the [extra] effort of [less] of you, for there to be more room for the extraordinary God to move. When you are blind, you can't do much, and it seems like you are heading nowhere. Yet even if you are in the middle of the desert feeling as lost as ever, if you have peace, then in all actuality, you are very much *found*. The blindfold removes "I" limited thinking for God to do unlimited wonders. It builds an ark with no rudder, motor, or steering wheel, trusting that what is not spoken does not need to be known. It lives by what is heard and not by what is seen. Those who take risks will find their rewards in Christ. Those who take blindfolds will find their home in Him. Your faith will always see much further than your sight, so in the terms of longevity, take the blindfold.

In the story of Noah, we remember the rainbow more than the dove—but both brought peace. The rainbow was a promise, the dove was hope. In Genesis 8:8 we read that Noah sent out a dove to see if the promised land had surfaced, yet when it returned to him with no sign, he waited again. By verse 11 we read, "When the dove returned to him in the evening, there in its beak was a freshly plucked olive leaf! → Then Noah *knew* that the water had receded from the earth."[dccv] (emphasis added) He waited seven more days, and sent out the dove once more, which he never saw again. Noah's ark may have not had a steering device, but it did have a dove. It was small, but significant, not coincidentally there, but intentionally placed. What could've limited Noah's trust by being built in, created space for God to move with all [I]limited elements out. As Luke 3:22 says: "The Holy Spirit descended on him in bodily form like a dove,"[dccvi] the same Holy Spirit is our guide! Faith is an adventurous journey that is best lived by no motor, no wheel, and no sight, but solely peace.

When God sends a rainbow, wait for the land. Live by what you hear and not by what you see. Don't limit your dreams to your [I]'s or eyes, but take the blindfold and follow His voice. You are right where you belong, and He is doing what you cannot. Your will being undone is a catalyst to His being done—and it will be a grand adventure of surprises. The more for you ahead is found with more of you left behind. For then you will *know* His peace like a dove, embarking on the most God-orchestrated paths toward the most unforgettable stories filled with such promise, favor, and glory to tell for generations to come!

305

ADVENTURING UNDERSTANDING

My favorite quote from the movie *Up* is, "Adventure is out there!"[dccvii] There's just so much to learn, see, and discover! But we have a tendency to get comfortable where we are rather than being awake to where God is leading us. In Proverbs 4:7 it says, "Wisdom is supreme; therefore get wisdom, though it cost all you have, get understanding."[dccviii] I think a great deal of understanding comes with adventuring, because every adventure holds a lesson to be learned. But I think we get so caught up in asking the small detailed questions that we overlook the simple answers that are right in front of us. There was a period in my life when I couldn't hear God as loudly as I wanted. I had so many questions, and I felt like I wasn't getting any answers. But one day I heard Him say so softly, "Walk straight." We read in Proverbs 4:11, "I guide you in the way of wisdom and lead you along straight paths."[dccix] And we start to see that sometimes the answer is simply to walk straight and allow Him to guide you. It's not that He is ignoring you; it's just that He knows you'll find the answer right in front of you if you'd just walk a little bit further.

Understanding comes with adventuring—but we tend to overlook the small promptings in our hearts with no second glance when that should be the direction of our focus. Adventure is found in the small whispers of our hearts that we push off as a thought; adventure is found in the unknown of the open doors, or even the closed. Adventure is found in the opportunities that are placed at our feet. And the greatest adventures are the ones that come unexpectedly. They are the moments that usually change our lives. It's in seeking understanding that we adventure down a road to discover things we would have never dreamed of, and they tend to be the lessons we never forget. Many times, we are the ones who seek adventure, but then there are those rare times when adventure seeks us, and we would be a fool not to follow it. God is always trying to show us new things, we just have to have the faith to keep learning, seeing, and discovering, because adventure is out there, and understanding awaits!

> *Our greatest mistakes, if we look at them and digest them, and interact with them, and learn from them... they can be the greatest moments of our lives.*[dccx]
> - Dan Pearce

306

CHILD OF GOD

In the book of Zechariah, we see the Lord's desire for His chosen all over it. He's speaking in every way possible trying to grab their attention. He sends visions, prophetic words, and even promises. But when you feel lost around you, it's easy to forget that which is within you. Have you ever heard, "God wants to reveal His will to you more than you want Him to?" This book screams this truth from the rooftops. Because here is the thing, Jerusalem has lost her way, and God isn't just going to let her go. The people of Judah were faced with a ruined temple and city, and in their eyes, all hope was lost. Yet, the real devastation wasn't in the ruins around them, but the ruins within them. Somewhere in the midst of losing their city, they also lost their identity as the people of God. They were searching for a way to rebuild a home in their hearts that only God could restore to them. In Zechariah 2, we read, "Then I looked up—and there before me was a man with a measuring line in his hand! I asked, 'Where are you going?' He answered me, 'To measure Jerusalem, to find out how wide and how long it is.' Then the angel who was speaking left, and another angel came to meet him and said to him: 'Run, tell that you man, 'Jerusalem will be a city *without* walls because of the *great* number of men and livestock in it. And I myself will be a wall of **fire** around it,' declares the Lord,' and I will be its glory within.'"[dccxi] (emphasis added) He sends out an invitation with a stamp of honor saying, "Come, O Zion! ... For this is what the Lord Almighty says: 'After he has honored me and has sent me against the nations that have plundered you—for whoever touched you touches the apple of his eye—I will surely raise my hand against them…'"[dccxii]

We see a King rise from His throne in a holy anger against the enemies who have attacked, demolished, and destroyed a people so dear to His heart. All along, He was there waiting for them to cry out to Him, but they depended on their ability over their identity, and never called. So He speaks up, and He stands up and says, "I myself will be a WALL of fire around her." Instead of Jerusalem needing to build a wall of protection to begin rebuilding, God promises His protection so He can start restoring their identities as His. The only thing they have to do is trust Him. *It's risky trusting the Lord in the world's eyes; it doesn't measure up. But the measureless happens when we let down our walls.* As Isaiah 30:18 says: "Yet the Lord longs to be gracious to you; he rises to show you compassion. For the Lord is a God of justice. Blessed are all who wait for him!"[dccxiii] There is no doubt in my mind that God is speaking the same to us today. It's easy to find comfort in the digits of our jobs, the luxury of our homes, the words of our people. But when you're a child of God, it's not the embrace of comfort you need, but the whisper of promise from your Comforter's lips, and He *longs* to be gracious to you.

There was a time in my life when God started to open up doors beyond measure for me, and I had an ability-crisis which really was an identity-crisis. I replied to God's invitation, "I can't," and you know what He replied to me? "You are." I realized that day, *what you're able to do is not defined by your ability, but by your identity.* Jerusalem couldn't rebuild their home on their own, and I couldn't build what was placed in my hands. But what we have in common is that we are children of God. Marianne Williamson says, "Our deepest fear is not that we are inadequate. Our deepest fear is that we are powerful beyond measure."[dccxiv] I don't know what ruins the enemy has created in your heart where there was once beauty, but God longs to restore you. He is a *wall of fire* around you with His glory dwelling within your heart ready to be released, ready for you to let your walls down. You have nothing to fear. He knows the depths of His child's heart and the heights of His chosen's belonging. If you truly believe, your wildest of dreams will come true. Declare what God has spoken is yours and go after it for you are a child of God. Although you may be the bullseye of the enemy's eye, you are the apple of God's eye, so nothing will ever be too great before you. When you say, "I can't" remember He says, "You are." And that truth is measureless in beauty.

307

THE GREATEST CALLING

You are called to be a child of God, and that is the greatest position of all.

I believe this is the statement that will rock any person's world. In a world that holds position so highly, we tend to strive to make our image known. Let's be honest, most of us would rather receive credit for something we didn't do, than to not receive credit for something we did do. And that is hardest part of us to lay down because we strive to be known! But Matthew 23:12 puts it this way, "For those who exalt themselves will be humbled, and those who humble themselves will be exalted."[dccxv] It's not about how high of a status we can obtain, it's about doing our best for His glory instead of ours. We grow up with these crazy dreams that usually exalt our image, and then one day realize it's all about His. Then in search for our oncein-a-lifetime calling, we overlook the very person we are called to be. And that brought me to this humbling statement that I have learned to love, **"Who I am in Christ is greater than anyone I could ever be alone."** Without a doubt, I know from the bottom of my heart that if I was able to get to the highest position with my ability, it still would be nothing compared to the potential I'd have yet to obtain within God's abilities. I have come to this realization that your true calling is never seen, but is always sought. Your calling isn't a position, but a disposition before God. Your calling isn't a title, and it can't be named, but it's found in *the name* of "Jesus Christ." When you are on your face before God, you are fulfilling your calling. When you are studying the Word of God, you are fulfilling your calling. You see, it's not about what you do, but who you are, and that is found in seeking who He is. I am called to be a child of God, and so are you! So we can live our lives knowing that we each are set apart for a purpose, and it's all for His glory, always for His glory.

308

IN THE MIDST

> *If a kingdom is divided against itself, that kingdom cannot stand"*[dccxvi]
> Mark 3:24

Where there is division, there is no unity. But where there is unity, God's blessing is in the midst. There is nothing Satan wants greater than to see the church destroy itself, not even by its enemies, but by the division within its own walls. If the church is the bride of Christ, and we are the church, then we must learn to love and protect His bride. The church is perfectly chosen, yet imperfectly flawed. Look at your own life and you will see where grace was given and freely received. Look at the church and it should be demonstrated the same. The sooner we realize how to honor, protect, and cherish the bride, the sooner we will see breakthrough revealed in unity's midst. Division starts in the heart before the kingdom falls. The truth is the war around you cannot touch you; it is the war you allow to be created within you that embraces defeat. When we look at God's people standing up for what is right, we see Him standing in their midst. When Shadrach, Meshach, and Abednego walked through the furnace, they were not burned. There was a fire around them that they didn't allow within them. When Peter took a step of faith onto the waters, he didn't drown. Though there were

frightening waves around him, he didn't let the waves of fear hold him back. When Daniel was thrown into a den of lions, they didn't seize him, and neither did his doubts. God was with them all because they kept their eyes fixed on Him through the battle. In the division of their faith and their realities, He was in the middle creating a unity of blessing in their midst.

So what creates the war? It can be trying to grasp something we aren't meant to understand or chasing a promise before its due time. Division creates space between *what is* and *what could be*, what is *wanted* versus what is *needed*, or really, between two different views. The enemy wouldn't love anything more than to see a divided heart defeat itself while he sits back and watches. As long as we keep going back and forth between the two, we wear ourselves thin. Yet, if we FIX our eyes on Jesus, we will be able to see He is in the middle of the two where unity is present. If we can pull the two flames *together,* imagine the light that would **shine**. In drawing closer to Jesus, things in our hearts will start to die naturally, but it's okay. There is a sweet freedom found in the unity of surrender, where death is not the poison but a sweet oil. If we can lay ourselves behind and bring Jesus to the forefront of our hearts, we can declare a war of love against the enemy within the unity of His church, as one and as the body. That's where unity thrives and blessing is demanded. It's not so much of standing against what is flawed in the church; it's standing for His Word and standing for His bride. For united we stand, divided we fall.

309

FIXATED

To have one's full attention is to have one's full heart. Thus, the enemy wants you to remain fixated on you—the good you, the bad you, the flawless you, the imperfect you—whatever you it takes to keep you distracted from *Him*—Jesus. To be fixated on Christ is to be fixated on good, to see His goodness all around you, to open your heart again to the One who is known as good Himself. In the midst, we love ourselves— with every bit of the good, the bad, the flawless, and the imperfect "us," because we find Christ, or simply *remember* Him again. The plot twist is that we then find ourselves by becoming who we were originally created to be—His. We don't fix ourselves for Him, we fix our gaze on Him, and thus become ourselves with Him, which the enemy secretly knows and keeps quiet. To remain fixed on the One who is fixed on you is to die to one's self naturally. His love drives out all fear; it drives out every darkness; it drives out each selfish ambition—to where all that is left is just Jesus and just you—fixated on each other—in a divine romance, a transformation of two becoming One—and it is *good*.

> *How blessed is God! And what a blessing he is! He's the Father of our Master, Jesus Christ, and takes us to the high places of blessing in him. Long before he laid down earth's foundations, he had us in mind, had settled on us as* **the focus of his love**, *to be made whole and holy by his love. Long, long ago he decided to adopt us into his family through Jesus Christ. (What pleasure he took in planning this!) He wanted us to enter into the celebration of his lavish gift-giving by the hand of his beloved Son.*
> (Ephesians 1:3-6, MSG)

310

LEGACY

Did you know your life is a legacy in the making? That amongst the ordinary acts and monotonous activities, a legacy is being left behind. When I think of people who were intentional with their legacy, I think of David who left provision for his son Solomon to build upon. Solomon then created a great temple for the Lord and reigned in wisdom. Eventually, king Asa did what was "good and right in the eyes of the Lord" and removed the foreign altars. Following his reign came Jehoshaphat, and "the Lord was with Jehoshaphat" for "he walked in the ways his father had followed."[dccxvii] I could go on, but I believe this verse summarizes the line of David, "For the eyes of the Lord range throughout the earth to strengthen those who hearts are fully committed to him."[dccxviii] (2 Chronicles 16:9) I do not believe a legacy is limited to just who you are but is measureless in what you leave behind for others to build upon. David's family line wasn't perfect, neither was he. But he was known for his heart after God's, and a legacy later, Jehoshaphat is following in his footsteps. One's legacy can truly only be created by trusting God to build it beyond oneself. In 1 Chronicles 17:10-12, God makes a promise to David, "I declare to you that the Lord will <u>build</u> a house for you: when your days are over and you go to be with your fathers, I will raise up your offspring to succeed you, one of your own sons, and I will establish his kingdom. He is the one who will build a house for me, and [I will establish his throne forever.]"[dccxix] (emphasis added) The greater David trusted, the greater he was strengthened, and the greater his confidence in God deepened. But there is risk involved with trusting God. It's not easy and it requires an eternal perspective throughout the journey, but it does build, and it does last beyond one's years.

One example is when Jehoshaphat faces war against the Moabites, Ammonites, *and* Meunites. Instead of turning to his limits, he turns to God proclaiming: "O Lord, God of our fathers, are you not the God who is in heaven? You rule over *all* the kingdoms of the nations. **Power** and **might** are in your hand, and

@bulgerjoseph

no one can withstand you... we do not know what to do, but our eyes are upon you."[dccxx] (2 Chronicles 20:5,12,15; emphasis added) God responds: → "Do not be afraid or discouraged because of this vast army. For the battle is not yours, but God's." Sometimes we fear the battle because we can't prepare for it. Sometimes we fear our own legacy for the same reason. But when it comes to the war the enemy is declaring against your legacy, learn to proclaim, "We do not know what to do but our eyes are upon you." The Lord did give victory to Jehoshaphat, but only after he took the risk of standing on God's word. Then "the kingdom of Jehoshaphat was at peace, for his God had given him *rest* on every side." (vv.30) <u>Beyond the risk there is rest in the aftermath.</u> My question to you is: "What legacy are you carving out for others to follow?" *For legacy does not happen in isolation.* When years have passed and people don't know your face, what will be left for them to build upon? What are you trusting God with that isn't for the here and now? Your ability to build a legacy is directly related to your ability to <u>trust God,</u> Whose loving eyes have *eternity* stamped upon them.

311

SEEK GOD

There are times in life when we will be resting in silence. Though they are some of the greatest times to grow, they can be some of the hardest seasons to stay in. Why? Because we are human, and our hearts desire assurance. However, we tend to pray and seek God about the questions we have, overlooking the fact that we're seeking our own desires instead of His. When you seek an answer, you seek your heart's desire; when you seek God, you seek His heart's desire. Jeremiah 29:13 says, "You will seek me and find me when you seek me with all your heart."[dccxxi] When you seek the answer, you become impatient. But when you seek God, His peace leads you in patience and assurance that He has everything in His hands. Thus, seek God and not the answer, and you will find Him, where all else and anything else does not matter besides Him. Right there, He will be ardently waiting for you.

312

INTO THE SEA

When you think about the story of Jonah, what comes to your mind first? A big fish? Or a big calling? We often know Jonah for his detour through the sea, but overlook the detour of his heart. What was going on in that heart of his that made him run from what God had called him to do? I mean, if we were in his shoes, we would jump at the command without hesitation right? Maybe, just maybe, it's not that simple. Maybe Jonah had a plan of the calling he wanted to live out and this wasn't according to his plan. And when God spoke this word, it created more of a war within Jonah than a calm. Maybe it went against all that Jonah had pictured for his life. "God I know you've called me to preach, but not… there." We can't be so quick to remember Jonah for his detoured calling rather than the vulnerability within his raging heart. I mean… God did call Jonah, and He doesn't just send anybody. Have you ever wondered why that was? Why did God send Jonah if He knew Jonah was going to run? If anything, it shows God had a specific call on Jonah's life that only Jonah specifically could do for it to come to pass. It just wasn't according to his specific plan. He ran,

@ kathleenmadethis

only in the wrong direction. He ran his direction, and so God began to direct the waves and winds to send a direct message to Jonah—a message we can all take heed to today: "Many are the plans in a person's heart, but it is the Lord's purpose that prevails."[dccxxii] (Proverbs 19:21) As the storm grew wilder around the boat, the war within Jonah calmed as he came to this point of surrender. With his words, he proclaimed as much as he spoke "Pick me up and throw me into the sea."[dccxxiii] (Jonah 1:12) I don't believe they were just words from his lips for the men to contemplate, but words from his heart for the Lord to hear. It was in a way saying, "God, have your way, let Your will be done." I think every one of us will come to a place someday where we are faced with His promise and purpose for our lives, and it may not look *exactly* like we thought it would. Instead of being an exciting whisper, it's a questioned statement. Instead of voyaging straight towards His sovereign Word, we sail sideways into self-created storms. But I'm glad God doesn't let us sail away to less than His best. If the waves are high around you, I think it'd be a good time to start praying these powerful words: "Pick me up and throw me into the sea. When I start to pursue my own plans, when I start to exalt my own dreams, when I start to chase my own desires, pick me up and throw me into the sea. Lord, I surrender. Let Your will be done." The war only comes because a purpose is declared that only you specifically have been gifted, chosen, and set apart for. So take heart. The waves around you aren't intended to sink you, they're intended to speak to you. At the most beautiful moment of surrender is when God will meet you right where you're at. He provided a fish for Jonah. I wonder what extraordinary miracle He will meet you with? I know the odds seem impossible for God to keep His Word, but just be brave and proclaim, "Pick me up and throw me into the sea," and He'll meet you, unquestionably, every single time.

313

IGNITE

We need to stop desiring for dreams to come to life *more than* we need to come alive. We need to stop desiring feelings *more than* the need for us to touch the lives others. We need to stop desiring to stay safe *more than* we need to move. We don't just need to stop; we also need to go. Let our lives be more than a confession. Let our lives be a declaration of faith. All for Jesus is what we say, but it's also how we should live. There is power in purpose **if** it is acted upon. Passion ignites a spark, determination starts a fire, faith will give height to your flames, and love will bring an unfathomable brightness to your light. All for Jesus!

> *Then Jesus came close to them and said, "All the authority of the universe has been given to me. Now go in my authority and make disciples of all nations, baptizing them in the name of the Father, the Son, and the Holy Spirit. And teach them to faithfully follow all that I have commanded you. And never forget that I am with you every day, even to the completion of this age."*[dccxxiv]
> Matthew 28:18-20

314

JUST WAIT

"Mom! I really want this bicycle!"
"Just wait, honey!"
"But, I want it now!"
"Maybe another time."
"Ugh, Mom! This is so unfair!"
Twenty minutes later, they pull into the driveway as, lo' and behold, a brand new bicycle is in the driveway waiting with a big red bow.
Just wait.

Have any of you ever had these moments? Where you want something incredibly bad, and then you hear this still soft voice telling you, "Just wait." Through the years, patience has been a strength of mine... until it came to waiting for something I wanted in that moment. Many of us see waiting as a bad thing, when really, I haven't ever seen a "con" to waiting. But there is a difference between procrastinating and waiting.

Procrastination is pushing something off until the last minute; waiting is trusting in God's timing. Psalm 27:14 reads, "Wait for the Lord; be strong and take heart and wait for the Lord."[dcxxv] I want us to see that there is a double emphasis in this verse to wait for the Lord, and in between the waiting, we are to be strong and take heart. First off, I think waiting is one of the greatest expressions of trusting. Second, we see that we don't only have a call to be strong and take heart, but we also have a call to be patient. Third, the longer we wait for something, the more we will cherish its value. It is easy for us to lose heart when God calls us to trust in Him, because we sometimes don't see what is happening on the surface. But our trust shouldn't be based on what we see, but should be confident in what He knows.

To put our waiting into an analogy, I want you to think of it as a tree. It starts with the moment our hearts decide we want something of value, which can be a relationship, a job, or an answer, and that is the seed that is planted in the ground. We tend to want the seed to grow quickly into this glorious tree, strong and beautiful, but it doesn't work that way. Even the magic beans of "Jack the Giant Slayer" took time to grow into a tree with deep roots. The roots are the most crucial part of our waiting; it's where we place the seed in God's hand and see if "the want" will grow into something beautiful or will never break through the surface. It's a way of trusting God because we know that He knows us better than we know ourselves. It is in this time that we usually grow anxious, but God lets our roots grow deep. However, it is below the surface, and so we can't usually see what He is doing. It's not until the tree starts to grow that our hearts finally feel peace from the long moments of waiting. *But our greatest moments of trust aren't found when the tree grows, but when the roots grow.* Psalm 37:7 says, "Be still before the Lord and wait patiently for Him."[dcxxvi] Psalm 62:5 goes on to say, "Let all that I am wait quietly before God, for my hope is in him."[dccxxvii] In other words: being still is knowing what you want, but trusting God with what He knows. The word "wait" usually is seen as a delay, but the phrase, "just wait," is a way of saying, "I have something greater for you, if you'd just trust me." It's not working against our good, but for our good. As Andy Warhol says, "The idea of waiting for something makes it more exciting."[dccxxviii] That is exactly the attitude we should have! That waiting isn't a burden, it's a blessing. It's not terrible, it's exciting! So, "just wait," be strong and take heart, and see what God has in store for you!

315

WITH HONOR AND BEAUTY

"Sometimes the questions are complicated and the answers are simple,"[dccxxix] said the wise Dr. Seuss. Quite often, they are so simple that the heart can't wrap itself around what the mind is saying. It's like the phrase, "Let go and let God." It's always easier said than done. How do we convince the heart of doing the same? How do we hold our honor and beauty in light of this nugget of wisdom? Well, first, it starts with realizing who you are to God, and who He is to you. Who you are to God is immeasurably valued, unquestionably loved, and inexpressibly beautiful. Here's how I see it: before God, you have two different parts of your heart that are stunning: your honor and your beauty. Our honor is part of our self-worth; it roots in what we believe we deserve. Our beauty is deeply grown from the inside-out. It is what we often put more emphasis on—making sure everything looks adjusted and put together. Our honor is more of a placement before God with what is to come; our beauty is more of a reflection of our love for God through passions He's placed within us. But instead of trusting God with either of these, we tend to take matters into our own hands. This is where we dive into—let go and let God.

Proverbs 3:5-6 says: "Trust God from the bottom of your heart; don't try to figure out everything on your own. Listen for God's voice in everything you do, everywhere you go; he's the one who will keep you on track."[dccxxx] Trusting God with our honor is taking our ideas of a perfect life, and holding them loosely. Letting them not be a plan but a dream so that He can show us what is BEST for us. A plan can so easily limit God. A dream allows us to not have everything figured out. Then there's trusting God with our beauty. We all have an immeasurable value. But when we source our value from an outside perspective, we limit the worth God created us to share from the inside out. Who you are to God is literally who you *are*! Song of Songs 4:7 says, "There is no flaw in you."[dccxxxi] "But humans are imperfect, Kaytee!" Yes, I know. *But our worth isn't found in our mistakes just as much as it isn't found in our successes.* Jesus said, "I am the way, the truth, and the life."[dccxxxii] (John 14:6) That coming to *Him* reminds us of who we are and what we were made for. So what in the world am I trying to say? Well, I am trying to say that you won't ever feel enough apart from the knowledge of knowing who you are in Christ.

Your beauty and honor are the most beautiful parts of your heart. But when you try to keep one from God or the other, you hold yourself back from feeling the *true* freedom in Christ. Letting go means trusting that there is nobody like you, and that rarity was purposely intended to be shared with the world. That yes, you can dream and make plans, but to try to run your own life instead of running to God with every inspiration, aspiration, and motivation is a dangerous thing. But placing them both before the Lord… Wow! What wonders He could do in and through your heart. As He speaks to all of us, "Don't make a path or cut off a path, let the path unwind before you." Letting go is a way of being; it isn't forced. As the Beetles song goes, "Let it be." By trusting Him with the greatest desires of your life, He works even in the smallest details of your heart. So *trust Him*. Know that with every waking moment, the *best* is yet to come through Him. Believe this. Repeat it. Meditate on it. Pursue this thought until your heart reflects this truth onto knowing the value of this for every person you run into. Strangers will become foreign and sons and daughters will be seen with this knowledge. Frustration comes when you try to figure out everything on your own, when you try to take matters into your own hands. You can't. We all can't. His thoughts are higher than your thoughts and His plans higher than your own, says Isaiah 55. But when you realize letting go is for His best, it makes trusting Him so much easier. Honor Him with your heart by placing your beauty before Him, and guard your thoughts from settling for anything less. The answers truly are simple. We only need to believe in the depth of His wild love for us.

316

PERSPECTIVE

You can see waves of fear
Or oceans of mystery.
You can see mountains of disbelief
Or kingdoms of truth.
You can see fields of fury
Or plains of passionate fire.
You can see pieces of brokenness
Or shapes of beauty.
One person sees a glass half-empty
Another sees it half-full.
One person sees endless closed doors
Another sees countless open.
One person sees a burden
Another sees a blessing.
One person sees coincidence
Another sees a miracle.
Every day is not a focus of what you see,
But a view of how you see it.
For everything comes down to your perspective,
And your perspective comes down to your Everything.

"For though I fall, I will rise again. Though I sit in darkness, the LORD will be my light."[dccxxxiii]
Micah 7:8

317

THE DECEPTION OF GLAMOUR

> *In the land of Uz there lived a man whose name was Job. This man was blameless and upright; he feared God and shunned evil. He had seven sons and three daughters, and he owned seven thousand sheep, three thousand camels, five hundred yoke of oxen and five hundred donkeys, and had a large number of servants. He was the greatest man among all the people of the East.*[dcxxxiv]
> Job 1:1-3

Many people remember Job, not by how highly favored he was by the Lord, but by the testing he faces in the 40 chapters of his story. Satan, all high and mighty, comes to God, proud of all the wreckage he has caused: "The Lord said to Satan, 'Where have you come from?' Satan answered the Lord, 'From roaming throughout the earth, going back and forth on it.' Then the Lord said to Satan, 'Have you considered my servant Job? There is *no one* on earth like him; he is blameless and upright, a man who fears God and shuns evil.'"[dcxxxv] (emphasis added) As we read on, we see Satan fully believes that if God takes everything away from Job, he will turn away from God. God replies, "Very well, then, everything he has is in your power, but on the man himself, do not lay one finger." (vs 12) Yet Satan comes around again, failing in his first attempt against Job's integrity, still believing if Job had not been well physically, then he would turn away, and the Lord says, "Very well, then, he is in your hands, but you must spare his life." (2:6) And yet Job remains loyal to God as he speaks, "Shall we accept good from God, and not trouble?" (vs 10) In the following chapters we see his closest friends question him and mock God, creating a dangerous weapon against Job— doubt.

As Job's life continually worsens, and he tries to hold onto the God who had been so good and faithful to him, doubt enters in and starts to make him question if that was by coincidence. Doubt creeps into your dreaming and shuts it down with fear. Doubt slides into your hopes and steals them from believing for greater things ahead. It knocks on your door and wants to have a one-on-one conversation so faith can leave and be locked out for longer than expected. [Doubt is distracting and doubt is dangerous because it alters the truth of God.] Its greatest attempt is to trick you to believe one of the greatest lies—He doesn't love you. If you feel your heart has become hardened or you're missing out on the fullness of life, then dear friend, I'm here to warn you that you've already let doubt in, and he has been robbing you of your integrity, loyalty, and beliefs, diminishing the knowledge of God's love for you. I not only believe, but also know, that God has a plan for you that has been dear to your heart for years. One that sounds too good to be true but is destined to be yours. And there was a time in your life where you once believed in it and were going for it— full of hope, integrity, and belief. But like the arrogant thief the enemy is, he decided, "Enter your name wouldn't keep pursuing God if they had this taken away, if they had such and such happen to them, if so and so attacked them physically. They'd quit." Maybe you were about to, or maybe you already did. So let me tell you some truths. 1) Sometimes, the enemy might come knocking at your door because God was up in heaven bragging, "Have you seen my servant, *your name*? There is no one on earth like them. (He/she) is blameless and upright. A person who fears God and shuns evil." God is so proud of you and your devotion to Him. It doesn't go unseen by Him, and that's why the enemy wants you to believe you are invisible. He wants to plant that doubt in your heart so you think God's prior provision was only a coincidence. If you only knew how much God believes in you. He is still speaking over you, "Have you seen my servant, my son, my daughter?" 2) God only allows trouble to come because he has a plan in mind to turnaround the enemy's scheme into something **greater.** The enemy came knocking at your door believing he was going to win when God already had victory in mind. By Job 42 we read, "The Lord restored his fortunes and gave him twice as much as he had before... the Lord blessed the latter part of Job's life more than the former part."dccxxxvi You see, the enemy's pride believed he could knock you down, when God's belief in you knew you could not be shaken, and He couldn't be more proud. In other words, while the enemy had great pride against you, the Lord had a greater pride in you.

It reminds me a lot of the book I'm reading called: *Cinder*. Within the story is this race called the Lunars.dccxxxvii They are a people from the moon that are able to "glamour" their beauty in a way that makes other people see what they want them to see and feel what they want them to feel. They can make a person fall in love with them and see them as flawless, even if it's what they aren't, or make someone afraid of them, even if they weren't before. It's funny how much the story parallels to how the enemy is like a Lunar to us. He makes himself seem so much bigger than he is, when indeed he is so small. He tries to project beauty in other people's lives as perfection to where we feel so small and insufficient ourselves. But the silly thing about Lunars is that they don't like mirrors because they can't "glamour" or fool them; the mirrors always reflect who they truly are. How much more is the Word of God a mirror in our lives! It not only reminds us of how God sees us, but it also sees through the enemy's schemes and sees him for what he truly is—a deceptive and lying creature. The mirror is the greatest weapon against his schemes because it will always reflect the truth. The more we dig into the Word of God, the more we surround ourselves with godly influences, and the more we remind ourselves of His whispers over us, the stronger we become in fighting back against the enemies lies and moving forward into God's promises before us. I have heard time after time where people feel like God is speaking to them that they're called to something so much greater, but because they feel so ordinary, they don't feel like they'll go anywhere. Then child, get in the Word and fight back! Stop letting the enemy rob your house of joy, hope, and passion! Don't let him glamour you anymore! As my teacher said, "When the enemy creates doubts, God whispers."

God isn't silent right now. Seek and you will find! Listen to Him—He doesn't make false promises. Stop fearing that He is going to sell you short. He won't let you settle for any less than His best. As Job says, "I know that you can do all things; no purpose of yours can be thwarted. You asked, 'Who is this that obscures my plans without knowledge?' Surely I spoke of things I do not understand, things too wonderful for me to know." (42:2) Doubt is but a glamour the enemy will use to belittle who you are and ultimately what He has before you. But get this! God wasn't bragging to Satan on your purpose. He was bragging to him about *your heart*. Know that God wants to pursue your heart before you pursue your purpose. Yes, He created you with a purpose. But your heart is ultimately the greatest prize God is after and the greatest treasure the enemy wants to steal—but that's the ONE thing God told the enemy he couldn't have, "but you must spare his life." The enemy tried to glamour Job's integrity away, but the Lord knew Job's heart that had His Word hidden in it. Likewise, God is pursuing you because He cares about your heart more than anything in the world. {Your purpose will unfold naturally as He pursues you personally.} I tell you this so that you may know God is whispering more to your heart than to your purpose. His whispers will forever remain hidden in your heart, which is the one place the enemy can't penetrate. As long as you love Him fully, you can't fail Him. It's when we pursue His promise before His presence that we feel like we are failing. Yet if we learn to pursue His presence, we'll see His presence is pursuing us. Never let the enemy deceive you of any less, like Job, you will die "old... and **full** of years." (vs 17)

318

DON'T LET GO

Instead of giving up, we should get up. George A. Custer says, "It's not how many times you get knocked down that count, it's how many times you get back up."[dccxxxviii] I think it is in the wildest storms that we forget our wildest dreams; and it's when we discover our greatest loves that we discover our greatest fears. Why? Because when we finally find a love that is so great, we are either afraid of failing in trying to chase after it or are afraid of falling in trying to reach it. Even more so, in the beginning steps of our journey, our faith can be strong, but it's when we reach that mountain in the middle that we have two decisions to face: go up or around. The way around builds no strength but it is easier; the way up is challenging, but worth it. Both hold the opportunity of victory, but one holds more worth than the other.

Before I went rock climbing for my first time, my friend asked the trainer, "Do you have any advice for her in a few words to start climbing." And his words impacted my heart, "Don't let go." In that moment, a thousands thing run through your mind: *But I am not as good as you; I will fall; I'm not strong enough,* and the list goes on. But even when you are hanging on by a thread—don't let go. Sometimes, we need to change our perspective to take the risk of holding on for longer rather than to let go for the inevitable. Yes, you will fall many times, but failure isn't when you fall, but when you don't get up. In hard times, Paul reminds us of this, "Not only that, but we rejoice in our sufferings, knowing that suffering produces endurance, and endurance produces character, and character produces hope…"[dccxxxix] (Romans 5:3-4) I think we tend to want to rest in a gravityless world in the now, instead of facing character building circumstances for the later. The thing is, if we had no gravity, we would never grow stronger; and thus, when we finally walked into gravity's field, we would crumble because we never grew in strength. In other words, the easy way now isn't always the easy way out. When you're building muscle, it rips to then grow back stronger. Or if you break a bone, it will heal double as strong and most likely never be able to break again. It's in our falling that we break, our failures that we rip, but in our perseverance that we rise to victory. Ecclesiastes 9:11 puts it this way, "I have seen something else under the sun: The race is not to the swift or the battle to the strong, nor does food come to the wise or wealth to the brilliant or favor to the learned; but time and chance happen to them all."[dccxl] When time and chance come around, don't let go, and don't be afraid. You don't have to be enough, and you don't have to be the greatest, you just have to be courageous. For you are either a step closer to being made stronger or a step closer to victory, and both are well worth the risk.

319

ENOUGH

What is "enough"? Is it a measurement, a quantity, a quality; a goal, a dream, a finish; a want, a hope, a love? Is it found in what can be obtained or can it be held within our very own hands? Can it be seen or even sought? Or, is "enough" simply not enough since it is the constant drive a person has in life, throughout a lifetime? And has enough ever been found, has it ever been reached? Because enough to a rich man may be different from enough to a poor man. Enough to someone who is full may be different from enough to someone who is hungry. Enough for an adult may be different from enough to a child. Enough may be different for someone who has everything—compared to one who has nothing at all. And it has brought me to this thought, *"Is enough ever really enough at all?"* I love the scripture of 2 Samuel 12:8 where the Lord speaks to David, "And if all this had been too little, I would have given you <u>even</u> more."[dccxli] (emphasis added) I used to read this and wonder why David didn't just *ask* God for what he wanted instead of *going* after what he desired without God's hand in it. But that was from the perspective of a rich man, one who was full. But when I looked through the other's eyes, I realized David already had enough. He just saw the one thing he didn't have compared to **all** of the uncountable blessings he already possessed. He had a kingdom under his feet, victories in his hand, and favor all around him, but David lost sight of what "enough" truly was. Enough cannot be measured; enough cannot be reached, and enough has no end—because only God is enough and He is limitless, with no boundaries, Who is constantly more. To one, enough may be an image at the end of a journey. But I have realized enough is at the feet of Jesus—laying everything down and yet having everything in the same moment. Enough has always been right in front of us. It's not at the end of life; it's the beginning of life every day with Him.

320

ALWAYS AND FOREVER

My love,

I have loved you at your worst, and I have loved you at your best. I have loved you in the valleys, and I have loved you in the mountains. I have loved you from before the beginning and will love you beyond the end. My love has no limits; it has no boundaries. My love is infinite; it is beyond what you could ever imagine. My love for you is extraordinary; it cannot be explained. My love is yours, always and forever. I am yours, forever and always. Always remember this, and you will never forget my forever love for you.

Jesus

"The steadfast love of the Lord never ceases; his mercies never come to an end; they are new every morning; great is your faithfulness."[dccxlii]
Lamentations 3:22-23

321

REMEMBER THE SPARROWS

The thought makes my heart leap when I ponder how the Creator of everything beautiful sees us—and cares. Not just a little either. It's so deep and vast and beyond the limits of our imagination. But I've come to know, not everyone knows God like this. They see their lives more as a dystopian novel rather than a fairytale. But I can't help but feel that most of us have had it all wrong. Take a good relationship between a child and a father. The child runs up all gladly to his rich and loving Father screaming, "Dad! Can I have money to get an ice cream from the ice cream truck?" The dad pulls out his wallet and hands his son a $5 bill, the very key to treasure in the child's eyes. Now if the kid asks, "Can I please have two ice cream cones? Pleeeassee!" I'm sure the dad's heart would want to give his son what he asks, but instead replies, "One is enough, son," knowing one is all he'd need, while two would leave him sick. We have experienced both moments with God throughout the years, ones where he does what we request, and others where he will act in love to protect us rather than please us. This is where most decide, "My life is a dystopian novel. Something always happens." Although it is true that life happens, life happens in fairytales too. The difference is we experience the struggle instead of just flipping over its story. If there ever was a fairytale without a struggle, let me know. Here's the reality you're placing your perspective in → in a dystopian novel, you feel doomed; in a fairytale, you have hope for a greater story to form from your struggle into a happy ending. The question is which will you choose to believe? You have a Father who has the capability to make <u>all</u> your dreams come true. Maybe you're in debt and don't know how to get out of it. Maybe you are waiting on healing. Maybe you've been knocking on a door that just won't open. Let me remind you: God cares. There is a purpose to your pain, a story to your struggle, and a promise to your persistence.

@sarahbgraves

When you can't comprehend a thing He is doing—"Remember the sparrows." The sparrows referenced in Matthew 10:31, "So don't be afraid; you are **worth** more than many sparrows."[dccxliii] (emphasis added) Or in Matthew 6:26, "Look at the birds of the air; they do not sow or reap or store away in barns, and yet your heavenly father feeds them. Are you not much more valuable than they?"[dccxliv] He is telling us, "Do not worry. Cast all your anxieties on Me. All the ones you've been hiding from Me because of the fear of fully letting go and handing them to Me. Are you not much more valuable than the birds of the air? I care for each one of them, yet **you** are worth *more* than many sparrows. You do not need to be afraid. For <u>I care</u> for you. Remember the sparrows and you will always be reminded of My love for you. You will never be able to forget; as they fly freely, so I give My love freely to you." He may not give you everything at once in the world, but He'll give you the dearest things to show you, you mean the world to Him. No matter the answer of yes, no, or not yet, forever know, He <u>cares</u> for you.

322

SOMEHOW

Somehow He loves us—with every imperfection, with every flaw, with every mistake.
Somehow He longs for us—knowing all that we do, think, say, and desire.
Somehow He waits for us—in the valleys, the mountains, the fires, and the storms.
Somehow He desires us—even when we walk away, even when we fall,
even when we don't choose Him. Somehow I fell in love—with how He
loved me, how He cared for me, how He saw me, inside and out.
Somehow I longed for Him—to be closer, to know Him more, and hear His heart.
Somehow I was embraced—when I was lost and broken to become new and free.
Somehow I chose Him—simply because He chose me.

Now it is an extraordinary thing for one to give his life even for an upright man, though perhaps for a noble and lovable and generous benefactor someone might even dare to die. But God shows and clearly proves His [own] love for us by the fact that while we were still sinners, Christ (the Messiah, the Anointed One) died for us.[dccxlv]
Romans 5:7-8

323

BEAUTY IN THE SIMPLICITY

It's so easy to have this perfect image of life made up in our minds, crafted and shaped by TV shows, movies, songs, and books which constantly impress this unimaginable dream for us to live up to; it's no wonder so many people can turn greedy and selfish with their desires. It's as if we believe that somehow we can defy reality to achieve our dreams by ourselves. But it is because of such a loud influence that we overlook life's silent beauty. The beauty of life is found in God, and everything else is just make-up, or a cover-up, that we see as perfection. Proverbs 13:7 says, "A pretentious, showy life is an empty life; a plain and simple life is a full life."[dccxlvi] **There is an extravagant beauty found in simplicity.** It is not made-up or covered-up, it is *real*, which is really what most of us are looking for all along. Simplicity is something that gives life authentic meaning, and honestly, it's not going to be found in something that is fake. In the end, **being content isn't having everything, being content is being God's.** Philippians 4:12 tells us this, "I have learned the secret of being content in any and every situation… I can do everything through **Him** who gives me strength."[dccxlvii] (emphasis added) It's not about being able to do anything; it's about having Him who **is** everything we need. He is *real*. He is sufficient. He is omnipresent. He is beautiful. He is love. He is ours. Yes. Life is beautiful even with the make-up, but the point is to realize that it is just as beautiful without it.

@ kathleenmadethis

324

FROM THE OUTSIDE IN

There is a quote that says: "You are either as beautiful or as ugly as you believe you are. You define your beauty. That's not a power anyone can have over you."[dccxlviii] And as much as I'm sure we might not want to admit it, this statement is 100% true. There is a movie I recently watched with my friends called, *Howl's Moving Castle*.[dccxlix] In the movie, the witch curses this young woman to age from around twenty-years-old to eighty-years-old, and the girl was absolutely mortified. But throughout the movie, she changes between ages of eighty to fifty to twenty back to fifty all depending on how she viewed herself. In the end, the curse wasn't kept on the young woman by the witch, but by the thoughts the young woman had of herself. When she felt beautiful, she went to her normal age. But when she felt ugly, she went back to eighty. She was as beautiful or as ugly as she believed herself to be. And it makes me wonder, even for ourselves, what age would we reflect based on how we view ourselves? *Our beauty from the inside out is only a reflection of what we allow from the outside in.* Many of us are and will be faced with hurt, anger, bitterness, jealousy, and insecurity. And even if we have spent our entire lives rooted and strong in the Word, if we ever let these thoughts into our hearts to spread and dwell, who we are, and how we think and act, will start to change. It will affect not only how we view others, but how we view ourselves. But I love how 1 Peter 3:4 defines beauty, it's a beauty from within: "Instead, it should be that of your inner self, the unfading beauty of a gentle and quiet spirit, which is of great worth in God's sight."[dccl] The thing is that beauty is believed before it is seen.

Knowing that your beauty comes from within will radiate your beauty outside for all, even you, to see. And when those thoughts of hurt or anger, bitterness, or jealousy come, your security of beauty in the Lord will purify your insecurity of thoughts to be for good instead of what the enemy intended for evil. It begins with seeing the beauty God created within you to see all the beauty God has placed around you to bring to life.

325

SHAPED IN ADVANCE

We see the motions; He sees a plan. We see the mountain; He sees strength. We see the journey; He sees the steps. We see appearance; He sees the heart. When we think we know what is best, it is only with the few pieces we have put together from our understanding. But "he who searches our hearts knows the mind of the Spirit, because the Spirit intercedes for God's people in accordance with the will of God."[dccli] (Romans 8:27) The MSG puts it this way, "He knows us far better than we know ourselves."[dcclii] And that is what gives us faith to trust God beyond our own understanding. The beautiful thing is that God knows our hearts better than we do ourselves. Our hearts can fall in love with appearances so easily, but God knows the depths of each man's heart. (1 Samuel 16:7) So when he whispers, "Trust in Me," we can walk in faith that one door closed means another door opened. And through it all, we experience even greater depths of His heart. Romans 8:28 says, "That's why we can be so sure that every detail in our lives of love for God is worked into something good."[dccliii]

We can only see the appearance of a want, a desire, a dream, but He sees every detail of the dream, the want, the desire, and He knows that desires don't lead to knowledge, but seeking leads to understanding. And in understanding, we find knowledge of whether we loved the dream or just the appearance. Proverbs 2:3-5 says, *And if you call out for insight, and cry aloud for understanding, and if you look for it as for silver and search for it as for hidden treasure, then you will understand the fear of the Lord and find the knowledge of God.*[dccliv]

In other words, if we ask God for understanding, and adventure for the answers, we will then discover knowledge. But you'll never know if you never go. The crazy thing is that God has this all planned in advance, but it is through steps of faith that we experience His plan. However, faith doesn't always mean impulse. We may act impulsively on our desires, but we act by faith on God's desires; and this is where each of our journey's truly begin—in seeking His heart over our own. Ephesians 2:10 puts it this way, "For we are God's workmanship, created in Christ Jesus to do good works, which God prepared in advance for us to do."[dcclv] He has prepared everything in advance for us. That's why déjà vu is so incredible! It is like Ephesians 2:10 coming to life! It's a way of God showing us how incredible He is, but also reassuring us that we can trust fully in Him. Psalm 37:25 says, "I was young and now I am old, yet I have never seen the righteous forsaken or their children begging for bread."[dcclvi] Because God never fails and always provides.

As much as our life is shaped, our heart is shaped in advance for us to live in Him. Romans 8:29 reads, "He decided from the outset to shape the lives of those who love Him along the same lines as the life of His son. We see the original and intended shape of our lives there in him."[dcclvii] Everything about us is shaped in advance to live out the purpose that He already has planned for us. And so our paths are already paved in advance, and our hearts shaped in precision, to bring glory to Him; and that is a beautiful thing. 1 Corinthians 2:9 says, "No eye has seen, no ear has heard, no mind has conceived what God has prepared for those who love Him."[dcclviii] In Isaiah 64:4 it closely relates to, "No one has heard, no ear has perceived, no eye has seen any God besides you, who acts on behalf of those who wait for Him."[dcclix] Those who love God, wait on God, for they'd rather wait in faith than act on impulse, to see His kingdom come above all else.

326

WAITING ON A WORD IN BLOOM

> *Don't dig up in doubt what you planted in faith.*[dcclx]
> -Elisabeth Elliot

Have you ever been in a season that's serene? It's surrounded by green pastures and flowers of all sorts. Goodness and blessings are at your left and right. Sure, there are cloudy days and some rainy, but overall, your season is quite lovely and quite comfortable. But in that garden, there's a secret place within your heart that you keep hoping for, looking for, and desiring to find in your daily walk through it's familiar white gates. But it still is just a bud, still closed, still hasn't come to bloom.

Song of Songs is a book some scholars describe as a story between two lovers, others say it could also be a metaphor of Christ and His church. But I believe, either way, the heart is the same in this passage:

I belong to my lover, and his desire is for me. Come, my lover, let us go to the countryside, let us spend the night in the village. Let us go early to the vineyards to see if the vines have budded, if their blossoms have opened, and if the pomegranates are in bloom—there I will give you my love.[dcclxi] (Song of Songs 7:10-12)

Here we are with our One true love, and yet, we still have desires? When you see it through the lens of a couple, it makes sense. But how easy is it for us as a church to dismiss our desires because we say we are dying to ourselves. I'm not saying the desires of our flesh that we are to put off, I'm saying the desires of our hearts where sweet dreams bloom and pure hopes grow. We can honor desires for their worth with a fellow lover, but bury in wastelands what should be planted in gardens the desires we have with the One who loves us ***most***. Verse 10 says, "I *belong* to my lover, and his desire is *for* me."[dcclxii] (emphasis added) Sounds like a verse I've heard before. Maybe Jeremiah 29:11... or Psalm 37:4... or is it Psalm 37:23?

Here's my point. God is a Father to us, and as a child of God, we don't have to be ashamed of having desires. Often, God places them within you. The key is to not let them go, nor hold onto them too tightly, but to keep them in surrender with your Love.

There are words that God has spoken over you, promises that were to be planted, dreams with intentions to flourish; but your disbelief in your identity of the One you're in relationship with has locked up a secret garden that once was a sacred place where you used to walk around and to discover which flowers were blooming and which ones you were still being patient for. In the MSG version it says, "Let's look for wildflowers in bloom."[dcclxiii] I know His words sound *wild*, and I know you were expecting it to be {here} already, but believe it is a *planted promise*. It's being nurtured, taken care of, and prepared. I know you thought the Word would have shown signs of blooming by now, but be faithful. Keep watering, keep letting light in, and keep it <u>planted.</u> God cares for what you care for, and He wants to reveal the secret things to you more than you want to see them blossom. But there's a beauty when you know the blossoming is worth waiting for. Just because it's hidden from your sight doesn't mean it's a secret from His sight. Just wait to see the beauty it will cultivate when it does come into full bloom.

327

VENI. VEDI. VICI.

> *We plan the way we want to live our lives, but only God makes us able to live it.*[dcclxiv]
> Proverbs 16:9

We imagine the way our lives will plan out, but God always fills in the gaps that we can't see. And it is those gaps that become the moments we will never forget; they're the hidden treasures we couldn't have dreamed up. Yet, when it comes to the future, there are two emotions that tend to come to my heart, fear and hope—fear of failing, hope of living. But when we look to the moment we are in right now, there are usually two emotions we feel: peace and comfort. In other words, there's no reason to have had fear at all in the past, because you're okay in the now. But in the gaps, there are no expectations because we couldn't see them coming, and it is there we come alive. So instead of being anxious of the future, be fully where you are now. Expect the unexpected and live the unlived. Because the greatest moments you can hope for will be found in the gaps. The greatest fears you dwelled on have more existence in the now than in the future. Your peace will come from God and your comfort from your vision. Vision of whether you will live [now] or [later] begins with if your heart is in the *now* or the *later*. Between your plans, you will discover the gaps. *And in those gaps we find ourselves, we lose ourselves, and we become ourselves.* As a Roman soldier would put it: "Veni, vedi, vici."[dcclxv] "I came, I saw, I conquered." Before you can see, you have to go. Before you can conquer, you must have vision for where you are. And it is *then* that we will live fuller lives than we could have ever imagined.

328

A PRAYER OF FREEDOM

Verse of the Day:

*Could it be any clearer? Our old way of life was nailed to the cross with Christ, a decisive end to that sin-miserable life—no longer at sin's every beck and call! What we believe is this: If we get included in Christ's sin-conquering death, we also get included in his life-saving resurrection. We know that when Jesus was raised from the dead it was a signal of the end of death-as-the-end. Never again will death have the last word. When Jesus died, he took sin down with him, but **alive he brings God down to us**. From now on, think of it this way: Sin speaks a dead language that means nothing to you; God speaks your mother tongue, and **you hang on every word**. You are dead to sin and alive to God. That's what Jesus did. That means you must not give sin a vote in the way you conduct your lives. Don't give it the time of day. Don't even run little errands that are connected with that old way of life. Throw yourselves wholeheartedly and full-time—remember, you've been raised from the dead!—into God's way of doing things. Sin can't tell you how to live. After all, you're not living under that old tyranny any longer. **You're living in the freedom of God**.*[dcclxvi]

Romans 6:6-14 (emphasis added)

Prayer:

Dear God,

Take me as I am. Take all of me. Leave everything behind. Wash away every fear, hope, paradigm, dream, criteria, desire, and plan that's ruled my mind. Let's start over. Let's do this again. I give You my hand. Lead me, guide me, but mainly, be close to me. I need You. I want You. As my friend said, "Let Him lead, and you just make Him look flawless as He guides you." I have no expectations for tomorrow. I have no knowledge. I have no plan. I am standing at the wilderness' edge. I see the rows of vineyards inside, they've been nurtured and are ready to reap. You have prepared them for me. So let's do this. I give my heart to You, and I am ready to fall deeply and madly in love. I'm ready to be sold out → to sing in the mist, to dance through the fog, to see light reveal glimmers of passion. The thought of dying to myself has never sounded so sweet. I leave myself behind. I am now **new**.

Amen.

329

RENEWED

> *Do not conform to the pattern of this world, but be transformed by the renewing of your mind. Then you will be able to test and approve what God's will is—his good, pleasing and perfect will.*[dcclxvii]
> Romans 12:2

To conform is to be similar in character, which is exactly how society tries to mold the world into their likeness. It's not so much us being set apart in our style or personality, but how we react to things, what we do or don't do, what we speak and how we speak as this new person we've become. When we look at reality and its "patterns," it's easy to become discouraged and lose sight of God's will to focus on ours. However, when we look at God's truth, our minds are renewed to refocus and see God's perfect will for us. To test and see that His word is greater than any patterns this world could offer. His word is His personalized promise to us. As Frederick Buechner said: "By believing against all odds and loving against all odds, that is how we are to let Jesus show in the world and to transform the world."[dcclxviii] Always remember, the world is not to transform us, we are to transform the world. Beginning with love, continuing with love, and finishing well with love, sanctity will rise above conformity every time.

330

ROYAL

We are all royalty, every girl, a princess, every guy, a prince, all enchanting, all heroic. Whether you've already thought, "This isn't me," or started to allow your disbelief to surface, I want you to push pause on the now and rewind to you as a child. We are going to see *your* fairytale. Girls, I think we all have had a few days of dress up, a few dreams of being a princess, and a few nights of watching the royalty we wanted to be in Disney. Guys, I'm sure you can remember the men you wanted to be from a young age. It may not have been a prince, but it was a hero of some sort. A firefighter coming to the rescue, a sports player making the final score to win the game, or wanting to be just like your dad who you thought the world of your entire childhood. There are two words that each of these fairytales begin with—belief and wonder. Now let's go back to the beginning of creation—formless, empty, and dark. But then comes an exhaled breath, a voice speaks, and the orchestration begins. Out comes light, waters expand, ground rises; creation is made. But this is just the beginning. It's beautiful and pure, just as Adam and Eve were made.

Yet it is here the thief of wonder comes with disbelief. "Did God really say…" (Genesis 3:1, NIV) as Eve begins to wander away from what she believed to be true. We know how it goes from there. Isn't it interesting how the moment she let disbelief into her heart, she lost sight of all the wonders around her? Before Satan crossed onto their path, they probably were curious to all that was around them. "What makes these things called trees grow?" "What does that animal do?" "What is water for?" Just thoughts upon thoughts of wonder. Just as we were growing up. "I want to be just like Cinderella. To be beautiful, a princess, and find true love." Or for the men, "I can't wait to grow up, be a hero, and be the guy everyone wants to be." (Taken from what little I know about a boy's mind.)

We lived in wonder. But as we grow up, we become swayed by the disbelief of what beauty and worth God has within us and before us. Somewhere and somehow, someone stripped away the belief of happy endings from your heart, robbing you of the pure joy and wonder of believing that when God orchestrated your story, He stepped back and thought, "This is good," as He did with the light, the waters, the land, and so on. I personally want to say, I'm so sorry for that. But even more, I pray that today that belief and wonder can revive in your heart. Resume to the now and *remember* that awe as a child, because still you are that child of God, and you always will be. You are that princess, and you are that hero, because we are children of the highest King. Girls, you are your very own Cinderella. You'll have troubles come, but God will always be the prince to rescue you and to bless you with gifts and joys that He *knows* you love. Men, you are the superheroes, the knights in shining armor, being brave when all is not well and being strong in tough times. We are not flawless, but we don't need to be when we serve a God who is perfect for us. So believe in the wonder God had in creating all things good, and you'll see the wonder in yourself that He believes in you. For you, my friend, are royal, and great dreams lie ahead.

331

SPARKS OF FIRE

Your words contain power
That man can't defeat
It can set this world on fire
And spread igniting heat
Yet choice can bring victory
But it also leads astray
From where the path was chosen
Can bring life or take away
So with the power of choosing
We can run or we can fight
We can use it for His glory
Or be consumed in our delights
Let not our hearts decide so quickly
On what is the truth
For wisdom is a discovery
It is sought and revealed to you
Choose your words wisely
A blaze can be contained
It can spark a revolution
Or create a war of flames

Consider what a great forest is set on fire by a small spark.[dcclxix]
James 3:5

332

SPEAKING WORDS INTO EXISTENCE

How many of us have had thought things differently in our minds, but said things differently with our words? It's like once we have said it, our mind quickly things, "Why did I say that?" When we are used to speaking without thinking, we lose control of thinking of what to speak. And the thing is words have power, so we **need** to have self-control over them. Proverbs 18:21 says, "The tongue has the power of life and death, and those who love it will eat its fruit."[dcclxx] Our words are a fuel. They can ignite or they can destroy. They can be warmth, or they can burn. James 3:5 says, "Likewise, the tongue is a small part of the body, but it makes great boasts. Consider what a great forest is set on fire by a small spark."[dcclxxi] The MSG version of James 3:6 says, "By our speech we can ruin the world, turn harmony to chaos, throw mud on a reputation, send the whole world up in smoke and go up in smoke with it, smoke right from hell."[dcclxxii] Our tongue speaks words into existence. Thus, if our thoughts are already glorifying God, so then should it be with our words. Set your hearts and minds on things above, so that people can praise the God above for the words you give. Purify your heart so your thoughts can be clean and uplifting for your own self. Then, when people see you, you will reflect the confidence in who God made you to be. Speak words of warmth to draw others close to God, instead of words of fire to turn them away. Tame your tongue and control your words → for they hold great power. May you quest not to destroy, but to rebuild.

@ kathleenmadethis

333

IN AND OUT

It is a part of our every day life and yet goes so easily unnoticed. Not only that, it is our very reason for life, for existing, for being. It is our constant, our necessity, our beginning. It's the very reason why we are. It is *breath*. We can become so focused on the moments that take our breath away that we overlook the value breath has. Here are a few facts about breathing:

1. Most emotional issues, including breathing related anxiety and depression, result from the nervous system being out of balance. Breathing drives the nervous system.
2. Shortness of breath and heart disease are directly linked; the heart goes into spasm when it is deprived of oxygen.
3. Science has proven that cancer is anaerobic; it does not survive in high levels of oxygen.
4. Breathing provides 99% of your energy. Without energy, nothing works.[dcclxxiii]

Crazy, right? And those are only a few uncovered truths. I wonder how many of us take the time each day to pause for a deep breath. To just breathe, inhale and exhale, in and out, coming back to the moment we're in, cherishing the moment for its worth. Job 33:4 says, "The Spirit of God has made me; the breath of the Almighty gives me life."[dcclxxiv] He is the breath we breathe in and out that balances our lives, that brings content to our hearts, that allows worries to subside, and remakes us as *us* again. The very breath that brought us to life in the beginning is the very breath that keeps us alive every day. Sometimes, all we need to do spiritually, emotionally, and physically is just *breathe*. To remember that He is still for us, that we are still His, and that everything is in His hands. Because it is when we breathe that His spirit sustains us and completes us. As Isaiah 42:5 says, "This is what the Lord God says—he who created the heavens and stretched out the earth and all that comes out of it, who gives breath to its people and life to those who walk on it."[dcclxxv] He gives *breath* to His people, and as it flows in and out of His heart, it flows in and out of our lives. He's always with us and forever for us—sometimes we just have to pause long enough to take a deep breath: to then remember, to again come alive.

> Take a deep breath, remember your God.
> Take a deep breath, remember He is good.
> Take a deep breath, remember His love for you.
> Take a deep breath, remember your love for Him.
> Come alive.

334

YOU WON'T

> *An attacker advances against you, Nineveh. Guard the fortress, watch the road, brace yourselves, marshal all your strength! The Lord will restore the splendor of Jacob like the splendor of Israel, though destroyers have laid them waste and have ruined their vines. The shields of the soldiers are red; the warriors are clad in scarlet. The metal on the chariots flashes on the day they are made ready; the spears of juniper are brandished.* dcclxxvi
> Nahum 2:1-3

When it comes to sport, there are always two teams: one offense, the other defense; thus making it a competition. Yet when it comes to the enemy, when it comes to war, it's not merely a game, it is a fight. It is not a fight in which we can swing swords or fists, it is a lifestyle that either advances or retreats. There will be victories, there will be defeats, but ultimately, the Great Victor lives in our hearts. We are conquerors, but only when we rise to believe so. Revelations 3:11-13 says:

I'm on my way; I'll be there soon. Keep a tight grip on what you have so no one distracts you and steals your crown. I'll make each conqueror a pillar in the sanctuary of my God, a permanent position of honor. Then I'll write names on you, the pillars: the Name of my God, the Name of God's City—the new Jerusalem coming down out of Heaven—and my new Name. Are your ears awake? Listen. Listen to the Wind Words, the Spirit blowing through the churches. dcclxxvii

There is a deep fire in my spirit against the advancing troops of evil. Sometimes life distracts us from the great map of lost territory due to the enemy's advancement in our world. With modeling, fashion, movies, music, families, poverty, wealth, and government, he doesn't rest in trying to destroy the conquerors, the elite, the heroes of goodness. Some of us need to hear these words: "Keep a tight grip on what you have so no one distracts you and steals your crown," for the enemy has been trying to discourage you from fighting. He is speaking, "You can't." My words to you are: "You won't."

I'm not speaking these two words to shut you down, but to wake you up, spur you on, and make you see... you actually can.

I love the moment when someone's face is perplexed, debating on whether to act on a whim, when their friend speaks up, "You won't," therefore, sparking a fire in the person's eyes to want to do it all the more, and then, they do! That is the phrase I am insinuating to your strong, courageous, undefeatable heart. It's time to guard the fortress, watch the road, brace yourself, and marshal your strength, for it's time to start living on offense. Stop watching the land perish away, and see it flourish with His anointing again. It's time to take back what is ours today. As Isaiah 62:10-12 says:

Walk out of the gates. Get going! Get the road ready for the people. Build the highway. Get at it! Clear the debris, hoist high a flag, a signal to all peoples! Yes! God has broadcast to all the world: "Tell daughter Zion, 'Look! Your Savior comes, Ready to do what he said he'd do, prepared to complete what he promised.'" Zion will be called new names: Holy People, God-Redeemed, Sought-Out, City-Not-Forsaken. dcclxxviii

I am urging you to take stance against the enemy and look at where he has taken you out. What does the enemy whisper to your heart cannot be conquered? What has he said is impossible to redeem? What does he shout cannot be forgiven? It's time to stand on the truth of God's Word, to advance the kingdom for His glory. When an opportunity of good arises, may you hear, "You won't" whispered in your ear, and may it ignite a fire within you to act in love. When your family, your friendships, or your church is under attack, speak truth, speak light, speak revelation, and swing that sword of truth, destroying the enemy's attempts to take out your people. This is not a time to retreat, but to rise; it's not a time to hold back, but move forward; it's not a time to stay silent, but to declare victory! He is here, He is alive, and every lie, plot, and attempt the enemy has been planning against you is already finished, in Jesus' name!

335

ETERNAL FOUNDATIONS

Fear.

It is a crippling factor in our pursuit of all that God has for us. Why? Because it is a masked disbelief that leads us astray from His truth and His <u>Word.</u> The man who was given one talent hid it because he was → afraid. The Israelites never walked into their promise because of their → disbelief. The enemy didn't keep either of them out, they themselves did. That completely boggles my mind. When it comes to God's word, it is vital to *treasure* it as if it were a bag of talents, where, with <u>determination,</u> we risk everything to see His word come to pass. **We** lead, ***not*** our fear. We *declare* His promises, not *hide* them in disbelief. We **fix** our eyes on an unseen city with real eternal foundations, not **settle** in a desert in weariness. We should not grow weary in doing good, for at the right time, we *will* reap a harvest. It's not a question, but a promise. In the end, the man who had risked the most was richly rewarded. So this is my advice for the devoted dreamer in the wilderness: {Be content in the process, consistent in the pursuit, and in the promise, you will live a *full* life. For the risk may be great, but the reward is so much greater.} There is a [purpose] to the word He has given you, not to be hidden and disbelieved, but to be uncovered and unraveled in His truth.

Believe it, go after it, and discover its eternal foundations that are real and right before you.

> *By an act of faith, Abraham said yes to God's call to travel to an unknown place that would become his home. When he left he had no idea where he was going. By an act of faith he lived in the country promised him, lived as a stranger camping in tents. Isaac and Jacob did the same, living under the same promise. Abraham did it by keeping his eye on an unseen city with real, eternal foundations—the City designed and built by God.* [dcclxxix]
> Hebrews 11:8-10

336

BEGIN STRONG. FINISH STRONGER.

I believe *every* time God whispers, a flower buds within the secret garden of promises, where designs are always taking place. The bud doesn't say much, and it surely doesn't look like much, but it is there with all its certainty. We are certain we heard a whisper; we are certain it was from God. But the uncertainty comes as we wonder when its green layers of promise will open. It's in this place of intimacy that we know God and find Him every time. But sometimes, when we leave the garden where certainty is on hold to bloom, the world offers us designs that we can see and bring into our garden. What we don't realize is that the enemy was the mastermind of placing that piece in our heart that would bring, not a flower, but a weed into our most precious of places. Once inside, it weaves around our budded certainty to create a vine that looks promising but is deadly. We must live by faith and not by sight, for His promise is always living. All along, life was there, flowing beneath the "seen-ery," and it's direction flowing faithfully into a promised place of gold.

In reading Genesis 2, I was drawn to the passage of the garden in verses 10-11, "A river watering the garden flowed from Eden; from there it was separated into four head waters. The name of the first is the Pishon; it winds through the entire land of Havilah, where there is gold."[dcclxxx] I've always heard to guard your heart for everything you do flows from it. But what we should be reminded of just as equally is that *the guarded and sacred water is flowing into places of gold.* I'm not sure what four areas your secret garden is pouring into beyond what you see, but what I do know is they are worth guarding everything for. One area may be your disciples, another your work area, another your family, but one is all for you, and it's worth investing in and believing for. I have come to know that *belief is the one thing that keeps you from settling for anything less than God's promise.* As long as you believe that what He has spoken is created, anything of less worth won't be worth taking into your most treasured of secret gardens. Belief keeps doubt out and certainty in → for it is in the garden where God whispers secrets and gold is reaped where flowers bloom.

The key to belief is listening. Listening at all times in all places to His voice which allured you gently to the secret garden in the first place. The same voice guides you and shines truth all around you in protection. For "His faithful promises are your armor and protection"[dcclxxxi] (Psalm 91:4) and "the Lord gives victory to his anointed."[dcclxxxii] (Psalm 20:6) We build upon the eternal with who we listen to and what we allow into our garden, for we can only see through His eyes when we listen to His voice—it's where the unseen blooms into something unquestionably beautiful. We are constantly pursuing one thing or finding rest in another, and we will have two different kinds of sight for that one thing, one that's here and one that is eternal. The enemy will remind you of what is and God will remind you of what is to come, the seen and the unseen. Listen with an open mind and be faithful with an open heart to *see* with an eternal perspective. <u>Then you will begin strong and end even stronger.</u> As the secret garden lives in your heart, so does the land of gold. The beauty is that you will never leave the garden the same way you came in; for when you come to the garden, God will always meet you there, and you'll believe what He has spoken all over again. Who we become in the waiting is who we are in the promise. So be intentional, not just with what you do with your days, but who you become within its secret gardens. For it is there you'll see your Father's designs come to life—for He does have a plan, and it's flowing into lands of gold.

337

TRUSTING > UNDERSTANDING

I am known so much more through your trust than through your understanding. It's about staying close to Me, even when you don't feel Me near at all. It's about loving Me with all that you are even when you feel like there's no love left. It's about trusting in Me when you see nothing changing, when you feel like you have no more faith. It is in those moments I am found in you the most. Yes…"My power is made perfect in weakness."[dcclxxxiii] *(2 Corinthians 12:9) Though you don't see Me in these situations over your circumstances, I am there. And when those situations pass, you'll see Me there, where I've never left, and you'll see all that I've done. I don't mold you out of pain; I mold you out of love. I am the loving Potter and you are my beloved clay. You are Mine as I am yours.*

338

WITHOUT WORDS

Dear children, let us not love with words or tongue, but with actions and in truth.[dcclxxxiv]
1 John 3:18

I want you to close your eyes for a moment and just imagine a world without words. One where you couldn't say how you felt, but could only express it, a life full of designs, signs, and handcrafted wonders. A heart can speak through words, but it is heard ever more powerfully through art. It can range from your high intelligence to your athletic ability, from your ear for songwriting to your eye for design, from your pen and pad to your paint and brush. All of these are expressions of your heart, which is widely known as art. Art voices your heart's depths and heights in unfathomable ways. To love without words is to tell His story in everything you do. It is a form of art, a new method of speaking, for the voiceless to hear, for sometimes it takes using our gifts for His glory to be heard at all. It may be the only chance we can say, "God loves you," without words when we release our art as a voice in the desert of the secular world. May you begin to love without words and live beyond your limits for His fame and name and glory to be made known to all.

339

LOCK YOUR EYES

Friends, my heart is alive and awake today. *Alive* in the freedom the Lord's goodness brings, *awake* to His glory dwelling among us. But even more, I am alert to the enemy's schemes, and I am furious. Furious as a child of God to see him moving in his pride thinking he is winning, taking as many conquerors out as he can. I am very aware of the path that the righteous are to follow, and I look around and see too many of the destined following the side paths the enemy is alluring them to. Mighty warrior, fight! Mighty warrior, remember whose you are, who your Father is! My best friend was telling me about a woman she met recently who had just got delivered from having hundreds of demons in her... *hundreds*. She went on to tell me that this woman used to speak with Lucifer. Lucifer himself told this woman that he was her dad, and he sent her to a bible college with specific names to destroy their destinies. Thankfully, now she is saved, and loves God undeniably and passionately. But, I cannot describe the fury, flamed by a wild love, that birthed in my heart at that moment to not be silent about the good news that could free so many captives!

Friends, the enemy is not under the rug! He is prowling around to destroy destinies and rob gifts. He is sneaking around doing everything out of sight in a way that *almost* goes unnoticed. Yet, we are to do two things in seasons of attack: one, lock eyes with God, and two, lock eyes with the enemy. Let me explain. Locking your eyes with God is a revelation of who He is. Psalm 18:2 describes him as our rock, our fortress, and our deliverer. An example of this is found in Matthew 16:18 where Jesus declares: "You are Peter and upon this rock I will build my church, and all the powers of hell will not conquer it." (Matthew 16:18, NLT) In the next chapter, Peter sees the transfiguration of Jesus by the high mountain, or what could also be described as this really great rock. As he caught the glimpse of who Jesus truly is as the Rock, I can imagine he had a revelation of what God spoke over him as the rock in him. Not only does Peter's name mean rock itself, but he is staring at the greatest rock while remembering these words that were declared over him. In that moment, Peter, the doubting and fearful, yet devoted and courageous Peter, saw Jesus, saw the Rock, and saw himself as God saw him, and then he went off to change the world.

I believe we all have a gift that God has spoken over us. It is the gift that we are most passionate about and most afraid of. It is *the gift* that the enemy wants us to keep from using for it is out greatest weapon to release a warfare against him. You just first need to lock eyes with Jesus to have a revelation of who He is and who you are. Then fight back, for destinies are under attack, and your greatest weapon can't be locked up in a closet, hidden, and unseen. Be bold and unashamed for greater is He that is in you than he that is in the world. (1 John 4:4) Second, lock eyes with the enemy with that fiery passion, and drive him out in Jesus name! Stop letting him exhaust you, stop letting him place insecurity in you, stop listening to doubts, and you will see, he can't look you in the eye, for he cannot stay where God's glory dwells. As 2 Timothy 1:6-7 says, "Fan into flame the spiritual gift God gave you... for God has not given us a spirit of fear and timidity, but of power, love, and self-discipline."[dcclxxxv] The flame within you is greater than the flames he is trying to cause around you, and it transforms what he intended for evil into something good. There is a world that needs to know *Who* their great heavenly Father, or Dad, is. Outside your walls of fear and comfort are people who are lost. It's not a scary thing, but a serious thing, and friends, we are all called to rise up and all destined to conquer! Lock your eyes with Jesus, know who He is, see who you are, and fan into flame the very gift He has placed in your heart. You never know the impact your flame could have in spreading a wildfire of love, shining bright the glory of Jesus for all to see!

340

PERFECT LOVE

God is love. Whoever lives in love lives in God, and God in them. This is how love is made complete among us so that we will have confidence on the day of judgment: In this world we are like Jesus.[dcclxxxvi]
1 John 4:16-17

The world is constantly striving for perfection, satisfaction, and contentment. But who are we, as followers of Christ, to strive to be perfect when we already have the perfect God? Sometimes we seek for a love to make us feel like we have worth because we haven't acknowledged the One love who was sent to pay the price for our worth. Jesus believed we were worth the cross. Even then, He died for us all to live, and truly live, in His freedom. In freedom, all strife and perfection lay to rest at His feet, and our worth is found forever in His love. We tend to let our eyes drift away from the Love that perfects by trying to perfect a love that cannot be. *You don't perfect love; His love perfects you*. It's not that you're not enough; you just forgot that God is enough for you. Your worth is still found in His worth, and forever will be.

341

TEN DEGREES

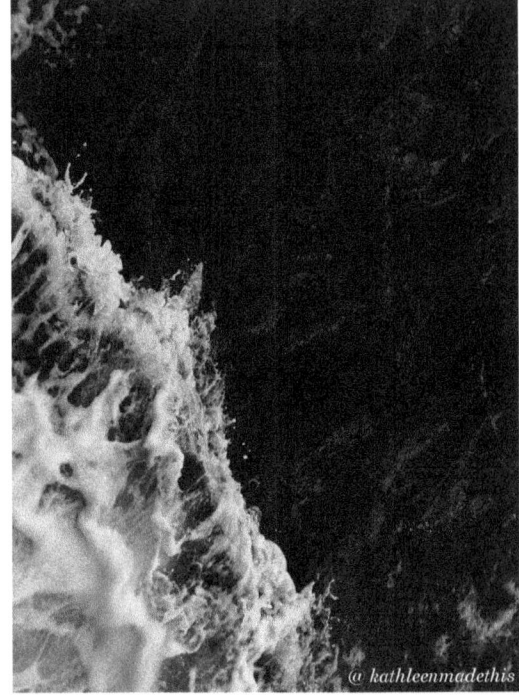
@ kathleenmadethis

When it comes to the impossible, many of us dream of experiencing it. But that's just it, we like to dream of it, because we can still wake up from it. Dreams are like the safety-harness to our reality. We can go over them step-by-step in our heads, but when it comes to actually taking a step, all of a sudden the safety-harness falls off and says, "Go." Reality is where belief turns into faith—because there is no waking up if something goes wrong. A man by the name of Charles Blondin dreamed big, but his faith was even greater. On June 30th of 1859, he was the first person in history to walk across a 1,100-feet long tightrope over the Niagara Falls, without a safety net or a safety harness. He even went a step past the impossible and did the unimaginable,→ he took a chair and a stove to cook an omelet and eat it… all while balancing on a line 160 feet above the Niagara Falls.[dcclxxxvii] Now I'm sure he recited all of these things a thousand times in his head, but he decided to have faith without a safety-harness and actually do it. That's the faith we need.

In 2 Kings 20:1-11, we read about Hezekiah's illness. It was so severe he was at the point of death. Isaiah reported that God said he was going to die, and so Hezekiah cried out to God. Thus, Hezekiah was healed to live for fifteen more years, but he wanted to make sure it was by God and not by the figs they gave him. This is the climax of the story because the safety-harness falls off of Isaiah's prayer when he asks, "Do you want the shadow to advance ten degrees on the sundial or go back ten degrees? You choose."[dcclxxxviii] Hezekiah realized that going forward ten degrees would be more possible, and so he decided to have the shadow go back ten degrees, which was unimaginable. And so Isaiah called upon the Lord and the shadow moved back ten degrees. There are two main points here. One: that our prayers should be faith-filled. Two: that once we let go of the safety-harness with the impossible, we start to do the unimaginable. Exodus 33:11 says, "The Lord would speak to Moses face to face, as a man speaks with his friend."[dcclxxxix] There is no reason why our prayers should not be as bold as Isaiah's or Moses', for prayer is simply communication with God. If our prayers have the ability to make a shadow move backwards ten degrees, can you imagine what else they can do?

To finish with the story of Charles Blondin, he asked the crowd if they believed he could push a man across the Niagara Falls sitting in a wheelbarrow. He spotted one of the men who screamed yes. And when he told the man, "Get in," the man refused. Our prayers are almost the same. We tend to whisper as if God can't do anything. When God is saying, "I can do all things." It is when we begin to pray bold prayers that we become courageous in heart. When we pray quietly, it's more of a, "I'll accept what You'll do." But when we pray boldly, it becomes, "I expect God to move." A perspective change happens when the impossible breaks through our reality, but sometimes it takes letting go of the probabilities to see all the possibilities God has in store. Dare to dream and dare to pray. Because when you pray for God to move ten degrees, your reality will surely shift 180 degrees, and nothing will ever be the same.

342

DELICATE DESIRES

> *What causes quarrels and what causes fights among you? Is it not this, that your passions are at war within you? You desire and do not have, so you murder. You covet and cannot obtain, so you fight and quarrel. You do not have, because you do not ask. You ask and do not receive, because you ask wrongly, to spend it on your passions.*[dccxc]
> James 4:1-3

If we ask, we must ask God. If we do not receive, we must check the motives of our hearts: "Is it for our sake or for His?" We must be conscientious about what we desire. Our desires may seem delicate and harmless, but if they are preoccupying our minds, then they are ruling us. If we are killing and coveting, doing whatever we can to make these desires come true, then we have already been overcome. We ask God because the desires from our hearts can be deceiving. (Jer. 17:9) [dccxci] So we must learn to not follow our own hearts unquestionably, but to look to His sight dependently every time, for when our hearts are blind, His remains Sovereign. We then fix the eyes of our hearts on what is unseen, "For what is seen is temporary, but what is unseen is eternal,"[dccxcii] and always pursue God harder than we ever pursue our desires. It is then that we will follow His heart over our own. As Brooke Ligertwood said: *Don't pursue your dreams, pursue Jesus.*[dccxciii] For He is always to be trusted.

343

AN OPEN JOURNEY

Our lives are led by open and closed doors, by things seen and foreseen, by signs and wonders. Yet, we tend to see a closed door as a dead end instead of an open journey. When we invest so much into something that has been on our heart, we see it as a slap in our face when the door shuts. It hurts our confidence and even our ego—because we just don't understand. It's almost like the story of Jonah. Many people see him as a coward for running from God's calling on his life, yet we overlook that we tend to run from the small promptings He asks us to do in obedience. Jonah eventually did obey God, but his ego was hurt in the process because God's plan was different from his plan. Like God provided and then took away the vine, Jonah became disappointed in God's will triumphing his own. And that's like the small promptings in our hearts, we begin to be led by them, but the way we plan them isn't always what God has planned for them. But the thing is that whether many doors are opened or many doors are closed, our faith should be the same, because a closed door isn't always a dead end. Actually, a closed door is an open journey, and an open door is a closed journey. In a journey, we see and discover new things that God is preparing us for; an open door closes off the other journeys we could have taken to lead us with a purpose to the place we belong in the now. Jonah saw the closed doors as a slap to his heart and so he became angry with God. God puts it this way, "You have been concerned about this vine, though you did not tend it or make it grow."dccxciv (Jonah 4:10) And that's just it! When we invest our emotions into something we love and it is taken away, we become so hurt and confused even though we weren't the one who created it or made it grow. But when it is all about the One we love, it doesn't matter what He gives and takes, because we know it's for a purpose that is for His glory, and yet in His mercy, still for our good. 2 Corinthians 4:15 reads: "Every detail works to your advantage and to God's glory."dccxcv So no matter how many doors are opened or how many are closed, let your faith stay the same because we know that He knows what is best for you. As long as your eyes are set on Him, you will see closed doors as an open journey, and an open door as a set purpose. *Open doors are <u>prepared</u> from the past, so continually trust Him and look to Him, for closed doors are <u>known</u> for the future, and His best is always ahead.* xx

@bulgerjoseph

344

ALWAYS

Do you know how precious your love is to Me? Do you know how dear your heart is to Mine? You see how others value you, but can you imagine how prized you are in My eyes? I know you so much more. I created you! I am always with you! Yet, still you have no idea of how much your heart truly means to My heart. I love you as I love My son; you are My child, and I am your Father. I will never leave you nor forsake you. I know the plans I have for you. I will never stop loving you until eternity ends. Always, I am for you, and always I am with you, that you may never doubt My love for you, that you may never forget our love.

It's easier for us to let love go than to let love hold us; but it's in the holding that we behold His majesty, becoming just like Him. In the beholding, we are set free within Him, as we wrestle from the inside out. When darkness is close, destiny is that much closer. At the sense of darkness, we run. But at the sense of destiny, we wrestle. The wrestle is always the last dance before destiny approaches. At the end of the wrestle, we will be the ones holding onto Him, as we find our everything, our every uniqueness, our every kindness, our every heart's piece within His peace, within His hold. He holds *us* together; His love holds all our pieces in peace. He keeps us, His treasure, in our rarity, close to His heart. To never forget the beat of His love for us never ends, never ends, never ends...

> *No, despite all these things, overwhelming victory is ours through Christ, who loved us. And I am convinced that nothing can ever separate us from God's love. Neither death nor life, neither angels nor demons, neither our fears for today nor our worries about tomorrow—not even the powers of hell can separate us from God's love. No power in the sky above or in the earth below—indeed, nothing in all creation will ever be able to separate us from the love of God that is revealed in Christ Jesus our Lord.*[dccxcvi]
> Romans 8:35-39

345

SHAPED IN PRECISION

> *God is within her, she will not fall; God will help her at the break of day.*
> Psalm 46:5

Have you ever thought about how rare you are? How you were well-thought-out beforehand and perfected before your very first breath. Like a jar of clay, beautifully put together as a stunning treasure to behold. Have you ever realized how valuable your heart is? That the very God of the universe desires it? That He reminds us not once, not twice, but multiple times throughout the scriptures to guard and protect it— knowing you don't deserve less, but the best. Have you ever tried to grasp how loved you are? It's not even possible. When you look at the sun rising or setting, the stars shooting or shining, the clouds moving or shaping, the rainbow's promise, the rain's peace, the wind's presence, it's all for you. For believing doesn't start with seeing, seeing begins with believing. When you start to believe these things, you start to see how rare, valued, and loved you are through *all* the things God has done, is doing, and has in store for you. *So why do we feel, insufficient, inadequate, and inferior? Maybe in a way, we are... yet then again, with God we're not at all.* As Psalm 46:5 says, "God is within her, she will not fall."[dccxcvii] God is our sufficiency. God makes us adequate. God is our strong tower. Apart from God, we can do nothing, but with God, anything can happen. You see, we've been built up in such a lie, that in order to fit in we have to do this, wear that, be strong, do more, and be this certain image of perfection that the world hasn't even specifically defined yet. When all along, you've always been more than enough, more powerful, more unique, and more cared for, than you could imagine. The real truth is, you don't have to *fit in* because you were *shaped in* precision, you've just been told to seek for it in different shapes and sizes for as long as you could remember. Yet as Song of Songs 4:7 says, "All beautiful you are my darling; there is *no* flaw in you."[dccxcviii] (emphasis added) Your heart has no flaw. Your personality has no flaw. Your figure has no flaw. You don't need to try to fit perfection when you are already shaped

perfectly. Lies will start to fall around you when you start to believe the beauty of God lives within you. You are dangerous, and the enemy knows that. That's why he tells you that you're not enough; but as you write God's scripture on your heart, (Psalm 119:11) you begin to know fully the truth that He is enough, and because He lives within you, you're incredibly more than enough in Him. As Charlotte Gambill said, "A creator doesn't create something wondering what it's for; you have a purpose."[dccxcix]

346

HIS VICTORY

Inspired by Ephesians 5:22-27 and Proverbs 31

She rests in beauty
And walks in strength
All the days of her life written
Every single step paved
She is hidden in His image
And seeks His heart
Life flows from within her
His peace is her guard
She embraces in grace
And loves the weak
She comforts the broken
Listens more than speaks
She defines beauty
Treasures don't compare
There's none like her
She is rare
She is clothed with strength and dignity
And laughs without fear
She is bold and resilient
A safe place for those near
Her heart remains beautiful
Her love remains pure
Her life ever powerful
Her future secure
She rises when darkness falls
She stands when fears arise
She falls when destiny calls
And looks to God at all times
She is the pride of His heart
The very Bride of the King
His victory is her alone
For His crowning glory is she

347

I LOVE YOU

Have you ever heard those awkward stories where the guy tells the girl, "I love you." And then the girl, by surprise, says, "Thank you." I keep wondering how many times we do the same to Jesus? As He continually tells us, "I love you." And we are just like, "Thanks! Glad you do." Instead of saying back, "I love you too." Because I think how we react to Jesus' words is a mirror of how we view our relationship with Him. It shouldn't be a one-sided receiving relationship; it should be loving on both ends. That's what I've discovered the healthiest relationships to be like, reciprocal. So here's a little thought to leave you with today: How is your life answering God's "I love you"?

> *Love the Lord your God with all your heart and with all your soul and with all your mind and with all your strength.*[dcc]
> Mark 12:30

348

"MIRROR, MIRROR"

A year passed away, and the King took another wife... She possessed a wonderful mirror which could answer her when she stood before it and said, "Mirror, mirror on the wall, Who is the fairest of them all?" The mirror answered- "Thou, O Queen, art the fairest of all," and the Queen was contented, because she knew the mirror could speak nothing but the truth.[dccci]

Now, I know that in Snow White, the Queen is asking this to be reassured of her beauty. But I also believe we ask the mirror this same question when we are looking for "the one whom we will marry." *Who is the fairest of them all?* Growing up, I have heard from many women to make a list of what we would like to see in our spouse, and to then never settle for less. At the end of their statement, they would conclude with: "My husband is everything that was on my list." As a girl who watched both Disney love stories and Titanic romances her entire life, my expectations went skyrocketing! And so the list began. Yet, that list didn't keep time standing still, instead, it almost stilled my heart from who God wanted *me* to be. Instead of looking in the mirror for my beauty, I was looking through it for the beauty I sought. Yet, what if instead of just making a list of what we want our *someday spouse* to be for us, we also made a list of what we want to be for God?

As a teenager, I read a blog that changed my perspective on this "list." She wrote: "I lived like I was waiting for something. I just didn't want to wait anymore—didn't want to live like I was waiting on anyone to get here. I already have Him ... and He is everything."[dcccii]

When we use "the list," not as a mirror, but a magnifying glass, we wait, stand still, and forget to "live." We set all of these expectations on a significant other to see if they are "the fairest of them all." Seeing not who they are, but who we want them to be. Even more so, we don't need to keep waiting for our "fairest of them all" to arrive, because we already have Him. Proverbs 27:19 reads, "As water reflects a face, so a man's heart reflects the man."[dcccii] In other words, a man's heart "mirrors" his identity, as our hearts mirror our identity. The very mirror we should ask these questions to is God's Word. My friend once said: "Don't let a day go by where you spend more time looking into a mirror than into your Bible." As we read the Word and allow our hearts to reflect on its beauty, we start to become more like Him.

2 Corinthians 3:16-18 says, "But whenever someone turns to the Lord, the veil is taken away. For the Lord is the Spirit, and wherever the Spirit of the Lord is, there is freedom. So all of us who have had that veil removed can see and reflect the glory of the Lord. And the Lord—who is the Spirit—makes us more and more like him as we are changed into his glorious image."[dccciv] He is the mirror where we find contentment in His beauty for His Word is the mirror that only speaks truth. He is the very source of beauty that we seek, discover, and desire. And so, we should make a list for **ourselves** to be the "fairest" we can be as a child of God. But what I hope for us to realize, most of all, is that we already have "the fairest of them all," and He is even far more beautiful than we were hoping.

349

DEFEND THE DESTINED

Have you ever had the inkling that... I don't know... you're destined for something greater than where you are at? That there's something bigger than you before you? That maybe, just maybe, you have a purpose? Maybe the thought has crossed your mind once or twice, but in the mundane days, you really never knew why or when or what this unshakable feeling was for. But this purpose didn't begin within you the moment you accepted Jesus into you life; no, it was planned long before then. You just became aware of this purpose the moment you realized you were adopted into a royal priesthood, that you were no longer a slave to sin, but free in righteousness. Freedom opened up your eyes to see that there's so much more for you. God knows that, He always has. But here's the thing, the enemy does too. The enemy knew the day you were born that you were destined for greatness, and he's done everything in his power to keep you unaware and distant from it. But I'm so glad that God, on the other hand, is never distant to us. He is always near, and He is always fighting for us. Can I encourage you to do something? Stop reading and grab a pen and just listen for a second. Ask God to speak to your heart three words He thinks about you. It may be three phrases even, but write them here: _____, _____, _____

Now let me ask you, have these three words been the very parts of your heart that have been being attacked? In fact, you were feeling the exact opposite from these three words. However, these three words are some of the greatest strengths to who you are: they're your light, your radiance, your glimmer of Jesus to others; and the enemy wants to snatch those truths away, because he is jealous of them. But there's a purpose to knowing you have a purpose, and it's not discovered in disbelief or by backing down. No, you are destined, and deep down, you've always known it. It was what you were created for! I don't believe God reveals our destinies in advance for just any reason; I believe He whispers so we can defend that which we have been destined for. This knowledge and confidence gives us an advance against the enemy by armoring our hearts with the words of His faithful promises over us. The enemy is set out to defeat you before you reach your destiny, but as long as you cling to this hope for which you have been called, he won't stand a chance against you. Psalm 91:4 says: "He will cover you with his feathers. He will shelter you with his wings. His faithful promises are your armor and protection."[dcccv] There is power in knowing you are destined for a purpose, and that sends the enemy shuttering in fear. When you wake up, he shakes in terror; when you pray, he runs, and when you rise, darkness falls.

It is our divine duty to defend the destined. And yet, we don't have to only live on defense with what's been entrusted to us, but we can live on offense taking back what the enemy has stolen from us. As Psalm 45:3-5 says,

Put on your sword, o mighty warrior! You are so glorious! So majestic! In your majesty, ride out to victory defending truth, humility, and justice. Go forth to perform awe-inspiring deeds! Your arrows are sharp, piercing the enemies' hearts. The nations fall beneath your feet.[dcccvi]

So rise up, o warrior, defend that which you have been destined for and live every promise God has whispered into the recesses of your soul, for it is beyond you and it is great!

350

WHAT IF, NOT EVER?

There's a saying that's been knocking on my heart this week: *If not you, then who? If not now, then when?* Every time I hear its doorbell chime, a sense of urgency beats in my heart. That urgency resonates in my soul like a track on replay. Because I know it wasn't by accident something was delivered to my home, and I know that as soon as I turn the handle, I am opening my door to a miracle baby—one that needs a caretaker. A miracle baby that I will love passionately, yet will also require a lot of grace and patience in its timely endeavor to grow into its design. One that will not only require all that I am, but also require all that God is for its days to come. Because ready or not, this is the miracle you prayed for, and the moment you prayed for it is the moment your everything was about to change.

As quickly as our hearts are moved by what we see and hear, God is as quick to say yes to those who pray: "Send me." *For there is a world of orphaned miracles waiting to happen for those willing to act for their justice.* Why am I calling it a miracle baby, you may be wondering? Because babies take time and commitment. Sometimes we ask for them without knowing what we are asking for. They are more than a cute child to love; they also require lots of discipline and forgiveness, time and time again, for you and for them. This isn't to discourage you from praying openhearted prayers; it is to empower you to prepare for what you are declaring. As you say yes, God replies: "Here is my servant, whom I uphold, my *chosen* one in whom I delight; I will put my spirit on him and he will bring justice to the nations."[dcccvii] (Isaiah 42:1, emphasis added) It starts with a prayer and begins with turning a door handle to an answered urgency. If not you, then who? If not now, then when? Some of you have a voice, a gift of prophecy, an anointing to lead worship—don't stay silent. Some of you have means that you've never invested into the body of Christ with—use your blessing to be a blessing. Some of you have a wild, artistic ability—bring glory to God's name through it. We are called to glorify His name in all spheres of life.

Maybe it's best to stop pushing off the starting date and set a deadline, despite any unfortunate circumstances. The Lord doesn't need perfection, He just needs a willing heart; He doesn't need the practical to do the impossible either. A man once told me: "I was waiting and saving up money to marry my fiancé for three years. I wanted to have enough saved for us to marry on. Looking back, I would have married her sooner. We will always feel like we never have enough for the perfect life. I just wanted her, and now I know, that would've been enough." It's the same with our miracle babies. The sooner we say yes, the longer we can be with the promise we love. Do they require a lot? Yes. Will everything go perfectly? No. But they will be the greatest risk we say yes to and the greatest adventure we endeavor for. When it's what you love passionately, mountains are worth climbing and rivers are worth swimming through, for you know, love is what orchestrated it all together. The fire burning in your heart isn't by accident. It's a gift ready to be released, a voice ready to be heard, means ready to be used. Because if not now, then what if not ever? What endless possibilities and wonders await to ever unfold?

351

BE MORE

> *Do your best to present yourself to God as one approved, a worker who does not need to be ashamed and who correctly handles the word of truth.*[dcccviii]
> 2 Timothy 2:15

It is in the moments that we want to do the least that we are called to be more, in the moments we want to be human most, that we should be like God most. We have to push past our tired day, our hard situation, and our flesh screaming to do it another time. To be honest, most of our most powerful and unforgettable memories will come in the most uncomfortable moments and inconvenient times. Waiting will only become something to upkeep, while doing will become an expansion. We just have to *be more than human and less than God,* and step out so that He can step in. You don't have to be enough, just be more. As Sheila Walsh says: "We're not called to pursue perfection, we're called to pursue Christ, who is perfect."[dcccix] Being more isn't about being perfect, for He is our perfection; it's about being stronger through Him and for His sake by going a step further no matter the time, no matter the weight. Steve Penny puts it this way, "When you are called to represent the King of Heaven in the nations of the earth—be more!... We **never** eclipse the need to be more for Him. It's a lifelong endeavor, a wonderful journey that He takes with us."[dcccx] At the end of ourselves is when we are most like Christ. So be brave in being more, and you will experience the more He already has planned ahead of you.

352

YOU ARE WHAT YOU EAT

There is a little saying that I've heard since I was little, "Be careful little eyes what you see. Be careful little ears what you hear." But what has been on my heart lately is to *be careful little heart what you seek,* because where your heart is, there your treasure will be also (Luke 12:34). Sometimes we are looking for security, approval, or completeness; and these desires aren't bad, but we can easily go down the wrong road trying to fulfill them. When we see someone or something that looks promising to our desire, we can easily mold and shape our own selves to try to have these rocks to stand on. But the great news is that there is a Rock that pre-molded and pre-shaped our lives for us to constantly cling and hold onto. It's the Rock that endures any storm and the Rock we are made stronger on. It's the Rock that never moves. In the book of Nehemiah, the beautiful walls of Jerusalem are broken down, but it's here in the ruins that Nehemiah experiences God's favor so strongly on his life. By Nehemiah 2, he starts to take steps of boldness to rebuild the walls, and in verse 18, God places people around him to help him on the journey: "Let us rise up and build. So they strengthened their hands for the good work."[dcccxi] But before this we read that he had never been sad before the king, and yet this very day his desires were moved. *Likewise, when our desires are moved in our own lives, and we go before our Great King, He will place the right people around us where our walls have been broken down, to help us be rebuilt and restored back to wholeness.* And yet in the rebuilding of the walls, adversity came. However, like Psalm 31:24 says, "Be brave. Be strong. Do not give up,"[dcccxii] the men did not give up. Instead they either had guards or more powerful weapons to protect them as they continued to rebuild under God's favor. We are called to do the same.

A common health phrase is, "You are what you eat." And the same goes for your heart. Whether you are feeding your spirit or your flesh, one will guard you and the other will defeat you. There are times where you are going to be in the ruins of your life and it is there where you will hear the will of God the clearest. And He will place people around you who believe in you and lift you up, people who will pour life and love back into your heart, and people who will stand behind you encouraging you in your walk, but you also must rise up and guard your heart by where you seek security, approval, and completeness. Adversity will come and try to tear you down, and if you listen to your flesh and fear, you will fall. But if you feed your spirit by being cautious with what you allow into your heart and being bold in the face of adversity, you will be <u>restored.</u> He is the Rock of our salvation, and He is the protector of our hearts, but we too must keep vigilant watch over our own heart that we may fulfill the will of God for our lives. And it is there in the rebuilding of your brokenness that you will find a security, approval, and completeness in God that cannot be shaken.

> *You gave bread from heaven for their hunger,*
> *you sent water from the rock for their thirst.*
> *You told them to enter and take the land,*
> *which you promised to give them.*[dcccxiii]
> Nehemiah 9:15

353

BEING LOVING
BEING RIGHT

There's a point in life where you just have to lay down your fight, lay down your deepest insecurities, and face reality... through God's eyes. We have all experienced moments where people have done wrong to us, whether it's intentional or not, it still hurts. However, we are quick to point out the faults in others before we check the very own reflection of our hearts. In a world that builds up self-image so high, you'd think we'd see ourselves pretty clearly, but sometimes, our focus just needs to be readjusted. Instead of looking through our eyes, we need to start looking through His, for God can see what man can't. Man can only see appearance, when God sees the heart. So before you point fingers, let God point out to you what your eyes can't see but His can. *Being loving is always better than being right*, so be slow to speak, quick to listen and patient to understand. It's not about us, it's about Him; and if we make it about our image, then we start to cover up His image with our lives when it should be the other way around. When we fix our attention on His heart, we will see their hearts through His own, and they will be able to see His heart through us in return.

> *But the wisdom that comes from heaven is first of all pure; then peace-loving, considerate, submissive, full of mercy and good fruit, impartial and sincere. Peacemakers who sow in peace reap a harvest of righteousness.*[dcccxiv]
> James 3:17-18

354

FIT FOR THE KINGDOM

Have you ever heard: "They let themselves go." (Please see my heart in this.) Typically, it's said in the gap between the last time you saw a person to seeing them for the first time decades later. They may have gained weight, stopped trying to look perfect, or quit properly grooming themselves. I think all parents can relate that it's not as easy at it looks, but there's also the factor that our bodies naturally change with time. However, when it comes to being "fit," there is an effort we all can make in keeping our bodies healthy. Imagine the sweet grandparents who join walking groups, families who change to healthier diets, or young adults who discover the benefits of working out even thirty minutes a day. Each have little to do with time and more to do with priority. When it comes to being fit for the kingdom, it is so much the same.

In the beginning of relationships, there's so much emphasis on trying to impress one another. The girl dresses up a bit more, the guy buys flowers to surprise her. Then after the engagement, both start to get ready to look their finest for the big day: typically by working out and eating healthier. They prioritize wellness to be at their utmost beauty. Imagine you are the bride and Christ is the groom, and you have been in a relationship for quite some time, yet now that you have chosen one another fully, you want to look your best for the big day! 2 Thessalonians 1:5-8,11-12 says:

All this trouble is a clear sign that God has decided to make you fit for the kingdom. You're suffering now, but justice is on the way. When the Master Jesus appears out of heaven in a blaze of fire with his strong angels, he'll even up the score by settling accounts with those who gave you such a bad time. His coming will be the break we've been waiting for. Because we know that this extraordinary day is just ahead, we pray for you all the time—pray that our God will make you fit for what he's called you to be, pray that he'll fill your good ideas and acts of faith with his own energy so that it all amounts to something. If your life honors the name of Jesus, he will honor you. Grace is behind and through all of this, our God giving himself freely, the Master, Jesus Christ, giving himself freely.[dcccxv]

When becoming fit, you will feel the burn. Sacrifice will be required. No more sweets all the time, and healthier meals need to be chosen. In a relationship with Christ, it is choosing good over evil, being generous and not stingy, being forgiving and not holding grudges. The burn comes when facing things within us we typically like to hide. I have learned in facing temptations that it's not about the resistance but the conviction. When you know why you're remaining pure, love casts that struggle far away. It may come back, time to time, but keep choosing love and remembering the why over the law. Conviction sets the heart ablaze with power to withstand any evil, and the Word is a fortress in which you can hide and a sword you can mightily use!

All of this is not for nothing, it is for the one thing you've been waiting for. As weeks go by, you'll look in the mirror and see your skin glowing, your face slimming, your body becoming more toned, and you will see and feel radiant. Likewise, when looking in the mirror of the Word, you will see how freeing it is to live out the truth, and you'll start to love it! It may be difficult at first, but with time, you'll learn to love the feeling of being fit! As the church, the bride of Christ, we are called to constantly become fit for our big days ahead. They are the promises we have been praying and waiting for; they haven't been forgotten, they've actually been in preparation for us as we have been in preparation for them. Therefore, when we move in with the groom into a new "home," we will not move into a house of straw or a house of sticks, but a house of stone, built by the bricks of His Word that cannot be knocked down by the enemy. That when others see us years after we gave our lives to Christ, they won't see someone who resents the church, but one who walks radiantly in the promise, or beautifully towards the promise ahead! You're only becoming more fit for the kingdom with the more trials you face, and how much stronger, more beautiful, and more ready you will be when you enter its doors! He who promised is faithful and that which is promised is coming!

355

MORE THAN A FEELING

We have all heard that love is so much more than a feeling! That love is a commitment and a choice; it's a trust beyond sight and a hope in the midst of disbelief. I love the way this article describes love:

"Love is not just a feeling, it's not just about chemistry and connection; it's about what we do with that connection, how we honor it or whether we dishonor it. Two people can meet, be brought together in this crazy world, have all of the rush and intoxication of automatic or romantic love and infatuation—have all the external raw materials necessary—but if one or both of these people are not also genuinely loving people, then the relationship will sooner or later, and more likely sooner than later, go badly, fall apart, crash on the shore."[dcccxvi] 1 John 4:8 tells us that "God is love."[dcccxvii] And so we can reread this paragraph replacing the word "love" with "God," and it shows us a different perspective of our relationship with Him. "God is not just a feeling, it's not just about chemistry and connection; it's about what we do with that connection, how we honor Him or whether we dishonor Him." Love is great, and it feels good; but love is also honorable and valuable. Love is a way of expressing the worth you see in someone. It's not based on an emotion, but it is built on a commitment. We often overlook the fact that God is love and so He is also more than a feeling; and so when we don't feel him, we become confused, anxious, and often frustrated. But just because we can't feel Him doesn't mean He isn't real, because God is always with us. I believe that it is in the times that we can't feel Him that we truly

@rachellegrace_

show Him what His worth is to us: if His love is an emergency fund or if it is a lifetime investment; if His value is an impulse of desire or a treasure worth fighting for. When we truly love Him, it will be more than a rush or intoxication of feelings, it will be a genuine love that is worth giving up everything for. Genuine love is not just from the heart, but it is also expressed with the mind, soul, and strength. Because when all feelings are gone, the heart will still love, the mind will still believe, the soul will still worship, and the strength will still fight. He is more than a feeling—He is love.

> *I will praise the Lord no matter what happens. I will constantly speak of his glories and grace. I will boast of all his kindness to me. Let all who are discouraged take heart. Let us praise the Lord together and exalt his name.*[dcccxviii]
> Psalm 34:1-3

356

IDK

"I don't know." I'm not sure why these three words like to be foreign to my lips, yet, they seldom come. I know not knowing everything is, in fact, okay. Yet I still find myself scrambling to give an answer of any sort when asked a question. I'm not sure if I feel like it's my duty, but really there is much worth… and humility… in this one certain uncertainty. And maybe it's a journey worth taking to see its design. I have realized it's engraved in my DNA to find any answer when a teacher asks me a question. If I didn't know the answer to a question, my blank eyes and complete silence answered them first, but "idk" rarely came out of my mouth. I find it quite easy to do the same with faith. Faith with the unseen, the uncertain, the unimaginable— when questioned—we can be scrambling for answers, trying to speak up for something that honestly makes no sense. Yet when it comes to faith, hope, love… they can't be figured out like a Rubik's Cube, they'll always remain complex and indefinable. "Idk" sums up just that. Think of a caterpillar, for example: does it go into cits cocoon knowing how it's going to be transformed in the process? Does it try to find answers to give other caterpillars once transformed? I would say not very likely. It just soars as it was meant to. Yet, we as complex beings try to create an answer that is quite beyond ourselves, when the simplest, most profound, most stilling answer is, "I don't know." (smile)

In the hidden, we don't see much, we don't know much, and we can't explain much, but it is there we are transformed. *Typically, change takes the world by surprise.* Andrew Smith says: "People fear what they don't understand and hate what they can't conquer."[dcccxix] Yet if nothing ever changed, there would be no butterflies. The world can be afraid to dream beyond themselves, yet I believe, we who know God should be the greatest risk-takers in going after those God-sized dreams in our hearts, for it shouts to the world of His faithfulness.

There's just one thing, you must be okay with being hidden first. You must be okay with the "idk's," with still silences to what the world cannot grasp; for in the hidden, you are transformed, and there's really no explanation necessary in the process. Faith may know you're in a cocoon, it just probably doesn't know much beyond that—because it has to be all God. 2 Corinthians 3:18 says: "And we all, who with unveiled faces contemplate the Lord's glory, are being transformed into his image with ever-increasing glory, which comes from the Lord, who is the Spirit."[dcccxx] The MSG says: "becoming brighter and more beautiful as God enters our lives and we become like him."[dcccxxi] For in the hidden, miracles take place.

I love the idea of fairytales! The truth is that happily ever after tales do come true. Yet even fairytales have hidden seasons that set them up for the miracle's coming. *The reason fairytales don't always come true is not because we hope not, but because we wait not.* Within this world's feared unanswered questions, we step out of hiding with explanations to offer and forfeit the creativity of the Spirit within us. Some things won't be grasped to begin with or even to end with; "it just happened" may become your new "idk" if you'll wait just a little bit longer. Don't drown before you sink because you can't comprehend what God is doing. Be okay with the process and be patient with God. His timing is perfect and His Word is His Word. If God gave you a word to hold onto, don't let go. Hold onto His word like it's the only certainty you have. There's much worth and humility in trusting God with the design of how His Word will unfold. Yet when it does, know you'll be ready, for you'll be transformed, and what once was hidden in your heart, will be undeniably bright and beautiful for all to see. There really won't be an explanation, just maybe an, "Idk. It just happened." Paired with the famous answer: "Jesus."

357

HALLELUJAH

*Who can fathom a more beautiful King? Who can begin to comprehend His kindness to us? How He calls us beyond ourselves but pursues the deepest desires within us. No thing is left unseen. He reigns in **majesty** and **glory** and yet cares for [us]. He's above and beyond what knowledge can obtain. His hands move in grace; His heart flows of goodness and mercy. His ears always listen for beauty's restoration, His feet ready to run to any who come home. And yet, how holy and unblemished He remains. There are no flaws to His acts, no evil in His doings. His works are wonderful–and we are but one of them. Is there anyone who can catch up with His designs? Is there anyone who can touch the faintest of His miracles? Oh! There is <u>no one</u> like Him. There's no one more deserving of my heart, my all. May my life be an unending devotion to such an everlasting King, one whose scepter is always of grace. All I have left is but an utterance of hallelujah, for that's all I can think to say.*

"For God is great, and worth a thousand Hallelujahs."[dcccxxii]
Psalm 96:4

358

EMBRACED IN GRACE

Perfection: "the condition or state of being free or as free as possible from all flaws or defects."dcccxxiii This is what our society has learned to seek; but it is also what has blinded us all. Striving to be more than human is exhausting; striving more to be like God is life-changing. *There is a difference in trying to be perfect, and trying to be like the One who is perfection.* Because it doesn't become all about us, but all about Him. And I think that is what we all need to be reminded of—that perfection is not ours but His. Grace is "the free and unmerited favor of God, totally unexpected and totally undeserved."dcccxxiv You see, beauty is not being free from flaws; beauty is being free in grace! I think the only problem is that we see the disgrace we've been in, and therefore displace our hearts in seeking the wrong freedom. But Psalm 18 puts it this way,

@ kathleenmadethis

*In my distress, I called to the Lord; I cried to my God for help. From His temple he heard my voice; my cry came before him, into his ears. He reached down from on high and took hold of me; he drew me out of deep waters. He brought me out into a spacious place; he rescued me because he delighted in me.*dcccxxv

I could read that over and over, because the imagery is powerful and the message clear. We are embraced in grace and freedom *because* He delights in us. His love is unexpected and undeserved, and that makes it beautifully wild. His perfect love for us is one hundred percent grace. It's always been Him—**He** is our perfection.

359

BEAUTIFINEMENT

Dear reflection in the mirror: you had this sweet notion that one day you would grow into someone you had always wanted to be. Looking at the future, there was much wonder and possibility. But within the journey, you lost the light in your eyes for your passion. As you came to the mountaintop, you thought life would feel full. Instead you were left wondering where am I? Because this person looking back wasn't you. It looked a lot like you on the outside, but on the inside, there were a million lost pieces. You couldn't imagine how anyone could love someone who didn't love their own self. Yet somehow, God does. He is wild for your heart, and He's ready for all your million of pieces that came undone.

Gaining every want in life isn't worth much if you lose your heart for God. But no matter how far we run… no matter how long we've run….God wildly pursues us, and with us, those crazy dreams He stirred within us long ago. After all, He is the One who placed them there in the first place—the only thing that we may have forgotten on the chase is Who we were to keep first. As Matthew 6:33 says: "But seek first his kingdom and his righteousness, and all these things will be given to you as well."[dcccxxvi] You may be on a mountain wondering where to go from here, yet if you look hard enough, you'll see there's another mountain God is wanting to take you to. One greater than the one you imagined for yourself. But first, He wants to remind you of one thing, Himself. The more your thoughts remain fixed on yourself, the quicker your world shrinks. My advice, go after God with all your heart. God knew you would be here before you were even born, and He still chose you. It's okay to not like who you are at the moment, but never stop loving yourself. That's one of the enemy's sneakiest traps. Once you convince yourself out of love for yourself, it's harder for you to remember your love for God. To insult what God is doing within you is to have a distorted view of Who God is Himself as the Creator. But to love who you truly are, which can never change, is always the beginning of the process of beautifinement. (Yes, I did make that word up—*it's a lot like refinement but the emphasis is on the beauty throughout the process which leaves the fear/curiosity of change unnoticed.*)

Gold goes through a refining process more than once. A lot of the impurities come up the first time, and less will come up each time after, but the most toxic impurities are deep within the gold. The closer you draw to Jesus, the more the impurities come to surface, for you're in the process of being purified. It may not look like much to the eye, but impurities are far more deadly to the heart. *The deeper you go with Him, the greater the refining will be in Him.* Yet, you need not to be ashamed of what He may find because nothing escapes His sight. Jesus knew there would be a lot of beautifinement happening when He chose you. But He also knew He loved you more than anything and believed in you all the more. When He waits, He waits for a part of us to come to Him that we hardly know. It's in those still moments that we will see the best and the worst. But it is what will make or break our love for ourselves and our love for God. Here's the good news, you don't have to change yourself. Being with God changes who you are naturally, because He is good and His goodness rubs off on us. And here's another piece of encouragement—you can live your life fully, I can promise you this, based off the knowledge that He promises a hope and a future for you in Jeremiah 29. Trust Him in the beautifinement. If anything, you are as radiant now as ever.

> "You have tested us, O God; you have <u>purified us like silver.</u> You captured us in your net and laid the burden of slavery on our backs. Then you put a leader over us. We went through fire and flood, **but** you brought us to a place of *great abundance.* "[dcccxxvii] (emphasis added)
> Psalm 66:10-12

360

IN FEAR AND WONDER

You are a jewel, a treasure, a prize
There's no flaw hidden from My eyes
Before you came to be I knew your design
Made in fear and wonder, before and behind
I have placed within you a love so deep
But don't be fooled; don't be deceived
Your beauty was precisely made
From your greatest gifts to your DNA
These are a blessing, not a curse
They are rare, and they are yours
There's no one like you
I made it that way
Don't seek in comparison
You're all uniquely made
From your appearance, to your heart
I loved you wildly from the start
You hold My beauty that lies inside
Crafted with purpose and brought to life
I knew your every step and where each would land
I knew your story before time began
So trust in Me with all your heart, soul, and mind
For all I am is yours, as all you are is Mine

"Look with wonder at the depth of the Father's marvelous love that he has lavished on us! He has called us and made us his very own beloved children. The reason the world doesn't recognize who we are is that they didn't recognize him. Beloved, we are God's children right now; however, it is not yet apparent what we will become. But we do know that when it is finally made visible, we will be just like him, for we will see him as he truly is."[dcccxxviii]
1 John 3:1-2

361

REFINED

I watched a video recently of an artist molding and shaping a lump of clay. And I felt the greatest sense of love while watching her careful fingers be so precise and gentle, yet purposeful and in control. It left me in awe of wondering what had to be going through her mind while doing so. Did she already know what she was going to create? Will it be different from anything I've ever seen created? What details will she use? How long will it take? How many times will she restart to have the perfect masterpiece come together? Because obviously, I am used to seeing the coffee mugs, the flowerpots, the plates, and the other works of art when they're finished. But I never thought about all the thought of beauty in the process. I never thought about the refining.

We tend to see the finished look of the product, of the picture perfect life, not really giving a thought of the story behind its making or its creator. And like our lives, we only see so much of what God is doing, if anything. We typically live not truly knowing the process we are in of being refined or not really giving a second thought to the refining process it requires for the picture perfect life we seek. But coming from a woman who has finally realized, "God isn't finished yet," trust me when I say → there is a story behind your refining; its author is a flawless creator who is precisely and gently holding you in His hands at this moment with the most beautiful and outstanding design in mind.

The key to being joyful in the refining is this: you have to do nothing. Crazy, right? "But Kaytee, I need to fix things in my life in able to change." Yes. Change is a part of the refining. But that comes from God. So what is it that you are called to in the refining? To simply—**be**, and just that. To be moldable and not stuck in your ways. To be open to what He has to say. To be obedient with what He places before you or doesn't.

And to be His—knowing He is working out the smallest and greatest details of your heart to have the most outstanding finish. Romans 5:3-5 says,

There's more to come: We continue to shout our praise even when we're hemmed in with troubles, because we know how troubles can develop passionate patience in us, and how that patience in turn forges the tempered steel of virtue, keeping us alert for whatever God will do next. In alert expectancy such as this, we're never left feeling shortchanged. Quite the contrary—we can't round up enough containers to hold everything God generously pours into our lives through the Holy Spirit![dcccxxix]

These verses give me so much hope, and I hope stir the same hope within you. Likewise Psalm 139:5 says, "You hem me in—behind and before; you have laid your hand upon me."[dcccxxx] The same hand that is hemming us behind and before, orchestrating the details of our lives, is the same hand hemming us even through troubles with a promise in mind. That same artist who created us fearfully and wonderfully in Psalm 139:14, is the same artist who is purposefully shaping us now with a little bit of pressure and heat for refining. Sometimes one detail takes more precision than the others, but as Brian Houston once said, "God wastes nothing, but He weaves everything together for His glorious future."[dcccxxxi] It's in the refining that we see the Artist's heart, and in the finishing that we see His reflection. And like the gold that is described in Revelation 3:18, having been "through the refiner's fire," our value will come to surface in ways we never could have dreamed.

362

THE AROMA OF HEAVEN

Breathe. I imagine a counselor saying this to still my mind and calm my heart. Yet when God speaks breathe, I imagine Him referring to something more than taking a deep breath, but rather to taking in the scent of the aroma of heaven. I imagine smelling the sweet fragrance of His presence. I imagine us smelling the aroma of something new and fresh, like pine trees, newly cut grass, or gardens of roses. I picture a place of peace, whatever that is for each of us, we catch a whiff of it when we breathe, and are then reminded of His home. Judith Lawrence writes: "The sense of smell has the power to transport us to another time and place, in this case to the spiritual house of God."[dcccxxxii]

@ kathleenmadethis

2 Corinthians 2:15 says: "We have become the unmistakable aroma *of the victory* of the Anointed One to God—a perfume of life to those being saved and the odor of death to those who are perishing."[dcccxxxiii] I have a theory that as we smell the aromas of heaven, we become a fragrance of heaven to the world around us. Like after we leave a bonfire with the fragrance of smoke, we go to the heavenly courts and leave with the fragrance of Love. It is this sort of fragrance that makes unbelievers sense there is a God who exists. As John 12:3 talks about the woman who poured out her alabaster jar of perfume upon the feet of Jesus, it states: "And the fragrance of the **costly** oil filled the house."[dcccxxxiv] (emphasis added) Some sense the love of Christ through the acts of kindness we go out of our way to do for them. 2 Corinthians 2:14 says, "God always makes his grace visible in Christ, who includes us as partners of his endless triumph. Through our yielded lives he spreads the fragrance of the **knowledge of God** everywhere we go."[dcccxxxv] (emphasis added) There is also a sweet fragrance to the knowledge of God that we overflow because of His grace. What we see as a palace garden others may see as a maze, yet we who know the paths are able to show guests the way towards meeting the King Himself! Furthermore, Ephesians 5:2 states: "His great love for us was pleasing to God, like an aroma of adoration—**a sweet healing fragrance**."[dcccxxxvi] (emphasis added) His great love brings an aroma of hope to those who need healing. We are able to lift them up in prayer, lay hands on the sick, and believe for

miracles! Lastly, Song of Songs 4:11 reads: "Your loving words are like the honeycomb to me; your tongue releases milk and honey, *for I find the Promised Land flowing within you*. The **fragrance of your worshiping love** surrounds you with scented robes of white."[dcccxxxvii] (emphasis added) When we lift up our praise to God, our worship becomes the robes we enter the palace in. That sense of heaven we seek around us dwells in our hearts when we praise Him! I leave you with Song of Songs 2:13:

Can you not discern this new day of destiny breaking forth around you? The early signs of my purposes and plans are bursting forth. The budding vines of new life are now blooming everywhere. The fragrance of their flowers whispers, 'There is change in the air.' Arise, my love, my beautiful companion, and run with me to the higher place. For now is the time to arise and come away with me.[dcccxxxviii]

Can you smell it in the air? The fresh aroma of heaven stirring in the atmosphere? The fragrance of the flowers whispering, "There is CHANGE in the air!" Breathe in its sweet aroma, the aroma of heaven, and walk into His heavenly courts with scented robes of white.

363

IN YOU

Reading:
Here's what I want you to do: Find a quiet, secluded place so you won't be tempted to role-play before God. Just be there as simply and honestly as you can manage. The focus will shift from you to God, and you will begin to sense his grace… With a God like this loving you, you can pray very simply. Like this: Our Father in heaven, Reveal who you are. Set the world right; Do what's best— as above, so below. Keep us alive with three square meals. Keep us forgiven with you and forgiving others. Keep us safe from ourselves and the Devil. You're in charge! You can do anything you want! You're ablaze in beauty! Yes. Yes. Yes.[dcccxxxix]
Matthew 6:6, 8-13

Prayer:
God, I'm going to trust in Your ways when I can't see my own.
I'll trust in the timing of Your steps.
I'll trust in you with the rhythms of love,
As I keep my heart open to Your will.
I will learn to give You my pain and share with You my joy.
Even when I don't understand, even when it seems I can't stand any longer,
I will turn my eyes to You, to trust in what You know.
As You created this world day-by-day, so You are doing a work in my days.
I'll forever look to You as my compass; Your heart being my direction.
I will learn to accept what I cannot help, and give to You what I cannot see.
Humble me to walk in Your ways and lay my life down for Your own.
I pray for patience to wait for what is right and courage to fight for it.
When I am not sure of what You are doing, I will trust in who You are.
For You are my very breath, my very peace;
The portion of my heart that I wish to pour out,
And the love of my life I choose to confide in forever.

364

PUTTING HIS GARDEN TO BED

There are a few things I have learned to love recently: one, going on walks—it allows my creativity to wander to far, far off lands; and two, surprises of any kind—in a way, it reminds me that I am thought of and cared for. Today, I experienced both of them. As I went on a walk around my hometown park, I looked to the left and saw this cute little library post. Not like a library store, but almost like a library birdhouse, grounded right along its winding path. I was so surprised! There weren't many books, but there was one in particular that caught my eye. I opened its glass door, reached into its mystery, and pulled out a blue book about gardening. I'm not a gardener of any sort, but God speaks a lot to me through metaphors of gardens, so I opened the book, hoping a whisper would meet my heart, and it did. The title of Chapter 13 read: "Putting Your Garden To Bed." As I flipped through its pages, I astonishingly discovered that the greatest attention, given unto the garden, begun when the growing season was over! In fact, it was at the end of the season, in the winter's rest, that all was set in place to thrive for its next future harvest. Thus, when the garden awoke, it'd be surprisingly ready to grow again! Now let me decode: When a season is coming to an end, a shift starts to take place in the atmosphere. Because of the change in temperature, sunlight hours, and maybe even rainfall, the harvest may feel like it's coming to a close. So here we are, a garden God has been cultivating, with everything going perfectly! Yet all of a sudden, the season is ending, and it wasn't the harvest you were expecting. The good news is that even though the season is ending, God hasn't stopped gardening, because this is actually when he pays most attention to what He's doing in you. When it feels like your season is coming to a close, know an awakening for this next season is being prepared within you.

After my walk, I did a flick-and-pick in my Bible where it fell open to John 16 titled with two sections: "The Friend Will Come" and "Joy Like a River Overflowing." Here, Jesus starts to explain to the disciples that He's about to leave. He says in verses 4-7, 12: *I didn't tell you this earlier because I was with you every day. But now I am on my way to the One who sent me. Not one of you has asked, "Where are you going?" Instead, the longer I've talked, the sadder you've become. So let me say it again, this truth: It's better for you that I leave. If I don't leave, the Friend won't come. But if I go, I'll send him to you. I still have many things to tell you, but you can't handle them now. But when the Friend comes, the Spirit of the Truth, he will take you by the hand and guide you into all the truth there is.*[dcccxl] The disciples are having their "end of season" talk, where they've been walking with Jesus, seeing wonders, performing miracles, and still expecting more to take place, but when their trusted friend, who has been with them through the highs and the lows, says He is leaving, they have no words. If they knew what He was saying, they would have been praised Him then, but because they couldn't imagine it, sadness overcame their hearts. But I love how in verses 20-23 Jesus says: *You'll be sad, very sad, but your sadness will develop into gladness. When a woman gives birth, she has a hard time, there's no getting around it. But when the baby is born, there is joy in the birth. This new life in the world wipes out memory of the pain. The sadness you have right now is similar to that pain, but the coming joy is also similar. When I see you again, you'll be full of joy, and it will be a joy no one can rob from you. You'll no longer be so full of questions.*[dcccxli] When it comes to God putting His garden to bed, or you, His garden, simply transitioning into a season of rest, know that what will awaken within you will be joy, like a river overflowing. There's a joy in this new season that will wipe away the sadness of the temporary birth pain. It will be a joy that can never be robbed! The Friend is here and now, caring for you in your season of rest, preparing you for what's ahead, and preparing ahead what's for you. Though you can't imagine it, it doesn't mean He isn't worth praising now, for if you knew the depth behind His words, you'd be overjoyed at what is coming. Rest away, for God is creating while He's tucking your heart to bed, and when you awaken, you may just be surprised about how refreshed you are for this next season's beauty.

365

ADVENTURE ON

> *And as He spoke, He no longer looked to them like a lion; but the things that began to happen after that were so great and beautiful that I cannot write them. And for us this is the end of all the stories, and we can most truly say that they all lived happily ever after. But for them it was only the beginning of the real story. All their life in this world and all their adventures in Narnia had only been the cover and the title page: now at last they were beginning Chapter One of the Great Story which no one on earth has ever read: which goes on for ever: in which every chapter is better than the one before.*[dcccxlii]
> - C. S. Lewis

8:00 A.M. hits and the day must begin. The last drum hit is made and the conference explodes to a close. The last melody is sung and the worship night is greeted again by life's traffic. In reading every scripture, in knowing every story, in expanding on the generational heroes on repeat, there is always more to discover. No matter how closely we look, there's always a larger magnifying glass to draw closer to the Word and closer to the Creator; to see something we've never noticed before in another creative, magical, and even simpler way. It is the diversity of seasons mixed with the diversity of people and the complexity of life that makes the tune of each verse sweeter to the place we're in. Like hot chocolate by a fire in winter, lemonade on a sunny day, or sweet medicine to the sick... it's the same Word, but we change, life changes, and that makes it ever the more beautiful adventure. Shall we delve into the mystery it has to offer daily, we will build kingdoms with the treasures we find. In coming out of Narnia, the sweet place where chains were broken, hearts renewed, and lives abandoned—adventure awaits! Our next step will be forward and not backwards, towards the greater ahead, leaving the familiar behind. We must pack our bags with the fruits it offered, the water it supplied, and the bread it gave to sustain us for the journey ahead, and adventure on into the wild life that waits for us. Some of us may just be beginning our hike through the desert, others of us may be continuing through the maze of the wilderness, but for some, they will experience the rich reward to the persistent warrior's finish, as they take their next steps into their dearly beloved promised land. We all may be in different seasons, but we all have endless adventures into the unknown before us.

With each morning, prior to life's awakening, pack your bags for the reality that awaits. Life isn't always easy, but His Word is sweet, and it is a great fruit to grab when the world starts to look a little bitter. At the end of the Conference, where breakthroughs took place, and God's presence was as real as the atmosphere around you, simply don't forget. Take the source of life with you through the desert; when you start to feel faint, remember and ponder how faithful He was, knowing He is still the same, and keep going. When the worship song fades, and your heart is at peace, let it be bread that multiplies into your next season. Let that sense of Him overflow from your heart to those around you, that Eden will not only reside in your heart, but also become a reality to those placed in your world. Promising and commanding in the same breath, Jesus leaves His disciples with these final words, for He would not physically be crossing over into their next chapters with them:

All the authority of the universe has been given to me. Now go in my authority and make disciples of all nations, baptizing them in the name of the Father, the Son, and the Holy Spirit. And teach them to faithfully follow all that I have commanded you. And never forget that I am with you every day, even to the completion of this age.^{dcccxliii} (Matthew 28:18-20)

One Greek manuscript reads: "As My Father has sent me, so I send you." And in verse 20, the Aramaic reads: to "keep" or "guard," a fortress. Therefore, keep and guard the authority that lives within you as you trek into this next chapter.

As you walk into this next season, you will live most fully when you remember Narnia, yet adventure on. Not trying to remake the exact same life you've left behind, but to instead plant the seeds from the Narnian fruit in the new world around you. As you do, you will begin to see God, not as the lion you once knew, but in the small acts of love around you that could only be from and by Him. There's always more of Him—in His Word, through His people around you, within His pursuit of your heart, you need only look with new eyes. *The older you become, the more you will know coincidence to be Christ.* Those coincidences will be surprises to your heart that you may know He is still with you, even if you don't see him as a lion. They will spur you on as much as a great power preacher could. You may not have an atmosphere of worship surrounding you in your every step, yet laughter, love, joy, and peace create the same sense of freedom and ease that lift life's pressures off of your fragile heart into His mighty arms. Not every morning will be long enough, or may be a morning at all, but the smallest verse, the tiniest bit of bread taken, can multiply to those around you still. So always pack your bags with what you have. It will go much further than what you're expecting. As 2 Timothy 1:12-14 says: "The confidence of my calling enables me to overcome every difficulty without shame, for I have an intimate revelation of this God. And my faith in him convinces me that he is more than able to keep all that I've placed in his hands safe and secure until the fullness of his appearing. Allow the healing words you've heard from me to live in you and make them a model for life as your faith and love for the Anointed One *grows even more*. Guard well this incomparable treasure by the Spirit of Holiness living within you."^{dcccxliv} (emphasis added) Like a fortress, guard the treasures of promise, of peace, of life, carry them with you, and create kingdoms out of their beauty! Give generously to the poor in spirit around you out of the abundance God has built within you, for there's always more ahead of you for you to find from Him. Then you will live a full life and a great story, one which no one on earth has ever read: which goes on forever: in which *every* chapter is better than the one before.

@bulgerjoseph

What a Day that will be! No more cold nights—in fact, no more nights! The Day is coming—the timing is God's— when it will be continuous day. Every evening will be a fresh morning. What a Day that will be! Fresh flowing rivers out of Jerusalem, half to the eastern sea, half to the western sea, flowing year-round, summer and winter! God will be king over all the earth, one God and only one. What a Day that will be!^{dcccxlv}
Zechariah 14:6-9

ACKNOWLEDGMENTS

I hold so much love and adoration for my family who has believed in me since day one. Thank you for sending me across the world multiple times to learn, explore, be broken and mended. To find and capture who I am, and in the midst of this, to discover the love of God even more intimately.

To my mother, Ann Parker, thank you for igniting my fire in more ways than I can describe. I wouldn't be who or where I am without you. To my father, Darril Parker, thank you for releasing me to chase impossible dreams. To Jim Miller, and Cathy and Scott Dittman, thank you for empowering me by your blessings and love multiplied. To Daniel Mitchell and Crystal Koch, thank you for being my warriors.

To my friends, pastors, teachers and mentors, to whom I call my extended family, you are the gold found within these pages. Without you, I would have never reached for the out of the reach, or found the treasure troves within my fields. I owe you all my gratitude, for you gave me true courage through your belief.

To my artists, this vision would not have been possible without your art designed upon its space. Thank you for saying yes, for sharing your bravery upon white-open-pages. I know they will speak their own worth and enhance my own words. You are all brilliant stars in my eyes.

To my dear, Sophia Bustos, thank you for all of the beauty, precision, and care you put into editing this book in order to bring its story to completion. To climb up this victory-mountain with you has been everything magical!

To Wes Selwood, thank you for believing in me. I will never forget the words you spoke after I shared my heart behind *Closer* with you. "No matter what, we are going to get this book on a shelf." Your "no matter what" mattered so much to me. Thank you for being a catalyst to this dream's beginning.

To Jürgen Oschadleus, thank you for being the extra encouragement I needed to reach the finish line. I am grateful for the generosity of your time and insight, which sparked hope within my midnight hour.

To Sarah Ko, thank you for your selfless, courageous heart, that found my pieces and brought peace to their scattered shapes. Without you, this puzzle could not have been completed without your eye for divine designs and your courageous heart to reap gold.

To Darren Thomas, thank you for your kind heart, which sealed this dream from heaven to earth. Truly, a simple word can go so much further than we could ever image.

Lastly, thank you God, for entrusting me with such a wild and precious beauty to share.

The Artists:
*Rachelle Castro // @rachellegrace_*
Katie Hall // @k15_nicole
Kathleen Travers // @kathleenmadethis
Joseph Bulger// @ bulgerjoseph
Sarah Graves// @sarahbgraves
Abbi Beckett// @abbibeckett
Ashtyne Standage// @ashtynekole
Aimee Whitmire // @aimeewhitm

BIBLE TRANSLATIONS CITED

Scripture quotations are from the following sources:

THE AMPLIFIED BIBLE: OLD TESTAMENT (AMP) © 1962, 1964 by Zondervan (used by permission); and from THE AMPLIFIED BIBLE: NEW TESTAMENT (AMP). ©1958 by the Lockman Foundation (used by permission). *The Message* (MSG). by Eugene H. Peterson. © 1993, 1994, 1995, 1996, 2000, 2001, 2002. Used by permission of Tyndale House Publishers, Inc. The Holy Bible, New International Version®, NIV®. Copyright© 1973, 1978, 1984, 2011 by Biblica, Inc.™ Used by permission of Zondervan. All rights reserved worldwide. www.Zondervan.com. Holy Bible, New Living Translation (NLT). ©1996,2004,2007,2013 by Tyndale House Foundation. Used by permission of Tyndale House Publishers, Inc., Carol Stream, Illinois 60188. All rights reserved. The ESV® Bible (The Holy Bible, English Standard Version®). Copyright © 2001 by Crossway, a publishing ministry of Good News Publishers. Used by permission. All rights reserved. Scripture quotations marked TPT are from The Passion Translation®. Copyright © 2017, 2018 by Passion & Fire Ministries, Inc. Used by permission. All rights reserved. ThePassion-Translation.com. Scripture quotations taken from the (NASB®) New American Standard Bible®, Copyright © 1960, 1971, 1977, 1995, 2020 by The Lockman Foundation. Used by permission. All rights reserved. www.lockman.org. World English Bible (WEB). Public domain. The NEW AMERICAN STANDARD BIBLE® (NASB), © The Lockman Foundation 1960, 1962, 1963, 1968, 1971, 1972, 1973, 1975, 1977, 1995. Used by permission. All rights reserved. Scripture quotations marked (TLB) are taken from The Living Bible copyright © 1971. Used by permission of Tyndale House Publishers, Carol Stream, Illinois 60188. All rights reserved. Scriptures taken from the Holy Bible, New International Reader's Version®, NIrV® Copyright © 1995, 1996, 1998, 2014 by Biblica, Inc.™ Used by permission of Zondervan. www.zondervan.com The "NIrV" and "New International Reader's Version" are trademarks registered in the United States Patent and Trademark Office by Biblica, Inc.™ King James Version of the Bible (KJV). Public domain. THE NEW KING JAMES VERSION (NKJV). © 1982 by Thomas Nelson, Inc. Used by permission. Scripture texts in this work are taken from the New American Bible, revised edition © 2010, 1991, 1986, 1970 Confraternity of Christian Doctrine, Washington, D.C. and are used by permission of the copyright owner. All Rights Reserved. No part of the New American Bible may be reproduced in any form without permission in writing from the copyright owner. The Holy Bible, Berean Study Bible, BSB. Copyright© 2016, 2018 by Bible Hub. Used by Permission. All rights reserved worldwide. Scripture taken from The Voice™. Copyright © 2012 by Ecclesia Bible Society. Used by permission. All rights reserved.

NOTES

i   J. Oswald Sanders, quoted by CS Lewis Institute, *Four Circles of Intimacy With God* (Springfield: CS Lewis Institute, 2006), 1.
ii James 4:8 NLT
iii 2 Peter 1:3-8 NIV
iv Francis Chan, quoted in Brian Dodd, "26 Leadership Lessons And Quotes From Francis Chan," Brian Dodd On Leadership, February 15, 2014, https://briandoddonleadership.com/2014/02/15/26-leadership-lessons-and-quotes-from-francis-chan-passion-2014/ (accessed November 25, 2018).
v   J. Oswald Sanders, quoted by CS Lewis Institute, *Four Circles of Intimacy With God* (Springfield: CS Lewis Institute, 2006), 1.
vi Psalm 36:5-6 MSG
vii Proverbs 25:3 MSG
viii H. D. M. Spence-Jones; Joseph S Exell; Edward Mark Deems, *The Pulpit Commentary*. (Grand Rapids: Wm. B. Eerdmans Pub. Co., 1950).
ix Isaiah 7:4 NIV
x   Matthew 19:17 NIV
xi Dias, Ron, and Bill Lorencz. 1999. Walt Disney's Cinderella. New York, N.Y.: Golden Books Pub. Co.
xii Isaiah 51:11 NLT
xiii Jeremiah 31:2-6,22 MSG
xiv A quote by Helen Keller. (n.d.). Retrieved August 27, 2020, from https://www.goodreads.com/quotes/508624-it-is-a-terrible-thing-to-see-and-have-no
xv Proverbs 29:18 KJV
xvi Mark Batterson, *The Circle Maker,* (Grand Rapids: Zondervan 2011), p 180.
xvii John 15:5 NIV
xviii Leviticus 19:30 NLT
xix Kerri Weems, "God's Metronome," published August 18, 2017, https://www.faithgateway.com/sabbath-gods-metronome/#.XDQPos8zaRs.
xx Isaiah 58:13 NIV
xxi Ezekiel 20:12 NLT
xxii Revelation 1:8 NLT
xxiii Psalm 85:8-13 TPT
xxiv "Extravagant," Dictionary.com, accessed December 9, 2017, https://www.dictionary.com/browse/extravagantly.
xxv "Lise Friedman," GoodReads, accessed December 9, 2017, https://www.goodreads.com/quotes/435529-claire-dear-claire-what-and-if-are-two-words-as.
xxvi Joshua 3:5 NIV
xxvii G. W. (Director). (2010). *Letters to Juliet* [Motion picture on DVD]. United States: Sony.
xxviii Jeremiah 31:22 MSG
xxix Song of Songs 4:8 MSG
xxx Luke 12:34 NIV
xxxi Luke 12:34 TPT
xxxii "adventure." *Merriam-Webster.com*. 2013. https://www.merriam-webster.com (8 March 2013).
xxxiii 1 Corinthians 2:9 TPT
xxxiv Matthew 10:31 NIV
xxxv Philippians 4:12 NIV
xxxvi Judges 6:6 NIV
xxxvii Judges 6:12 NIV

xxxviii	Ibid.
xxxix	"Elisabeth Elliot Quotes," AZQuotes, accessed December 18, 2017, https://www.azquotes.com/quote/1366392.
xl	Isaiah 61:1&3 NIV
xli	"Fire," TheFreeDictionary, accessed December 4, 2017, https://www.thefreedictionary.com/fire.
xlii	Nehemiah 9:38 NIV
xliii	Haggai 2:5-9, 23 VOICE
xliv	English, M. (2019, July 19). 12 Facts Every Peony Enthusiast Needs to Know. Retrieved August 27, 2020, from https://www.townandcountrymag.com/leisure/arts-and-culture/news/g1236/12-peony-facts/
xlv	Isaiah 43:19 ESV
xlvi	Hebrews 10:23 NIV
xlvii	Proverbs 27:17 NIV
xlviii	Judges 16:20 NIV
xlix	Psalm 23 NIV
l	Zechariah 4:6 NIV
li	Jeremiah 29:11 NIV
lii	"Bernard M. Baruch Quote,"Goodreads, accessed September 3, 2015, https://www.goodreads.com/quotes/865-be-who-you-are-and-say-what-you-feel-because.
liii	Jonah 3:2 NLT
liv	sticks and stones may break my bones, but words will never hurt me. (n.d.) *McGraw-Hill Dictionary of American Idioms and Phrasal Verbs*. (2002). Retrieved September 21 2020 from https://idioms.thefreedictionary.com/sticks+and+stones+may+break+my+bones%2c+but+words+will+never+hurt+me
lv	Genesis 1:26-27 NIV
lvi	"Rudyard Kipling Quotes," GoodReads, accessed May 1, 2014, https://www.goodreads.com/quotes/1144205-i-am-by-nature-a-dealer-in-words-and-words.
lvii	Proverbs 18:21 MSG
lviii	Ezekiel 37:9-10 NIV
lix	Ezekiel 37:14 MSG
lx	"Voyage," OxfordDictionaries, accessed March 22, 2016, https://en.oxforddictionaries.com/definition/voyage.
lxi	"voyage." *Merriam-Webster.com*. 2018. https://www.merriam-webster.com (9 July 2018).
lxii	Genesis 15:5 NIV (emphasis added)
lxiii	Isaiah 43:19 NIV
lxiv	"Marcel Proust Quotes ," BrainyQuote, accessed July 9, 2018, https://www.brainyquote.com/quotes/marcel_proust_107111.
lxv	Nehemiah 8:10 NIV
lxvi	"Kintsugi," Pinterest, published January 13, 2014, https://www.pinterest.com.au/pin/567946202990252464/.
lxvii	"Imperfection," Dictionary, accessed December 13, 2018, https://en.oxforddictionaries.com/definition/imperfection.
lxviii	"Work In Progress,"Google, accessed December 13, 2018, https://www.google.com.au/search?q=Dictionary#dobs=work%20in%20progress.
lxix	Exodus 31:3-5 NASB
lxx	"What are some interesting facts about gold?" Quora, published June 24, 2017, https://www.quora.com/What-are-some-interesting-facts-about-gold-1.
lxxi	John 6:8-13 NASB emphasis added
lxxii	Isaiah 58:11-12 MSG
lxxiii	"Passages," BryantMcGill, accessed December 13, 2018, https://bryantmcgill.com/passages/beautiful-carry-distinctions-thing-damaged-beauty/.
lxxiv	Philippians 3:12-14 NLT

lxxv	Romans 12:2 NIV
lxxvi	Hosea 2:14 NIV (emphasis added)
lxxvii	Ephesians 6:10-18 NIV
lxxviii	2 Corinthians 3:18 NIV (emphasis added)
lxxix	Psalm 100:5 TPT
lxxx	Isaiah 40:31 NLT
lxxxi	"J.R.R. Tolkien Quotes," GoodReads, accessed June 11, 2014, https://www.goodreads.com/quotes/229-all-that-is-gold-does-not-glitter-not-all-those.
lxxxii	Hosea 2 NIV
lxxxiii	Ibid.
lxxxiv	"J.R.R. Tolkien Quotes," GoodReads, accessed June 11, 2014, https://www.goodreads.com/quotes/229-all-that-is-gold-does-not-glitter-not-all-those.
lxxxv	"Oswald Chamber Quotes," GoodReads, accessed January 1, 2018, https://www.goodreads.com/author/quotes/41469.Oswald_Chambers?page=26
lxxxvi	Psalm 139:16 NLT
lxxxvii	Hamlet, Act III, Scene I [To be, or not to be] by William Shakespeare -Poems | Academy of American Poets. (n.d.). Retrieved September 21, 2020, from https://poets.org/poem/hamlet-act-iii-scene-i-be-or-not-be
lxxxviii	"Jim Elliot Quotes," GoodReads, accessed September 21, 2020, https://www.goodreads.com/quotes/12747-wherever-you-are-be-all-there-live-to-the-hilt
lxxxix	"Be," Dictionary.com, accessed September 22, 2015, https://www.dictionary.com/browse/be.
xc	Acts 17:28 NIV
xci	Psalm 16:6 NIV
xcii	Psalm 37:23-24 NLT
xciii	"Ruwa," BibleTools, accessed June 25, 2016, https://www.bibletools.org/index.cfm/fuseaction/Lexicon.show/ID/H7321/ruwa%60.htm.
xciv	Psalm 145:3 MSG
xcv	"Radicle," Wikipedia, accessed November 29, 2018, https://en.wikipedia.org/wiki/Radicle.
xcvi	Mark 4:20 MSG
xcvii	Isaiah 58:11 MSG
xcviii	Matthew 13:32 NIV
xcix	John 14:23-26 TPT
c	"C.S. Lewis Quotes," GoodReads, accessed February 6, 2019, https://www.goodreads.com/quotes/66683-but-first-remember-remember-remember-the-signs-say-them-to.
ci	Stasi Eldredge, *Captivating* (Nashville: Thomas Nelson, 2005), 15-16.
cii	John 12:3 NIV
ciii	Isaiah 52:7 NIV
civ	"Veronica Roth Quotes," GoodReads, accessed February 4, 2017, https://www.goodreads.com/quotes/378945-fear-doesn-t-shut-you-down-it-wakes-you-up-i-ve.
cv	2 Timothy 1:7
cvi	Psalm 18:35 NIV
cvii	James Orr, "Entry for 'BELOVED,'" accessed April 4, 2017, https://www.chicagomanualofstyle.org/tools_citationguide/citation-guide-1.html#cg-website.
cviii	Ezekiel 28:12-14 BSB
cix	Stasi Eldredge, *Captivating* (Nashville: Thomas Nelson, 2005), 85.
cx	Song of Songs 4:12 NIV
cxi	"Rick Warren Quotes," AZQuotes, accessed September 8, 2014, https://www.azquotes.com/quote/560965.
cxii	2 Corinthians 5:17 NLT
cxiii	2 Samuel 22:24-25 MSG
cxiv	Esther 4:14 NIV
cxv	Psalm 16:2&5 TPT
cxvi	Lamentations 3:21-23 ESV

cxvii	Ephesians 2:21-22 MSG
cxviii	Ezekiel 16:7 NIV
cxix	Philippians 1:6 NIV
cxx	"Theodore Roosevelt Quotes," BrainyQuote, accessed September 13, 2014, https://www.brainyquote.com/quotes/theodore_roosevelt_100965.
cxxi	Luke 11:9 NLT
cxxii	Psalm 8:4 BSB
cxxiii	John 14:13 NLT
cxxiv	Luke 11:7-8 NLT
cxxv	Exodus 32:9-10 NIV
cxxvi	"Quotes," QuoteFancy, accessed October 25, 2015, https://quotefancy.com/quote/756884/Jim-Watkins-A-river-cuts-through-rock-not-because-of-its-power-but-because-of-its.
cxxvii	"Undeterred," OxfordDictionary, accessed January 27, 2017, https://en.oxforddictionaries.com/definition/undeterred.
cxxviii	Genesis 15:17 NIV
cxxix	Jeremiah 29:13 NIV
cxxx	Ephesians 6:12 NIV
cxxxi	2 Chronicles 20:12,15,17 NIV
cxxxii	1 Corinthians 13:8-13 TPT
cxxxiii	"Design," OxfordDictionaries, accessed December 2, 2018, https://en.oxforddictionaries.com/definition/design.
cxxxiv	2 Chronicles 20:2-3 MSG
cxxxv	2 Chronicles 20:20-22 MSG (emphasis added)
cxxxvi	Psalm 139:15 AMP
cxxxvii	Ephesian 1:11-12 MSG
cxxxviii	"C.S. Lewis Quotes," GoodReads, accessed December 12, 2016, https://www.goodreads.com/quotes/7288468-humility-is-not-thinking-less-of-yourself-it-s-thinking-of.
cxxxix	1 Peter 2:9 NIV
cxl	John 14:27 NIV
cxli	1 Samuel 17:33 NIV
cxlii	1 Samuel 17:47 NIV
cxliii	1 Chronicles 29:1 NIV
cxliv	"Quotes," QuoteFancy, accessed February 3, 2017, https://quotefancy.com/quote/1485077/Henry-B-Eyring-Don-t-worry-about-how-inexperienced-you-are-or-think-you-are-but-think.
cxlv	Psalm 81:10 TPT
cxlvi	Ecclesiastes 3:6b MSG
cxlvii	Lindsey, A. C., and Strand, B. (2015). You Don't Miss A Thing [Recorded by Bethel Music]. On *We Will Not Be Shaken* [MP3 file]. Redding, California: Bethel Music.
cxlviii	"William Shakespeare Quotes," GoodReads, accessed December 17, 2014, https://www.goodreads.com/quotes/276750-expectation-is-the-root-of-all-heartache.
cxlix	Ezekiel 36:26 NIV
cl	"Maurice Setter Quotations," Quoteland, accessed October 9, 2017, http://www.quoteland.com/author/Maurice-Setter-Quotes/7788/.
cli	Matthew 11:28 NIV
clii	John 15:5-8 MSG
cliii	Isaiah 52:1-2 NIV
cliv	Romans 12:1 MSG
clv	1 Peter 1:8 MSG
clvi	Psalm 92:10-15 TPT
clvii	Isaiah 54:2-3 MSG
clviii	Travis Smith, "A great reminder to the Channel from Mrs. Disney: "He did see it, that's why it's here," MoveTheChannel, published September 10, 2013, http://movethechannel.com/?p=610.

clix	Acts 2:17, 25-28 MSG
clx	Song of Songs 2:15 NIV
clxi	Daniel 3:16-18 NLT (emphasis added)
clxii	Psalm 46:10 NIV
clxiii	"Harry's Curious Wand," Pottermore, accessed January 9, 2017, https://www.pottermore.com/book-extract-long/a-curious-wand.
clxiv	C. C. (Director). (2009). Harry Potter and the philosophers stone; Harry Potter and the chamber of secrets [Motion picture on DVD]. Los Angeles: Warner Brothers.
clxv	Isaiah 48:3-5 MSG
clxvi	Amos 3:7-8 MSG
clxvii	Isaiah 48:6-7 MSG
clxviii	Proverbs 16:9 MSG
clxix	Mark Batterson, *The Circle Maker,* (Grand Rapids: Zondervan 2011), p 71.
clxx	Zechariah 4:10 NLT
clxxi	Colossians 3:3 NIV
clxxii	"Kristin Martz Quotes," GoodReads, accessed August 27, 2015, https://www.goodreads.com/quotes/732290-we-lose-ourselves-in-things-we-love-we-find-ourselves.
clxxiii	Jeremiah 6:16 NLT
clxxiv	Matthew 5:4 MSG
clxxv	Job 37:5 NIV
clxxvi	"Walt Disney Quotes," GoodReads, accessed January 20, 2015, https://www.goodreads.com/quotes/656385-we-keep-moving-forward-opening-new-doors-and-doing-new.
clxxvii	1 Kings 19:3 NIV
clxxviii	"Cave," Merriam-Webster, accessed December 18, 2016, https://www.merriam-webster.com/dictionary/cave.
clxxix	Romans 8:31 NIV (emphasis mine)
clxxx	Jeremiah 29:11 NIV (emphasis mine)
clxxxi	Isaiah 41:10 NLT (emphasis mine)
clxxxii	Jeremiah 17:9 NIV
clxxxiii	Proverbs 4:9 BSB
clxxxiv	"Quotes," GoodReads, accessed January 5, 2014, https://www.goodreads.com/quotes/7102704-we-lose-ourselves-in-books-we-find-ourselves-there-too.
clxxxv	William Shakespeare, *Hamlet*, SparkNotes, accessed January 5, 2014, https://www.sparknotes.com/nofear/shakespeare/hamlet/page_110/.
clxxxvi	Ezekiel 22: 30 NIV
clxxxvii	1 Peter 5:7 NLT
clxxxviii	Hebrews 4:16 NLT
clxxxix	Esther 4:16 NLT
cxc	"Jonathan Edwards Quotes," GoodReads, accessed July 1, 2015, https://www.goodreads.com/quotes/331863-lord-stamp-eternity-on-my-eyeballs.
cxci	Ecclesiastes 3:1 NIV
cxcii	Philemon 1:15 TPT
cxciii	Genesis 6:9 NIV
cxciv	2 Corinthians 12:9 NIV, emphasis mine
cxcv	"Man Of Steel," Quotes, accessed April 4, 2014, https://www.quotes.net/mquote/1037992.
cxcvi	Psalm 33:4 NLT
cxcvii	Luke 1:45 NIV (emphasis added)
cxcviii	"Pisteuo," BlueLetterBible, accessed February 7, 2021, https://www.blueletterbible.org/lang/lexicon/lexicon.cfm?t=kjv&strongs=g4100.
cxcix	Jeremiah 17:9 NIV
cc	Hebrews 6:13-15 NIV
cci	"The Hunger Games Quotes," IMDb, accessed November 14, 2016, https://www.imdb.com/title/tt1392170/quotes/qt1666897.

ccii	Hebrews 11:12 NIV
cciii	Hebrews 6:19 NIV
cciv	Hebrews 10:35 NIV
ccv	Hebrews 11:1 NIV
ccvi	Luke 1:37 NKJV
ccvii	Luke 1:37 NIV
ccviii	1 Peter 5:8 NIV
ccix	Proverbs 28:1 NLT
ccx	Psalms 45:3-5 NLT
ccxi	Genesis 4:15 MSG
ccxii	Hebrews 6:16-18 TPT
ccxiii	"Quote," QuoteCatalog, accessed September 2018, https://quotecatalog.com/quote/atticus-her-heart-was-w-g7O4XRp/.
ccxiv	Genesis 18:17 MSG
ccxv	r.h.Sin tweeted: "She was fire enough to light the way and burn anything attempting to stop her." (@byRHSin, September 18, 2017).
ccxvi	Song of Songs 8:6 NIV
ccxvii	Esther 4:16 NIV
ccxviii	"Mark Twain Quotes," QuoteFancy, accessed December 1, 2016, https://quotefancy.com/quote/861374/Mark-Twain-Courage-is-not-the-lack-of-fear-It-is-acting-in-spite-of-it.
ccxix	Psalm 27:4 NIV
ccxx	Acts 16:26 NIV
ccxxi	"Darlene Zschech Quotes," GoodReads, accessed January 9, 2017, https://www.goodreads.com/quotes/749607-praise-is-declaration-a-victory-cry-proclaiming-faith-to-stand.
ccxxii	"C.S. Lewis Quotes," GoodReads, accessed July 9, 2015, https://www.goodreads.com/quotes/13641-imagine-yourself-as-a-living-house-god-comes-in-to.
ccxxiii	Matthew 7:25 NIV
ccxxiv	Psalm 45:13-15 NIV
ccxxv	1 Chronicles 29:1 NIV
ccxxvi	Micah 5:4-5 NIV
ccxxvii	Kenneth Barker, NASB Study Bible, (Grand Rapids: Zondervan, 1999) p 1463.
ccxxviii	"C.S. Lewis Quotes," GoodReads, accessed July 10, 2017, https://www.goodreads.com/quotes/685177-wrong-will-be-right-when-aslan-comes-in-sight-at.
ccxxix	Proverbs 16:32 ESV
ccxxx	John 4:13-14 NIV
ccxxxi	Robert Madu, *The Water and the Wilderness,* spoken at Hillsong Church 2017.
ccxxxii	Isaiah 26:15 NLT
ccxxxiii	Proverbs 3:5-6 MSG
ccxxxiv	"Elisabeth Elliot Quotes," AZQuotes, accessed December 1, 2015, https://www.azquotes.com/quote/1366392.
ccxxxv	Ezekiel 3:1-3 MSG
ccxxxvi	Psalm 139:7-12 MSG
ccxxxvii	"Catalyst," Dictionary.com, accessed July 8, 2016, https://www.dictionary.com/browse/catalyst.
ccxxxviii	Jeremiah 33:3 NLT
ccxxxix	1 John 5:14 NIV
ccxl	Genesis 6:22 NIV
ccxli	Psalm 37:23 NLT
ccxlii	Psalm 84:10 TPT
ccxliii	"A.P.J. Abdul Kalam Quotes," GoodReads, accessed November 27, 2015, https://www.goodreads.com/quotes/5732134-you-have-to-dream-before-your-dreams-can-come-true.
ccxliv	"The Circle Maker Quotes," GoodReads, accessed November 27, 2015, https://www.goodreads.com/work/quotes/16839389-the-circle-maker-praying-circles-around-your-biggest-dreams-

	and-greates?page=4.
ccxlv	"Thomas A. Edison Quote," GoodReads, accessed November 27, 2015, https://www.goodreads.com/quotes/8287-i-have-not-failed-i-ve-just-found-10-000-ways-that.
ccxlvi	2 Samuel 7:3 BSB
ccxlvii	Proverbs 29:18 KJB
ccxlviii	Psalm 139:5-6,13-16 NLT
ccxlix	*NIV/The Message Parallel Study Bible*, (Grand Rapids: Zondervan, 2008), p 23.
ccl	"C.S. Lewis Quotes," GoodReads, accessed July 15, 2017, https://www.goodreads.com/quotes/101369-only-a-real-risk-tests-the-reality-of-a-belief.
ccli	Deuteronomy 7:9 NIV
cclii	1 Corinthians 2:16 TLB; Proverbs 15:8 NIV; Matthew 21:22 NIV; Philippians 4:6-7 NIV
ccliii	"Prayer," MerriamWebster, accessed August 22, 2014, https://www.merriam-webster.com/dictionary/prayer.
ccliv	Msgr. Charles Pope, "A simple but powerful definition of prayer," ADW, published October 21, 2013, http://blog.adw.org/2013/10/a-simple-but-powerful-definition-of-prayer/.
cclv	Quote from the LiveDead Journal
cclvi	Matthew 7:7 NIV
cclvii	Romans 12:1-2a MSG
cclviii	John 15:9-13 TPT
cclix	Exodus 14:13 NLT
cclx	Psalm 96:2-3 MSG
cclxi	Job 37:5-7,13-14 NIV
cclxii	Ruth 1:16 NIV
cclxiii	2 Kings 2:2 NIV
cclxiv	1 Samuel 22:23 NIV
cclxv	Isaiah 43:1-4 NLT
cclxvi	Psalm 119:105 NKJV
cclxvii	Psalm 45:10-11 MSG
cclxviii	Proverbs 25:28 NAB
cclxix	2 Timothy 1:14 NIV
cclxx	1 Corinthians 13:4-8 NIV
cclxxi	Ann Voskamp, *The Broken Way,* (Grand Rapids: Zondervan, 2016), p161.
cclxxii	Isaiah 51:3 NIV
cclxxiii	Isaiah 30:21 NIV
cclxxiv	Galatians 5:22-23 NIV
cclxxv	Mark 11:22-24 MSG
cclxxvi	Haggai 2:4-9 MSG
cclxxvii	"Lao Tzu Quotes," GoodReads, accessed October 1, 2016, https://www.goodreads.com/quotes/36323-time-is-a-created-thing-to-say-i-don-t-have.
cclxxviii	Matthew 11:28 NIV
cclxxix	Luke 12:34 TPT
cclxxx	John 15:13 NLT
cclxxxi	Romans 5:8 NLT
cclxxxii	Psalm 25:5 TPT
cclxxxiii	*Poetry on Fire: The Psalms,* (BroadStreet Publishing Group LLC, 2017) p 44.
cclxxxiv	Drew Coffman, "Those who believe in God can never in a way be sure of him again," published September 12, 2015, https://extratextuals.com/those-who-believe-in-god-can-never-in-a-way-be-sure-of-him-again-6a481be32518.
cclxxxv	Psalm 27:14 TPT
cclxxxvi	Zelda Fitzgerald, GoodReads, accessed September 2, 2018, https://www.goodreads.com/quotes/866237-she-quietly-expected-great-things-to-happen-to-her-and.
cclxxxvii	Proverbs 23:7 NKJV
cclxxxviii	Psalm 84:5-7 MSG

cclxxxix	Frank Damazio, "Become a Game Changer Leader," published October 28, 2017, https://www.citylifechurch.ca/wp/wp-content/uploads/2017/11/Become-a-Game-Changer-Leader-Session-Notes.pdf.
ccxc	Jeremiah 18:3&6 NIV
ccxci	Charlotte Gambill, *Turnaround God,* (Nashville: W Publishing Group, 2013), p 22.
ccxcii	"Charles Haddon Spurgeon Quotes," GoodReads, accessed January 3, 2018, https://www.goodreads.com/quotes/1199735-i-have-learned-to-kiss-the-waves-that-throw-me.
ccxciii	Ezekiel 47:3-5 MSG
ccxciv	Beautifully In Over My Head [Recorded by Bethel Music Publishing (Jenn Johnson)]. On We Will Not Be Shaken [MP3 file].
ccxcv	Isaiah 26:3-4 NLT
ccxcvi	"Exist," OxfordDictionaries, accessed March 1, 2015, https://en.oxforddictionaries.com/definition/exist.
ccxcvii	Mark 12:30 NIV
ccxcviii	Acts 17:28 NLT
ccxcix	1 John 4:19 NIV
ccc	Psalm 19:1-4 TPT
ccci	Psalm 64:3 NLT, emphasis mine
cccii	Jeremiah 9:8 NIV
ccciii	Rev. Dale Kuiper, "Arrows," accessed December 4, 2017, http://www.prca.org/Word%20a%20Week/word48.htm.
ccciv	2 Chronicles 7:16 MSG
cccv	Song of Songs 8:6-7 NLT
cccvi	2 Corinthians 3:16 NIV
cccvii	"Green Lantern Quotes," IMDb, accessed June 4, 2016, https://www.imdb.com/title/tt1133985/quotes.
cccviii	Ecclesiastes 4:9 NIV
cccix	Matthew 18:20 NIV
cccx	Hebrews 11:1 NIRV
cccxi	Hebrews 11:10 MSG (emphasis added)
cccxii	Nehemiah 9:12 NIV
cccxiii	Robert Frost, *The Road Not Taken,* accessed September 14, 2015, https://www.poetryfoundation.org/poems/44272/the-road-not-taken.
cccxiv	"Jennifer Lee Quotes," GoodReads, accessed November 19, 2017, https://www.goodreads.com/quotes/7430302-be-fearless-in-the-pursuit-of-what-sets-your-soul.
cccxv	Luke 1:28 MSG
cccxvi	Charlotte Gambill, *Turnaround God,* (Nashville: W Publishing Group, 2013), p 203.
cccxvii	Luke 2:51 NIV
cccxviii	Mark 4:26-27 MSG
cccxix	"Vincent Van Gogh Quotes," BrainyQuote, acceseed December 21, 2017, https://www.brainyquote.com/quotes/vincent_van_gogh_120866.
cccxx	Nehemiah 13:2 NIV
cccxxi	Philippians 4:7 NIV
cccxxii	Quote from Christine Caine at Passion Conference 2014.
cccxxiii	Hebrews 12:1 NIV
cccxxiv	Hebrews 10:36 NIV
cccxxv	Isaiah 45:2-3 ESV
cccxxvi	Mark 6:3 MSG
cccxxvii	John 14:12 MSG (emphasis added)
cccxxviii	Psalm 90:1-2 MSG
cccxxix	Psalm 8:3-4 ESV
cccxxx	Hebrews 2:6 AMPC
cccxxxi	Psalm 139:14 NIV

cccxxxii	Romans 8:28, 31 NIV
cccxxxiii	Matthew 28:20 NIV
cccxxxiv	Ephesians 2:10 NLT
cccxxxv	Ephesians 3:12 MSG
cccxxxvi	Mark Batterson, *Primal,* (Colorado Springs: Multnomah, 2009), p 135.
cccxxxvii	Joshua 1:9 NIV
cccxxxviii	Tressa Ripp, "15 Disney Quotes To Live By," Odyssey, published May 16, 2016, https://www.theodysseyonline.com/15-disney-quotes-live.
cccxxxix	Richard La Gravenese, dir. *PS I Love You.* 2007. [S.I.]: Warner Brothers. DVD.
cccxl	2 Corinthians 12:9 NIV
cccxli	Proverbs 4:4-5,21-23 TPT
cccxlii	J. R. R. Tolkien Quote," GoodReads, accessed June 27, 2016, https://www.goodreads.com/quotes/1390286-a-single-dream-is-more-powerful-than-a-thousand-realities.
cccxliii	Hebrews 10:23 NLT
cccxliv	Genesis 50:20 NLT
cccxlv	"Roald Dahl Quote," GoodReads, accessed January 17, 2016, https://www.goodreads.com/quotes/7032-and-above-all-watch-with-glittering-eyes-the-whole-world.
cccxlvi	Ephesians 3:20 MSG
cccxlvii	Ephesians 6:12 NIV
cccxlviii	2 Corinthians 12:9 NIV
cccxlix	"Fear Quotes," Spiritual Cleansing, accessed Jan 17, 2021, https://spiritualcleansing.org/i-think-part-of-the-reason-why-we-hold-on-to-something-so-tight-is-because-we-fear-something-so-great-wont-happen-twice/
cccl	Isaiah 33:5-6 MSG
cccli	"R.C.Sproul," AZQuotes, accessed October 11, 2016, https://www.azquotes.com/quote/707385.
ccclii	Hebrews 10:23 NIV
cccliii	"C.S. Lewis Quotes," GoodReads, accessed January 28, 2016, https://www.goodreads.com/quotes/641380-i-do-not-know-why-there-is-this-difference-but.
cccliv	Isaiah 40:28 MSG
ccclv	Philippians 3:13 NIV
ccclvi	Isaiah 30:21 NIV
ccclvii	Proverbs 3:6 TLB
ccclviii	1 Samuel 14:6 NIV
ccclix	1 Samuel 14:12 NIV
ccclx	"Quote," Pinterest, accessed August 9, 2016, https://www.pinterest.com.au/pin/20407004535054711/?lp=true.
ccclxi	Matthew 5:14 MSG
ccclxii	"Frederick Buechner Quotes," GoodReads, accessed January 18, 2021, https://www.goodreads.com/quotes/1333354-life-batters-and-shapes-us-in-all-sorts-of-ways
ccclxiii	Proverbs 18:21 MSG
ccclxiv	Ephesians 5:14 NIV
ccclxv	Steven Pavlina, "How to Get Up Right Away When Your Alarm Goes Off," published April 25, 2006, https://www.stevepavlina.com/blog/2006/04/how-to-get-up-right-away-when-your-alarm-goes-off/.
ccclxvi	Colossians 3:1-4 NIV
ccclxvii	Earle Wilson, *Galatians, Philippians, Colossians.* (Indianapolis: Wesleyan Publishing House, 2007), 243.
ccclxviii	Earle Wilson, *Galatians, Philippians, Colossians,* (Indianapolis: Wesleyan Publishing House, 2007), 248.
ccclxix	Earle Wilson, *Galatians, Philippians, Colossians,* (Indianapolis: Wesleyan Publishing House, 2007), 137.
ccclxx	Matthew 11:30 NIV
ccclxxi	Brian J. Walsh, "Late/Post Modernity and Idolatry: A Contextual Reading of Colossians 2:8-

	3:4," EBSCO*host* (1999): 6.
ccclxxii	Romans 8:38 NLT
ccclxxiii	Joshua 1:6-9 NLT
ccclxxiv	"God's Heartbeat," YouthForChrist, published September 19, 2011, http://www.yfc.net/deafteenquest/blog/gods-heartbeat.
ccclxxv	Ibid.
ccclxxvi	Psalm 46:10 NIV
ccclxxvii	1 John 4:18 NIV
ccclxxviii	Ephesians 6:26-27 MSG
ccclxxix	Revelation 4:8 NLT
ccclxxx	Psalm 16:2 NIV
ccclxxxi	Galatians 6:9 MSG
ccclxxxii	Mark 4:26-29 MSG (emphasis added)
ccclxxxiii	Genesis 3:1 NIV
ccclxxxiv	Song of Songs 2:10-13 NIV
ccclxxxv	"Once Upon A Time," GoodReads, accessed January 12, 2021, https://www.goodreads.com/quotes/8392006-all-magic-comes-with-a-price-dearie.
ccclxxxvi	Song of Songs 3:5 NIV
ccclxxxvii	James 1:22-24 MSG
ccclxxxviii	Psalm 139:1 NIV
ccclxxxix	Psalm 31:19 TPT
cccxc	Nathan Greno and Byron Howard, dir. Tangled. Written by Dan Fogelman. Music composed by Alan Menken. Performed by Mandy Moore, Zachary Levi, Donna Murphy, and Brad Garrett. Walt Disney Animation Studios, 2010. DVD.
cccxci	Psalm 37:34 MSG
cccxcii	Psalm 86:11 MSG
cccxciii	Ann Voskamp, *The Broken Way,* (Grand Rapids: Zondervan, 2016), 53.
cccxciv	*Psalm 111:1-5 TPT*
cccxcv	Philippians 4:11-12 NIV
cccxcvi	"Quotes," TvFanatic, accessed January 3, 2017, https://www.tvfanatic.com/quotes/when-we-say-things-like-people-dont-change-it-drives-scientist/. cccxcvii "Lao Tzu Quotes," GoodReads, accessed March 14, 2016, https://www.goodreads.com/quotes/282740-if-you-correct-your-mind-the-rest-of-your-life.
cccxcviii	"Cinderella Quotes," IMDb, accessed January 9, 2018, https://www.imdb.com/title/tt1661199/quotes/qt2422176
cccxcix	Matthew 23:26 NIV
cd	Psalm 37:29,31,34 TPT
cdi	James 4:8 NIV
cdii	Zephaniah 3:17 NLT
cdiii	"Ernest Hemingway Quotes," GoodReads, accessed June 4, 2017, https://www.goodreads.com/quotes/53157-every-man-s-life-ends-the-same-way-it-is-only.
cdiv	1 Samuel 16:7 ESV
cdv	Luke 8:16-17 TPT
cdvi	2 John 1:2-3, 5-6 (AMPC)
cdvii	John 10:10 TPT
cdviii	Ecclesiastes 11:9 MSG
cdix	2 Timothy 1:14 TPT
cdx	Ephesians 3:20 NIV
cdxi	Russell, Teagan. "Hillsong United on Wonder, Trust and the Next Generation." *Eternity news*, July 7, 2017. https://www.eternitynews.com.au/australia/hillsong-united-on-wonder-trust-and-the-next-generation/
cdxii	Genesis 28:15, 20,22 NIV
cdxiii	Luke 18:27 TPT

cdxiv	2 Corinthians 4:16-18 NIV
cdxv	1 Timothy 6:11-12 NLT
cdxvi	Romans 15:4 NLT
cdxvii	"Rodney Williams Quote," Pinterest, accessed July 3, 2015, https://www.pinterest.com.au/pin/6051780733461448/.
cdxviii	Psalm 46:10 ESV
cdxix	Psalm 46:5 NIV
cdxx	Genesis 12:1-3 MSG
cdxxi	"16 Peter Pan Quotes About the Beauty of Innocence," GoalCast, published April 17, 2018, https://www.goalcast.com/2018/04/17/16-peter-pan-quotes/ (emphasis added)
cdxxii	Genesis 15:5 NIV
cdxxiii	1 Samuel 3:9 MSG
cdxxiv	Psalm 139:3 AKJV
cdxxv	Psalm 143:8 NIV
cdxxvi	Exodus 4:10 NIV
cdxxvii	"Henry David Thoreau Quotes," BrainyQuote, accessed August 28, 2016, https://www.brainyquote.com/quotes/henry_david_thoreau_145971.
cdxxviii	Deuteronomy 29:29 NIV
cdxxix	Habakkuk 3:19 KJV
cdxxx	Ecclesiastes 3:1 NIV
cdxxxi	"20 Quotes about Living in the Moment," habitsforwellbeing, accessed December 18, 2018, https://www.habitsforwellbeing.com/20-quotes-about-living-in-the-present-moment/.
cdxxxii	Shauna Niequist, *Present Over Perfect*, (Grand Rapids: Zondervan, 2016), p 130.
cdxxxiii	Psalm 46:10 NIV
cdxxxiv	2 Corinthians 12:9 AMP
cdxxxv	1 Samuel 17:44 NIV
cdxxxvi	Proverbs 31:25 NIV
cdxxxvii	Ephesians 6:11 NIV
cdxxxviii	Isaiah 55:9 NIV
cdxxxix	Hebrews 6:15 NIV
cdxl	Hebrews 6:13 NIV
cdxli	Hebrews 6:18 NIV (emphasis added)
cdxlii	Psalm 37:7 NIV
cdxliii	1 Thessalonians 5:17 ESV
cdxliv	Luke 9:58 NIV
cdxlv	Ibid.
cdxlvi	David Platt, *Radical*, accessed October 3, 2015, http://www.radicalthebook.com/movement.html.
cdxlvii	"Lang Leav Quotes," GoodReads, accessed February 9, 2017, https://www.goodreads.com/quotes/7942262-her-time-she-has-been-feeling-it-for-awhile--.
cdxlviii	Marshall, G., Chase, D. M., Houston, W., Iscovich, M., Rhimes, S., Andrews, J., Hathaway, A., ... Buena Vista Home Entertainment (Firm),. (2004). The princess diaries 2: Royal engagement.
cdxlix	"The Princess Diaries 2: Royal Engagement Quotes," IMDb, accessed December 21, 2016, https://www.imdb.com/title/tt0368933/quotes/qt0333894.
cdl	Psalm 108:12-13 TPT
cdli	Isaiah 62:10-12 MSG
cdlii	"Suzanne Collins Quotes," GoodReads, accessed January 22, 2015, https://www.goodreads.com/quotes/290707-you-love-me-real-or-not-real-i-tell-him.
cdliii	Psalm 119:15-16 AMP
cdliv	Psalm 31:24 AMPC
cdlv	Isaiah 54:10 NLT
cdlvi	"Oprah Winfrey Quote," GoodReads, accessed January 8, 2015, https://www.goodreads.com/

	quotes/48624-you-get-in-life-what-you-have-the-courage-to.
cdlvii	Ezra 10:2-3 MSG
cdlviii	Ezra 10:4 NIV
cdlix	Proverbs 21:21 TPT
cdlx	John 14:27 NIV
cdlxi	John 16:33 NIV
cdlxii	J.S. Park, "GRACE: TO REST, TO FIGHT," published July 11, 2015, http://jspark3000.tumblr.com/post/123813599153/grace-to-rest-to-fight.
cdlxiii	1 Corinthians 16:13-14, 23 MSG
cdlxiv	Psalm 91:4 NLT
cdlxv	Colossians 3:1-2 ESV
cdlxvi	Job 26:14 NIV
cdlxvii	Job 42:1-3 NIV
cdlxviii	Job 42:1-3 MSG
cdlxix	Job 34:29 MSG
cdlxx	Zephaniah 3:16-20 MSG
cdlxxi	1 Kings 19:11-13 NIV
cdlxxii	Psalm 59:16 NLT
cdlxxiii	Proverbs 3:5 NIV
cdlxxiv	Proverbs 3:5 MSG
cdlxxv	Genesis 15:5 NIV
cdlxxvi	1 Corinthians 1:25 NIV
cdlxxvii	1 Samuel 2:2,9-10 NIV
cdlxxviii	2 Corinthians 2:14 MSG
cdlxxix	"Ocean Facts," NationalGeographicKids, accessed May 3, 2014, https://www.natgeokids.com/au/discover/geography/general-geography/ocean-facts/.
cdlxxx	"15 Fun and Surprising Facts about the Earth's Oceans," MotherEarthNews, accessed May 3, 2014, https://www.motherearthnews.com/nature-and-environment/nature/fun-surprising-facts-about-the-oceans.
cdlxxxi	Proverbs 20:5 NIV
cdlxxxii	1 Corinthians 2:10 NIV
cdlxxxiii	Hebrews 11:8-10
cdlxxxiv	Proverbs 30:5 MSG
cdlxxxv	"V. Raymond Edman Quotes," GoodReads, accessed December 14, 2018, https://www.goodreads.com/quotes/814981-never-doubt-in-the-dark-what-god-told-you-in.
cdlxxxvi	Psalm *18* TPT
cdlxxxvii	Malachi 1:2-3,5 MSG
cdlxxxviii	*NIV/The Message Parallel Study Bible*, (Grand Rapids: Zondervan, 2008), p 1879.
cdlxxxix	Malachi 4:1-5 MSG
cdxc	"Theodore Roosevelt Quotes," BrainyQuote, accessed January 11, 2018, https://www.brainyquote.com/quotes/theodore_roosevelt_136001.
cdxci	Genesis 28:15 ESV
cdxcii	Colossians 3:12-14 MSG
cdxciii	Colossians 3:12 TPT
cdxciv	Isaiah 32:8 NIV
cdxcv	Isaiah 61:10 NIV
cdxcvi	"Hacksaw Ridge: the Movie," DesmondDoss, accessed July 11, 2017, https://desmonddoss.com/hacksaw-ridge-movie/.
cdxcvii	"Hacksaw Ridge: the Movie," DesmondDoss, accessed July 11, 2017, https://desmonddoss.com/hacksaw-ridge-movie/.
cdxcviii	Jeremiah 20:9 NIV
cdxcix	Ephesian 6:19 NIV
d	Isaiah 49:4 NIV

di "*Finding Nemo* Quotes," RottenTomatoes, accessed January 29, 2021, https://www.rottentomatoes.com/m/finding_nemo/quotes/.
dii Rob Lammle, "6 People Who Accidentally Found A Fortune," published February 26, 2014, http://mentalfloss.com/article/22449/get-rich-quick-6-people-who-accidentally-found-fortune.
diii Ibid.
div Matthew 5:4 MSG
dv Helen Cadler, "How To Dig A Well And Make Room For God To Move," published March 28, 2010, https://www.enlivenpublishing.com/blog/2010/03/28/how-to-dig-a-well-and-make-room-for-god-to-move/.
dvi Psalm 37:27 + 28 NIV
dvii Jeremiah 29:13 NIV
dviii Matthew 5:5 MSG
dix 1 Corinthians 3:9 AMPC
dx Isaiah 61:11 AMP
dxi Matthew 20:16 NIV
dxii Proverbs 4:23 NIV
dxiii Lisa Bevere, "*Without Rival* Quote," Pinterest, accessed August 11, 2018, https://www.pinterest.com.au/pin/386746686737242571/?lp=true
dxiv Psalm 78:1-4 TPT
dxv *Isaiah 54:3 MSG*
dxvi "C.S. Lewis Quotes," GoodReads, accessed November 24, 2016, https://www.goodreads.com/quotes/350927-and-as-he-spoke-he-no-longer-looked-to-them.
dxvii "C.S. Lewis Quotes," GoodReads, accessed November 24, 2016, https://www.goodreads.com/quotes/41523-it-isn-t-narnia-you-know-sobbed-lucy-it-s-you-we.
dxviii Jeremiah 33:3 MSG
dxix Jeremiah 6-7,10 MSG
dxx Daniel 6:23 MSG
dxxi "Acceptance," Wikipedia, accessed February 11, 2021, https://en.wikipedia.org/wiki/Acceptance
dxxii "Cinderella Quotes," GoodReads, accessed October 27, 2017, https://www.goodreads.com/quotes/7680998-perhaps-the-greatest-risk-any-of-us-will-ever-take.
dxxiii "Charles H. Spurgeon," QuoteFancy, accessed April 19, 2017, https://quotefancy.com/quote/786609/Charles-H-Spurgeon-You-will-never-know-the-fullness-of-Christ-until-you-know-the.
dxxiv "William Sharp - A Crystal Forest & Other Poems (Poetry from 2017 "Beauty & the Beast")," R.E. Slater blog, published March 26, 2017, https://reslater.blogspot.com/2017/03/william-sharp-crystal-forest-other.html.
dxxv Condon, B., Chbosky, S., Spiliotopoulos, E., Menken, A., Ashman, H., Rice, T., Hoberman, D., ... Buena Vista Home Entertainment (Firm),. (2017). Beauty and the Beast. dxxvi Titus 2:1-7,14 NIV dxxvii Revelation 2:7 MSG dxxviii Habakkuk 2:3 MSG
dxxix Habakkuk 2:3 NIV
dxxx "Prize," NET Bible, accessed February 12, 2021, http://classic.net.bible.org/dictionary.php?word=Prize.
dxxxi 1 Corinthians 9:24 AMPC
dxxxii Exodus 14:13-15 NIV
dxxxiii 1 Corinthians 9:24 AMPC
dxxxiv Isaiah 60:22 NLT
dxxxv "Frank Jackson," AZQuotes, accessed July 1, 2017, https://www.azquotes.com/quote/520066.
dxxxvi Lisa Bevere tweeted: "There is something new inside you that fear wants to contain. Don't let it. #WithoutRival" (@LisaBevere, June 13, 2017).
dxxxvii 2 Corinthians 12:7-10 TPT
dxxxviii 1 Corinthians 13:13 MSG

dxxxix	Shauna Niequist, *Present Over Perfect*, (Grand Rapids: Zondervan, 2016), p 125-126.
dxl	Buck, C., & Lee, J. (2013). *Frozen*. Walt Disney Studios Motion Pictures.
dxli	Isaiah 59:16-20 ESV
dxlii	"Saint Augustine Quotes," BrainyQuote, accessed July 3, 2017, https://www.brainyquote.com/quotes/saint_augustine_105351.
dxliii	Psalm 18:6,16,19 NIV
dxliv	1 Chronicles 19:12-13 NIV
dxlv	Psalm 138:3 NIV
dxlvi	John 3:16 AMP
dxlvii	2 Corinthians 4:7-9 NIV
dxlviii	Wright, Joe, Tim Bevan, Eric Fellner, Paul Webster, Debra Hayward, Liza Chasin, Deborah Moggach, et al. 2006. *Pride & Prejudice*. Universal City, CA: Universal Studios Home Entertainment.
dxlix	"Pride and Prejudice," WikiQuote, accessed October 21, 2015, https://en.wikiquote.org/wiki/Pride_and_Prejudice_(2005_film).
dl	"C.S. Lewis Quotes," GoodReads, accessed July 9, 2015, https://www.goodreads.com/quotes/344874-but-there-must-be-a-real-giving-up-of-the
dli	Philippians 1:6 AMPC
dlii	Jude 1:21 KJV
dliii	Disney, Walt, Hamilton S. Luske, Clyde Geronimi, Wilfred Jackson, Bobby Driscoll, Kathryn Beaumont, Hans Conried, et al. 2007. *Peter Pan*.
dliv	Matthew 9:27-29 MSG
dlv	Galatians 4:18 MSG
dlvi	Joel 2:28 + Acts 2:17 NIV
dlvii	Romans 8:26 NIV
dlviii	1 Corinthians 2:12 MSG
dlix	Psalm 45:1 TPT
dlx	"The Karate Kid," IMDb, accessed May 19, 2015, https://www.imdb.com/title/tt1155076/characters/nm0000329.
dlxi	Micah 4:1-4 MSG (emphasis added)
dlxii	"The Karate Kid," IMDb, accessed May 19, 2015, https://www.imdb.com/title/tt1155076/characters/nm0000329.
dlxiii	Proverbs 3:11-12 MSG
dlxiv	Psalm 91:1-16 TPT
dlxv	Deuteronomy 31:8 MSG
dlxvi	Isaiah 40:3 AMPC
dlxvii	"Camel Facts," AnimalFactsEncyclopedia, accessed October 28, 2017, https://www.animalfactsencyclopedia.com/Camel-facts.html.
dlxviii	Isaiah 40:31 AMPC
dlxix	Psalm 68:13 TPT
dlxx	Hebrews 10:25 NIV
dlxxi	Bobbie Houston, *Stay the Path*, (Castle Hill: Shout! Publishing, 2017), p 83.
dlxxii	Hebrews 10:39 NIV
dlxxiii	"Francis Chan Quotes," GoodReads, accessed November 22, 2017, https://www.goodreads.com/quotes/655369-god-will-not-be-tolerated-he-instructs-us-to-worship.
dlxxiv	1 Samuel 1:9-17 MSG
dlxxv	1 Samuel 1:7 MSG
dlxxvi	Ephesians 1:14 TPT
dlxxvii	Isaiah 54:1 NIV
dlxxviii	1 John 4:19 NIV
dlxxix	Ruth 3:18 NIV
dlxxx	Steven Furtick, *Greater*, (Colorado Springs Multnomah, 2012), p 44.
dlxxxi	Isaiah 55:10-11 NASB

dlxxxii	Luke 8:22-24 AMPC
dlxxxiii	Lori Thomason, "Love Like the Ocean – A Devotion," published July 15, 2010, https://lthomason.wordpress.com/2010/07/15/love-like-the-ocean-a-devotion/.
dlxxxiv	Ephesians 3:17-19 MSG
dlxxxv	Romans 8:1-2 TPT
dlxxxvi	"1 Peter 2 Bible Commentary," Christianity.com, accessed September 15, 2017, https://www.christianity.com/bible/commentary.php?com=jfb&b=60&c=2.
dlxxxvii	"Quotes," AtticusPoetry, posted March 24, 2016, https://www.pinterest.com.au/pin/AXOzcBDOmRoL4aGVGg0jc17DTYVEqOmjnuSAa_7aJA5LuQg5vgEU7Es/.
dlxxxviii	2 Corinthians 5:20 NLT
dlxxxix	"Crown," BibleStudyTools, accessed September 15, 2017, https://www.biblestudytools.com/dictionary/crown/.
dxc	3 John 1:5-8 TPT
dxci	"Frederick Buechner Quote," GoodReads, accessed January 9, 2018, https://www.goodreads.com/quotes/701695-your-life-and-my-life-flow-into-each-other-as.
dxcii	1 John 4:20
dxciii	Song of Songs 7:9 TPT
dxciv	John 4:26 TPT
dxcv	"Sleeping Beauty Characters," SparkNotes, accessed February 15, 2015, https://www.sparknotes.com/film/sleepingbeauty/characters/.
dxcvi	Psalm 45:11 NIV
dxcvii	Psalm 139:16 NIV
dxcviii	Ecclesiastes 3:1 NIV
dxcix	"Charles Spurgeon Quote," GoodReads, accessed December 6, 2018, https://www.goodreads.com/quotes/1403154-god-is-too-good-to-be-unkind-and-he-is.
dc	John 10:10 NIV
dci	Deuteronomy 30:11 NIV
dcii	Judges 4:8 NIV
dciii	Genesis 28:13,15 NLT
dciv	Genesis 31:13 NLT
dcv	"Anna Wintour Quotes," BrainyQuote, accessed April 15, 2015, https://www.brainyquote.com/quotes/anna_wintour_637511.
dcvi	"Jack Canfield Quotes," GoodReads, accessed September 29, 2017, https://www.goodreads.com/quotes/495741-everything-you-want-is-on-the-other-side-of-fear.
dcvii	2 Corinthians 10:5 NIV
dcviii	Ephesians 3:14-19 TPT
dcix	Proverbs 4:23 NIV
dcx	"Joel Osteen Quotes," AZQuotes, accessed March 4, 2014, https://www.azquotes.com/quote/1260294.
dcxi	Psalm 45:3-5 NLT
dcxii	1 Corinthians 16:13-14 NIV
dcxiii	1 Samuel 30:6 MSG
dcxiv	1 Chronicles 28:8-10 NIV
dcxv	Hebrews 11:1 NLT (emphasis added)
dcxvi	Esther 7:3 MSG
dcxvii	James 5:16 MSG
dcxviii	Isaiah 33:17 NIV
dcxix	Romans 5:5 NASB
dcxx	"Jeffery R. Holland Quotes," AZQuotes, accessed December 1, 2018, https://www.azquotes.com/quote/689134.
dcxxi	Proverbs 18:10 WEB
dcxxii	Obadiah 1:17-18 NIV
dcxxiii	Obadiah 1:17-18 MSG

dcxxiv	Isaiah 64:1-2 AMP
dcxxv	J.K.Rowling Quotes," GoodReads, accessed December 8, 2017, https://www.goodreads.com/quotes/3670-it-does-not-do-to-dwell-on-dreams-and-forget.
dcxxvi	Drew Coffman, "Those who believe in God can never in a way be sure of him again," published September 12, 2015, https://extratextuals.com/those-who-believe-in-god-can-never-in-a-way-be-sure-of-him-again-6a481be32518.
dcxxvii	Hillsong Conference 2018
dcxxviii	Luke 15:31 NIV
dcxxix	Psalm 145:6 MSG
dcxxx	"C.S. Lewis Quotes," GoodReads, accessed December 12, 2016, https://www.goodreads.com/quotes/1016787-i-would-rather-be-what-god-chose-to-make-me.
dcxxxi	Mark 8:36 NIV
dcxxxii	Mark 8:36 MSG
dcxxxiii	Hebrews 6:19 NIV
dcxxxiv	Luke 24:49 NIV (emphasis added)
dcxxxv	"10 Best Yoda Quotes," StarWars, posted November 26, 2013, https://www.starwars.com/news/the-starwars-com-10-best-yoda-quotes.
dcxxxvi	Numbers 13:27,28,31-33 MSG
dcxxxvii	Ibid.
dcxxxviii	Numbers 14:11 NIV
dcxxxix	1 Peter 1:16 NIV
dcxl	Philippians 3:13 TPT
dcxli	Revelation 19:12 NIV
dcxlii	Genesis 24:15-21 MSG
dcxliii	Bobbie Houston, *Stay the Path*, (Castle Hill: Shout! Publishing, 2017), p 124.
dcxliv	Ephesians 6:13-16 TPT
dcxlv	Mark 11:22 MSG
dcxlvi	Isaiah 14:24 and 27 MSG
dcxlvii	Psalm 31:24 MSG
dcxlviii	"Nayyirah Waheed Quote," Pinterest, accessed August 9, 2016, https://www.pinterest.com.au/pin/336714509614526487/?lp=true
dcxlix	Romans 8:26-28 AMP
dcl	"Intercession with groanings that cannot be uttered," commented on by James Anderson, published October 6, 2010, https://theosophical.wordpress.com/2010/10/05/intercession-with-groanings-that-cannot-be-uttered/.
dcli	Psalm 19:1-4 TPT
dclii	Joshua Kennon, "The Average Person Lives 27,375 Days. Make Each of Them Count," published July 14, 2012, https://www.joshuakennon.com/the-average-person-lives-27375-days-make-each-of-them-count/.
dcliii	Isaiah 30:18 NIV
dcliv	2 Peter 3:9 NIV
dclv	Psalm 139:5-10 MSG
dclvi	Matthew 18:1 HCSB
dclvii	Matthew 18:10 HCSB
dclviii	Matthew 18:4 HCSB
dclix	Matthew 5:8 NIV (emphasis added)
dclx	Mark Batterson, *In a Pit with a Lion on a Snowy Day,* (New York: Multnomah, 2006), p 44.
dclxi	Proverbs 4:20-23 MSG
dclxii	Take Courage [Recorded by Bethel Music Publishing (Kristene DiMarco)]. On Starlight [MP2 file].
dclxiii	Jude 1:2 MSG
dclxiv	Luke 12:34 NIV
dclxv	Psalm 104:24 TPT

dclxvi	Romans 10:9-10 MSG
dclxvii	Romans 10:11 MSG
dclxviii	Psalm 84:11-12 AMP (emphasis added)
dclxix	"Frances Hodgson Burnett Quotes," GoodReads, April 1, 2017, https://www.goodreads.com/quotes/315890-at-first-people-refuse-to-believe-that-a-strange-new.
dclxx	Mark 4:20 MSG
dclxxi	Exodus 4:2 NIV
dclxxii	"20 Amazing Facts You Didn't Know About Cacti," CactusWay, accessed January 7, 2019, https://www.cactusway.com/20-Amazing-Facts-You-Didn't-Know-About-Cacti/
dclxxiii	Job 8:7 ESV
dclxxiv	Exodus 14:16 WEB
dclxxv	Titus 1:2 MSG
dclxxvi	Ephesians 2:10 TPT
dclxxvii	Psalm 46:10 NIV
dclxxviii	Psalm 147:11 & 15-20 TPT
dclxxix	Judges 16:5-6 NIV
dclxxx	Isaiah 30:21 NIV
dclxxxi	Judges 16:26-30 NIV
dclxxxii	"Steven Furtick Quotes," GoodReads, accessed July 19, 2018, https://www.goodreads.com/quotes/837149-what-matters-most-is-not-what-i-think-i-am.
dclxxxiii	1 Corinthians 2:9 NLT
dclxxxiv	"Cinderella Quotes," GoodReads, accessed May 1, 2018, https://www.goodreads.com/author/quotes/2868789.Cinderella
dclxxxv	Psalm 119:41-48 MSG
dclxxxvi	Isaiah 64:8 NIV
dclxxxvii	Exodus 33:13 NIV
dclxxxviii	John 12:24 NIV
dclxxxix	C.S. Lewis Quotes, GoodReads, accessed May 15, 2015, https://www.goodreads.com/quotes/347103-aslan-said-lucy-you-re-bigger-that-is-because-you-are.
dcxc	Psalm 37:4 NIV
dcxci	Psalm 119:14-16 TPT
dcxcii	"The Vow Quotes," Quotes.net, accessed January 1, 2018, https://www.quotes.net/mquote/112140. (Emphasis added)
dcxciii	2 Chronicles 14-15 NIV
dcxciv	Exodus 3:14 NIV
dcxcv	"Phil Vischer Quotes," GoodReads, accessed January 24, 2018, https://www.goodreads.com/author/quotes/63353.Phil_Vischer.
dcxcvi	Psalm 46:10 NIV
dcxcvii	L. Gayle Orf, "Mirrors of Glory," published November 7, 2017, https://saintedolce.wordpress.com/2017/11/07/mirrors-of-glory-by-l-gayle-orf/.
dcxcviii	Exodus 14:14 NIV
dcxcix	Ibid.
dcc	Matthew 14:28 MSG
dcci	Ephesians 5: 14 TPT
dccii	Matthew 9:17 TPT
dcciii	New Wine [Recorded by Hillsong Worship (Brooke Ligertwood)]. On There Is More [MP3 File].
dcciv	Job 10:8 NIV
dccv	Genesis 8:11 NIV
dccvi	Luke 3:22 NLT
dccvii	"Up Quotes," IMDb, accessed November 29, 2018, https://www.imdb.com/title/tt1049413/quotes.
dccviii	Proverbs 4:7 NIV

dccix	Proverbs 4:11 NIV
dccx	"Dan Pearce Quotes, "GoodReads, accessed November 11, 2015, https://www.goodreads.com/author/quotes/3994285.Dan_Pearce?page=4.
dccxi	Zechariah 2:1-5 NIV
dccxii	Zechariah 2:1-21 NIV
dccxiii	Isaiah 30:18 NIV
dccxiv	Marianne Williamson, *A Return To Love: Reflections on the Principles of A Course in Miracles*, (Harper Collins, 1992) p190-191.
dccxv	Matthew 23:12 NIV
dccxvi	Mark 3:24 NIV
dccxvii	2 Chronicles 17:3 NIV
dccxviii	2 Chronicles 16:9 NIV
dccxix	1 Chronicles 17:10-12 NIV (emphasis added)
dccxx	2 Chronicles 20:5,12,15 NIV (emphasis added)
dccxxi	Jeremiah 29:13 NIV
dccxxii	Proverbs 19:21 NIV
dccxxiii	Jonah 1:12 NIV
dccxxiv	Matthew 28:18-20
dccxxv	Psalm 27:14 NIV
dccxxvi	Psalm 37:7 NIV
dccxxvii	Psalm 62:5 NLT
dccxxviii	"Andy Warhol Quotes," GoodReads, accessed March 1, 2015, https://www.goodreads.com/quotes/78319-the-idea-of-waiting-for-something-makes-it-more-exciting.
dccxxix	"Dr.Seuss Quotes," GoodReads, accessed October 11, 2015, https://www.goodreads.com/quotes/6805-sometimes-the-questions-are-complicated-and-the-answers-are-simple.
dccxxx	Proverbs 3:5-6 MSG
dccxxxi	Song of Songs 4:7 NIV
dccxxxii	John 14:6 NIV
dccxxxiii	Micah 7:8 NLT
dccxxxiv	Job 1:1-3 NIV
dccxxxv	Job 1:7 NIV
dccxxxvi	Job 42:10, 12 NIV
dccxxxvii	Meyer, M. (2012). *Cinder* (1st ed). Feiwel and Friends.
dccxxxviii	"Quotes," PassItOn, accessed August 8, 2016, https://www.passiton.com/inspirational-quotes/3274-its-not-how-many-times-you-get-knocked-down.
dccxxxix	Romans 5:3-4 NIV
dccxl	Ecclesiastes 9:11NIV
dccxli	2 Samuel 12:8 NIV
dccxlii	Lamentations 3:22-23 ESV
dccxliii	Matthew 10:31 NIV
dccxliv	Matthew 6:26 NIV
dccxlv	Romans 5:7-8 AMPC
dccxlvi	Proverbs 13:7 MSG
dccxlvii	Philippians 4:12 NIV
dccxlviii	"Quote," Pinterest, accessed July 7, 2015, https://www.pinterest.com.au/pin/128774870569682918/?lp=true.
dccxlix	Miyazaki, H., Suzuki, T., Lasseter, J., Dempsey, R., Lott, N., Docter, P., Hewitt, C. D., ... Buena Vista Home Entertainment (Firm),. (2006). Hauru no ugoku shiro =: Howl's moving castle.
dccl	1 Peter 3:4 NIV
dccli	Romans 8:27 NIV
dcclii	Romans 8:27 MSG
dccliii	Romans 8:28 MSG

dccliv	Proverbs 2:3-5 NIV
dcclv	Ephesians 2:10 NIV
dcclvi	Psalm 37:25 NIV
dcclvii	Romans 8:29 MSG
dcclviii	1 Corinthians 2:9 NLT
dcclix	Isaiah 64:4 NIV
dcclx	"Elisabeth Elliot Quotes," GoodReads.com, published October 15, 2013, https://www.goodreads.com/quotes/915294-don-t-dig-up-in-doubt-what-you-planted-in-faith.
dcclxi	Song of Songs 7:10-12 NIV
dcclxii	Ibid.
dcclxiii	Song of Songs 7:12 MSG
dcclxiv	Proverbs 16:9 MSG
dcclxv	"Veni, vidi, vici," Oxford Learner's Dictionaries, accessed February 28, 2021, https://www.oxfordlearnersdictionaries.com/definition/english/veni-vidi-vici
dcclxvi	Romans 6:6-14 MSG
dcclxvii	Romans 12:2 NIV
dcclxviii	Ann Voskamp, *The Broken Way,* (Grand Rapids: Zondervan, 2016), p 141.
dcclxix	James 3:5 NKJV
dcclxx	Proverbs 18:21 NIV
dcclxxi	James 3:5 NIV
dcclxxii	James 3:6 MSG
dcclxxiii	"Secrets Of Breathing," QuigongTraining, published January 25, 2011, http://developyourenergy.net/2011/01/25/secrets-of-breathing/.
dcclxxiv	Job 33:4 NIV
dcclxxv	Isaiah 42:5 NIV
dcclxxvi	Nahum 2:1-3 NIV
dcclxxvii	Revelations 3:11-13 MSG
dcclxxviii	Isaiah 62:10-12 MSG
dcclxxix	Hebrews 11:8-10 MSG
dcclxxx	Genesis 2:10-11 NIV (emphasis added)
dcclxxxi	Psalm 91:4 NLT
dcclxxxii	Psalm 20:6 NIV
dcclxxxiii	*2 Corinthians 12:9 NIV*
dcclxxxiv	1 John 3:18 NIV
dcclxxxv	2 Timothy 1:6-7 NIV
dcclxxxvi	1 John 4:16-17 NIV
dcclxxxvii	"Daredevil crosses Niagara Falls on tightrope," History.com, published July 21, 2010, https://www.history.com/this-day-in-history/daredevil-crosses-niagara-falls-on-tightrope.
dcclxxxviii	2 Kings 20:9 MSG
dcclxxxix	Exodus 33:11 NIV
dccxc	James 4:1-3 ESV
dccxci	Jeremiah 17:9 NIV
dccxcii	2 Corinthians 4:18 NIV
dccxciii	Quote from Brooke Ligertwood at VOUS Conference 2018
dccxciv	Jonah 4:10 NIV
dccxcv	2 Corinthians 4:15 MSG
dccxcvi	Romans 8:35-39 NLT
dccxcvii	Psalm 46:5 NIV (emphasis added)
dccxcviii	Song of Songs 4:7 NIV (emphasis added) dccxcix Quote from Charlotte Gambill at Colour 2018
dccc	Mark 12:30 NIV
dccci	*Snow White*, StoryNory, accessed March 11, 2017, https://www.storynory.com/snow-white/.
dcccii	Grace Thornton, *I Don't Wait Anymore,* GracefortheRoad, published February 3, 2012,

	https://gracefortheroad.com/2012/02/03/idontwait/.
dccciii	Proverbs 27:19 ESV
dccciv	2 Corinthians 3:16-18 NLT
dcccv	Psalm 91:4 NLT
dcccvi	Psalm 45:3-5 NLT
dcccvii	Isaiah 42:1 NIV
dcccviii	2 Timothy 2:15
dcccix	Sheila Walsh posts: "We're not called to pursue perfection; we're called to pursue Christ, who is perfect." (@sheilawalshconnects, September 19, 2018).
dcccx	Quote from Steven Penny at Hillsong Church, December 9, 2017.
dcccxi	Nehemiah 2:18 AMP
dcccxii	Psalm 31:24 MSG
dcccxiii	Nehemiah 9:15 AMP
dcccxiv	James 3:17-18 NIV
dcccxv	2 Thessalonians 1:5-8,11-12 MSG
dcccxvi	"Love Is More Than A Feeling—Much More Than A Feeling; It's A Virtue," RealTrueLove, published January 5, 2012, https://realtruelove.wordpress.com/2012/01/05/love-is-more-than-a-feeling-much-more-than-a-feeling-its-a-virtue/.
dcccxvii	1 John 4:8 NIV
dcccxviii	Psalm 34:1-3 TLB
dcccxix	"Andrew Smith Quotes," GoodReads, accessed June 14, 2018, https://www.goodreads.com/author/quotes/26810.Andrew_Smith.
dcccxx	2 Corinthians 3:18 NIV
dcccxxi	2 Corinthians 3:18 MSG
dcccxxii	Psalm 96:4 MSG
dcccxxiii	Kim Lier, "What Is The True Meaning Of Perfection,"Odyssey, published June 26, 2017, https://www.theodysseyonline.com/teens-perfection.
dcccxxiv	"Grace and Christianity," Wikipedia, last modified November 22, 2018, https://en.wikipedia.org/wiki/Grace_in_Christianity.
dcccxxv	Psalm 18: 6, 16, and 19 NIV
dcccxxvi	Matthew 6:33 NIV
dcccxxvii	Psalm 66:10-12 NLT
dcccxxviii	1 John 3:1-2 TPT
dcccxxix	Romans 5:3-5 MSG
dcccxxx	Psalm 139:5 NIV
dcccxxxi	Brian Houston, *Live, Love, Lead,* (Sydney: HarperCollins*Publishers*, 2015), p 277.
dcccxxxii	Judith Lawrence, *Prayer Companion: A Treasury of Personal Meditation*, (Toronto: Pathbooks, 2001), p 104.
dcccxxxiii	2 Corinthians 2:15 TPT
dcccxxxiv	John 12:3 TPT
dcccxxxv	2 Corinthians 2:14 TPT (emphasis added)
dcccxxxvi	Ephesians 5:2 TPT (emphasis added)
dcccxxxvii	Song of Songs 4:11 TPT (emphasis added)
dcccxxxviii	Song of Songs 2:13 TPT
dcccxxxix	Matthew 6:6,8-13 MSG
dcccxl	John 16:4-7, 12 MSG
dcccxli	John 16:20-23 MSG
dcccxlii	"C.S.Lewis Quotes," GoodReads, accessed January 25, 2019, https://www.goodreads.com/quotes/350927-and-as-he-spoke-he-no-longer-looked-to-them.
dcccxliii	Matthew 28:18-20 TPT
dcccxliv	2 Timothy 1:12-14 TPT
dcccxlv	Zechariah 14:6-9 MSG

www.ingramcontent.com/pod-product-compliance
Lightning Source LLC
Chambersburg PA
CBHW061752290426
44108CB00029B/2967